MUSTANGS
over Korea

This book is dedicated to Captain Mike Hindman, USAF

MUSTANGS over Korea

The North American F-51 at War 1950-1953

David R. McLaren

Schiffer Military History
Atglen, PA

Acknowledgements

This book actually began as a research project for the American Aviation Historical Society, AAHS. It origionally was envisioned as a simple story of one of the more famous aircraft types employed in a war that has been largely forgotten. The F-51 Mustang, nee P-51, was flown in combat over Korea for almost as long as it was utilized during World War II, but because most of the aviation "press" during the Korean War was devoted to the exploits of the emerging jet fighters, the story of the Mustang and those that were involved with it in Korea just never received the mention that they deserved.

The length of this project just grew with the research involved, and although I fear that portions of this book will read like a litany of losses, I do feel that it could not have been properly written otherwise, lest it would result in a disservice to those that participated, and particularly to those young men who gave their lives in the "Forgotten War."

As with any research project, the quality and quanity of support given to the author is critical to its success. In the beginning the AAHS lent its hand, and this was followed up by the Air Force Association, the Liberator Club, the 8th Air Force Society: various offices of the Department of the United States Air Force, particularly the Air Force Museum and the Simpson Library, Historical Research Agency; and the Air Force Historical Foundation. In addition, individuals, writers, historians, pilots, and the guys on the ground who "kept 'em flying" all contribuited support and motivation, and I am greatful to the following: Duane Biteman (18th FBW Association), Roger Besecker, Donald Brackenreg (77 Sq. RAAF), Gerald Brown (39th FIS), Clyde Carstons, Kathy Cassity, Richard Chard (40th FIS), Paul Coggan, Larry Davis, John deVires, Robert Dorr, Robert Dunnavant (39th FIS), Judy Endicott (Simpson Library), Robert Esposito, Jeff Ethell, Gene Evens (6146th BASUT), James Gasser (8th FBG), Robert Glisson, William Greenlalgh, Al Hollet (35th FIG), Perry Hundicott (45th TRS), Marty Isham, M.E. James (77 Sq. RAAF), H.J.W. Jooste (Embassy of South Africa), Dick Komperta, William Larkins, Carl McCamish (67th FBS), David W. Menard, Ron Neal, William O'Donnell (36th FBS), Merle Olmsted, Richard Penrose (39th FIS), Father B.C. Reed, John Sibert, Warren Thompson, Charles Trask, B.G. Van Donkelaar (77 Sq. RAAF), Horace Q. Waggnor (18th FBG), Vivian White, Ron Witt, R.D. Woods (18th FBG), John Yost (45th TRS).

Dustjacket artwork by Steve Ferguson, Colorado Springs, CO.

HORSE AND OXEN: After the historic amphibious landings on 15 September, 1950, at Inchon, North Korea, the hastily assembled American tactical air force was tasked with interdicting enemy supply routes from China. Understandably, the North increased its airborne interventions and as of November, Mustang and Yak were contesting the air space over the Yalu River valley.
Our cover depicts Lt. Jim Glessner of the 12 FBS knocking down one of his two victims in the fierce duel fought on the morning of November 2nd. Oddly enough, Glessner would have only one of the Yaks confirmed and it would be the only aerial victory for his squadron until the unit switched to the F-86 Sabre in early 1953.

Book Design by Ian Robertson.

Printed in China.
ISBN: 0-7643-0721-5

We are interested in hearing from authors with book ideas on military topics.

Published by Schiffer Publishing Ltd.
4880 Lower Valley Road
Atglen, PA 19310
Phone: (610) 593-1777
FAX: (610) 593-2002
E-mail: Schifferbk@aol.com
Please visit our web site catalog at www.schifferbooks.com
or write for a free catalog.
This book may be purchased from the publisher.
Please include $3.95 postage.
Try your bookstore first.

Contents

CHAPTER ONE

The Country Nobody Ever Heard Of

On June 25, 1950, at the ungodly hour of 0400 North Korean forces crossed the 38th Parallel. This surveyor's tangent had divided the land of "Morning Splendor" since the end of World War II. The decision to divide a country and a race in such an arbitrary fashion seems based upon dubious political wisdom, for it threw up a line that just had to be crossed by someone, and it hadn't worked before. Korea, itself, had never been particularly splendiferous, morning or otherwise, ever since the Sino-Japanese War in 1895 gave half of Korea to Japan and the other half to Russia, with the 38th Parallel dividing the "Spheres of Influence." As a result the country was always in a constant state of turmoil as the Japanese and the Russians haggled over ideology and the right of Korean sovereignty until August 29, 1910 when the Japanese took complete control of the country. This was a date the Koreans observed as "National Humiliation Day."

During this period, as far as the United States was concerned, Korea was just another piece of minor geography, and one that students usually overlooked while glancing at a map. The United States had shown little interest in the country at all prior to, and during World War II, although there was some bombing of Japanese held installations during the war.

A tentative agreement between U.S. President Franklin Roosevelt and USSR generalissimo General Joseph Stalin at Yalta in early 1945, which was reiterated at the Potsdam Conference later in July, and then confirmed when the Russians entered the war against Japan on August 8, 1945 stated that, "Korea should be prepared for independence by an international trusteeship." At this time there was a provisional Korean government which was located in Chungking, China and was led by Ku Kim, but neither the United States nor Russia desired to recognize it. The 38th Parallel was reestablished upon the collapse of Japan, so the Russians, who had already invaded Korea, could accept Japanese

Lt. General George Stratemeyer. Commanding General of the Far East Air Force until May 21, 1951. (USAF via B.C. Reed)

prisoner's of war north of that line, while the United States would accept responsibility for those on the south side of the line. Exactly what the Russians did with all their POW's is an unknown, although they probably wound up in forced labor for the communists. By September 1945 there were already 100,000 Russian troops in northern Korea, while the United States had 72,000 men in southern Korea, with both sides allegedly having them there for peace keeping duties and the establishment of an independent unified Korean government.

Beginning in December 1945 the Russian forces had commenced to fortify their side of the 38th Parallel, just to prevent anyone from taking away their holdings. They tore out all of the north-south railroads and blockaded the conventional roads. There were 21 million South Koreans who furnished the food and fabrics required for the nine million North Koreans who lived in the industrial northern half of the country, and who in turn furnished the water and electricity to the southern half. Both sides saw their economy collapsing, and heard the Russian propaganda broadcasts which claimed that it was the UN's, and in particular the United States' fault. Now the UN was trying to return political control to the Koreans, as Roosevelt, Churchill and Chiang Kai-Shek had originally promised in Cairo in November 1944, but Stalin, even though he had agreed to the proposals, now said the effort was "illegal."

In September 1947 the United States asked the United Nations to consider the problem of a unified Korea. Although Korea was of little political value to the Russians, it did contain many types of natural resources, and Stalin did not want to relinquish control of these to anyone. All of the UN's suggestions were rejected out of hand.

A United Nations peace commission oversaw the first free election in South Korea on May 10, 1948, which elected Syngman Rhee as President. His office would be in the traditional Korean capitol city of Seoul. Not to be outdone, elections were soon held by the puppet government of Kim Il Sung in North Korea. Sung named Pyongyang, the largest city in the north, as his capitol. Both Russia and the United States then started withdrawing their forces from Korea, with both sides having their men out by mid 1949.

Physically Korea encompasses approximately the same number of square miles as Minnesota. Geographically, the peninsula lays similar in latitudes as between Concord, New Hampshire and Wilmington, North Carolina, running approximately 600 miles long by 235 miles broad, with similar climate to the United States' eastern

General Earle E. Partridge. Deputy Commanding Officer of FEAF under General Stratemeyer until he assumed command himself on May 21, 1951. (USAF via B.C. Reed)

seaboard. The northern and central portions of Korea are characterized by having very hot summers and severe winters, while the southern portions are more like the Carolina's with temperatures moderated by the ocean breeze. Population wise, Korea is more than twice as densely packed as the average United States' state.

Korea could be as much of an asset or a liability to the United Nations as they wanted it to be. Strategically it was of little importance, for the actual land mass created little threat to anyone, as it was physically no closer to southern Japan than Manchuria was to the northern part. Yet, if an invasion would create a climax to post war political intransigence, a political line would have to be drawn. The United Nations, if it was going to be an United Nations at all, would have to take action, or wind up "as morally bankrupt as the League of Nations had when they compromised with the aggressors in Abyssinia and China."

A B-26 Invader of the 3rd Bomb Wing (Light) "Somewhere over Korea." The Invaders performed the yeomen's tasks during both day and nighttime combat operations throughout the entire Korean "peace action." (USAF)

The First Weeks of the War

To the few observers of the Korean political scene that there were, the attack on June 25, 1950 came with little surprise, It had been obvious to them for some time that the North Koreans were going to invade their brothers to the south. The only questions were when? How strong would the invading force be? And what would the ultimate goal be, to take the capitol city of Seoul and then bring about a political coup, or to attempt to conquer the entire Republic of South Korea?

The invasion started with an all-out attack on the lightly defended fortifications that the South Koreans had constructed along the 38th Parallel. The initial attack came at Onjin, a small city on a peninsula that was separated by water from the South Korean mainland along the western coast. It was indefensible. The attack then spread eastward, and two and one-half hours after the initial attack an amphibious force landed at Kang'nung, on the eastern coast. Three hours hence, United State's Ambassador John J. Muccio finally received word of the invasion, but the story was that the South Korean Army was holding. One hour later the cities of Kaesong and Ch'unch'on were captured.

The air war started at 1315 hours Korean time when the rains dissipated and the skies cleared. Two North Korean Yak's fighters made a low-level observation pass over Seoul's Municipal airport and the Republic of Korea's Kimpo Air Base, and then disappeared to the north. At 1700 two more Yak's returned to strafe Kimpo, damaging a parked USAF C-54D and setting some fires, while four more Yaks struck at the Municipal airport and virtually wiped out the South Korean Air Force, ROKAF, (Technically, Republic of Korea Air Force.) destroying seven

out of ten ex Canadian Mk. IV T-6 Harvards that had been parked there. Two hours later six more Yak's appeared and set about strafing Kimpo again, insuring the destruction of the Skymaster. There was no aerial opposition, as the last of the United States Air Forces' 5th Air Force fighters that had been stationed in Korea had been scrapped in September 1949 and their fighter group deactivated.

Republic of Korea's President Rhee had confidence in his ground troops as far as there effectiveness was concerned against other ground troops, it was the communist T-34 tanks that he was afraid of. The surviving ROKAF T-6s had already claimed three tanks, but this claim appears highly unlikely in light of the difficulty involved in stopping an armored tank from the air with the minimal 2.5 inch rockets carried by a T-6D. (It took a average of eight 5" HVAR's to stop a T-34 according to USAF figures). Rhee had also watched the Yak's work over his airfields and wipe out his air force, and this is one thing

A F-80C in an "air-to-mud" napalm strike against a North Korean target at tree-top height. The Shooting Stars took their losses, too, but they did their job. (Air Force Museum)

that really shook his confidence. If Rhee was anything, he was a believer in air power. He had been clamoring for an air force of his own ever since he had attained political office. Rhee attempted to get ahold of General Douglas MacArthur without success, so he then implored Ambassador Muccio to get him "ten F-51 aircraft with bombs and bazookas." Rhee wanted these Mustangs delivered to Taegu where his pilots would be waiting for them. He got his wish, of sorts, for his few qualified pilots were picked up by a USAF C-47 the next day and were flown to Japan for training in these aircraft, and the era of the Mustangs over Korea began.

There were but ten Mustangs available for use at the time, as these ten were the only ones still operational within the 5th Air Force, and they were "tired tow-ships" at that. The training of the ROKAF pilots was delegated to Captain James P. Becket, who had been selected from the 36th Fighter Bomber Squadron at Itazuke Air Base to accomplish the task. Becket was given only enough time to give each ROKAF pilot one check-ride in the Mustang before they were sent back to Korea to join with the future "Bout 1" project, which was to oversee further ROKAF pilot training in the Mustang and to provide operational support to the ROKAF.

When the war started, FEAF, or Far East Air Forces, was commanded by Lt. General George E. Stratemeyer, a veteran of the India-Burma Theater during World War II. Under Stratemeyer was Major General Earle E. Partridge, who commanded FEAF's 5th Air Force, the largest of the three Pacific Air Forces, 5th, 13th, and 20th, which when combined then made up FEAF. Partridge was an ex bomber pilot from the Mediterranean and European Theaters during World War II, but he was now commanding a tactical air force, something he would accomplish with a flair. As Stratemeyer happened to be enroute from the United States at the onset of the Korean War, Partridge also was serving as the temporary commander of FEAF, and he had to carry the weight of the first two critical days decisions.

General Partridge finally received word of the invasion at 1130 hours, and he immediately implemented Operational Plan 4, a contingency program that had been developed the previous March. Plan 4 outlined the tactics to be used for the evacuation of American nationals from Korea. The major task for this being placed upon the 374th Troop Carrier Wing, which would stage from Itazuke Air Base to carry out the evacuation.

In a briefing General Douglas MacArthur advised General Partridge to prepare to attack only those forces

Mustangs of the 8th Fighter Bomber Wing attacking a North Korean held position near Seoul during the early months of the Korean Conflict, as photographed by a forward air controller, FAC. Napalm was the most versatile weapon of the war. (O'Donnell)

that might interfere with the evacuation, but not to do so without his specific orders. Partridge in turn passed these instructions on to Colonel John M. Price, Commanding Officer of the 8th Fighter Bomber Wing, which included tactical control of the 374th TCW. Nine hours later Price informed FEAF that all of his units would be ready to commence any assigned task by the following morning.

For a period of time on June 26 it appeared that the Republic of Korea (ROK) Army was holding their own and possibly the invaders would be thrown back across the 38th Parallel. The proposed airlift of the American civilians out of Seoul was called off, and the scheduled transports were released from their staging assignments. All non-essential American's were still to be evacuated, but since time did not seem to be critical any longer, they would leave by ship. Just to be on the safe side, however, F-82 Twin Mustangs of the 68th and 339th Fighter (All-Weather) Squadrons would be detailed to fly armed reconnaissance and surveillance missions over the Seoul-Inchon area while the evacuees were being boarded upon Norwegian merchant ships that happened to be the best available vessels. The F-82s were jumped by a Russian built La-7, but since they had not been released by FEAF to return fire, they were forced to take evasive action until the threat passed. That evening President Rhee called Ambassador Muccio and told him that he feared that his ROK Army was now close to collapsing and that he was going to have to move his government to Taegu, in central South Korea. It was now obvious that Seoul could not be held, and that the invasion was more than a simple boarder skirmish. Muccio had no choice but to again ask for emergency evacuation of all remaining American personnel.

A FAC party working fighter-bombers on a close air support strike. The Jeep's windshield is covered with a mat, so the glass does not reflect the sun and give away their position. (O'Donnell)

Eleven C-47s and two C-54s, with a top fighter escort cover of F-80 Shooting Stars and a low cover provided by F-82s left Itazuke Air Base to commence the airlift on the morning of June 27. Due to communist pressure on Seoul, the airlift was carried out from both Kimpo and Suwon, a small town and airstrip twenty miles south of Seoul. The evacuation would take all day, but by the time it was over 851 individuals had been flown out of Korea without injury.

That same afternoon at FEAF Headquarters General's Partridge and Edward J. Timberlake, Deputy Commander, 5th Air Force, arrived at the decision that it was necessary to send further military assistance to Korea, in the form of more F-51 Mustangs. It was already recognized that it was going to take too long to train the ROKAF pilots in Japan, so any further training they would receive would have to be "on the job," A request for USAF

volunteers to instruct the present ten, and any future ROKAF pilots, while simultaneously providing limited air support to UN ground forces was immediately dispatched to all 5th Air Force units. The request for these pilots was received by Colonel Virgil L. Zoller, commanding officer, 35th Fighter Interceptor Wing.

FEAF specified that they wanted ten qualified Mustang pilots, four ground officers, and one hundred enlisted men to start the program, to be titled as "Bout 1." Colonel Zoller happened to be discussing the situation with Major Charles Bowers, 39th Fighter Interceptor Squadron Operations Officer, as he had to select a commanding officer for the new unit, when Major Dean Hess got wind of what was going on. Through the luck of the draw Hess beat out Bowers to become the first Commanding Officer of Bout 1.

Since all of the available F-5ls were already slated for the ROKAF, a rapid program was started to pull those awaiting salvage in the storage area at Johnson Air Base, Japan before they were scrapped, but this number amounted to only a couple dozen aircraft. FEAF immediately requested a mass shipment of additional Mustangs from the United States to alleviate the shortage. The USAF in turn contacted the National Guard Bureau, and orders were sent to selected Air National Guard Squadrons for them to send a specified number of F-51Ds to the U.S. Naval Air Station at Alameda, California, for shipment to Korea on the U.S. aircraft carrier Boxer. Altogether the ANG furnished seventy-nine Mustangs during this first shipment, while sixty-six more were taken from a storage area at McClelland Air Force Base, It was also suggested at the time that the USAF should also ship F-47 Thunderbolts to Korea, but this request was turned

Ex Air National Guard Mustangs shipped from the United States on the aircraft carrier Boxer upon arrival in Japan. Both of these F-51Ds had once belonged to the Indiana ANG, with #538 having been assigned to the 113th FS at Stout Field, Indianapolis, (And still bearing their insignia.) while #362 belonged to the 163rd FS at Baer Field, Ft. Wayne. (USAF via Witt.)

down, primarily because there was only one USAF training unit still operational with the type, and gathering in those from the Air National Guard would create logistical problems. Also, there were plenty of spare F-51 parts still in Japan, but none remaining for Thunderbolts.

(General Hoyt Vandenberg, USAF Chief of Staff, again denied General Stratemeyer's request for F-47s on May 4, 1951, as he did not want two obsolescent fighter aircraft types in Korea. He also informed Stratemeyer at this time that the F-51 was going to be replaced, and if the F-51s were beginning to become "war weary" they should be returned to Japan for defense of the Islands. Consequently, 40th Fighter Interceptor Squadron was relieved of combat duties, but it would take another eighteen months to replace to remaining F-51 squadrons).

On June 28 Seoul fell to the communist forces. The North Korean southward push was on in earnest, and before the day was over the east coast port of Mukhojin-ni had also fallen. President Truman directed the 5th Air Force to achieve air superiority, to isolate the battlefield through interdiction, and to provide close air support for the ground forces. That the 5th Air Force had air superiority was never in doubt , although the North Korean Air Force was capable of extended harassment, but the rest of the President's directive was going to require some effort.

The first of the Mustangs to be ferried to the Republic of Korea departed Japan on the afternoon of June 29. As it happened, General MacArthur was already enroute to Suwon to look over the tactical situation in his C-54 "Bataan" at the time, under an escort of 8th Fighter Bomber Wing F-80s that were flying top cover, and two

The temporary 5th Air Force Headquarters in downtown Taegu. The site was known as "Comet." (USAF via Reed)

F-82s that were at his aircraft's altitude, so the Mustangs being ferried just tagged along behind.

The C-54 landed and MacArthur was in conference when the airfield came under attack by North Korean aircraft, which just happened to coincide with the arrival of the Mustangs overhead. Ambassador Muccio, President Rhee and MacArthur went outside to watch the show. It was the field day for the F-51s in the Korean air war, 2nd Lt. Orrin Fox, 80th Fighter Bomber Squadron shot down two Yak-9s, 1st Lt. Richard Burns, 35th Fighter Bomber Squadron, got an Il-10, 1st Lt. Harry T. Sandlin, 80th Fighter Bomber Squadron, got himself a La-7, and 1st Lt. Eugene R. Hanson, 36th Fighter Bomber Squadron was credited with a "probable" Yak-9. (Indicative of the tragedies of war, of these four volunteer Mustang pilots in this fracas, Burns, Sandlin and Hanson would all be killed while flying F-80s before the year ended).

When MacArthur returned to Japan on the evening of June 29 he discovered that the Australian Prime Minister, R.G. Menzies, had announced that Australia had offered the support of their 77 Squadron. Both MacArthur and his Air Force Generals were elated, for these Mustangs of 77 Squadron had been readied for combat during the previous four days as a result of the Australian's initiative. With thirty Mustangs they would be able to bolster the 5th Air Force's tactical strength of F-80s and B-26s until FEAF could obtain additional aircraft of their own.

Bout 1 became established at Taegu airstrip on June 30, 1950 and started flying combat missions soon thereafter with six South Korean and ten American pilots. The six ROKAF pilots were eager enough to get into action, and most of them were experienced fighter pilots, having

What's left of a 51st Fighter Bomber Squadron (Provisional) F-51 at Taegu in August 1950. This Mustang had been in storage at McClellan AFB, California prior to shipment to Korea and only had 365 hours on it at the time when it was written-off. Note that it still carries the tail-warning radar antennas on its vertical stabilizer, an item that was removed from ANG Mustangs. (U.S. Army via Ethell)

Headquarters 5th Air Force at Itazuke Air Base, Japan. (O'Donnell)

flown with either the Chinese or the Japanese air forces during World War II. Unfortunately, the F-51 had a considerably higher wing loading than those aircraft they had previously flown, and because of the press of the events they did not have enough time to learn this fact for themselves until it was dramatically shown to them the hard way. Their first loss was that of their Troop Commander, Colonel Lee, who was an ex Japanese ace with over twenty American kills during World War II. He tried to split-ess his Mustang during a bomb run against North Korean tank, but did not have sufficient altitude left to recover.

The morning of June 30 saw the fall of Suwon and its airstrip, designated K-13, The North Korean Army relentlessly pushed south along a coast-to-coast line. They soon forced the evacuation of the Taejon airstrip, K-5, and then captured the east coast port of Samch'ok before this day ended. Orders were transmitted to the U.S. 24th Infantry Division, pulling garrison duty in Japan under the 8th Army, to prepare to move to Korea. The next day, July 1, elements of the 24th Division were flown to Pusan, South Korea in C-54s of the 374th Troop Carrier Wing, becoming the first United States and United Nations ground forces to enter the Korean Campaign. The first battalion was then trucked to positions north of Osan, where they were committed to battle on July 2.

With Mustangs and some pilots in the United States already being prepared for duty in Korea, an additional plan to get more pilots had to be arrived at. The ideal number being three pilots per each aircraft, so as to reduce fatigue from having to fly more than once a day. On July 3 General Stratemeyer directed the 13th Air Force, which was headquartered at Clark Air Base, Philippine Islands, to screen the three squadrons of the 18th Fighter Bomber Group for pilots with recent proficiency in the F-51. The 18th Fighter Bomber Group was then directed to form a provisional squadron, to be known as the "Dallas Project," and to fly these people to Japan where they would be assigned thirty Mustangs that were now being refurbished from storage at Johnson Air Base. From Johnson, their next move would be to Taegu, where they would absorb the Bout 1 unit, and thus become the 51st Fighter Bomber Squadron (Provisional).

The orders forming the Dallas Project were received at Clark on July 5, and by July 10 the men were enroute to Japan. As the pilots arrived and were recertifying in the F-51, (Or checking out in them in the first place, as many had never flown the type at all, but did have some lengthy period remaining on their overseas tour, which made them eligible under military logic.) the ground echelon drew their required supplies and were on their way to Taegu.

It was now found that enough Mustangs were available in the storage depots at Johnson and Tachikawa Air Bases' to equip one additional squadron after the Dallas Project was established, so the 40th Fighter Interceptor Squadron of the 35th Fighter Interceptor Group was instructed to prepare for conversion from F-80s to F-5ls. The "Fighting Fortieth" had already moved from Johnson to Ashiya Air Base, Japan to conduct combat operations, but at the same time it had become obvious that the short-ranged Shooting Stars were not going to be able to fill the desired tactical role the unit was committed to. The problem wasn't with the aircraft as much as it was in the location of the air bases that could handle it when it was heavily loaded with ordnance. The F-80 needed more runway than was available at the time on any airfield in South Korea, and the Japanese airfields were just to far away from the targeted areas to be feasible for support missions. This forced a trade-off between the long range fuel tanks which permitted the F-80 to get to the targeted area to begin with, or the bombs that it needed to carry there in the first place, thus at this time ordnance was restricted to rockets and machine guns.

The 40th FIS was slated to move to Po'hang, South Korea, numbered K-3, as soon as transition training into the F-51 could be accomplished. For most pilots this was literally done "on the fly," as they received their first Mustangs on July 10, and the 40th FIS moved to Po'hang on July 14, 1950 without a break in combat operations. The next day, July 15, the newly formed 51st Fighter Bomber Squadron (Provisional) started flying their first combat missions. General Timberlake was quite pleased with these Mustang operations, stating, "one F-51 adequately supported and fought from Taegu airfield is equivalent to four F-80s based on Kyushu."

There were many factors effecting the air war over Korea during these first few weeks. Support of the ground troops was not nearly as effective as it should have been, due to a lack of adequate air-to-ground control. There was an element of Staff Officers within FEAF that thought they could run the war from their cushy offices in Japan, and it took some effort to persuade them otherwise. Communications and coordination had to be established with the U.S. 8th Army Headquarters and the U.S. Navy's Task Force 77 that would bypass inter-service rivalries before attention could even be given to working out the technical bugs and tactical problems associated with running a war.

Plans were formulated to move a section of FEAF Headquarters to Korea in conjunction with EUSAK, (Eighth U.S. Army in Korea), under General Walton Walker, to help solve the coordination difficulties. But there remained numerous problems with trying to support the

Night missions were never intended by the Mustang's designers, but they were just a part of the job during the early months of the war. Captain William Hook, 40th Fighter Interceptor Squadron, is preparing for a mission in August, 1950. Hook was killed on January 5, 1951 while flying his 117th combat mission with the 35th Fighter Interceptor Group. (USAF via Ethell)

ground forces, The pilots were unfamiliar with the terrain, and they virtually had no maps. The ground Forward Air Controllers (FAC's) were all army troops and did not know how to call targets in over the limited radio frequencies in a method the pilots could use to locate them. An air strike would be called in to take out a tank, and a entire squadron might show up, or no aircraft at all! FAC's fought among themselves on the radios to get control of an air strike, which confused the pilots to no end. To solve some of these problems the 6147th Tactical Control Squadron was formed and sent to Taegu with L-5s, L-17s, and soon afterwards with T-6s for observation and target marking. In addition, Air Force pilots were "selected" to serve with ground units to also serve as FAC's. A Joint Operations Center, JOC, was established at Taejon, South Korea, and in spite of a myriad of communications problems that were brought on by a lack of radios, telephones and Teletype equipment they managed to get defensive operations underway.

Unfortunately, the envisioned "Call Strike" tactic turned out not to be workable. The primary tactical aircraft, F-80s and B-26s, were usually just to far away at their bases in Japan to be effective at a target when they were needed. It took just too long to get them scrambled off the ground and to the target area. As an alternative, flights were launched at timed intervals, and as they approached the combat arena the flight leader would check in with the JOC, who would then assign him to either a FAC who would give him the position of a target, or send the aircraft somewhere beyond the bomb line to pick out a target of opportunity if he did not have a worthwhile target for him.

Under ideal conditions support could be supplied to the requester in under twenty minutes. If there were more aircraft than the air or ground FAC could handle, or needed, the pilots were again released to find targets on their own. Due to the lack of compatible radio frequencies, the later was all to often the case. Actually, there was usually no shortage of aircraft during daylight hours, but the communications problems often resulted in flights flying around trying to find worthwhile targets to dump their ordnance on after the first month of the war. It was all a learning experience, for he lessons learned during World War II had never been refreshed.

Armament Loads for all of the tactical aircraft were essentially the same, .50 caliber machine guns, rockets of both the 2.5 and 5" varieties, light case 500 pound thermite or fragmentation bombs, occasionally para-frag bombs, and the invincible napalm. Targets were tanks, artillery positions, troop concentrations, and supply dumps. Initially the F-80s were used almost exclusively, as the B-26s were being employed on longer range rail-busting interdiction or night missions. After the later Pusan breakout the B-26s were also employed along the battle line, and they were considered particularly effective, due to their heavy armament, but they also proved to be more vulnerable to ground fire because of their slower speed and larger size. They were soon returned to almost exclusive night flying.

After the Mustang entered combat in July 1950 the brunt of the low-level tactical work along the front lines fell to them, and the F-80s were released for interdiction missions, where they could stay at higher altitudes longer in consideration of their fuel consumption. It was during these critical days of July and August that the Mustang started to receive its greatest accolades of the Korean War, as observed in retrospect by the USAF historian Robert Futrell, "The Mustangs based at Taegu and Po'hang displayed great utility during the critical days of mid-July." Perhaps the noted Australian author George Odgers said it even stronger, "Mustangs and napalm won the war for the UN in the early days, if it hadn't been for them we all would have been doing the backstroke across the sea."

CHAPTER TWO

The Opponents: The North Korean Air Force

The North Korean Air force, NKAF, had its beginnings in September 1945 while still under the dominance of the occupying Russian Army. At this time it was identified as the North Korean Aviation Society, but in 1946 is was reorganized as a quasi-military organization and was renamed as Aviation Division, North Korean Army.

Most of the airfields utilized by this Division were of Japanese construction and were still intact at the end of World War II. These airfields were also known to be in use by the Soviets from August 1945 until they withdrew from North Korea in 1948. There were some indications that the Soviets had also left these airfields intact, while some others were of the opinion that they had been stripped of everything that might be considered as worthwhile. It mattered little at this time for the fledgling NKAF was totally dependent upon Russian generosity, and the NKAF were not to receive any aircraft resembling sophisticated by Western standards during the years immediately proceeding the Korean War.

Early in 1948 the Aviation Division did begin to receive Polikarpov Po-2s, NATO coded as "Mule," and Yak-18s, "Max," for training purposes. These aircraft did not require much more than a thousand yards or so of a cleared grass area to fly from, nor did they require expensive or modern maintenance tools. The North Korean Army established its primary training base at Pyongyang, and used their other major base at Sinuiju for liaison purposes, (Later identified as K-23 and K-30, respectively, by FEAF. The USAF designations being given if later occupied or so designated.) permitting all of their other bases within their domain to molder. Later on during 1948 the Aviation Division was once again renamed, as the "Korean People's Army Air Force." At this time it was commanded by Colonel Wang Yen, and Yen subdivided it into three regiments, training, ground attack and fighter. Solely in a tactical format.

In 1949 the ground attack regiment began receiving Il-2M3s, NATO designated as "Bark," which were an early version of the Il-10 "Beast," the noted Shturmovik. The fighter regiment received some La-5s, which were uncoded, and La-7s and 9s, which were coded as "Fin" and "Fritz," respectively. They also received a lesser number of Yak-3s, 7Bs and 9Ps, with the first two outmoded examples being uncoded and the Yak-9P designated as the "Frank." (There is no relationship between this "Frank" and the World War II Japanese Nakajima Ki-84 that had previously been named as a Frank.) It was also reported that they had received several examples of Lend-Lease Bell P-63Cs Kingcobras, coded "Fred." Proof of this latter type remains unverified, for although reports circulated through the press during the early stages of the

The ravages of war, the remains of a North Korean Air Force Il-10 on a scrap heap at Kimpo. The Shturmovik was powered by a 2000 horsepower engine and carried three 20mm cannons for offensive armament. (Needham via Olmsted)

The remains of another Shturmovik, this time at K-27, Yonpo. The photograph was taken after the 35th FIG took possession of the base in November, 1950. The buildings in the background were relatively undamaged during the fighting and were used to house the men of the 35th FIG. (Penrose)

Korean War that the P-63 and F-51 engaged in aerial combat, no official documentation could be discovered.

The exact details of the operation of the NKAF prior to and during the Korean War have yet to come to the Western World, although some light has been shed by statements by POW's or defecting NKAF pilots. In September 1949 it was reported that an agreement had been reached between the Soviet Union and North Korea, where the Russians would assist the North Koreans by furnishing Soviet instructors, military advisors and aircraft. This was to have commenced on May 20, 1949 and it was to continue for at least a year. At the time this intelligence was received by FEAF Headquarters in Japan it was estimated that the NKAF strength would approximate 800 men of all ranks and thirty-six aircraft of various types.

Later, during September 1949, additional reports indicated that sixty North Korean Air Force and seventy Russian pilots had arrived at Pyongyang's Heijo Airfield on June 16. These reports also indicated that the North Korean pilots had already received some training in an unidentified Soviet maritime province and that they were now commanded by a Korean Army Senior Colonel.

In April 1950 it was estimated by FEAF intelligence that the mission of the NKAF was strictly one of training and proficiency, but they admitted that further details were lacking. The types of aircraft, and more importantly, their numbers, remained elusive. Oddly enough, there was still some suspicion within FEAF that most of the NKAF's tactical strength was made up of captured Japanese fighters and that they were only supplemented by Russian built aircraft. It was also believed that the NKAF pilot ranks

had been expanded by the inclusion of seventy or more ex Japanese and Chinese pilots who had gained their experience during World War II. The only major concern raised by this information was that it was now estimated that the NKAF had grown to approximately 1,500 men. There was little apparent thought given to the idea that the NKAF might become an eventual opponent, much less a formidable one.

Just prior to the summer of 1950 there came further reports of a large influx of combat aircraft into North Korea. Intelligence sources indicated that some sixty-odd Il-10s and seventy Yak-9Ps, along with twenty-two Yak-18s and eight Po-2s has suddenly appeared on North Korean airfields. However, total figures never seemed to add up properly, for a defecting North Korean pilot stated that he believed the NKAF to consist of thirty-five Yak's of various versions, three twin-engine bombers, two twin-engine transports, and thirty-five Soviet or Japanese built trainers, totaling approximately seventy-five aircraft altogether.

Nevertheless, the expansion of the NKAF also brought an increase of their available airfields. Two additional airfields were rebuilt well inside of North Korea at Yonpo and Wonsan, (K-27 and K-25, respectively.) on what had originally been Japanese airfield sites. To supplement these permanent field, three more airstrips were constructed at Kansong, Kumchon and Sinmak, all in close proximity to the 38th Parallel.

Even with this information, no one in Japan evidenced any great concern. Although the NKAF was showing signs of expansion, they certainly did not appear to be strong

Carl Frazer, (right), 68th Fighter (All-Weather) Squadron and two other members of his squadron inspect the remains of another North Korean aircraft at Kimpo. It would be difficult to confirm whether it had been a Yak-9 or an Il-10 after such damage. Frazer and his pilot, "Skeeter" Hudson, were the first to destroy a North Korean aircraft during the conflict while crewing a F-82 Twin Mustang. (Frazer)

enough to pose any sort of a threat to peace to warrant any actual counter preparedness effort. At this time FEAF was actually in the process of scrapping their tactical air power with over two hundred Mustangs having been rendered scrap.

The NKAF air war began at 1:15 pm kst on June 25, 1950 with little significant action. Two Yak's were observed over Seoul at this time on an apparent reconnaissance sweep, and they then turned north without firing a shot. Later that afternoon two additional flights of four Yak's each again approached Seoul. One flight broke away from the other to strafe Seoul's Municipal Airport, while the other strafed Kimpo Airdrome. At Kimpo it took five strafing passes to destroy the one undefended C-54 that was parked there. At Seoul Municipal Airport seven ROKAF T-6s were set ablaze and they burned to hulks. The Yak's came back the next day, with two striking Seoul Municipal once again, while four strafed Kimpo, and four more set about strafing Seoul, itself. All of these attacks on the second day created a panic, but actually caused little material damage.

The following day, June 27, North American Aviation F-82 Twin Mustangs shot down a Yak and two La-7s out of a flight of five NKAF aircraft that were encountered between Seoul and Suwon. A few hours later the Lockheed F-80 scored for the first time when a flight of Shooting Stars shot down four out of eight Il-10s that they had intercepted.

On June 28 four more Yak's attacked Suwon and destroyed a B-26 and a F-82 on the ground. They came back again the following day with four more Yak's and strafed Suwon once again, but by this time there wasn't anything remaining there that was worth hitting. Still, they returned once again that afternoon with six Yak's and a mixed bag of Il-10s and La-7s, and two of these attackers were shot down. The final attack of the day was mounted by four Yak's, which were intercepted by USAF piloted Mustangs enroute for delivery to the ROKAF. Four NKAF Yak's were shot down and another was probably shot down and the fifth was damaged in the aerial combat. These two battles on June 29 were the first major combats between the Mustang and conventionally powered Russian built fighters during the Korean War, and the last of any magnitude until November.

The last dogfight over Suwon had been witnessed by General MacArthur, who, reportedly, was impressed with the skill of the American pilots in their Mustangs. He also was impressed by the maneuverability of the Yak aircraft and the aggressiveness shown by their pilots. Since the strength of the NKAF remained an unknown, MacArthur realized that they could not be permitted to either grow in size or to roam at will, thus he authorized FEAF to seek out and destroy the NKAF wherever they might be, least their numbers might be increased through the dallying on the part of the United Nations. Before the day ended American bombers struck the two airfields at Pyongyang and crippled the NKAF.

The NKAF had mounted its strongest efforts during this last week of June. It was reported on June 29 that a P-39 had attacked a USAF B-29, although it may be surmised that this was actually a Yak-9 that had been misidentified. Also on this date two Yak's made passes on another B-29. Both encounters were uneventful. The NKAF also looked to the sea this week, making repeated

The appearance of the MiG-15 over North Korea in the fall of 1950 violated the very first tenant of USAF intelligence: Do not be surprised. When they first became operational they suffered from a combat range problem, having a combat range of only 100 miles. This was only sufficient to cover as far south from their Manchurian bases as the North Korean capitol of Pyongyang. Later, when external fuel tanks were fitted, they could fly as far south at the 38th Parallel. (Sommerich via Esposito)

Down in the rough! Everything considered, Mustang pilots were able to fight the MiG-15 to a draw, but it was through the talents of the F-51 pilots and the fact that the MiG's had to attack the Mustangs at their optimum altitudes that gave them a fighting chance against the faster fighters. (Sommerich via Esposito)

strafing passes on HMS Black Swan and two ROK vessels. Damage was negligible in all cases, and only on rare occasions thereafter did the NKAF operate beyond their own shoreline.

The first conformation of the 5th Air Force's assumption of the strength of the NKAF also came on June 29 when a NKAF Major shot down near Suwon was interrogated.

The Major stated that a Soviet Colonel had taken command of the NKAF two days after the war had started, and that he had fifteen other Soviet advisors on his staff. The Major went on to say that he knew of no instance of where the Soviets were actually flying combat missions. He then proceeded to give the locations of the squadrons that were flying forty Yak-7Bs, fourteen Yak-11s, and sixty-eight Il-10s, with these numbers pretty well matching FEAF's estimated strength of the NKAF.

It appeared that after these first few days of the air war that the NKAF would only attempt an offensive operation in the absence of UN aircraft. Whether this was due to a lack of qualified pilots or a shortage of tactical aircraft was an unknown. One theory was that they were attempting to conserve their pilots by judicious deployment. It might have also been just blind luck that the NKAF happened to be where UN aircraft were not, as there were many unconfirmed sightings of NKAF aircraft by UN or South Korean ground personnel.

The NKAF did return to strafe Suwon on July 2, but there were no worthwhile targets for them to hit and little damage was done. Of interest, however, was the reported sighting of a Tu-4 under escort by two La-7s over Suwon that were flying on a northerly heading. According to the observers none of these aircraft bore any identifying markings. This reported sighting might be completely erroneous, for this same day 77 Squadron, RAAF, was escorting B-29s with their Mustangs on a mission to Yonpo. Additionally, the USAF also had several RB-29s operating from Japan without any identifying markings. (In fact, Lt. Harry White, 339th Fighter (All-Weather) Squadron, was once ordered to intercept with his F-82 one of these RB-29s that had suffered a radio failure and provide it an escort to Misawa Air Base, Japan. He was under orders to shoot it down if it made any aggressive moves, since it was virtually identical to the Tu-4 and its actual identity could not be ascertained until it was on the ground).

Also on July 3 it was believed that the NKAF assumed a small but lethal role of ground support for their own forces when four Yak's dropped anti-personnel bombs on ROK army troops south of Kimpo, killing sixty-eight soldiers. (Since the state of reporting was in such confusion at the time, this incident may actually have been one involving 77 Squadron Mustangs. Conformation either way has proven impossible). Several Yak's were active this day, nevertheless, for Suwon was strafed again, and this same flight of four Yak's then went on to strafe Pyongtaek. This was followed on July 4 by four unmarked Yak's that strafed Osan, and one further strike by Il-10s that came in to destroy the town's radio station.

The NKAF was credited with its first aerial victory on July 12 when two Yak's attacked a B-29 over Haeju, causing enough damage that the Superfortress crew had to bailout. Another B-29 was attacked by Yak-9s over Seoul, but it managed to evade the encounter without incurring damage. Operating at a lower altitude, two more Yak's attacked and shot down a hapless L-5 over Chochlwon. Two days later the NKAF shot down a B-26 Invader over Kaejon.

Between July 15 when four Yak's strafed the MLR of the 21st Regimental Combat Team near Taejon and August 23 the NKAF was only moderately active. They made limited attacks against UN liaison aircraft and attempted to cut off several flights of F-80s that were returning to Japan short on fuel. All of these attacks were unsuccessful with the exception of the death of Lt. Howard O'Dell, 36th Fighter Bomber Squadron. O'Dell was shot down by a Yak on July 19.

It was assumed that the NKAF's first jet fighter, also assumed to be a MiG-15, was operational on July 16 when a swept-winged fighter was spotted over Chongju. Little concern was evidenced in reaction to this sighting at the time. There were then only a few sightings of NKAF aircraft until August when two Yaks were destroyed on the ground by 67th FBS pilots on August 3 and three more on August 10. In the air the NKAF remained dormant until August 23 when two Yaks again headed out to sea to strafe HMS Conus, which was approximately twenty miles southeast of Haeju, but they did little damage.

It was during the first two months of the Korean War when the NKAF had their strongest potential. During this period they were only limited by the radius of action of their aircraft and the armament they could carry. Still, one major questions arises and that is, if they were going to wage a war, why was their air force so weak in numbers and so unsupporting of their ground forces? Surely, in light of the role that air power had played during World War II the communists knew of the importance of aerial supremacy over a battlefield. The Yak aircraft were noted for their maneuverability and speed, yet they were not suited for ground support. The Il-10 however was the premier ground support in the entire world. It was virtually impossible to knock down with antiaircraft fire, due to its heavily armored undersides. As a team the two aircraft could have played havoc with the South Korean and UN forces. It may be surmised that the NKAF intended to only participate in a "lightning war," and that they considered that what they had was adequate. If this was the case, then they sadly underestimated the resolve of the United nations and the speed in which they reacted, which although it was barely in the nick of time it was sufficient to counter the North Korean forces.

At the beginning of the war the 5th Air Force Intelligence Office estimated that the NKAF was capable of mounting 138 combat sorties during each twenty-four hour period. They also concluded that the NKAF included some P-39s and P-63s that had been destined for Russia during the World War II Lend-Lease, and maybe they had some F-51s that they had obtained from China either during or after the war. Oddly enough, the Mustangs were supposed to have been painted all black! With these types FEAF estimated that the NKAF had a radius of action from their North Korean airfields to encompass all but the very southern tip of Korea, and also 50% of the Japanese home islands.

Two months later, and based upon claims for NKAF aircraft destroyed, the 5th Air Force estimated that the NKAF could only launch a total of twenty-three sorties per day. This figure was derived from the estimated thirteen fighters and twelve Il-10s that remained in their inventory. There was no estimation made as to a resupply from the Soviets. The 5th Air Force also assumed that the NKAF continued to have adequate maintenance capabilities.

Prisoner of war interrogations that took place in mid October revealed that the NKAF had moved their entire training operation from North Korea to Manchuria. On October 18 a 31st Strategic Reconnaissance Squadron RB-29 flew down the Yalu River and spotted between seventy-five and a hundred aircraft parked at Antung, Manchuria, just across the river from Sinuiju. Another RB-29 went back to the area the next day, and no aircraft could be seen at all. The question then was, was this an observation of a tactical deployment, or were they trying to draw a reconnaissance aircraft across the river to create an escalation of the war? Also, during the last five days of October there was a marked increase in observed NKAF air activity, but whether this indicated a build-up in forces or a last gasp tactic remained an open question.

By October 31 the NKAF was believed to have been reduced to only five tactical aircraft and somewhere between ten and fifteen trainers. Even so, they were expected to be capable of flying fifteen to twenty combat sorties per day. At this time the North Korean Army was pressed well back into their own countryside, where they retained only their four most northern airfields. Even if they did use their trainers in a tactical role, it was now felt that the NKAF no longer posed a threat to UN forces.

With the entry of the Chinese Communists into the Korean war there came a marked increase of communist aerial activity. By November 5 the NKAF's role had changed from making a few sneak harassing attacks across the Yalu River to aggressively seeking out and attacking UN aircraft. It was, however, considered remote that the NKAF was actually participating in these actions, due to their attrition of experienced pilots.

Yet, during this same period six Yak's that supposedly no longer existed were shot down by 18th FBG Mustangs! Then there was also the appearance of the swept-winged, (Or, reportedly, elliptical-winged.) jet fighters, possibly either MiG-15 or Yak-15 types, and some additional sightings of identified Tu-4s. All of these were aircraft that the NKAF were not supposed to either possess or be capable of operating. Therefore it was logically assumed that these aircraft were being flown by other than NKAF pilots or crews.

Further assumptions being made by 5th Air Force Headquarters estimated that 250 aircraft of the Soviet Air Force operating in China would be obtainable prior to the communists launching an all-out air effort. This figure was derived through an intelligence report that indicated that an estimated 250 fighters, 175 ground attack aircraft, 150 twin-engines bombers and seventy-five transport aircraft were available in the regions in close proximity to North Korea. It was also expected that the Soviets would probably be able to furnish between 400 and 500 more aircraft to the NKAF from a storage depot in the area of Dairen.

By the first of November the estimated NKAF inventory figures were revised to show that the NKAF might posses around fifty Yak-9s, believed to come from a staging area in Manchuria. This potential became a minor concern for FEAF, for if all of these aircraft were utilized in the war, a sizable diversion of UN support aircraft, ie: F-51s and F-80s of the USAF and F4Us of the U.S. Navy, would have to take place in order to continue proper air defense functions. The UN airlift program into Korea would definitely be hindered, as the transports would then have to be given fighter escorts. Attacks against UN shipping could be expected. The threat of the communists commencing tactical support of their ground forces could not be discounted. In all, it would probably mean that the UN effort stood a good chance of being driven out of the country before they could react to the onslaught once again.

All of this was not to mention the potential of the communists actually attacking some, or all, of the Japanese home islands, every bit the sanctuary for the United Nations as Manchuria was for the communist forces.

Through November and December the communist air forces made and broke contact with UN air power at will, taking every advantage of their Manchurian sanctuary whenever they needed to. By the end of 1950 things were apparently going so well for the NKAF and the NKA, (And whomever their counterparts might be that were now appearing on a regular basis with the MiG-15.) that they had been able to regain the use to some degree of twenty of their airfields in North Korea that had previously been held by UN forces.

In spite of the arrival in Korea in December of the USAF's 4th Fighter Interceptor Wing with F-86As and the 27th Fighter Escort Wing with F-84Es, there was little doubt that the communists had gained immediate control of the skies over North Korea at this time. They had taken some losses when they broke into the fighter bomber strikes, but by these same interruptions they had in many cases forced the fighter bombers to jettison their ordnance short of their targets and rendered the missions as negligible.

By the end of 1950 there had been eight encounters between F-51s and MiG-15s, with the Mustang pilots claiming five MiG probables or damaged with no losses of their own. Several other flights of MiGs had been observed by Mustang pilots, but combat had not been joined.

Yet there was no question after these encounters that the Mustang was now well out of its element when it came to dogfighting with jet propelled aircraft, and for them to remain as a viable combat aircraft they were going to have to be afforded some fighter escort protection.

As the 27th FEW had become operational in Korea on December 6 and the 4th FIW ten days later, the entire spectrum of air warfare changed from twisting and turning at low altitudes by conventional vs. jet to climbing and diving and pulling high G's in the stratosphere by jet vs. jet over a piece of geography to be known as "MiG Alley." The focus of the attention became directed toward the Sabres and MiGs and how they fared in respect to each other, both in aircraft capability and pilot techniques. Jet battles were exciting press.

Little interest was now shown in the NKAF by FEAF intelligence, for the bully on the block had brought in a "ringer." It was generally believed that the MiG was far to complex for the NKAF to handle, and there had never been any indication that they had ever received any training in jet propelled aircraft to begin with. There was a great amount of talk as to whether the Chinese were able to fly the aircraft in combat, and it was generally agreed that at the very least whomever was flying the MiG was receiving strong Soviet technological assistance.

Whether Soviet pilots were flying the MiGs or not is really an academic issue of value only to vanity. In reality, it made not one iota of difference, for in comparison, the USAF did not permit ROKAF pilots to fly the Sabre or engage in combat with the MiG, either. One can only imagine the bar room talk in Manchuria about whether the F-86s flown by the Canadians or Royal Air Force exchange

A NKAF Mitsubishi Ki-54 "Topsy," (World War II name, no NATO designation.) abandoned at K-24, Pyongyang East Airdrome, in November 1950. Most interesting is the tail of the F-80 on the right side of the photograph, as it had to have wound up at K-24 through some sort of an emergency since Shooting Stars were never based there. (Tidwell via Thompson)

pilots were better flown than those from Australia or the U.S. Navy or Marine Corps pilots versus those flown by USAF pilots?

Just because the MiG 15 and the apparent Chinese Air Force were now fighting over Korea did not mean that the NKAF no longer existed. Although never strong by comparison to any of the participating United Nations air forces, the NKAF still remained in evidence, with most of their combat sorties now being flown at night. These missions became known as "Bedcheck Charlie's" by the UN forces. On November 20 one of these missions struck the 8th FBG Mustang parking area at Pyongyang and damaged eleven F-51s.

After the UN forces were routed from North Korea in December 1950 the NKAF followed them south and continued to nip at their heels with nightly raids along the MLR. These attacks did little actual damage but they did force a demand for an increase in vigilance, which added to the fatigue of the retreating forces and hampered their effectiveness. These "Charlies" took advantage of the predominant bad winter weather conditions and worried the airfields at Suwon and Kimpo. Usually flying Po-2s that flitted in and out under USAF radar coverage, they made their presence known just often enough to force FEAF to devote F-82s, F7F-3Ns, F4U-5Ns, F3Ds and then in April 1951 F-94Bs to airfield defense during periods of inclement weather and darkness. The entire situation was just one more logistical and budget problem for FEAF and UN planning officers, akin to having to provide multi-million dollar fly swatters to attack gnats.

There appeared to be very little cooperation between the apparent Chinese MiG-15 operations and the NKAF missions at this time. At high or low altitudes the MiGs intercepted UN aircraft, or ignored them at will. The few observed NKAF daylight operations were mostly composed of either Yak-9s or Il-10s, and they also appeared to be operating independent of each other. Usually they flew in flights of four aircraft or less at altitudes that were compatible with those flown by F-51s or F-80s on interdiction missions, which also permitted them to enter into or evade combat at their discretion.

These fighter missions of the NKAF were fairly dormant as 1950 ended and 1951 began. On December 27, 1950 several unidentified NKAF aircraft chased a B-26 and several Yak-9s were seen by a B-29 over Cheju Island, but they did not press an attack. A few more Yaks were observed over Pyongyang in January 1951 but for the most part they only made feints at the B-26s they saw and then they returned to Manchuria. After this only a few more general encounters took place until mid-year.

An abandoned NKAF Il-10 at Kimpo Air Base, K-14, in late September 1950. It appears to be unscathed. (Rockwell via Thompson)

On June 17, 1951 a single Po-2 dropped a pair of twenty-five pound bombs on the 335th FIS flight line at Suwon, destroying one F-86A and damaging four more.

Then on June 20 eight Il-10s were intercepted by 18th FBW Mustangs over the Yellow Sea. The Shturmovik's were headed for Sinmi-do, a small island outpost some seventy miles south-southeast of Sinuiju and west of Chongju. The Mustangs shot down two and damaged three more, and the remainder turned north and fled across the Yalu River. That afternoon, in a rare cooperative action, six Yak-9s were provided a top cover of MiG-15s as they also headed for Sinmi-do. They also were intercepted by 18th FBW Mustangs, but only one Yak was destroyed, and one F-51 was shot down by a MiG that broke through the escort provided by 4th FIW F-86s.

NKAF Po-2 nocturnal raids continued through the end of June and the first week of July, with two being shot down by USMC night fighters.

There wasn't much in the way of reported NKAF observations until September when something very unusual occurred in the way of sightings of communist aircraft, and this has never been confirmed as to who was actually flying the aircraft. On September 5 a flight of 18th FBW Mustangs was jumped by a F-80C that had to be flown by a communist pilot. The Shooting Star bore no national markings, but it did have its entire nose painted red, all the way back to the canopy. This rogue F-80 was seen again on November 1, and again on December 3, but on this latter occasion it was not carrying any tip tanks.

On December 10 two more rogue F-80s attacked a flight of Mustangs, and on this occasion both carried the underslung tip tanks, and neither bore national markings. A flight of three rogue F-80s was then encountered on January 3, 1952, and then a single one on February 27,

The remains of a NKAF Yak-9 at Kimpo after being well and truly worked over by fighter-bombers during the course of the Inchon Invasion. Interesting is that the engine and propeller rotation is opposite to that used by Western aircraft manufactures. (Fahlberg via Thompson)

but after this date they were never seen again. It can only be assumed that they were rebuilt USAF Shooting Stars that had gone down in North Korea and that the NKAF (Or someone.) had rebuilt them.

The NKAF had started flying twin-engine Tu-2s, NATO named "Bat," in combat in November 1951. On the last day of the month the NKAF had launched a flight of twelve "Bat's" under an escort of MiG-15s. They were jumped by a flight of F-86s and all of the Tu-2s and seven MiGs were claimed as shot down. From this point on until the spring of 1952 there was very little indication that the NKAF still existed during daylight hours, yet they did continue their nocturnal forays along the MLR with their Bedcheck Charlies. Some of these were still Po-2s, but Yak-18s and La-7s were also being used according to FEAF reports.

The NKAF started "bed checking" Inchon, Suwon and Seoul with a serious intent during the winter of 1952. On the night of February 28, 1952 the 68th Fighter Interceptor Squadron lost their first F-94 while chasing a Po-2. It was believed, but not confirmed, that the Po-2 was shot down, but the F-94 stalled out and crashed into the sea, killing both crew members.

A combination of USAF, U.S. Navy and Marine Corps night fighter operations only served to hamper NKAF nocturnal operations for the next eighteen months. On October 13, 1952 four Po-2s struck Cho-do Island, wound-

ing two USAF airmen and killing five ROK civilians. They would return three more times until on December 10 when a USMC F3D destroyed a Po-2. They continued into January 1953, then had a short respite until April 15 when they returned to Cho-do, killing two antiaircraft gunners. On April 23 Po-2s, La-11s and Yak-18s hit Kimpo damaging five RF-80s. In May 1953 a pair of NKAF aircraft, credited only as "Prop" were shot down by F-94s.

On the night of June 16-17, 1953 the NKAF struck Inchon with fifteen aircraft and blew up five million gallons of fuel that was in unprotected storage. In the next three weeks of nocturnal counter-air operations the U.S. Navy gained their only ace of the Korean War when Lt. Guy Bordelon shot down his fifth night victory while flying a Corsair. Between June 30 and July 16 he destroyed two Yak-18s and three Po-2s. (Bordelon also was the only pilot to gain ace status during the war while flying a conventionally powered aircraft).

It was reported that the NKAF had started training in MiG-15s during the winter of 1953 and that they had become operational with them in the spring. Prior to this time only selected individual pilots had been permitted to fly the MiG, and these individuals were forced to fly in formations with Chinese pilots, and not with their own countrymen. There is no record that any of the NKAF pilots ever destroyed any UN aircraft while flying the MiG, although they did engage in several encounters that were touted for their propaganda value.

As the conflict closed the NKAF attempted a last minute rebuilding of their airfields in North Korea. But as these were kept under close scrutiny by USAF reconnaissance aircraft, and as soon as it appeared that a runway might be serviceable, it was bombed. On the last day of the war there was an attempt to repair and fly into these airstrips a number of aircraft, for according to the treaty they could only have what was in place on July 27. On the 27th it was determined that all but one airfield in North Korea was unserviceable for jet operations, ie: less than three thousand feet of runway remained usable, and the last one at Uiju, northeast of Sinuiju, was in dubious condition. It was thought, however, that the NKAF had imported two hundred aircraft of mixed types and secreted them by "cave and crate" in anticipation of rebuilding their air force in a more peaceable environment.

CHAPTER THREE

The Republic of Korea's Air Force

Prior to the Korean conflict the Republic of Korea had only a small air force that was economically and politically forced to concentrate solely on training and pilot proficiency in light aircraft. The Republic of Korea Air Force (ROKAF) had separated from the Korean Army on October 1, 1949 as a direct result of intervention by President Rhee. This was due to political pressure brought upon Rhee by the ex Chinese and Japanese pilots that comprised the majority of the "capable" pilots within the South Korean Army. It appears that there had been a considerable number of internal power plays within the South Korean Army during the post World War II period, and it was to avoid further of these internal conflicts that had prompted these pilots to seek a separate air force, lest they lose their identity as aviators.

At the time the ROKAF was formed it was composed of 400 officers and 1499 enlisted men, all who had at least three years experience in aviation. The greatest

Maintenance on the cooling system of the first F-51D supplied to the Republic of Korea's Air Force at Sachon Airdrome, K-4. November 19, 1951. The Mustangs oil and water radiators were both located in the belly airscoop and were vulnerable to any and all sorts of damage. (Reed)

percentage of these men were of Japanese heritage or were those who had been conscripted into the Japanese Air Force during World War II and for one reason or another elected to remain in Korea after the war ended. The new ROKAF Chief of Staff was General Kim Chung Yul.

The new South Korean Air Force was built around a force of eight Piper L-4s, four Stinson L-5s, and ten Canadian-built North American Aviation T-6 Harvards that had been obtained from surplus stocks in Japan at the end of the war. The one aircraft that President Rhee really wanted for his new air force was the Lockheed F-80, and he had started pressuring the 5th Air Force for them in 1949, but they kept. turning him down. (They didn't even have enough for their own requirements!) Rhee then requested Lockheed P-38s, for there were known to have been ninety of them at Seoul, and they were all "low time" aircraft, but this would have upset the "balance of power," and the Lightnings were all scrapped when the USAF withdrew from Korea in 1949.

When the North Koreans invaded on June 25, 1950 the ROKAF was without any tactical air power at all. Their training aircraft were virtually wiped out in one attack by North Korean Yak's. The three remaining T-6 Harvards were hastily fitted with jury-built bomb-racks, and their pilots dropped Korean made bombs until their limited supply of them was consumed three days later. The few surviving liaison aircraft were also pressed into service, to drop leaflets to warn their own people and to try and discourage the invaders. They were also used as reconnaissance aircraft, but they were soon so shot up by both ground and air-to-air fire that they had to be withdrawn.

Immediately President Rhee implored FEAF for ten "Mustang IV" fighters to rebuild his air force. Possibly he

Every squadron seemed to have at least one aircraft named "Miss Manooky" (Or some variation of the spelling), and the ROKAF was no exception. This lonely aircraft, (or pilot) was at Taegu in September 1950. (Brackenreg)

was thinking of those F-51s belonging to the Royal Australian Air Force that he knew were slated to return to Australia when 77 Squadron rotated home. But since 77 squadron had been had been placed on alert and were expecting to be volunteered by their government for United Nations service in Korea, ten USAF F-51D Mustangs were furnished instead. This was viewed as disappointing since somehow Rhee either knew or suspected that the Australian aircraft were in better flying condition.

Initially the ROKAF selected ten of their more experienced pilots for training the F-51, and they were flown to Johnson Air Base, Japan where this task was to be accomplished. Most of these ten pilots had some experience in fighters, but no recent flying time in anything larger than the T-6. On July 2, 1950 Mustangs, now bearing the freshly painted yin-yang insignia of the ROKAF were ferried to South Korea by the first six of the ROKAF pilots to have qualified in the Mustang.

They took off from Itazuke Air Base, Japan and headed for Taegu, K-2, and there was an immediate expressed concern as to whether these pilots could handle themselves well enough in the aircraft to begin with, and even a greater concern in respect to their being able to land at Taegu when they got there. This was due to two factors, their inexperience, and the potential of the airstrip having been overrun by the North Koreans while the Mustangs were enroute. The Mustangs carried enough fuel for a return trip to Japan should it prove necessary, and the pilots hoped that some effort would be directed toward improving communications in the future so they could find out if they were going to land in a trap, or not. As it was, Taegu was never over run, with a good portion of the credit for this going to the ROKAF Mustangs whose vary presence helped hold the Pusan Perimeter during the "dark days" of August when the few

ROKAF Mustangs actually represented the only tactical air power the United Nations had in Korea, all of the other tactical units having been forced to withdraw to Japan.

The movement of these ROKAF Mustangs into the combat arena was originally identified as "Detachment 1, 36th Fighter Bomber Squadron. But by the time the Detachment was packed and were ready to leave Japan they were renamed as "Bout 1," and another "Detachment 1" was formed, with this second unit becoming what would eventually be known as the 5lst Fighter Bomber Squadron (Provisional).

The Detachment was to have included a Ground Controlled Intercept (GCI) radar site, communications equipment consisting of radio, telephone and Teletype circuits for air-to-air and air-to-ground communications. They did receive the radar equipment, which did not work, and received little of the remainder, but they made do with the what they had.

Another ROKAF Mustang receiving maintenance on its cooling system, showing the "doghouse" removed for access. August 3, 1950. (U.S. Army via Ethell)

Major Dean Hess's "By Faith I Fly" was photographed at Miho Air Base, Japan on March 31, 1951. For a period ROKAF # 18 (USAF s/n 44-74629) also bore the name "Last Chance." This ex Air National Guard aircraft had 481 hours on it when transferred to the ROKAF. (Reed)

"Bout 1" was led by Major Dean Hess, who flew to Taegu in a "donated" C-47 to set up combat and training operations for the ROKAF in the F-51. To maintain some semblance of both a combat and training role the ROKAF pilots, themselves, were forced to fly out of the airstrip at Chinhae, which later became better known as simply K-10, The ROKAF pilots would fly a combination of aircraft familiarization and, or ground support strikes, depending upon their individual expertise, and then fly to K-1, Pusan-West Airdrome, where they would land. The ROKAF pilots would then be flown back to K-10 in a liaison "ferry" while the Mustangs were flown back by a USAF "instructor." At this time the runway at K-10 was deemed as far to short for the inexperienced ROKAF pilots to attempt landing there and K-2 was too crowded with transport aircraft providing logistical support to the UN operations. It was hardly an efficient operation, but it was necessity, lest a scarce fighter might be damaged in an accident.

"Bout 1" had hardly gotten started in its roll of a fighting/training air force when it was deactivated. The combat situation had become so desperate that FEAF was forced to recall all their USAF personnel and the F-51s.

The USAF men and aircraft were now used to form the provisional 6002nd Fighter Bomber Squadron, which became attached to the also newly created 6002nd Fighter Bomber Wing, which was placed under the command of Colonel Curtis R. Low. Among other factors, this move amounted to the virtual total destruction of ROKAF morale, as the South Korean pilots and ground crews were just beginning to feel that they were of some value to their own country. An irate Dean Hess finally was able to catch the ear of General Timberlake and managed to

convince him that his Bout 1 squadron actually did have some value of its own, and Timberlake then consented to return six of the ten conscripted Mustangs to the ROKAF, but only Hess and one other USAF pilot was allowed to return to the unit.

At this time the remnants of "Bout 1" was redesignated as the 6146th Base Unit, (BASUT). The second USAF pilot, Captain Mike Bellovin, and Hess were then permitted to select thirty pilots and airmen of various skills to get the BASUT operational, and these men became the nucleus of a unit that would slowly increase in size. By the time the Korean War ended the 6146th BASUT had expanded to a force of forty-two officers and 222 airmen, becoming identified as the 6146th Korea Air Force Advisory Group.

On July 10, 1950, after a week of massive confusion, the American volunteer pilots were finally authorized to beginning flying limited combat missions in the ROKAF aircraft without having ROKAF pilots in tow. Prior to this time, Hess had pulled two Mustangs from their training roles and kept them armed for combat, anyhow. It was during this period that he earned the nickname of "one man air force," while flying officially unauthorized combat missions as often as ten times a day in support of the UN ground forces.

During the afternoon of July 10 the first ROKAF Mustang was lost. A flight, led by Major Hess was headed for Chonan when one of the newly assigned USAF pilots, Lt. A.E. Helseth, a young pilot himself with only 200 hours flying time in the F-51, discovered that his radio had failed. Helseth then spotted two North Korean tanks, but he could not attract the attention of the rest of his flight, so he broke off on his own to attack them. He dove down and knocked one of them out, and then discovered that he was lost.

ROKAF # 19 after coming to grief via a runway over-shoot at K-4, Sachon, in 1952. (Chard)

The ROKAF also flew a mixed bag of other types of aircraft, including the Taylorcraft L-4. These young ROKAF pilots were waiting at K-4 for the arrival of some additional Mustangs to be ferried in from Japan. (Chard)

skills, as there were no electronic navigational aids in service in Korea during these first months of the war.

Another major problem was the total lack of maps. During the postwar occupation of Korea the entire southern half, and a fair portion of the northern half of Korea had been photographed and mapped by F-6s (RF-51Ds), F-7s (B-24s), and F-I5 Reporters, a reconnaissance modification of the P-61, of the 8th Photo Reconnaissance Group. What ever benefit these photographs and maps might have been was lost, as they disappeared during the 1949 USAF withdrawal from Seoul. Thus pilots had to rely upon "pilotage" and "dead reckoning" techniques for navigation, and these accounted for the loss of many aircraft within all of the squadrons flying in Korea until proper maps and navigational aids became available. As in England and Europe during the previous war, each village, mountain, or rice paddy looked like its neighbor from the air.

While searching for a recognizable landmark he proceeded to knock out nine trucks and a half-track, and then he headed south. With darkness approaching and nothing familiar in sight, Helseth decided to belly land his Mustang before it ran out of fuel. He settled for a field at Haedong, which turned out to be the town's park, and put it down without injury. It took him five days to walk and hitchhike his way back to Taegu.

The additional pilots that slowly filtered into the 6146th averaged considerably more experience than Helseth. Most of then had been flying around Japan with the occupation forces for several years, and several had seen action during World War II. A few of them had been a part of the first fighter sweeps over Seoul during the evacuation in June, which helped in their "pilotage" navigational

One of the smaller units supporting the 6146th and the United Nation's effort was the Korean Military Advisory Group (KMAG). They would remain in existence until they were combined with the Advance Command and Liaison Group in Korea, (ADCOM), and they became the communications contact between operational FEAF units and Eighth United States Army in Korea (EUSA). The initial senior air advisor of the KMAG to the ROKAF was Major Ervin Ethell, formally the Commanding Officer of the 39th Fighter Interceptor Squadron. Most of the officers assigned to the KMAG served in the field with the Republic of Korea army units, and upon them had fallen the task of determining whether the initial assault on June 25 had been a real act of war or just a minor boarder

A line-up of Mustangs at Kisarazu Air Base, Japan awaiting application of ROKAF insignia. The nearest, 44-73263, previously belonged to the 152nd Fighter Squadron, Rhode Island Air National Guard. It was supplied to the ROKAF in November 1952 and it was salvaged in July 1957. (T.P. Ingrassia via Menard)

Another Mustang for the ROKAF as it prepares to depart Kisarazu for Sachon. The 160 gallon Fletcher Aircraft Corporation drop tanks, a variation on their T-33 tip tanks, gave the Mustang a ferry range of 1600 miles. (T.P. Ingrassia via Menard)

skirmish, and once this decision was established, how to best deploy the forces to try and turn the enemy back.

On June 26 the KMAG Headquarters had reported an "increased steadiness" on the part of the ROK army troops, but with the coming of darkness that very night it became obvious that the ROK army moral was cracking. It was Colonel W.H.S. Wright, Chief of the KMAG, who then had the task of reporting that the enemy would take Seoul the next day, and he and Ambassador Muccio had made the decision to ask for the emergency evacuation of American personnel.

Because flexibility and availability was the key to survival, it was fortunate that the KMAG and the 6146th BASUT were stationed at the same location for the first few weeks of the war. Obtaining an air strike often be-

ROKAF #'s 69 & 81 at Suwon while paying a visit to the 4th Fighter Interceptor Wing in 1953. Note that the tail wheel doors have been removed and the tail wheels are locked in the down position. (via Davis)

came simply a matter of yelling across the office space in the 6146th operations tent and asking for air support at a given location. In fact, it was commonplace for General Dean or General Walker of the 8th Army to conduct their own operations briefings from the 6146th operations tent, as the pilots' reports provided the quickest appraisal of the movement of ground forces.

Because of the relentless pressure of the invading North Koreans, the 6146th BASUT and their ROKAF contingent was kept constantly on the move. From Taegu they went to Sachon Airdrome, K-4, and then back to Taegu, and then to Chinhae, their staging base. All of these moves were accomplished within three weeks, but they would stay at Chinhae until after the Inchon Invasion in September.

Chinhae, itself, was an old Japanese constructed airfield that eventually became the modernized home of the 18th Fighter Bomber Wing, but it was just a mudhole when the 6146th Base Unit arrived. The twenty-seven hundred foot runway that was available at the time was deemed far to short for the inexperienced South Korean pilots to use, and Major Hess and his fellow USAF pilots had to use extreme caution with their combat loaded Mustangs, trundling them off the ground in support of the U.S. 25th Infantry Division that was embroiled in battle only ten miles away. Through the South Korean government, indigenous labor was hired to lengthen the runway to thirty-five hundred feet, which then permitted the ROKAF pilots to also fly combat missions. But in the meantime, it was back to the old "ferry" routine of shuttling Mustangs and ROKAF pilots between Chinhae and Taegu or K-1 so the ROKAF pilots could build up their flying experience.

In a non-sequitur, the first "official" combat mission of the ROKAF was flown from Chinhae on August 6, 1950 with Dean Hess and ROKAF wingmen, The ROKAF was not officially committed to the Korean War until September 27, 1950, when they flew to Kwangju, where a communist banner had been strung across the main street by the invading army. The banner was strafed, along with five trucks, a car and a motorcycle. Missions of this sort would continue throughout the month, alternating with interdiction and ground support. Most of the ground support sorties were directed to the main line of resistance in front of the U.S. 24th and 25th Infantry Divisions. Air support was also given as often as possible to the hard pressed ROK divisions, as it was a real morale booster for them to see Mustangs overhead that bore the insignia of the Republic of Korea.

On August 29, 1950 a firepower demonstration was put on by Hess and Captain Wilson for President Rhee. They strafed 50 gallon oil drums and napalmed a small island off-shore from Chinhae. Rhee was impressed, and put in yet another request for more Mustangs. August, in itself, had been considered a good month for the fledgling ROKAF. They had flown 109 combat sorties, and in them they claimed 19 trucks, 7 motorcycles, 7 jeeps, and one tunnel sealed off. 216 two-hundred-fifty pound fragmentation bombs were dropped, and 196,300 rounds of .50 caliber ammunition were fired. There were no ROKAF casualties and no ROKAF aircraft were lost or damaged.

September 1950 did see a marked reduction in combat operations, however. This was due to a lack of ordnance to expend. The ROKAF was definitely on the low end of the FEAF supply priority lists, because of their commitments to other Mustang units and their own limited resources. Only twenty-one effective combat sorties

were flown. Emphasis was thusly directed to checking out as many ROKAF Mustang pilots as possible.

To assist in this training, Detachment 4, 3499th Training Aids Wing was assigned to the 6146th BASUT on temporary duty. This unit, known as F-51-4, was led by Lt. Robert Denomy, and was composed of twenty men whose home was Chanute Air Force Base, Illinois. They arrived at Chinhae just in time to watch one ROKAF piloted Mustang invert itself into the bay because of pilot error, just the type of incident they were there to teach the pilots how to prevent.

The ROKAF assigned interpreters to surmount a first major obstacle, language. The USAF/ROKAF interpreter team set to the task of translating the F-51 maintenance and pilot's handbooks into Korean and drew up bilingual charts for the classroom which showed the various F-51 internal systems. When the ROKAF later moved from Chinhae to Seoul, Detachment 4 went with them, setting up shop in the Yongdongpo Middle School. They shepherded one class through the intricacies of the Mustang and then returned to the Zone of Interior, leaving the ROKAF instructors with all the required training aids and some expertise for instruction of additional classes.

The actual move to Seoul was carried out during the last week in September. Most of the men and equipment were moved in an old LST named the City of Tangyang, that was a "smelly old rust bucket whose fumes made and kept most of the men sick for the entire voyage." They arrived at Inchon Harbor in the midst of rain and high winds, and then were transported via trucks to Kimpo, K-14. But, due to a poor "political climate," brought on by a USAF Colonel, the ROKAF unit immediately started looking for another location. Actually, the "political climate" situation involved Colonel Curtis Low and his 18th Fighter

The original ROKAF Base Operations section at Sachon was more than a little seedy in 1952. (Chard)

The same area at K-4 after the United States started pouring money into the ROKAF, creating a first class Base Operations area. (Evans)

A ROKAF Mustang taxiing out for takeoff for a training flight from K-4 with a marshal to insure wing tip clearance between the ROKAF C-47 and L-26. (Evans)

The USAF's 6146th Base Unit eventually grew to reach Group status before the Korean War ended. Left to right are USAF advisors to the ROKAF Major Marvin Evans, Captains McDermatt and Taylor, and Lt. Colonel Harrison, the Group commander. (Evans)

Bomber Group who were trying to run a war and did not want a bunch of Mustangs on training missions their way, particularly when most of the pilots could not speak English and whose own language spooked the American pilots when they were overheard on the radios.

The ROKAF found another airstrip south of Seoul, at Yogdungpo. This airfield, originally Seoul City, became known as K-16, and it looked more "like a wheat field in Kansas than an airdrome." What few buildings still standing had been "cheese holed" by B-26s that had bombed the area while it was in communist hands. The North Koreans had even based some Yak's and Po-2s there for a period, but certainly made no effort to keep the airstrip operational after the Invaders had done their work. Again, indigenous labor was hired to clean things up.

The first ROKAF F-51 combat missions were flown from K-16 on October 11, 1950, bringing the loss of the first aircraft and pilot in two months. 1st Lt. Sang Soo Lee, one of the more experienced ROKAF pilots, crashed while attacking a fuel dump near Pyongyang. He was last seen diving into the smoke and fire from the 5" HVAR's he had unleashed, and apparently he had target fascination, for he never pulled out of his dive. Before the month was over another pilot was lost in the same area. The squadron Operations Officer, Captain Dean A. Crowell, became missing in action, with his loss being reported without a great amount of detail by his ROKAF wingman, because of his shock and the language barrier. Apparently Crowell got into a grudge match with an anti-aircraft battery, a situation where the pilot usually does not keep the upper hand.

On October 27 an advance party of ROKAF personnel left K-16 for K-24, on the outskirts of Pyongyang. The contingent was led by Captain Melvin Jackson, and the convoy of twenty-five trucks crossed the 38th Parallel at 1013 hours kst. To say that the men of the ROKAF were elated would be an understatement. They moved into an old abandoned school building, and once again indigenous labor, this time North Korean, were impressed to clean up the damage created by UN air attacks. Living conditions would remain spartan as ever, with the buildings being heated by inadequate oil stoves, and the wind blowing through the many gaps in the battered buildings and tents.

During November the ROKAF was on limited combat status, once again due to a limited amount of ordnance that they had to expend. The pilots dropped one hundred 250-pound general purpose bombs and fired 300 5" HVAR's, which consumed their entire supply, and then they just sat chaffing for more action. One F-51 was lost, on November 11 when Captain Jackson was forced to belly it in after his Merlin engine was damaged by communist antiaircraft fire. Jackson had been flying with Hess near Sinanju when they came under fire. And upon discovering that he had been hit, Jackson headed southeast for Pyongyang, managing to put his Mustang down just a few yards inside of friendly lines. He received severe lacerations to his face and a slight concussion when his head struck the aircraft's K-14 gunsight. He was evacuated, first to Pyongyang, and then to Osaka, Japan to recover from his injuries.

A ROKAF Mustang on the gunnery range near Chindu. The puffs of dust are from the .50 caliber rounds that have already penetrated the targets. (Evans)

The Temco Corporation modified several Mustangs to two-seat trainers, designated as TF-51Ds, in the early 1950s. The ROKAF received five of these to facilitate transition training between the T-6 and the single-seat standard F-51. (Menard)

Due to the massive intervention of the Chinese communists, it soon became obvious that the ROKAF was going to have to pack up their things and move once again. The original plan was to return to K-16, but more "political pressure" from Colonel Low and his 18th FBG was felt.

Colonel Low now wanted K-16 for his own squadrons that were also pulling back from Pyongyang. The advance party of the ROKAF was already headed for K-16 in the squadron's C-47 when they received orders to divert to K-5 at Taejon. K-5 was another battered airstrip, described as "short, narrow, and terribly muddy." On December 5 they started tearing down the old structures at Taejon in the midst of snow and rain showers, to make room for new tents and quonset huts. Meanwhile three USAF C-47s started evacuating the rest of the ROKAF from Pyongyang. They got out of North Korea only twelve hours ahead of the Chinese troops arrival.

It appeared that Taejon was to be the ROKAF's permanent home, which was something they really desired for after all their moves and the problems with the 18th FBG they felt like unwanted nomads. Before they were forced to evacuate K-5 they had almost made it like a home for themselves, having constructed brick walks, put up screened-in tents, built an outdoor movie theater, new showers, and even built revetments to protect their aircraft.

ROKAF # 97 "Somewhere in Korea." This Mustang was USAF 44-84968 that had previously belonged to the 195th Fighter Squadron, California ANG. (Charles Trask via Besecker)

Combat flying was reduced to a six month low, with only thirty-nine combat sorties being flown, once again due to the lack of ordnance. It was decided that since this shortage had become a way of life there was little point in trying to instruct ROKAF pilots in a combat environment and risk loosing a pilot and his aircraft for a nebulous gain. With the exception of a few highly proficient ROKAF pilots and the USAF pilot advisors that pulled combat alert assignments, the ROKAF was virtually withdrawn from combat responsibilities.

On December 17 1st Lt. Earnest Craigwell, Jr., took seven USAF enlisted men to Cheju-do Island to establish a permanent training camp for the ROKAF in a sterile environment. Cheju-do was a volcanic island off the coast of South Korea that was nearly two miles long, and otherwise was of little interest, but it did have an immediately usable 6,500 foot runway at K-40 and would later have a secondary airstrip, K-39. At this time the 6146th BASUT was formally relocated to Cheju-do to oversee the base and train ROKAF pilots, while a detachment remained at and assumed control of K-5. Before the month ended training operations were in full swing at K-39 and ten new ROKAF pilots had become certified in the F-51.

The syllabus consisted of flying in the morning and classroom activities in the afternoon. This type of program had actually started the previous August, but had never been particularly effective because of the commitment to combat operations, Even so, there remained many problems to contend with at Cheju-do, primarily in the form of the continuing language barrier. It became customary to use bilingual ROKAF officers for classroom instruction, with USAF airmen overseeing the lessons. Eventually, as experience and language difficulties were overcome both the speed and the accuracy of instruction improved. During this transition and training period the more experienced ROKAF Mustang pilots were flying as instructor pilots, and the assigned USAF pilots were flying the combat missions in Mustangs bearing the ROKAF insignia.

1950 ended with the loss of two ROKAF Mustangs under these conditions, On December 29 Captain George Metcalf's Mustang developed engine trouble on takeoff from Taejon and he had to crash land 500 feet off the end of the runway, He suffered a wrenched back and facial cuts, and was treated at the Taejon Hospital. On December 31 2nd Lt. James Gilliespie had to bailout of his F-51 after his engine quit near the front lines. Gilliespie was picked up by an American infantry patrol and returned to the squadron after two days. Fuel contamination due to water in the fuel lines caused the loss of both of these aircraft according to the investigating team.

Logistical problems became the largest deterrent to ROKAF operations during the first months of 1951. All supplies had to be flown into Cheju-do, and a continuing shortage of aircraft parts kept most of the aircraft out of service for maintenance. The Taejon installation had only twenty men available to keep that base operational, and

ROKAF # 21. Even though this Mustang bears a "low number" it was not assigned to the ROKAF until March 26, 1953; from the 40th Fighter Interceptor Squadron. There is no known correlation of ROKAF and USAF Mustang serial numbers. Their # 10 bore such a stigma through their national aversion to the number ten that ROKAF pilots refused to fly it. (GI #1, you ass hole #10!) It was then renumbered by the USAF when it went through overhaul at Kisarazu and had no further problems. (Trask)

these men had to work in a quagmire of mud, which often mired both aircraft and vehicles. It was felt that K-5 was impregnable as a base, because no one could make their way through the mire, On the brighter side though, four new Mustangs were delivered to the ROKAF by the USAF, which brought the unit up to authorized strength for the first time since their initial allotment the previous July. (Still only ten aircraft, versus the standard twenty-four for a USAF squadron.) Four of the F-51s were now kept at K-5 for operational use, and the other six were based at K-40 for training. Three of the K-5 F-5ls were constantly kept loaded for combat, while the fourth was reserved for use as a spare. With Seoul and Suwon having fallen to the communists once again, K-5 was now the northern most airfield in UN hands.

On January 14 one of the hazards involved with air-lifting supplies in and out of Korea became all to apparent. A C-54 loaded with aviation fuel missed its landing approach to Taejon in foggy weather. The pilot made a missed approach, but on his second attempt to find the runway he still could not locate the air strip and again started a missed approach, crashing against a hillside, There were no survivors. In spite of the mud and weather there were no ROKAF Mustang losses for the January, but only thirty-seven effective sorties were flown against the enemy.

Because of the cold and the inadequate housing a lot of jury-rigged heating equipment was fabricated, some not so successfully. Three major fires occurred in February alone. On the 14th a quonset hut belonging to the 6147th Tactical Control Group at K-40 burned to the ground. It's oil stove was fired with a combination of oil and 100 octane gasoline, a volatile mixture that flared up while the hut's occupants were sleeping and burned one man to death. This loss was notable because the 6147th worked closely with the ROKAF training program. On Feb. 19 another oil stove exploded and burned down the control tower at K-5. This fire was followed by another which destroyed the combination Base Operations and Weather Office at K-5. All of these fires may have been avoidable, but the men ran the stoves as hot as they dared in an effort to keep warm in the zero temperatures.

On February 19 Major Harold Wilson was forced to crash land his Mustang two miles west of Taejon. Wilson had just taken-off when his Merlin engine hiccuped and then quit cold. He settled for a muddy flat along the Kum River and belly landed without injury to himself. The Mustang was reduced to spare parts. A simple diaphragm in the carburetor had ruptured.

The weather hampered combat operations for all FEAF Mustangs during the winter and spring months. However, since the ROKAF was located considerably closer to the front lines, they often were able to fly ground support missions while the other squadrons could not penetrate the clouds to get into the target areas. The pilots navigated by rail and by roads, basic pilotage techniques, in areas familiar only to themselves. The biggest fear was in taking on a load of ice, for the F-51 was not equipped with a deicing system. Wing ice on a heavily loaded fighter would mean instant death, for at the altitudes the Mustangs were flying there would be no chance to recover from an ice induced stall or a spin.

March continued with reduced combat operations, still due to the adverse weather and a lack of ordnance to expend. For some reason FEAF was still not taking the capabilities of the ROKAF seriously, even though they were aware that most of the missions were still being flown by USAF or experienced ROKAF pilots. With the UN finally being able to reverse the communist flow in the Spring, the battle line again being move to the north, and the ROKAF once again returned to K-16, only to find it a shambles, When the 18th FBG had been there they had made many improvements to the field, but then the communists had retaken it during the winter and once again B-26 Invaders had to come back and attack it, destroying all of the improvements that the 18th FBG had made and everything else. Consequently, the ROKAF had to start another rebuilding program from scratch. Toward the end of the month the ordnance supply line finally caught up with them, but it was too late for them to mount any sustained combat operations and run up any notable statistics during March.

During April a total of 182 combat sorties were flown out of K-16 by the ROKAF. These missions accounted for the destruction of 180 enemy vehicles as well as some supply dumps and enemy held buildings. The figures may seem minute, but considering that the communists were rarely seen by day and that they made heavy use of camouflage the figures are more impressive.

These missions also brought on losses. On April 16 four Mustangs we launched to strike north of Inchon. The first three aircraft made their strikes on the heavily defended supply dump without incident. But when the flight started to rejoin the pilots were watching for the number four aircraft to complete his attack and then also join up. The latter Mustang, flown by Captain Choi Chong Bong, was seen climbing off the target on a southwesterly heading. As Bong approached one thousand feet his F-51

A Mustang out to pasture. This example was one of fifty awaiting salvage in 1957. (Komperta)

suddenly nosed down and plunged into the ground. The impact was so great that no trace of the Mustang remained.

On April 19 Major General Kim Chung Yul, Commanding General of the ROKAF, presented the 6146th Air Base Unit with the Republic of Korea Presidential Unit Citation. As was customary, Major Hess, representing the BASUT, was awarded an ox along with the Service Streamer. Hess gave the beast to a local farmer.

A second Mustang mishap occurred on April 21. Capt. Lee Se Young was hit by antiaircraft fire while he was strafing an enemy supply dump. His F-51 was seen to climb to 500 feet and then start a left turn and descend in a tightening turn until it crashed. Again there was no chance of survival.

Two days later a near fatal accident involved Major Metcalf. While on an armed reconnaissance flight the mission was diverted by the Joint Operations Center to provide a rescue cap (RESCAP) for a downed army pilot. As the Mustangs arrived over the downed pilot's location they came under heavy antiaircraft fire. The F-51s still were carrying their ordnance so they then dove down to suppress the ground fire and to try and prevent the encircling enemy soldiers from capturing the pilot.

As Metcalf climbed away from his strafing pass his F-51 was hit by a burst of antiaircraft fire which blew off three feet of one wing's leading edge and seriously damaged the aileron. Despite the damage Metcalf braced himself against the cockpit longeron and maintained a steady pressure on the stick and rudder to maintain the F-51 in a normal flying attitude. Testing the controls he found that the F-51 would stall out at 250 mph, so he was forced to land "hot" in order to keep directional control. It bounced and skidded, but it stayed on the runway and the damage was repairable.

Finally the pipeline of supplies and ordnance opened up and permitted the ROKAF to begin mounting sustained combat operations in squadron strength. During May 1951 several maximum effort missions were flown in support of the troops on the main line of resistance. They flew 164 missions, and no aircraft were lost during the month. Dean Hess completed his 250th mission during May also, while Major Metcalf and Lt. Gilliespie both got in their 100th. Hess was relieved at this time, being replaced by Major Harold Wilson. It was against Wilson that Hess had "cut the cards" back in June 1950 when he was selected to lead "Bout 1," so Wilson got his wish after all. Two additional USAF pilots were also assigned to the ROKAF at this time, 1st Lt.'s John Wigglesworth and Lewis Largo.

On June 15, 1951 the ROKAF again received orders to move. This time they headed for K-4 at Sachon. This airstrip was somewhat remote from the combat arena, but it was close enough for the fighters to be called upon if needed. The primary emphasis was now directed toward training the ROKAF instead of flying combat support missions and the men were informed that they would not be utilized except in the case of a dire emergency. As expected, this did not set well with the South Korean pilots. The 6146th Base Unit also was officially relieved from any potential combat assignments as of June 15, Both ground personnel and indigenous laborers set to work to build a new runway for liaison aircraft so the smaller aircraft would not interfere with the F-51s traffic patterns. The existing runway was cleared and made available for the expanded complement of twenty Mustangs. The main section of the ROKAF from Cheju-do was now withdrawn from the island and they also moved to K-4 which consolidated the ROKAF at one airfield. This movement, and the construction efforts kept the ROKAF occupied for the remainder of the summer, and since the ground war was now at a virtual standstill along the front lines, they were never called upon for any combat operations.

During September 1951 the 1st Fighter Wing of the ROKAF was formed. The Wing consisted of sixty-three ROK officers and 222 airmen. Twelve Mustangs were detached from training commitments and were used to form the nucleus of the 12th Fighter Squadron, (Not to be confused with the USAF's 12th Fighter Bomber Squadron of the 18th Fighter Bomber Group). Also established was Detachment 2 of the 6146th Air Base Squadron, with 1st Lt. Largo commanding, and seven airmen to serve as advisors to the new 12th Fighter Squadron. The 12th FS and Detachment 2 then moved to K-18 at Kangnumg (Koryo) during the first week of October and they were considered as combat operational on October 11, 1951.

One of the three known remaining ROKAF Mustangs on display in South Korea. (Dorr)

They flew their first combat mission on this date, being led by the commanding officer of the 12th Fighter Squadron and monitored by Lt. Largo. The mission was flown as briefed and was completed without mishap, and the ROKAF was back into the game. The 12th Fighter Squadron flew 236 combat sorties through the end of October, and flew an additional 250 sorties in November. All of these were with "excellent results."

On December 1, 1951 all of the Mustangs at K-18 were flown back to K-4 to participate in Operation Rattrap. This effort was a "clean-up" campaign that was in conjunction with the Republic of Korea's army. The mission was to eradicate any guerrilla activity the communists were conducting behind the United Nation's lines. These guerrillas had created problems for the UN forces ever since the UN had broken out of the Pusan Perimeter. Most of the guerrillas were those communists who had infiltrated into the hills during the counteroffensive to escape capture or death. They moved mostly at night on harassing strikes, and never created a great amount of damage, but their potential and very existence was intolerable.

The first half of the campaign concluded on December 14, and the 12th Fighter Squadron returned to K-14 to fly a week of interdiction missions along and just behind the Red front lines while their efforts during Rattrap were assessed. They then flew to Chinhae, where they set up operations for the second half of Rattrap. Since all of the Rattrap missions at this time were a South Korean effort, most of the results were unpublicized, but they did serve to curtail guerrilla attacks on road and rail movements behind the UN lines. There would later be a follow-up Operation Rattrap which also involved USAF fighter-bombers.

Commencing in January 1952 the ROKAF assumed an autonomous role, which they would continue in through the end of the war. The front line areas had been subdivided into areas of responsibility that now conformed somewhat to the nationalities of the ground forces in each particular sector. The USAF's 18th Fighter Bomber Group had the areas from the central part of the country to the west coast of Korea. U.S. Navy and Marine aviation covered the U.S. Marines on the east coast, and the ROKAF covered their own infantry divisions, primarily along the western ridges of the Tabaek Smanek Mountains.

Since the ROKAF was now basically independent from FEAF in their combat role, their reporting of losses an exploits became an internal affair, and their records have become unretrievable from their archives. It is known that the ROKAF did suffer heavy losses of both aircraft

A ROKAF Mustang of another sort, this time in Peking, China. In October 1953 its pilot walked into Base Operations at K-4, grabbed a parachute, and defected to North Korea. The USAF's comment was that "They didn't get much, it was not only obsolescent, it was obsolete." It is ex-USAF 44-73870. (Coggan)

and pilots while flying armed reconnaissance, interdiction and ground support missions, although these figures will probably never be disclosed.

One exception to the lack of notice accorded to the ROKAF occurred on July 11, 1952. This was the day that "Operation Pressure Pump" took place. The target was Pyongyang, and within this capital city thirty targets were designated for destruction. Just about every available fighter-bomber in the Theater was slated far action, including the Mustangs of the ROKAF. The attacks went off better than expected, considering that there were over 150 known large caliber antiaircraft guns in the area that had been alerted by a leaflet raid that the attack was going to take place. Three of the thirty targets in the city were totally destroyed and all of the rest heavily damaged, for the loss of three jet fighter-bombers. Radio Pyongyang announced, after they came back on the air after being off for three days that over 1,500 building had been destroyed with the city suffering more than 7,000 casualties. Quite proudly the ROKAF pilots noted that they had hit and destroyed their assigned target and then returned without a loss.

The ROKAF now expanded further to include one Training Wing and one Transport Wing, in addition to their Fighter Wing. The Transport Wing was now equipped with C-47s, while the Training Wing started receiving Cessna L-19s from the U.S. Eighth Army, and these were soon followed by Ryan L-17 Navions, which gave them a light aircraft strength of twenty-six aircraft. In addition to using their older T-6s in a training role, their utilization was expanded for use in forward air controller duties. Unfortunately, the longevity of the ROKAF Mosquitos' was not any better than their L-4s two years previously, and losses in this mission were reportedly high.

A "Three Year Plan" had been established by the ROKAF in April 1952 in hopes of expanding and improving their force. Assisting in this plan was FEAF's forecast of reequipping both 2 Squadron, South African Air Force and the ROKAF with F-80s as they were withdrawn from operational service with the 8th Fighter Bomber Group. A second proposal by FEAF was considered as even better. This would provide the ROKAF with F-84s from the 136th Fighter Bomber Wing when they were rotated home in Fiscal Year 1953. Under these propositions the F-51s and the F-80s of the ROKAF would equip two fighter squadrons by the end of 1953, and then in 1954 they would expand to three fighter squadrons of Thunderjets, while the F-51s and F-80s would be relegated to training roles. All of this was to be contingent upon an early cease fire, which did not occur. Consequently 2 Squadron kept their Mustangs until December 1952 when they traded them in for F-86s, while the ROKAF had to continue with F-51s. They never did receive any F-80s or F-84s.

When the Korean War ended many of the F-51s within FEAF's inventory were turned over to the ROKAF. This made them the largest air force in the world at the time that was equipped with Mustangs. In fact, they had so many that they could not use them all, so a dozen were recalled by FEAF and then transferred to the Philippine Air Force. The ROKAF continued to fly the F-51 into 1957 when they were finally phased out, being replaced by F-86s. These Sabres, both the tactical F-86F and the all-weather capable F-86D, finally brought a full-fledged status to the ROKAF and South Korea became recognized as a major airpower.

CHAPTER FOUR

77 Squadron
Royal Australian Air Force

Sergeant Pilot Raymond Trebilco was pulling operations duty at Iwakuni Air Base, Japan during the morning hours of June 25, 1950 when he received notification from 5th Air Force Headquarters at 1130 hours JST that the 5th Air Force had been placed on an alert status. Trebilco dutifully logged the information, and then informed his Squadron Leader, Graham Strout, who in turn passed the notification on to the Wing Commander, Lou Spence.

At this time there wasn't a great amount for the Australians to do with this information but to sit on it and await further developments. 77 Squadron, Royal Australian Air Force, although attached to the 5th Air Force, was not actually assigned to it any longer. In fact, they had just been relieved of their occupation duty in Japan and were preparing for their return to Australia at the time. Yet it stood to reason that they soon would be recalled to duty if their government decided to support the United Nations as a result of the boarder incursion in Korea. Thus while awaiting further developments, Spence ordered the squadron, who were virtually packed up and ready to return home, to prepare themselves for possible commitment to action.

77 Squadron's Mark IV Mustangs were towed from the hangars where they had been in the process of being "pickled" for transport home and ammunition was loaded into their gun bays. At Spence's direction, long-range fuel tanks were hung from the bomb racks and filled with gasoline. Spence also called FEAF and requested two hundred more of these disposable fuel tanks. There was some grumbling among the men, for they were psychologically prepared to go home and not off to war, but there was also an excitement with the potential of finally being able to realistically do something that they had been preparing for for years.

General MacArthur's comments to news reporter MacCartney during MacArthur's C-54 trip to Suwon were not unfounded. MacArthur wanted 77 Squadron, and brought political pressure to get them into action. The squadron had placed second in the 1949 FEAF Gunnery Meet and Flight Lt. John "Bay" Adams, "B Flight" leader, had been the top scoring fighter pilot in FEAF. Adams, himself, had flown with the Royal Air Force during World War II and for a period had been the French ace Pierre Clostermann's wingman. Clostermann had stated that "Adams feared neither God nor the Devil," and this was the type of pilot that was going to be needed.

77 Squadron was released to FEAF for combat on June 30 by the Australian government. It was an inauspicious beginning, for the Australian newspapers had barely

A line up of 77 Squadron Mustangs at Iwakuni. The nearest Mustang is A68-808, which was utilized for pilot proficiency for squadron Mustang pilots after 77 Squadron converted to Meteors in April 1951. It was wrecked in an accident on November 8, 1953. (Royal Australian Air Force)

An Australian Mustang Mk.4. It was virtually identical to the USAF F-51D except that it was a bit lighter, possibly because of less radio equipment?

missions to be flown by 77 Squadron would be to escort C-47s evacuating wounded from South Korea, and then to escort 3rd Bomb Group B-26s, to be followed by escorting B-29s to Yonpo. It would be a busy day.

On July 2 at 0500 hours, one week and one hour after the North Koreans had began their attacks, the first Australian Mustangs took off from Iwakuni to become the first non-American combat unit to support the Republic of Korea. The first flight was composed of Squadron Leader Strout and Flight Lt.'s Bradford, Cottee and Murphy. Since it was a predawn takeoff into an unknown condition, an operating radio was a necessity and "Brick" Bradford had to abort because of a radio failure.

Crossing the Japanese Sea, Tom Murphy noticed that it was time to clear the Mustang's Merlin engine, lest the spark plugs foul, and he advanced the throttle, pulling ahead of the remainder of the flight and becoming the first to cross the coast of Korea. The mission orbited over a town they took to be Taejon, but there was no sign of the C-47s, so they had to return to Japan without any "breathless deeds" to report.

The second mission became airborne after daybreak with Wing Commander Spence leading Flight Lt. Adams and six other Mustangs. One, flown by Sgt. James Flemming, had to abort because of a mechanical problem. Seventeen B-26s were joined over Tongnae, on the outskirts of Pusan, and were escorted to Seoul where the Invaders bombed railway bridges across the Han

even mentioned the invasion of South Korea, being more concerned of flooding on Australia's northern coast and in New South Wales. Little publicity was given to Australia committing their forces to a war in an unheard of country.

On July 1 the weather was just to bad to fly. 77 Squadron personnel checked and rechecked their aircraft at Iwakuni to make sure that they would be ready when the clouds lifted, and then they waited. The previous day's newspapers arrived from "down under" and asked, "Will the American's go, will the Russians intervene, is this the beginning of World War III?" The "word" came in, the first

The personal mount of Wing Commander Spence, commanding officer of 77 Squadron until his death on September 9, 1950. Note the Commander's Pennant under the cockpit. (Royal Australian Air Force)

Photographed at Iwakuni, this 77 Squadron Mustang now bears the "split spinner" scheme in common use by the 35th Fighter Interceptor Group, to which 77 Squadron was assigned for the last seven months of their Mustang combat period. (Royal Australian Air Force)

River. The Mustangs were jumped by F-80s from an undetermined squadron, which forced Flight Officer William Horseman and his wingman, Sgt. Brian Nicholls to turn inside of the Shooting Stars which were making a "hot pass," but the flight returned to Iwakuni without further difficulties.

The third mission for the day was composed of seven Mustangs carrying long-range fuel tanks. Takeoff was at 1325 hours and they headed for Kangnung, some twelve miles south of the 38th Parallel on Korea's east coast. As they arrived over the rendezvous they spotted the first of the B-29s that were just commencing to enter an orbit to await their escorts and the remainder of the B-29s to arrive from Okinawa. The target was Yonpo and the nearby North Korean Airfield at Hamhung, K-28. There initially appeared to be heavy weather over the targets, but it turned out to be only industrial haze and the Superfortresses had little trouble in laying their bombs square upon their targets. The return leg of the mission was broken by a short, unsuccessful, search for a reported submarine off the coast of Korea. the participating pilots were elated as a result of their first day's efforts. Sixteen successful sorties without any losses.

The next mission took place on July 3 and it turned out to be a demoralizing event. Spence had received a

"Frag Order" to take 77 Squadron to Korea to strafe the main highway between Suwon and Pyontaek. he would lead the mission with one flight of four Mustangs, while Adams would lead a second flight, also of four aircraft. The eight Mustangs were loaded with full ammo bays and carried six sixty pound rockets each. (The Australian rockets were some twenty pounds heavier than the U.S. 2.75" projectiles). The mission orders were changed by a telephone call prior to takeoff, "to targets of opportunity." For some reason the revision in orders did not set well with Spence and he called FEAF Headquarters at Itazuke Air Base for conformation. He talked with a U.S. Marine Major, who also had misgivings, but the mission was to be flown as instructed.

Over the general targeted area there were still feelings of uneasiness, as it was impossible to determine whose army was in what position from the aircraft's altitude. Adams radioed the USAF Tactical Air Support Group and received clearance to commence attacking, and Spence's flight dove on a train composed of boxcars, firing their machine guns in combat for the first time in five years.

As Spence's flight pulled up, Adam's flight started down, and then pulled up when Adam's spotted Republic of Korea markings on the boxcars. They reconfirmed the target area on their maps, and then, having little recourse but to believe that the train had been captured by the North Koreans, they pressed their strafing and rocket attacks. They worked over the area for fifteen minutes before setting course for Iwakuni, feeling that they had accomplished a fair day's work.

Technically it had been a beautiful job. The press corps which witnessed it said so. The problem was that the targeted area was the ROK and U.S. 24th Infantry Division. Fortunately only one American sergeant was hit, the Division's first causality of the war. But the ROK Army suffered heavy losses. 77 Squadron was exonerated in the inquiry, as they were only following instructions, but the meaning of war was forcefully brought home to the pilots. And, just to make things worse, they found that one of their mates had drowned in the crash of his Mustang into the bay near Iwakuni while the rest had been over Korea. His engine had quit while he was test flying a maintenance overhaul.

Due to inclement weather the squadron did not fly again until July 6. Spence then led two flights of Mustangs to Seoul to cover B-26s that were forced to bomb through an overcast with undetermined results. That afternoon another Frag Order was received from FEAF Headquarters alerting them for another mission that afternoon.

The second strike did not get off until 1737 hours. Strout's Mustang acted up and he had to return to Iwakuni, leaving Flight Officer Ken McLeod as mission commander. Approaching the bomb line the flight contacted a Forward Air Controller in a L-17 "Dragonfly," who had a bridge

Pilot 3 Dick Turner is congratulated by a "mate" upon receiving the U.S. Air Medal. (Brackenreg)

at Pyontaek picked out for destruction before North Korean T-34 tanks could use it. The Mustangs dove and cut loose with their rockets, but the particular bridge had been of Japanese construction during the previous war and it was impervious to the small rockets.

Since the Mustangs were not carrying drop tanks they started running short on fuel, so at the suggestion of the L-17 pilot they diverted to Taejon to spend the night, becoming the first Australians to land in Korea. It created quite a stir at Iwakuni, as the message transmitted of the diversion was not received at the squadron and all of the involved pilots became listed as missing in action for twenty-four hours.

June 7 would become another of many black days within 77 Squadron. Their target had been a railway sta-

Another nicely photographed line up of Australian Mustangs in Japan. The nearest aircraft, A68-716, was scrapped in February 1953. The second in line, A68-116, belonged to the sister squadron, the 76th, and did not see action in Korea, being shipped home with 76 Squadron before the conflict commenced. (Royal Australian Air Force)

77 Squadron brass after an award ceremony at Iwakuni. In the background are 3rd Bomb Wing (Light) B-26s. Note the officer in shorts, which the 3rd BW commander did not like. (Brackenreg)

Flight Lt. "Nobbie" Noble after receiving the U.S. Air Medal. (Brackenreg)

tion at Sanchok, and as the Mustangs crossed the Korean coast Squadron Leader Strout ordered the flight to drop their belly tanks. Unencumbered, they rolled into dives against the station and flight Lt. Desmond Murphy was flying in the Number Three position, and all that he saw in front of him was a blinding flash. Murphy thought at first that Strout had hit a "fat target," but it was Strout's Mustang that Desmond had seen explode. There had been no chance at all for Strout to escape and he became the first British Commonwealth serviceman to die in Korea.

Pilots are going to be lost in war, and they more than any others they realize the reality and inevitability of the fact. A dispatch was sent to Australia for volunteers to serve as replacements and to bolster 77 Squadron's compliment, and twelve pilots were selected. These men were flown to Iwakuni on a Quantas Airline DC-4, arriving in Japan on July 8, along with twenty-eight crew chiefs, armors, mechanics, and spare parts for the squadron's Mustangs.

The loss of Graham Stout also brought the somewhat expected orders for the dependents of 77 Squadron members to leave Japan. It was with mixed emotions that the men bade farewell to their families, for they knew that a combat airfield was no place for them to be. Iwakuni had been a good duty station for them, as houses had been built by the Australian government for those with dependents, and the pilots living in the barracks had "girl sans" to keep their room and personal equipment clean. All of these amenities would soon change, also, by the arrival of the 3rd Bomb Group (Light) from Johnson Air Base, Japan, for there arose a bit of a "personality con-

flict" between the leaders of the Invader squadrons and the Australians.

The movement of the 3rd BG, initially, was looked upon by the Australians with a bit of mirth, who had always carried on a bit of a rivalry with the tenant U.S. Navy organization and had established a solid rapport with both the USN and USAF fighter pilots. In fact, on hot summer days it was a common practice for U.S. pilots to suddenly develop engine trouble if they were in the vicinity of Iwakuni, as it was customary for the Australian "fitters" (mechanics) to first greet a visiting pilot with a cold beer, and then see what his problem was. When the 3rd BG arrived their new commanding officer not only refused to try and get along with the USN, he alienated the Australians by attempting to counter their practice of wearing their traditional shorts into the mess halls. For his attitude, enough pressure was mounted on FEAF to have him transferred to Korea.

July 14 was a field day for one flight of Mustangs from "Double Seven Squadron." Due to bad weather all but one mission led by Ken McLeod had to abort their assigned missions. McLeod had been briefed to contact "Mosquito Angelo" over Taejon, only he couldn't raise him on the radio, so he switched frequencies and contacted "Mosquito Dragonfly." Between the L-17 and a Direction Finding steer, McLeod found a juicy target.

A contingent of North Koreans was attempting to cross a river, with many troops either resting or feigning dead on the river's banks, but they panicked when the Mustangs dove down for a look-see. Two boats, loaded with troops, were spotted midway in the river. After the Mustangs finished their strafing the river literally ran red with the blood of the communists. The Mustangs pilots did not feel good about their strafing, but it had to be done to protect the UN ground forces.

On July 15 the replacement pilots to 77 Squadron flew their first combat missions, escorting 3rd BG B-26s to Seoul. During these first few days it had been hard for the new pilots to get on the roster for combat missions, as there just were not enough Mustangs to go around. By the end of July most of the replacement pilots only managed to get in three or four sorties, usually working with the B-26s at low level rocket and strafing runs along the MLR.

On July 24 the North Koreans mounted a major tank offensive. Working with "Mosquito Horseradish" four 77 Squadron pilots caught a bunch of tanks as they were just breaking through the MLR, and they bore in rippling off their rockets. Two lead tanks were stopped dead, and a third tried to turn around to retreat when four more Mustangs attacked and took care of him. Soon more Mustangs were called in, and for four hours they patrolled the area attacking anything that they could see moving. There was a great amount of antiaircraft fire thrown back up at the Mustangs in retaliation and Flying Officer William Horseman had a fuel line cut, which forced him to divert to Taegu. Two other Mustangs were also hit, but they returned safely to Japan.

Through the end of July the war continued along the same vein. The North Korean Army pressed south, ever tightening their hold on the beleaguered South Koreans and the U.S. 24th Division. They continued attacking regardless of their losses, with UN pilots reporting that the enemy often would not even attempt to seek cover while undergoing a strafing attack.

A big question was always in the pilots minds, where was the North Korean Air Force? Intelligence had postulated that the NKAF was not a strong force to begin with,

77 Squadron Mustangs at Taegu in September 1950. The mounted Australian rockets packed more wallop that the standard USAF 2.75" rockets, but it still took a direct hit to stop a Russian-built T-34 tank. (Brackenreg)

but it should have been in evidence somewhere if it indeed did exist. One thing was altogether obvious, and that was if the North Korean's had any air support behind their tanks and infantry they could have pushed the UN forces right into the sea post haste. Besides, 77 Squadron pilots wanted a chance to mix it up in aerial combat. Ground support was a hot and dangerous chore and it was not a mission that the pilots enjoyed. Nevertheless, the NKAF refused to appear and 77 Squadron pilots never did get a chance to engage the NKAF while they were flying Mustangs.

Late summer is nothing else but oppressively hot and humid in Japan and Korea. After a sweltering day spent over Korea strapped to the seat of a Mustang, a location many claimed to be the hottest spot in the world, the pilots returned exhausted to Japan to lay in their birthday suits under mosquito netting to swelter even more. Takeoffs were made prior to daybreak, so as to arrive over the target in the predawn light. Their attacks would be made, and then they would proceed to a base in South Korea, normally Taegu, where they often came under small arms fire while in the traffic pattern, to land, rearm and refuel.

Every effort was made to expedite the Mustangs through these ground functions, so usually the pilots did not even have the opportunity to get out of their cockpits to stretch their legs before they were dispatched once again. Once airborne they would contact "Mellow Control," the Joint Operations Control center, for their next target assignment. And then the process of striking a target and returning to rearm and refuel would continue. The last day's mission was timed so as to hit a target at dusk and get back to Iwakuni for a night landing.

One day in late summer these conditions caught up with a hapless pilot. After spending an entire day working in and out of Taegu, where they couldn't even find a drink of fresh water, the last sortie was diverted to Miho Air Base, Japan because weather had closed Iwakuni. The pilots were fatigued and dehydrated, and the radio in Pilot 3' Bob Hunt's Mustang had quit. The other pilots noticed that Hunt had forgotten to lower his landing gear, but they were accordingly unable to warn him. Hunt flared-out nicely on his approach and landed wheels-up. The USAF people at Miho took the tired pilots and made sure that they were freshened up and gave them fresh clothing and free meals in the Officer's Club, even though all four pilots in the flight were enlisted men. A RAAF Dakota flew in with spare parts the next day and the Mustang was jacked up and repaired. Hunt was grounded by an unsympathetic RAAF Headquarters officer and fined 5 Pounds for his transgression.

According to Wing Commander Spence, morale could not have been better after the first two months in combat. 77 Squadron had accounted for 35 enemy tanks, 182 trucks, four complete trains and numerous other tactical targets. Since the squadron had started staging out of Taegu their flying time to targeted areas was reduced enough to permit them to maintain almost constant operations and they had been able to amass 1, 745 combat hours in 812 combat sorties.

The last week of August brought the final North Korean push of their initial offensive. The North Koreans had crossed the Naktong River at seventeen locations, using barges, boats and by constructing fords. The USAF's 35th Fighter Bomber Group had been forced to evacuate their own staging base at Po'hang, but the airfield at Taegu was still secure for continued staging operations. At this time Dean Hess's 6146th Base Unit with its combined USAF and ROKAF pilots and ground personnel remained as the only Mustang unit still based in Korea. Through their efforts and those of the fighter bomber units operating from Japan, enough air support was provided to the UN ground forces to reverse the flow of the war. By the end of the first week of September the "Pusan Perimeter" was declared secure and the fighter bombers were finally able to take on an offensive role for the first time.

On September 3 Pilot 3 Bill Harrop and three other 77 Squadron pilots flew an escort mission to Pyongyang. Upon returning to the Pusan Perimeter area they then attempted to contact a forward air controller, so they could find a worthwhile target to expend their rockets upon before landing at Taegu. Landing with rockets still attached to their Mustangs was not permitted by policy. Harrop advised his flight that he was now low on fuel, and he was going to have to head for Taegu, regardless. Shortly thereafter Harrop was heard to announce that his Mustang was on fire and that he was bailing out.

For an unknown reason Harrop changed his mind, and then a T-6 Mosquito pilot spotted him making a belly landing along the Naktong River near Waegwan. The rest of the flight soon arrived over the area and two Mustangs started RESCAPing the site while the third pilot headed for Taegu to organize a rescue effort. The RESCAPing pilots saw Harrop run from tree cover to a rice paddy where he attempted to cover his white flying suit with mud for camouflage, and then run to a small hut in an orchard.

Harrop appeared once in the hut's doorway, waved, and disappeared back inside. The Mustangs continued their orbits overhead, at an altitude low enough that the

Australian pilot Lyle Klaffer in a Jeep at K-2. (Brackenreg)

pilots could see part way into the hut's interior, but when a rescue helicopter arrived no trace of Harrop could be found. His body was found in a rough grave the following December without any explanation from the local Koreans, who were apparently afraid of North Korean partisans in the area.

On September 9 Flight Lt. Roscoe "Ross" Coburn found himself with his hands full that resulted in a lifetimes worth of excitement. Upon making a rocket strike against Kigye Coburn encountered some small arms fire and his Mustang took a hit in its cooling system. With Flight Lt. Jack Murry as an escort Coburn headed home to Iwakuni, and while crossing the Tsushima Strait glycol fumes started to seep into the cockpit. The fumes soon condensed on the Mustang's canopy and Coburn was force to start flying on instruments, for he no longer could see out to the side. Not much later Murry stated that Coburn's Mustang was now streaming coolant from the radiator's shutter.

Approaching the coastline of Honshu Coburn's Merlin engine temperature "pegged out" and then the Merlin started running rough. When the Merlin started showering sparks out of its exhaust stacks Coburn started tiding up the cockpit and trimmed the Mustang for hands-off flight so he could bailout. Without further adieu the Merlin seized, and to Coburn's amazement the propeller sheared off and went pinwheeling into space. Oddly enough, the Mustang continued in a normal flight attitude while the prop spun ahead for a hundred yards before slowly spinning down into the water.

Coburn, very calmly then bailed out over the coast and was picked up by some Japanese farmers who took him to Iwakuni. It was a toss-up as to who was the most shaken by the incident, as Murry hadn't seen Coburn bailout, as his eyes were transfixed to the spinning propeller and thought that Coburn had gone down with his Mustang.

It was during these early days of the Korean war that 77 Squadron had to participate in one of the grimmest and controversial incidents of the war. Even though the Pusan Perimeter kept shrinking as a result of communist pressure, the battle line had gaps along its roadways. Through these openings civilian refugees poured through in columns or in unorganized masses. Po'hang had to be evacuated and Taegu continued to be threatened with NKA firing taking place within a mile of K-2.

Roadblocks were thrown up to stop, or at least slow down the refugees until they could be checked for North Korean infiltrators. The NKA interspersed themselves within the civilians, with some disguised as pregnant women while carrying satchels of hand grenades or small arms over their abdomens. The beleaguered soldiers on the roadblocks had neither the time nor the facilities to check each person trying to enter the Perimeter. Dressed in the traditional white garb of mourning, there was no way to tell friend from foe, but the masses had to be stopped. The columns were ordered to stop and disperse, but like lemmings they continued to the south.

Three flights of Mustangs, two from the USAF and one from 77 Squadron, were led by Wing Commander Spence to Taegu on night in a last ditch attempt to stop the refugees the next morning. The Mustangs were parked wingtip to wingtip across the airstrip, for if it appeared as if the airstrip, itself, might be captured during the night. If this were to occur the pilots were to toggle-off their napalm tanks where the Mustangs stood and then takeoff across the grass to save themselves and their aircraft.

The pilots spent that night attempting to sleep on the wooden floor of the operations tent. It was a fitful effort for the sporadic gunfire echoed from the hills. The perimeter guards held the airstrip, and the Mustangs were dispatched at first light to annihilate the southbound masses.

The people were spotted in open country, in a number in excess of 3,000, and they were ordered to stop their southward trek by broadcasts over both air and ground address systems, but they continued. The Mustangs bore in and commenced strafing and napalming. "It was a gruesome task, but it had to be done to hold Taegu at that point – things were that desperate."

It wasn't too much later when the process had to be repeated. The North Koreans were approaching the Naktong River line southwest of Taegu and were forcing civilians that they had rounded up to move ahead of them

as a human shield as they approached the unprotected rear of the UN forces. 77 Squadron pilots were called in by a forward air controller to stop this movement. The Mustangs flew down the length of the column, observing corpses along the sides of the road where the NKA had killed those who would not, or could not be driven. The Mustang pilots then laid down burst of .50 caliber fire across the front of the column, and at this time they stopped, knowing that if they continued that they would all be killed.

It should be noted that the Australian pilots were all professional fighter pilots who had to follow orders, but rest assured, they have never felt good about these incidents. It haunts them yet today. The fact remains, if the strafing and napalming had not been done, the UN would have probably been pushed off the peninsula within a week and the course of the war would have taken an entirely different direction.

On September 9 another pilot was lost, this time Wing Commander Lou Spence. Spence was leading a flight of four Mustangs, being flown by Pilot 3's Dick Turner, Andrew Hankinson and Ross Coburn. (Coburn's Mustang was carrying a special drop tank which contained a 35 mm camera which was used to obtain some film footage for the Hollywood movie "One Minute to Zero," which featured a modified version of the previously described strafing incidents).

Spence and his flight were soon working with a T-6 Mosquito against targets at Angang-ni, on the Pusan perimeter. Carrying napalm and four rockets each, they started their attacks from 700 feet under low cloud ceilings. Hankinson saw Spence roll in on the target in an unusually steep dive, and then attempt to pull out, form-

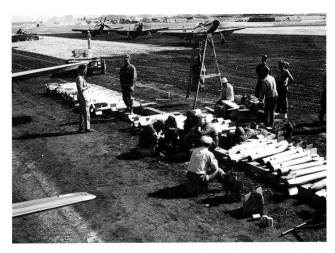

American 5" HVAR's being assembled at Taegu in September 1950. Three Aussie Mustangs are already armed and are taxiing for another mission. (Brackenreg)

Unloading 260 pound fragmentation bombs at Taegu prior to the Mustangs arrival at the loading area for rearming. The frags were lethal against ground troops, but otherwise did little damage. (Brackenreg)

ing vapor trails off his wingtips in the humid air. Spence crashed directly into the center of the town. Hankinson and the rest of the flight continued to strafe, but there didn't appear to be any worthwhile targets for their rockets, so they carried them home. Spence's loss was keenly felt as he had been truly a leader of men, having personally received the Legion of Merit from General Stratemeyer on August 22.

Leadership of 77 squadron passed temporally to Flight Lt. John Adams, and then was assigned to Squadron Leader R.G. Cresswell, as he had been one of the original members of 77 Squadron back in March 1942 and had become their third commanding officer during World War II. Cresswell was also noted for being the first Australian fighter pilot to score a kill at night when he shot down a Japanese bomber over Australia.

The Pusan perimeter was finally declared as secure on September 12. With this came the freeing of B-26s and B-29s for two solid nights of interdiction. This was not a totally feasible role for the Superfortresses, but it did work well as far as this particular goal was concerned. By September 14 all major movements of North Korean military supplies had been curtailed by UN air power.

In the few remaining days before the Inchon Invasion on September 15 77 squadron flew as often as their number of aircraft in commission permitted in an effort to soften up the areas around Inchon and Seoul. Flying conditions, however, were a major problem, as the remnants of a typhoon that had struck Japan and Korea had left low ragged ceilings and poor visibility in its wake.

On September 16 General Walker's 8th Army hit the front lines north of the Pusan Perimeter and began the UN forces' push to the north with the intention to meet the Inchon Invasion forces east of Seoul. Three days later the NKA broke and the 8th Army was able to mount a sustained drive toward their goal. MacArthur announced, in his fashion a bit prematurely, that Seoul was again free on September 26, but in reality it took another twenty-four hours to secure the capitol.

Unfortunately the fluidity of the ground battle lines brought on a repeat of the July 3 attack by 77 Squadron, only involving another Mustang squadron. Two companies of Argyll Highlanders were held up by enemy fire and called for air support. A flight of 18th Fighter Bomber Group Mustangs was in the area, and they promptly bore in and napalmed and strafed the UN troops, leaving thirty-eight casualties in the aftermath.

The 8th Army advanced north, often making as many as forty miles a day. 77 Squadron swept the areas in front of the advancing troops providing continual ground support and interdiction strikes. After the incident with the Highlanders the pilots were kept under a much tighter control of either a ground or airborne FAC, and there were no more problems with attacks on the wrong objectives.

The press against the NKA was relentless. 77 Squadron was assigned a beachhead to work over twenty miles north of Po'hang and after numerous attacks by the Mustangs, the Republic of Korea Army assigned to assault the area made an amphibious landing from their landing craft without loosing a man to enemy fire.

In spite of the UN advance there were still the dangers involved with attacking ground targets, for the NKA was not giving up without a struggle. The communists soldiers would simply lay on their backs when they came under fire from the air and fire their own rifles straight up into the air without any attempt at aiming them. Throw up enough lead and you are bound to hit something was the rational. Both Horseman's and Noble's Mustangs were hit in this manor while making low altitude attacks near Pyongyang. They both returned to base successfully, however.

Pilot 3 Dick Whittman encountered another danger that these type of missions brought about. He hit a tree. "I felt the Mustang shudder and then it veered violently toward the ground. I had to fight desperately to level off, and then I began a long battle, straining at the controls to get it back to Taegu." He had lost three feet of one wing, and his Mustang became a hangar queen for spare parts.

The bombline was moved steadily northward in front of the advancing UN forces. Because of this the mission's durations were also becoming longer and the pilots more fatigued. It was now a thousand mile round trip from Iwakuni to targets in northwestern North Korea and long range fuel tanks were a necessity. This reduced the Mustangs effective firepower to the six .50 caliber machine guns and four rockets, instead of the normal six, because of the weight factor.

On October 9 the UN ground forces crossed the 38th Parallel and the decision was made to relocate 77 Squadron to K-3, Po'hang. This, in itself, would reduce the anticipated long range missions by at least three hundred miles. The move started on October 10 and was completed by the 12th, with 77 Squadron moving into the USAF's 35th Fighter Interceptor Group's billeting area. In the process 77 Squadron lost its autonomy but their combat role was enhanced.

There had been some talk during this period of creating a true UN force by combining 77 Squadron with the 35th FIG, and then later adding 2 Squadron South African Air Force when they arrived in Korea. However the South African government had not been consulted on this matter beforehand, and they immediately rejected the proposal. Consequently 2 Squadron was assigned to the 18th FBG. There had never been any ill will between the Australians and the South Africans, each simply taking pride in their own independence. Each squadron considered the other to be composed of "tough boys," and pretty well stayed out of each others way on the ground. Rarely did they ever find themselves pitted against the communists simultaneously, and if they did, they just did their job and returned to their own home base with respect for the other pilot's ability.

Conditions at K-3 were a far cry from the comforts at Iwakuni. At Po'hang the men were billeted in drafty tents that whipped in every breeze. The tents were both lighted and heated by burning napalm in tin cans. Lt. Colonel

Aussie "fitters" waiting for their pilot to show up for the next mission. These men worked through typhoons and blizzards, and they never seemed to receive much credit for their efforts. (Brackenreg)

Jack Dale, Commanding Officer 35th FIG commented, "Where else but in Korea could you eat dinner at night to the light of napalm?" The temperatures were also dropping steadily at night with the approach of winter and the Australians had never experienced such cold. They immediately requested more appropriate clothing from the USAF, and gave up their characteristic uniforms for more realistic wear for the duration.

On October 19 the UN forces captured Pyongyang. The next day C-119s dropped paratroopers thirty miles to the north of Pyongyang in an attempt to cut off any escaping NKA troops. The Flying Boxcars were escorted to the drop zone by 77 Squadron, and after the paratroopers were on the ground they were released to seek targets of opportunity. Flight Lt. Ian Olorenshaw and Pilot 2 Eric Douglas joyfully spotted a train carrying NKA troops towards Manchuria, and they promptly destroyed it.

For a short period the war became stagnate as far as aerial operations were concerned. One pilot commented, "We're fresh out of shagging targets." The airborne 77 Squadron Mustangs, known by their tactical radio callsign of "Dropkick," were shunted from Mosquito to Mosquito FAC's who had difficulties in finding targets for the Mustangs to attack. The NKA, always masters at camouflage, was now moving only at night, if at all, and little could be seen from the air by day. The Mustangs sat armed with rockets, napalm or bombs, while their pilots chaffed for action.

Four of the original pilots did manage to complete their tours of duty and were permitted to return to Australia. Flight Lt.'s Desmond Murphy, Brick Bradford and John Adams, along with Flight Officer Ken McLeod. Their reception was similar to those received by USAF pilots returning to their own homes, they were ignored. Few cared about the returning warriors or the Korean War.

October 29 saw the NKA begin a last ditch stand in the vicinity of Chongju. The UN ground forces had their hands full, and the 5th Air Force staged a maximum effort to come to their support. The 8th Regiment of the 1st Cavalry Division was hit the hardest at Unsan, some eighty miles north of Pyongyang. By the time the NKA attack was over they had captured thirteen American tanks and the 8th Regiment had lost over five hundred men. In continuing the pressure on the UN forces on November 3 elements of a Chinese Division assaulted the Anglo-American 27th Brigade. 77 Squadron was called in to provide air support, marking the first time that the squadron was utilized to provide air cover for their own Australian people during the conflict.

Two days later the 27th Brigade launched a counter-attack with 77 Squadron's support. At 1500 hours KST Squadron Leader Cresswell had his Mustangs over the Pakchan area when the FAC Mosquito ordered them in to commence their attacks. the pilots had just been waiting for this opportunity, for from their aerial vantage point they had been watching the ground movements develop. Flight Lt. Olorenshaw led in the first strike, sweeping down the valleys and up along the rugged hills, dodging trees in the process. In relays, flights led by Flying Officers Horseman and Pilot 2 Thomas Stoney followed suite. The Chinese were strafed in their trenches until they fled in a panic into the open where they became even easier targets for the Mustangs, infantry and tanks.

"They (Olorenshaw's Flight) used up all their machine gun and rocket ammunition and saw enemy troops scattering all over the place," reported Squadron Press Officer Flight Lt. George Odgers.

"It was a good feeling to know you were supporting your own boys. Horseman and Stoney stooged around for awhile, and then the controller sent them rocketing and machine gunning the trenches on the same hill. They saw dozens of enemy troops dash out of their positions and run to the valley. Tanks were landing shells on them as the Mustangs attacked. The whole place was alive with aircraft. Squadron Leader Cresswell led a four ship flight against tanks and transport. His flight fired eleven rockets at a tank, which toppled over the edge of the road. They then knocked out two trucks, and attacked a village, which replied with antiaircraft fire but didn't score a hit."

"It was an all-Australian day," said Lt. Colonel Ferguson, battalion commander, "and the boost to morale was amazing when we recognized the planes of 77 Squadron overhead." Just to top off the day's activities the squadron also reported destroying one hundred communist food trucks.

But losses in war are not one-sided, nor in a fighter squadron, always in the air. Two 77 Squadron pilots, Flight Lts Craig Kirkpatrick and W.V. Grey were burned to death in their tent at Po'hang. An electrical short caused the tent to torch, and they were overcome before they could even get free of their sleeping bags.

In some circles, the presence of the Chinese was kept hush-hush, but it was obvious that something major was about to take place because of observed communist activity behind the MLR. On November 8 Squadron Leader Cresswell returned from a sortie to report that they had destroyed twenty communist trucks. On November 10 fifty more trucks, containing food and ammunition

were spotted by a flight of RAAF Mustangs led by Flight Lt. Harvey. They destroyed forty-three. Still, the U.S. Army and the USAF kept a clamp on any of their intelligence gathering about the Chinese intervention into the conflict.

November 18 was a banner day for 77 Squadron. On this day a battalion of the Chinese 41st Division entered the combat arena and they were set upon by flights of F-51s who commenced pounding them until they surrendered on November 22. This marked the first time in history that a ground unit of this size had surrendered as a result of Mustang attacks. Elsewhere on the 18th the Chinese 113th Division came under fire from 77 Squadron. Between four Mustangs and three B-26s that had been invited to join in over fifty trucks, containing fifty men each, and fifty more trucks loaded with supplies were destroyed.

Once again it was decided to relocate 77 Squadron, as Po'hang was now too remote from the MLR to be truly effective. On November 19 they moved, along with the 35th FIG into North Korea. Their new base was that of one of their early targets, the Yonpo Airdrome near Hamhung.

Creature comforts were an improvement over K-3, as the airfield had been built by the Japanese during World War II and all of the existing buildings were of either brick or stone construction and although they were battle damaged they were easily repaired. Since it appeared that the winter was going to be a severe one, particularly in the opinion of the Australians, it was generally agreed that any building was better than the flimsy and drafty tents.

Winter did arrive, almost coinciding with 77 Squadron's arrival at K-27 and temperatures plummeted. Rain changed to snow born on icy winds from Manchuria. The physical location of K-27 was desolation personified, on the coastal plains, and when the clouds blew away the men could see snow covered mountains in the distance where infantry troops were dug in. The living conditions became almost intolerable to the Australians viewpoint, for they had difficulty in acclimating themselves to such wintry weather conditions.

The ground crews fought an endless battle to keep the snow off the Mustangs and their canopies frost-free. Maintenance was a nightmare in the freezing temperatures, minus 21 degrees at night, zero during the day, and never adequate shelter from the ever prevalent winds. When an aircraft took off its "slipstream whipped up a miniature hurricane." Above all, the weather was always a major hazard for the pilots who had to fight through snow showers, which destroys visibility quicker than anything else: while contending with clouds, ice, and mechanical problems brought on by cold-soaked aircraft.

By the end of November 77 Squadron had surpassed the 2,000 combat sortie mark, and most of these missions had been involved with providing close air support for front line troops. At K-27 they continued in this role, with their main focus being support for the men of the U.S. 27th Infantry Division at Chongju. The ground war had been taken to the North Koreans, and the UN was now deep within their territory. There was talk of having the men home by Christmas – the same sort of conversations that had preceded the Battle of the Bulge in 1944. The 8th Army was moving northward in a mass movement of troops in the western portion of North Korea, but with limited logistical support, while the mountainous eastern side was largely ignored as an impassable area for anyone to do battle. The day after Thanksgiving Day the UN push began in earnest. Thirty-six hours later, the night of November 26-27, the Chinese retaliated in force and the rout began. The GI phrase was "bugging out."

Air support was provided by all of FEAF, but particularly by Marine F4U Corsairs and the Mustang units that were now based in North Korea. But it soon became obvious that these fighter-bombers were not going to be able to hold the UN effort this time, as they had during the Pusan ordeal. The USMC ground elements retreated to the Chang Jin Reservoir and every fighter bomber that was serviceable was flung into the air to provide them with a top cover.

Pilots swept the snow off their aircraft while ground crews struggled to get them armed, fueled and started in the cold weather. 77 Squadron pilots would take off at first light for the short forty mile trip to Chang Jin and all day long they would expend their ordnance against the enemy as quickly and accurately as possible and then whip around and head back to K-27 to rearm for another sortie and continue their shuttling back and forth in support of the Marines.

As night fell the aircraft were grounded and the ground forces were on their own. The men fighting in the hills suffered from frostbite along with combat induced wounds. The U.S. 2nd Division attempted a retreat, but they encountered the entire Chinese 40th Army head-on and hardly a vehicle escaped. As the battles continued it became more and more apparent that the UN had over extended itself. 77 Squadron pilots attempted to provide all of the air support that they could, switching to interdiction missions when they had the opportunity to cut the communists supply lines. Unfortunately it was soon discov-

Pilot 3 Donald Brackenreg at Taegu in September 1950. 77 Squadron flew under the radio call sign of "Dropkick," and Don's personal call sign was "Dropkick Zebra." The lowest ranked pilot in the squadron. (Brackenreg)

ered that their prime targets were abandoned UN equipment.

Orders came to abandon Yonpo, as not only were the Chinese getting closer, but there was now more air traffic in and out of K-27 to permit tactical operations. Priority had to be given to transport aircraft that were constantly staging through K-27 and the nearby K-46 with supplies for the ground forces on their inbound leg and for the evacuation of the wounded and severely frostbitten troops outbound. What little tactical support that might now be provided would have to come from Marine F4Us that remained there until the bitter end.

The air elements of 77 Squadron and the 35th FIG departed North Korea on December 3 with their Mustangs loaded with napalm and rockets. They fought their way through snow showers to find and hit their assigned targets, and then headed south for their new home at Pusan, K-9. Upon their arrival they rejoined with the remainder of the 35th FIG, which had been evacuated after the combat mission had become airborne.

Pusan Air Base had in essence been abandoned by FEAF after the 18th FBG had left there after the fall offensive was over. When the Mustangs returned all the personnel from the Group Commander on down pitched in to refuel and rearm the Mustangs for the next day's sorties. There could be no let up in their missions with the Chinese communists breathing down the UN's neck. Living conditions were a bit better than they had experienced at Po'hang, with concrete floored wooden huts which were heated by gasoline stoves for living quarters, but not as nice as what they had just abandoned.

K-9, previously known as "Dogpatch," was not considered the best airfield for fighter-bomber operations, or any flight operations at all for that matter. On three sides it was surrounded by rock strewn hills, and the fourth side was the waters of the Western Channel of the Korea Strait. An over water takeoff was usually the most comfortable for the pilots of a loaded down Mustang, for it did give them a bit more room to maneuver while they gained some airspeed. However the prevailing winds usually did not permit this luxury, which meant taking off toward the hills with corresponding anxious moments. Likewise, landing approaches had to be made from over the water, which often created depth perception problems for the pilots, as there were no visual clues for orientation.

The dust at K-9 got into everything, clothes, eyes, coffee and food. The Mustangs were plagued by this insidious grit also. It got into every part of the aircraft and its associated equipment, jamming radio tuners, contaminating fuel and clogging air filters. A rash of accidents on December 19 caused the 35th FIG and 77 Squadron to be grounded. One American pilot had crashed into the Strait. Another was forced to seek out a rice paddy for a belly landing. Flight Lt. Ross Coburn lost power while on his takeoff roll and barely got stopped before going off the end of the runway. Sabotage was suspected as there were many suspect indigenous personnel on and near the air base, but analysis of the Mustangs fuel storage showed it to be contaminated by impurities.

On December 22 77 Squadron lost another pilot. One of the replacements, Sergeant Donald Ellis was flying in the Number Two position in his Dropkick flight on a combat air patrol east of Pyongyang when he suddenly called his element leader and told him that he was going to crash. Ellis' Mustang was seen as a "ball of fire" when it hit the ground and there was no chance of survival. 20 mm antiaircraft fire was attributed as the cause.

The beginning of 1951 saw a continuation of defensive action on the part of the United Nations. Chinese troops were relentless in their southward movements. The fighter- bombers were hitting anything and everything that even looked like it could support the enemies drive. The weather conditions continued to be on the communists side, also, creating an even more brutal situation than antiaircraft fire. The insidious physical strain of having to fly a Mustang on instruments was wearing the pilots down. Flak areas could be identified and avoided, but flying a Mustang on instruments with its minimal navigational aids when it was made unstable by heavy fuel and ordnance loads to begin with was exhausting. 77 Squadron flew every day except those when the ceilings were to low for safe takeoffs and landing, or to low in the target areas to permit the pilots to locate their objectives.

Seoul fell again on January 4, 1951 and several F-51s were nearly lost while flying ground support missions south of the city, but to the north of the new MLR, when they encountered high tension power lines that were not shown on their maps. The Mustangs slashed through the wires and then had to limp back to K-9 with battered and nicked airframes. Usually it is the wires that win in such a situation, but this time the pilots were lucky.

Two days later Sergeant Geoffry Stephens did not have such fortune as he was believed to have been shot down by antiaircraft fire. His wingman did not see the actual crash, only the tail of a burning Mustang protruding from a one hundred octane fire was visible when he started a search for Stephens after his absence from his formation was noticed. Posthumously Stephens was promoted to Pilot Officer and awarded the American Distinguished Flying Cross for a mission he had performed on November 20.

January 11 saw an unusual occurrence for a 77 Squadron pilot. In fact, for any Mustang pilot. Pilot 3 Donald Brackenreg managed to ditch his Mustang and survive the incident! Brackenreg was performing a functional flight check when his engine started cutting out and when he returned to K-9 he was given a go-around by the control tower for another F-51 that was also experiencing difficulties. He then was instructed to extend his traffic pattern while on the downwind leg for a no-go-around C-119 that was arriving heavily loaded. While on a wide base leg turn at 900 feet Brackenreg's Merlin engine quit completely and it was obvious that he was too far out to glide to the runway, and too low to bailout.

Mustangs are not ditched with a great deal of success, as the belly air scoop tends to impact the water and immediately force the aircraft to violently dive. Only

Lt. Ross Coburn leads the first flight of Australian Mustangs into their new home at Yonpo Air Base, K-27, on November 19, 1950. (USAF via Ethell)

a dozen or so successful ditchings have been recorded. Brackenreg touched down in the bay at eighty miles per hour, and the Mustang pitched down. He wasn't too worried as he did not loose consciousness and he was a strong swimmer. He freed himself from the Sutton harness as soon as the aircraft's speed had dissipated in a methodical fashion, which prevented panic and mistakes, and popped to the surface without undue delay.

A tugboat was within a half mile of the location, and its skipper had seen the Mustang being ditched. Due to the winter season, and although he was picked up within minutes, Brackenreg was already turning blue from his immersion, but he did not even catch a cold and had only a minor cut from striking his head on the gunsight.

At the crash inquiry it was brought out that Brackenreg had landed straight into the water, instead of skewing the Mustang into a wave as prescribed in the Mustang's Pilot Handbook. About two years later another Australian pilot also ditched his Mustang in a similar manor. He also survived and credited his life to having read and followed Brackenreg's technique. The theory behind this technique permitted the aircraft's shoulder harness to restrain the pilot's forward movement, whereas skewing the aircraft as prescribed in the Handbook placed the pilot in an unrestrained position, due to the design of the harness, which would probably cause an incapacitating injury. (Eventually some South Koreans recovered the Mustang from the bay, but it was to large to be moved through the streets of Pusan, so it was left on the beach. Within two days every trace of it had disappeared).

The ground support role was starting to appear very futile to the pilots of 77 Squadron. The Chinese kept pushing south, but as usual they moved only by darkness. The Mustangs were up on constant CAP's and armed reconnaissance, but they could find few targets. The pilots started to complain, sometimes quite bitterly, of the waste of lives and effort, and that the infantry could not hold the communists long enough to give them something to shoot at. The floods of refugees again added to the problem, for it was estimated that over two million people were again moving south to escape the onslaught. And again, the hoards were suspected of containing many communist infiltrators. The Mosquito pilots attempted to single them out, but this was an inexact process, and many civilians were strafed once again.

On January 18 77 Squadron had the sad task of burying the recovered bodies of Squadron Leader Strout and Pilot 3 Harrop. After the services were concluded the men were gathered for a briefing on one of the most important and hazardous missions that they would ever encounter.

They were to fly to Pyongyang to bomb the Chinese Army Headquarters. This was forecasted to be the most heavily defended target in North Korea at the time. The mission had been scheduled before, but it had always been aborted because of poor weather conditions. The mission, scheduled for the 19th, would be made with two flights of six Mustangs each. One flight would carry 500 pound bombs, while the other carried napalm, and both flights carried four rockets on each Mustang.

The instructions were that after the first flight went in and bombed the target they would then sweep the area with rocket attacks which would hopefully silence any antiaircraft fire that might interfere with the following wave of Mustangs with napalm. It would be a maximum range mission at low altitude and the pilots found themselves getting edgy because of all the previous postponements, but then came the "go" and the Mustangs were started under leaden skies.

The first flight of Dropkicks arrived over Pyongyang and made their bomb runs as briefed. But, due to the prevailing weather conditions the second flight was forced to pick their way northward through the "clag" and were late in arriving over the target. The second flight consequently made their napalm runs through the falling bombs of a B-29 mission that was on schedule above them.

Flight Lt. Gordon Harvey reported that he had been hit, but that he was continuing with his attack. Smoke and flames were seen spewing from one of his napalm tanks, and Harvey reported that his Merlin engine was loosing power. Pulling off the target Harvey announced that he was going to make a belly landing along the Taedong River, and he put his Mustang down with a shower of sparks and mud. He was then seen to get out of his Mustang and run into a haystack. Other 77 Squadron pilots immediately set up a RESCAP, but it didn't look to good for the downed pilot. They were 150 miles deep into enemy territory.

The next day 77 Squadron mounted a rescue mission with sixteen Mustangs. Unfortunately when they arrived in the area only Harvey's footprints in the snow and the wreckage of his Mustang could be seen. The supporting helicopter was told to forget it. Later in 1951, when the first listing of POW's was released. Harvey's name was on it, much to the relief of his mates, and he was finally released from his prison camp on August 29, 1953.

January 25, 1951 was the day when the UN decided to once again take the offensive in the Korean War. The next day probing tanks and infantry found little of substance to the communist lines, and they started a forward advance with vehicles bumper to bumper as the again headed back to Inchon and Seoul. The Turkish Brigade was finally relieved from a hill that they had held during some of the bitterest fighting of the war. No less than 750 communist bodies were found on the slopes, many having perished as a result of napalm dropped by 77 Squadron pilots. Lt. Edward Stinson, a 39th FIS pilot who had served with the brigade as a FAC commented that the Turks, with bayonets and taken care of the rest. "Believe me, they are rough boys."

To continue the offensive a mass formation of 35th FIG Mustangs was scheduled. Forty pilots were briefed with sixteen Mustangs of the 40th FIS to take the left, twelve from the 39th FIS in the middle and twelve more on the right from 77 Squadron, which was led by Flight Lt. Olorenshaw. This mission would be the largest one dispatched by the 35th FIG during the war, and it was led by Major Thomas Robertson. The target was a bulge in the bomb line below the Han River with the F-51s armed with napalm and rockets, in addition to their machine guns. They clobbered every village and enemy soldier that they saw.

On February 1 the UN voted to end the Korean Conflict by "peaceful means." All this vote accomplished was a massive amount of morale damaging talk of being home by the 4th of July, or from the Australians viewpoint, being home for their winter season.

Two weeks later the Chinese communists commenced a counter-offensive. They were thrown back at Chipyong-ni, but UN casualties were heavy. The UN continued to move north, and they finally were able to retake Seoul on March 1. Hardly by peaceful means.

Australian war correspondent George Odgers, on the left, documented the history of 77 Squadron and the other Commonwealth forces during the Korean War. His book, Across the Parallel, is rare but highly recommended. In the center is "Pip" Olerenshaw. The third individual is unidentified. (Brackenreg)

77 Squadron had spent February by flying, primarily, interdiction missions. On February 18 Flight Lt.'s Ross Coburn and Fred Barnes became the first two squadron pilots to complete 100 missions. Two days later Olorenshaw completed his 100th, while flying as a top cover for helicopters evacuating U.S. Army troops that had been cut off behind communist lines.

The only multiple loss of 77 Squadron pilots while flying Mustangs occurred on February 14. A flight of four Mustangs led by Ray Trebilco was returning to Pusan from a strike when they encountered a thickening haze that soon developed into solid clouds. Caught on top of an overcast, Trebilco had no choice but to try and lead the flight down through the weather, and as they entered the clouds and he went on instruments he heard a voice exclaim that he was spinning and bailing out. It was never ascertained whether the transmission had come from Flight Lt. K.C. Matthews or Pilot 3 S.S. "Sink" Squires. Neither pilot actually had a chance to bailout, for they were to low and both perished in the crashes of their respective Mustangs.

In their first months of combat operations 77 Squadron had been able to mount 200 effective sorties per month. During February 1951 these sortie totals had been boosted to twenty to twenty-four per day, giving them over five hundred for the month. FEAF, in itself was launching an average of 2,000 per day at this time. These missions were mostly interdiction, and they were considered to be the most hazardous because of the low altitudes from which they were flown and enemy antiaircraft fire. The three biggest enemies of the fighter-bomber pilots being considered, respectively, as ground fire, weather, and mechanical failure.

On February 26 Sergeant Ken Royal crashed, becoming the eleventh 77 Squadron pilot to go down. Royal was on his 97th mission and was flying in the number two position in his flight, being wingman to Flight Lt. Desmond Murphy. Royal called Murphy and told him that his oil pressure was dropping, and it was reading only 15 pounds per square inch, which for a Merlin engine was virtually nil. Turning south and starting a climb, Royal hoped that he could at least get back to friendly territory before his engine "packed up," but the oil pressure dropped to zero and Royal said, "I'm going to have to get out of this." He released the Mustang's canopy to bailout but he apparently changed his mind, as he had a chance for a belly landing if he could spot a flat stretch of land.

Royal settled for a rice paddy near Kimpo and set the Mustang down nicely, but it slid into a dike and nosed over, falling upside down in the muck. A rescue helicopter came in, but could not land in the mud and water. "Sorry, fellas, There's no hope," said the chopper pilot. He was correct, as Royal died in the crash.

The word was out, 77 Squadron would soon convert to jets. Feelings ran high among squadron members at the news, for maybe now they would get out of the air-to-mud role and get a crack at the vaunted MiG's they had seen overhead. Initially the rumor machine said that they were to receive lend-lease F-86s, but this was soon squashed by the 5th Air Force, as they were not enough available for their own USAF units. 77 Squadron would receive the British Meteor, considered to be the second best jet fighter in the UN's resources.

Two Royal Air Force pilots were soon assigned to 77 Squadron to instruct on the "Meatbox." Flight Lt.'s Joseph Blyth and Frank Easley. On the quiet these two soon began flying combat missions in the squadron's Mustangs, which created a political headache. According to the British Government, Englishmen were not permitted to cross the 38th Parallel without their express approval. Soon four more RAF pilots went "on ops," including Sergeant Reginald Lamb, who would be killed on August 11, 1951 in a mid-air collision of two Meteors.

FEAF's Operation Ripper began on March 7 with the limited objective designed to out flank the east side of Seoul. The communist troops, fleeing from air and ground pressure, still had plenty of rice for food and ammunition to shoot, and they were not inclined to give up ground without inflicting their share of damage to the UN objectives.

Two 77 squadron pilots received major damage to their Mustangs while flying through "fusillades." This included the squadron's Meteorological Officer, Flight Lt. Bill Allen, who had the unarmored side windshield shot out of his Mustang, wounding him with shattered bits of Plexiglas.

The wily communists set up phony tanks in the middle of a road to sucker pilots into making a pass on them. Pilot 3 Lyall Klaffer and his wingman decided to even things up a bit and they started a pass at the tanks, and then eased their dives off to the sides of the road a bit, waiting for the unseen gun emplacements to open fire on them. When they did, they were destroyed. The Aussies could be wily, also.

March 15 was the day when Seoul was finally declared as a secure area. 77 Squadron was again up in force. Flight Sergeant H. W. Meggs was over-flying Munan when his Mustang took a hit from small arms fire and it started loosing oil pressure. Meggs headed south in an attempt to reach Kimpo, but his oil pressure kept drop-

ping until it hit zero. Running the Merlin engine at minimum power, Meggs managed to keep his Mustang in the air long enough to reach K-14, but by the time he got it lined up with the runway he was too low to lower the landing gear and he had to settle for a belly landing. As the security of Kimpo remained in doubt at this time, when Meggs was approached by armed soldiers he stood on his Mustang's wing with a drawn pistol to hold them off until he was able to ascertain their nationality as ROK. In the Meantime Desmond Murphy had called for a rescue helicopter, which then evacuated a very shaken Meggs.

Warrant Officer Ronald Howe was flying an armed reconnaissance mission that same afternoon when he too was hit by small arms fire and his engine started running rough. Howe immediately climbed to ten thousand feet and headed for Pusan, but his Mustang could not maintain altitude and Howe was forced to look for a spot to put it down. He settled for an island in the Han River and "parked it there nicely." He was also picked up by a rescue helicopter.

On March 19 Sergeant Harry Strange, who had only joined the squadron the previous month, developed engine trouble while over enemy controlled territory. Strange turned east for Wonsan Harbor, where friendly ships had been blockading and bombarding the harbor for months. He intended to bailout, and picked a ship to come down by and released his canopy, and he was seen to clear his Mustang when he bailed out, but his parachute never opened.

The next day another 77 Squadron Mustang went down. The pilot was Sergeant Cecil Sly, one of the original contingent from Japan. Sly and his wingman were on an armed reconnaissance mission just north of the 38th

A 77 Squadron Mustang on the ramp at Iwakuni. The hangars were of World War II Japanese construction. Note the bomb under the wing which used the characteristic circular fins of RAAF ordnance. (Brackenreg)

Parallel and were flying at only twenty-five to thirty feet high, so they could get a look into trenches and buildings. After coming under some antiaircraft fire Sly's wingman, Sergeant Meggs, called him stating that Sly's Mustang was streaming sparks. Soon thereafter smoke started to enter the cockpit from around the fuel tank gauges on the floor.

Sly then told Meggs that he was going to turn south for the MLR. By this time the cockpit had filled with smoke and Sly had to crank the canopy open to get rid of it, and they had climbed to one hundred-fifty feet. The Mustang then caught on fire, and Sly knew that he was too low to bailout, but the fire gave him little choice. He forced the protesting Mustang up to four hundred feet so he could jump, but his parachute then snagged on the aircraft's seat. Just as the Mustang stalled Sly managed to twist himself free and he went out of the cockpit backwards only to strike the vertical stabilizer with his back. Stunned, Sly popped his parachute open by instinctive reaction, never actually recalling that he did so, and at the moment the parachute blossomed Sly realized that he was now being shot at by the enemy troops on the ground. Sly and his Mustang hit the ground within one hundred-fifty feet of each other, which may have proven to be a record for the lowest successful Mustang bailout.

Meggs called for a rescue helicopter and then he had to leave, for his own Mustang was now damaged by enemy fire. Sly continued to be RESCAPed by other Mustangs that were called in to cover the helicopter's rescue attempt. The Mustangs laid down a withering fire upon the communist troops, so close to Sly that he had to duck the empty .50 caliber shell casings that were falling out of the Mustangs wings overhead and striking the ground all around him and "tinkling."

"The sweetest symphony I ever heard," Sly stated later. Two F-51s overhead took hits from the enemy gunners. Flight Lt. Joseph Blyth, the RAF instructor pilot, had two holes through a self-sealing fuel tank. Another Mustang had the leading edge of a wing crumpled by a flak hit.

A T-6 Mosquito came in to direct the rescue operation, and its observer was shot in the leg, so it had to quickly depart. Two more Mustangs came in, this time from the sister 39th FIS. Their two pilots, Captains Everett Hundly and Oakly Allen, laid napalm in the laps of the Chinese, and then followed these runs up with strafing.

After two hours on the ground Sly was by now in a real sweat. The Mustangs overhead were running low on fuel and ammunition and the communists were now within one hundred-fifty yards of his position. Another helicopter started in for one final rescue attempt, covered by sixteen Mustangs flying in-trail on their last permissible pass before their own fuel shortages would force them to head for home.

The 3rd Air Rescue Squadron helicopter, flown by Captain Lyndon E. Thomasson, literally plucked Sly from the grasp of the enemy. After two weeks rest at Iwakuni Sly was back on missions. Thomasson was decorated with the Distinguished Flying Cross for is part in the rescue effort.

A68-799 had been stored in Japan after 76 Squadron departed in 1949. It was pulled from storage and placed in service with 77 Squadron in November 1950. It was scrapped in 1953. (via Davis)

To provide an aerial top cover for the largest paratroop drop of the Korean campaign to date, 77 Squadron dispatched eight Mustangs, which covered the right flank of the C-46s and C-119s of Operation Tomahawk. This exercise took place at Munson-ni on March 23, 1951 with the objective of blocking the communist northward retreat along the Seoul-Kaesing axis. FEAF had mounted 800 combat sorties during Tomahawk, and in the process marked their 100,000th combat sortie of the war. Tomahawk was intended to trap 60,000 Reds south of the 38th Parallel, but all but a couple thousand managed to filter their way through to the north. Mostly the only thing that was proved through this effort was that air power was unable to provide all the answers to someone's battle plans.

The potential of the communist forces remained horrendous. The 5th Air Force decided that the only way there was to reduce the enemy's threat was to positively close all roads to communist vehicles. The tactic was to bomb the roads day and night at half-mile intervals. For this, each Mustang assigned to the daylight portion of these missions carried two 1,000 pound bombs each, with flights of four aircraft staggering their drops accordingly. Since the roads were generally of flimsy construction to begin with, they were easily repairable by the enemy: just shovel some dirt and rock into the bomb craters and continue on. The first of these missions was flown on April 3 and they coincided with Operation Rugged, an exercise designed to kill as many Red's as possible and place the UN forces in a position to take the "Iron Triangle" area.

Pilot 3 Rich Whittman preferred to do this type of bombing from a steep angle instead of from the more usual level flight attitude, and it almost cost him his life. The danger stemmed from the inherent tendency for the bomb to hang up in its shackle if the Mustang was dove too steeply, instead of falling away cleanly, as the weight of the heavy bomb could place undue pressure on the bomb release mechanism. On one bomb run it happened, the rear bomb shackle released, but the front one did not, and the bomb swung down on the front shackle and was bound in place.

Due to the unexpected weight of the bomb still hanging in place the Mustang almost mushed into the ground. Whittman was now faced with a Mustang that was aerodynamically unstable from the weight of the bomb and the imbalance of its wings. He quickly found that he could not climb back up to a safer altitude to experiment on how he might get rid of the encumbrance, and he dared not fool around with it at a low altitude, for in all probability if it did come off the blast would take him with it when it went off. On top of all this, he did not know if the rear fuse arming pin had been pulled when the bomb swung down, or not.

Whittman soon found himself headed for some electrical power lines that he could not evade. With little choice he managed to tuck the Mustang between the lines and the ground with just inches to spare. And, just before encountering a hilltop he managed to regain enough airspeed to permit a climb to a sufficient altitude to shake the bomb off and to head for home.

77 Squadron was relieved from combat operations at noon on April 6. They were scheduled to return to Iwakuni Air Base on April 10 to begin their conversion into Meteors. Whittman had hoped to get in his 100th Mustang mission on the 6th, but he had to settle for his ninety-ninth when he and three other squadron pilots made a successful strike against the road between Koksan and Singye where the destroyed a dozen communist trucks. This was the last Mustang combat mission for 77 Squadron and within the week they were all back in Japan, but it wasn't exactly a perfect return trip for them as a pair of Mustangs were destroyed in two accidents, one taking the life of Sergeant R. Robson.

During the nine month period of Mustang combat operations 77 Squadron had flown 3,800 combat sorties, an average of 400 per month. They lost a total of ten pilots in combat, two in the fire at Po'hang, two were killed in accidents, and one became a POW.

They were considered by the Commanding General of the 5th Air Force as the "squadron that set the pace."

CHAPTER FIVE

The 8th Fighter Bomber Squadron

The first United States Air Force tactical fighter group to carry the air war to the invading North Koreans was the 8th Fighter Bomber Group, whose motto, appropriately, was "Attack and Conquer." The Group was composed of three Fighter Bomber Squadrons, the 35th, 36th and 80th FBS's, and it was subordinate to the 8th Fighter Bomber Wing, whose other flying squadron was the F-82 equipped 68th Fighter (All-Weather) Squadron. At the time the conflict began the Group's three tactical squadrons were flying F-80Cs, and the Group, itself, was led by Lt. Colonel William Samways. Samways would score four ground kills in July 1950 while flying the Shooting Star, and thus became the highest scoring F-80 pilot in the Korean War.

The 8th FBW was commanded by Colonel John M. Price, and it was upon his shoulders that the responsibility for the tactical air war fell during the first critical weeks

A brand new Mustang being delivered to the 116th Fighter Squadron, Washington Air National Guard in March 1947. This F-51 was one of the aircraft carrier Boxer's first deliveries to the 8th Fighter Bomber wing. It was lost on October 12, 1950 to an unknown cause while on a combat mission. (McLaren collection)

of the war. The 8th FBW was operating under a peacetime Table of Organization and Equipment, TO&E, when the war started, as were all other flying units within FEAF, and strong credit must go to their personnel, both in the air and on the ground, for getting and keeping their aircraft operational in the face of heavy demands in an environment where the aircraft were definitely at a disadvantage.

Because there was not one single airstrip in South Korea that was deemed suitable for jet fighter operations, the 8th Fighter Bomber Group's F-80s were forced to fly all of their combat missions from Itazuke Air Base, J-13, Fukuoka, Japan. This created a constant concern in respect to fuel constraints for the F-80 pilots. Loiter time over a target in Korea was often a bare five minutes, which meant that a target had to be located before a pilot could start his descent down to an attack altitude, or that there had better be a forward air controller, FAC, there to pinpoint it out for him when he reached a lower altitude. If the target could not be immediately located, then the pilot had little choice but to make a quick search for a target of opportunity to expend his ordnance, for he was not permitted to return to Japan with any remaining underwing armament.

Due to a lack of adequate maps, or poor radio communication, many combat missions over Korea during the first weeks of the conflict were exercises in futility. Later, when the F-80s were fitted with underwing bomb racks, which then permitted them to carry both the normal wingtip fuel tanks and bombs, their loiter time was increased to ten to fifteen minutes, but this still remained an unacceptable short duration. Also, the weather over Korea during this period was predominately one of overcast skies, because of the typhoon season, and targets continued to remain difficult for the pilots to locate.

An "in the field" attempt to increase the range of the F-80 had taken place in January 1950 with the creation of the "Misawa" tip tanks. These simply were the conventional tank with an extra center section spliced in, which increased their capacity by over a third. Originally constructed without internal baffles, the fuel would flow forward in the tank when the aircraft was descending, and then when it was pulling up, it would slosh to the rear. If the aircraft was pulled up in an evasive action with a high "g" load after making an attack, as little as thirty gallons of fuel (180 pounds plus "g" forces) would be sufficient to over stress the F-80s wingtips. This would cause the tank and wingtip to snap off, which would then whip back into the horizontal stabilizer and rip it off, resulting in the loss of plane and pilot in a high speed snap-roll. The problem was not one that could have been readily foreseen in peacetime conditions, and it was quickly rectified through the installation of internal baffles, but not until after it caused the deaths of several pilots in Korea.

With heavy operational demands placed upon the 8th FBW, the corresponding loss rate of pilots and aircraft was quite high. During July 1950 the 8th FBW lost seventeen F-80s and six pilots were either killed or declared missing in action, with two more being wounded. Small arms fire over the target area, the loss of wingtips, or running out of fuel were the sequential causes of these losses.

Through hard work by the men of the 6002nd Fighter Wing, which had just been created in South Korea to support combat operations, it appeared as if the 8th Fighter Bomber Group might just be able to take their F-80s to Taegu Air Base, K-2, after all. In fact some of the

44-12943 was one of the oldest Mustangs to serve in Korea. In this instance it had slid off the runway at K-2 after the tail wheel failed to extend as a result of enemy gunfire. Note the battle damage just aft of the National Insignia. "Red Raider" was repaired and continued in service, being transferred from the 36th Fighter Bomber Squadron to the 18th Fighter Bomber Group. It was scraped in November 1953 after amassing 1540 flying hours. (Tanner via Davis)

ground echelon had left Japan for Taegu on August 4 to assist the 6002nd Fighter Wing in making K-2 suitable for jet operations. There was a definite need to get the airstrip open, for the press of aerial activities through Itazuke, along with the distances involved to targets was proving to be just too great of a hazard for the pilots to have to face on a daily basis.

However, the North Korean pressure on the ever tightening Pusan Perimeter appeared to be placing Taegu in jeopardy. Thus Colonel price decided to move the 8th FBW to Tsuiki Air base, J-36, Japan for the interim. Tsuiki, happily known as "Sun Valley," was located on the northern tip of Kyushu and it had previously been utilized as a staging base by the 8th FBW during peacetime exercises. The airstrip, in actuality, had been virtually abandoned since the end of World War II, but it now entered into a phase of rapid reconstruction.

Through August 10 the 8th FBW had run up a total of 865 combat sorties in the F-80. But because of the F-80 attrition, Headquarters FEAF decided to convert the 8th FBW back into Mustangs. For most of the men the transition would be effortless, for they had only switched from F-51s to F-80s six months previously. There were still several Mustangs assigned to the group, utilized as target tugs and as squadron hacks, and several of the pilots had continued to fly them just for the enjoyment of it all.

In addition, two small detachments of 8th FBW Mustangs had been established at the on-set of the Korean War. One was led by Captain James Becket, and as-

Mustangs bound for Japan and service in Korea on the aircraft carrier Boxer. (Robert Fogg via Davis)

44-74941 was "Red Eraser" & "Buckeye Blitz VI," the personal Mustang of Captain Joe Rogers, 36th FBS. The painted symbols indicate twelve tanks, two trains, and one hundred-thirty missions. It was lost to Code R on December 5, 1950 at Kimpo (Tanner via Davis)

signed the task of training the first batch of ROKAF pilots in Japan. This detachment had received ten of the first F-51s withdrawn from storage at Johnson Air Base.

The second section became identified as Detachment 1, 36th Fighter Bomber Squadron, and they had been formed on July 1, 1950. They then became attached to the newly formed 6002nd Fighter Wing, and through a process of evolution, the Detachment expanded to 37 officers and 303 airmen. With the expansion, the Detachment eventually became redesignated as the 51st Fighter Bomber Squadron (Provisional), and the chapter on the 18th FBW continues their story.

The majority of the F-51s that were assigned to the 8th FBW were those that had arrived on the aircraft carrier Boxer. Forty-eight were received altogether, and six of them became operational losses before the end of August, with one more being lost in an accident. It was felt that these Mustangs had been fostered off on the 8th FBW in "rather sad shape." Even though the Air National Guard squadrons that they had been taken from in July had worked hard to prepare them for overseas shipment, and some additional work had been done to them after their arrival in Japan, they were still considered to be in "poor condition." Apparently the ANG squadrons that had furnished them had seen fit to get rid of their maintenance hogs when they had the chance.

The 35th Fighter Bomber squadron started receiving their Mustangs on August 1, and by August 8 they had a Mustang and a F-80 for each pilot in the squadron! The pilots continued to fly their combat missions in the F-80 at this time, and then returned to fly transition training in the F-51 later in the day. The ground crews were virtually

working around the clock in the process while trying to keep the disparate types operational. It would be impossible to over-credit them for their efforts.

On the morning of August 11 pilots of both the 35th and 36th FBS's flew from Itazuke in their Mustangs for their first combat missions over Korea in the type, and then returned to Tsuiki. They flew fifty-three combat sorties during this first day of F-51 operations.

The 80th FBS, was now the only F-80 squadron remaining in the 8th FBW, and for logistical and tactical considerations they were separated from the 8th FBW and attached to the F-80 equipped 49th FBW at Misawa Air Base. The 49th FBW, in turn, became attached to the 8th FBW for support functions, which sounds a bit confusing in light of the USAF's "One base, one Wing" program, but the 8th FBW was the prime mover for all tactical air operations over Korea at this time and they included the 3rd Bomb Wing (Light) with B-26s under their control, also.

Morale among many of the 8th FBW pilots reportedly ebbed with the transition back into the F-51. Headquarters FEAF had told them that since they were the most recent Wing to switch from F-51s to F-80s, they were the most capable of reverting back to the Mustang. This same story had been told to the men of the 35th Fighter Interceptor Wing, and it didn't take very long for everyone to feel that they were being duped. They were also told that the F-51 was a better ground support aircraft than the F-80, which was a view not necessarily shared by the involved pilots.

Lt. Colonel William O'Donnell, commanding officer 36th FBS, was quite happy to get back into the Mustang, in fact he had requested them for his squadron. His best friend and previous commanding officer of the 36th FBS,

James Gasser's "Bad Check (Always comes back)" as assigned to the 8th FBG. It was lost in May 1951 while with an unidentified unit. (Gasser via Ethell)

Major Richard McNess, had been one of the F-80 pilots killed when his Misawa tip tank tore off his horizontal stabilizer after a wing tip failure. Comments ranged from the statement found in the 36th FBS history for July 1950: "When are we going to convert to the F-51 type aircraft so we can really give the enemy all we've got?" to the negative view that "Pilots thought the F-80 was a wonderful aircraft, easy to fly, after all, Lt. Wurster had brought one back with more than half the vertical stabilizer missing." (This was in reference to an incident where Wurster had hit a cable and sheared off his stabilizer and rudder, a situation that a F-51 was not likely to survive because of the torque associated with a propeller driven aircraft requires a presence of a rudder for stabilized flight). The younger pilots had a great amount of confidence in the F-80, while the older ones, those who had flown the Mustang in World War II, had mixed emotions. They knew that the F-51 was a good aircraft, but that it was vulnerable to ground fire, for they had seen many lost during ground support operations during the previous war. Yet it was difficult to argue with statistics:

In July the 36th FBS had lost its commanding officer and its adjutant to the failure of the F-80s wingtips. Another pilot, 1st Lt. Howard O'Dell, the squadron's engineering officer, was shot down by a more maneuverable Yak-9, and 1st Lt. Eugene Hanson had been shot down by ground fire. The 35th FBS had lost two pilots, 1st Lt. Leon Pollard because of weather and low fuel, and 1st Lt. Donald Sirman to ground fire. The issue was academic, for the F-80s were in short supply and they were going to have to be transferred to the 49th FBW and be replaced by F-51s. Period.

Lt. Reichman, 36th FBS, and his "Nightmare Alley," 44-74925, photographed while returning from a mission over Korea in murky skies. Lousy weather was the rule during the first months of the war. It was lost in February 1951 after being transferred to the 18th FBG. (O'Donnell)

Japanese girls rolling out barrels of napalm at Tsuiki Air Base in August 1950. When the 8th FBW converted back to F-80s in December 1950 45-11732 was transferred to the 18th FBG and it was a combat loss on September 22, 1951. (O'Donnell)

The 35th Fighter Bomber Squadron started out its Mustang era under the leadership of Major Rayburn Lancaster, who had just replaced Major Vincent Cardarello, who had been killed when his F-80 crashed on August 1 during a strafing mission. The 35th FBS and Lt. Colonel O'Donnell's 36th FBS became attached to the 6131st Fighter Bomber Wing while at Tsuiki. The 6131st FBW had originally been formed at Po'hang Air Base, K-3, South Korea on August 8 under the leadership of Colonel Charles Stark. It had been the intention for this Wing to oversee combat operations from Po'hang, but due to the forced evacuation of the airstrip on August 14, they had to be withdrawn to Tsuiki once again. The 8th FBG, en total, eventually joined with the 6131st FBW, and then the 35th Fighter Interceptor Group also was assigned to them for a short period.

Although not officially flying combat missions in F-51s until August 11, the 8th FBG had actually started flying them on August 8. Their first mission was to provide an escort for a SA-16 "Duckbutt." that had gone out to pick up a downed U.S. Navy pilot.

Lt. Omer Reichman, 36th FBS, flying as "Carrot Charlie," had a fire in his cockpit on the return leg of the third mission of August 11, a strafing attack near Pugoing-ni. Reichman then was forced to bailout ten miles east of Tsushima, but he was rescued by a Japanese fishing boat none the worse for wear.

When the "official" F-51 missions started on August 11 they marked the loss of another Mustang. Captain Charles Brown, 36th FBS, was strafing a North Korean T-34 tank, which decided to fire back at him instead of buttoning up its hatches. This is the only reported incident of a tank shooting down a fighter during the Korean

Conflict. Brown bailed out at 0931 hours KST, and was picked up by friendly troops at 0940, which also may be a record for the speedy recovery of a downed pilot from enemy territory. Brown suffered a broken ankle when he hit the ground, but he was evacuated through Mangun Airdrome, K-12, without delay.

On August 15 1st Lt. John Munkres, 35th FBS, was lost. Soon after a predawn takeoff Munkres reported that he was having engine trouble, and within minutes his Merlin engine caught on fire. Munkres, an experienced Mustang pilot, attempted to ditch his F-51 just off the northeast coast of Kyushu. Although the wreckage of his F-51 was located and inspected by divers, no trace of Munkres was found. He was declared as KIA on December 15.

That afternoon 2nd Lt. Paul Carlsen, 35th FBS, also developed engine trouble while crossing the Korea Strait on his way back from a mission over Korea. Carlsen elected to bailout, and he came down in the vicinity of where Munkres had gone down, and he was picked up by an air-sea rescue aircraft that was searching for Munkres.

Three days later 1st Lt. Charles Wurster, a 36th FBS pilot who had shot down two Yak-9s while flying F-80s, and the same pilot who had brought back the rudderless Shooting Star, experienced a traumatic crash in a F-51. Wurster had just taken off from Taegu in a fully loaded Mustang when his supercharger failed and he lost power at the most critical phase of flight. His Mustang stalled and then crashed with a violent thud, but with a stroke of luck both Wurster and his seat were thrown from the exploding wreckage. he was critically injured, but eventually recovered.

36th FBS pilots: Reichman, Goulait, Bennett, Fogg and Walton. (Then) Captain Chauncy Bennett was killed on April 30, 1951 while flying his 100th combat mission with the 12th FBS. (O'Donnell)

More 36th FBS pilots: Wine, Rogers', Doris and Peyser. The flight suits, Mae West life preservers et al, were hot and uncomfortable while flying in the cramped F-51 cockpits. (O'Donnell)

On August 22 1st Lt. Patterson Gilliam, 35th FBS, was hit by ground fire while strafing northeast of Andong. he headed back for friendly territory, but the Mustang was to damaged to make it, and he crashed behind enemy lines. His wingman had not seen any attempt by Gilliam to bail out, nevertheless he was carried as MIA until his death was confirmed on December 22.

The next day Captain James Canrahan and 1st Lt. Richard Zielke found themselves in the midst of a thunderstorm while returning from a mission over Korea. They headed for "Sun Valley," but were diverted to Ashiya Air Base because of the storm. In the midst of the weather the navigation lights on one aircraft went out, and the radio on the other one failed, and the two aircraft became separated. They individually found Ashiya and started their landing approaches, only to meet head-on on the runway. Both Mustangs suffered minor damage, but the pilots escaped injury.

The last loss of the month occurred on August 27 when 1st Lt. Arlin Mullet, 35th FBS, was killed while attempting an emergency landing at Taegu. His Mustang had suffered numerous hits from small arms fire, but it was believed that his loss came as the result of being caught in the prop wash of his element leaders' Mustang while in the landing traffic pattern, that caused him to loose control and spin-in from too low of an altitude to bail out.

In spite of the shortages of almost every critical item required to keep the Mustangs operational, not to mention the more mundane items for the men, as clothing, underwear and shoes, the 8th FBW squadrons were truly carrying the war to the North Koreans. They had flown 1,127 combat sorties and logged 2, 661 combat hours in August. An individual sortie record went to Captain James Gasser, 36th FBS "B Flight" commander, who had flown

All the comforts of home, an outdoor privy in use prior to a mission from Suwon Air Base. (O'Donnell)

five sorties on August 23 for a total of 9:20 combat hours. Gasser ended the month with a total of ninety-seven missions. The highest amount of flying time went to Captain Joseph Rogers, who had logged 124 combat hours.

On September 1 the 6131st FBW was redesignated as the 6131st Tactical Support Wing and in a reversal of roles it became subordinate to the existing 8th FBW. The relationship of the 6131st TSW is identical for all practical purposes to the 8th FBW and the 35th and 36th FBS for the period that they flew the F-51.

Most Mustang missions over Korea started with a predawn briefing and then a departure from J-36 as the sun was rising. The departure was timed so as to arrive over the target area just as their was sufficient light to pick out the target, in hopes of catching the North Koreans before they had a chance to camouflage themselves for the day. After these initial attacks were accomplished the fighters would then head for Taegu Air Base, to rearm and refuel. They would then stage from Taegu for the remainder of the day, with most of the pilots getting in between three and five missions. After the last strike of the day they would return to J-36, where they usually arrived after sunset.

These missions created an obvious strain on the pilots, but they also wore down the ground crews who were faced with an all-night job of preparing the Mustangs for the next days' missions. It did not take long for the Mustangs to start showing signs of wear, either, for most required some sheet metal patching as a result of small arms fire. There was no end of radio difficulties, as the SCR 522's with their tube-type transmitters broke down quite easily under the constant shocks of the jarring take-offs and landings on Taegu's poor runway. All of the Mustangs soon required fuel line replacements, as dry rot

had attacked the rubber junction hoses. The pilots were apprehensive as to whom was going to have to fly the 'Stangs equipped with peacetime non self-sealing hoses.

September had begun with the emphasis on ground support missions, and ended with missions of the armed reconnaissance nature. Both of these missions were dangerous in their own right, and cost the two squadrons several pilots each.

The first casualty for September was on September 2 and involved 1st Lt. James Anderlie, 36th FBS. Anderlie was flying as the Number Two man in a flight led by Captain Homer Hanson. The two Mustangs came under intense flak near Wonson and they broke formation to evade they enemy fire. After clearing the area Hanson called for Anderlie to rejoin him, but he received no response, and no trace of the F-51 was to be found. Anderlie was declared MIA at the time, and as KIA in December 1953.

Two days later Captain Robert Wayne, 36th FBS, was leading a two-ship flight with Captain Raymond White as his wingman. The two pilots headed north to provide ground support to UN troops north of Po'hang when Wayne's Mustang was hit by ground fire just after they crossed the MLR. Wayne was forced to bail out at a low altitude, less than five hundred feet above the ground, and his parachute barely had time to blossom before he hit the ground. Wayne landed in a rice paddy and quickly found himself being pursued through the mire by North Korean troops.

Captain White, observing the action transpiring below, dove down with his machine guns blazing to cover Wayne, while at the same time he was broadcasting on the emergency frequency a Mayday call for a rescue helicopter. Fortunately a chopper was nearby and an-

A briefing of 8th FBW pilots at Tsuiki Air Base prior to the 8th FBG's departure for Korea. The "Hobo" on the box indicates the Group's mission relocation name, and became memorialized as "The Spirit of Hobo" after five moves. (O'Donnell)

"My Baby II," 44-74138 belonged to the 36th FBS. Here it has its canopy removed for access to the radio equipment. (Moir via Davis)

"Mox Nix" (makes no difference) of the 35th FBS at Tsuiki Air Base. It was another of the aircraft carrier Boxer's initial cargo to Japan, and it was lost on March 1, 1951 after transfer to the 12th FBS. (USAF)

swering the call, hove-to and flew to the area. Both the helicopter and White's Mustang then came under heavy ground fire, with the F-51 receiving several 40mm and small caliber machine gun hits. Again, and fortunately, "Wolfhound Jig," a flight of 49th FBW F-80s had overheard White's initial Mayday call and had come in to provide a RESCAP. Wayne was picked up by the chopper crew and evacuated for treatment of burns on his hands and legs, for which he received the Purple Heart. He also received a Distinguished Flying Cross for having shot down two Il-10s on June 26 while flying a F-80. Raymond White was put in for a Silver Star for his part in the rescue effort.

On September 10, 1st Lt. Ralph Hall, 35th FBS, was slightly injured when a single round of small caliber ammunition penetrated the wing of his Mustang and then traversed through his cockpit. Hall received a minor burn from the hot fragments and was wounded in the arm by the bullet as it ricocheted around the cockpit. Hall had been one of the three 35th FBS pilots that had gone to fly with Bout One during the early weeks of the war, but he had not scored a victory on the "shoot-out" on June 29 as they were delivering Mustangs to the ROKAF. He would, however, get one ground kill, believed to be a Yak-9, on September 28 after recovering from his injuries.

On September 12 all serviceable Mustangs of both squadrons were flown from Japan to K-2 to avoid damage by Typhoon Kezia. The storm passed over Tsuiki, causing only minor damage, and since the aircraft had been evacuated, no loss of operational flying. The ensuing combat missions did become more hazardous as a result of the storm's low-laying clouds over Korea, as they forced the pilots to fly at lower altitudes and also silhouetted them against the cloud bases, which made them enhanced targets for the North Korean antiaircraft gunners.

This typhoon residue was a contributing factor in the next Purple Heart awarded within the 8th FBW. On September 13 1st Lt. Russell Rogers, 35th FBS, who had just returned to flying duties after a stint as a forward air controller, had his canopy shattered by machine gun fire. Rogers was on a low-level strike and was caught between the clouds and the enemy gunners. Fortunately the bullets missed him, but he received several cuts from shards of shattered Plexiglas.

Captain Harold Webster, Armament Officer, 36th FBS, was lost on September 14. Webster was seen ducking under low clouds while attempting to make a strafing pass against some enemy vehicles near Kunchon, but he flew into to some high tension electrical power lines. His Mustang did a complete snap roll and then struck the ground upright, which was followed by a high speed slide into a dike ringing a rice paddy, where it exploded.

Captain Walter Russell, Assistant 8th FBW Operations Officer, was flying a mission with the 35th FBS when he was killed on September 16. His flight of Mustangs had been providing ground support to UN troops in the Nagan area until they ran out of ordnance. The flight then rejoined after this last pass and headed back to Tsuiki, but suddenly Russell's Mustang was seen to plunge into a dry river bed. He had not reported any injury or battle damage, but apparently his Mustang had taken several strikes while on its last strafing pass, for it was found to have several holes in it when a UN patrol examined the wreckage and recovered Russell's body.

James Gasser, who has since retired from the USAF, commented: "It was distressing to return to home base with only three aircraft when starting with four." Yet this seemed to be the pattern that was becoming to be all to prevalent. On September 18 Captain Edward Onze, 36th FBS, was lost on a ground support mission. Onze became separated from the rest of his flight in bad weather and simply disappeared. he was declared MIA, and his death was confirmed in December 1950.

On September 22 Captain Joseph Rosenfield, 36th FBS, had a narrow brush with death, himself. He was struck in the forehead by an enemy bullet that had come up through his Mustang's floorboard and just grazed his scalp before exiting through the canopy. Three days later 1st Lt. Lea Pagan, 35th FBS, also got his forehead banged up, this time by the Mustang's K-14 gunsight. Pagan was landing at Tsuiki and was rolling down the runway in a "wheel landing" when he discovered that the aircraft's tail wheel had failed to extend when he had lowered its landing gear. As the F-51 lost flying speed, directional control was lost and it went into a severe ground loop, which caused minor damage to Pagan and major damage to the Mustang.

A major problem the 8th FBW was having with their Mustangs at this time was due to the fact that the pilots could not fire their rockets when they needed to. The pilots were becoming quite disgruntled, as they found it both frustrating and hazardous to be making a rocket attack on a target only to discover that while they were being shot at by the North Koreans, they could not retaliate. As it was discovered, the problem was not with the F-51, but with sabotage. A close inspection of the rockets showed that someone had tampered with the rockets

Captain Joe Rogers and his "screamer," a set of pitch pipes attached to a rocket rail that set up a horrendous wail as the air passed through them. (O'Donnell)

Captain Paul Carlisle, 8th FBG, and "Jr's Troubles." Below the S is the oil breather vent, while just below the T is an access for inserting a hand crank to manually start the Merlin engine. Rarely, if ever used. (O'Donnell)

"pigtails," which were plugged into the Mustang's lower wing and were used to supply the electrical charge that would ignite the rocket's motor. When the pilot squeezed the trigger to fire a rocket, the sabotage caused the electrical charge to short out the Mustang's electrical system.

After the success of the Inchon Landing, FEAF asked the U.S. Army's X Corps for authority to move two Mustang Groups to Korea from Japan, as the amount of flying time could be drastically reduced. From Tsuiki to the Yalu River was five and a half hours of drudgery for the pilots. The current group of pilots were all older than their World War II counterparts had been, in fact most were the same individuals with five more years added to their ages. Their average pilot's rank was that of a captain and a flight of four aircraft all piloted by captains was the norm. Both the pilots and their aircraft were beginning to show their age. In addition, the Mustangs had to carry their drop tanks to make the trip, which reduced their ef-

The insignia of the 36th FBS dated back to World War I. The "Flying Fiend" was more commonly known as the "puking pup." (O'Donnell)

Lt. C. S. "Little" Thomas, 36th FBS, at Kimpo. "Deacon Butler III" was a well known race horse at the time, as well as Mustang 44-74484. It was lost on April 26, 1951 with the 18th FBG. (O'Donnell)

fectiveness by likewise reducing the ordnance they could carry. X Corps was more than happy to agree to this move, as it would place the fighter-bombers much closer to the army's front lines. X Corps supplied engineers to repair and improve the retaken airstrip at Suwon, K-13, for the 8th FBW's use. They even agreed to provide the security for the airstrip, which was a FEAF prerequisite.

Since the runway at Suwon had been so torn up by FEAF bombing when the airfield had been in enemy hands, Marston Mat, PSP, had to be laid over what good runway remained, which helped provide an all-weather capability for the airstrip. This was a true necessity, for when it was dry there was so much dust in the air, stirred up by jet or prop wash, that the runway was almost always under virtual instrument flight conditions. When it was wet, only the runway, itself, was safe for use, and aircraft had to be towed on the slick grass areas to pre-

vent accidents. Because of these problems, and air traffic congestion, the 36th FBS was forced to remain in Japan for several more weeks, with no respite from the longer ranged missions.

The Headquarters Section of the 8th FBG and the 35th FBS were airlifted to K-13 on October 7, 1950, and the next day the 35th FBS was back on combat operations from their new home. Only one-half of the runway was available for use by the Mustangs at the time, due to the pasting it had received by B-26s when it had been occupied by the North Koreans. Nevertheless, the short runway was shared with the 80th FBS and their F-80s who staged through K-13 on missions of their own.

At Suwon Air Base the ground crews were pushed to their limits. There was no refueling equipment, so the F-51s had to be refueled by hand. If an unscheduled aircraft landed that had to be refueled, the Wing's mission

Lt. Colonel William Samways, commanding officer 8th FBG. Samways had scored four ground kills while flying F-80s with the 8th FBG and was the top scoring Shooting Star pilot. (O'Donnell)

"Mac's Revenge," the personal Mustang of Lt. Colonel William O'Donnell, commanding officer of the 36th FBS. His Mustang, 44-84974, was named for Major Richard McNees, O'Donnell's best friend who lost his life in a F-80 crash. (O'Donnell)

The starboard side of "Mac's Revenge" was "O'L Anchor Ass," named by O'Donnell's crew chief, Sgt. "Andy" Anderson. Anderson had been in the U.S. Navy during World War II, hence the name. Previously O'Donnell, Anderson and this Mustang had been in the 95th Fighter Interceptor Squadron and Anderson spotted it being off-loaded from the Boxer and claimed it for O'Donnell. (Brackenreg)

fuel allotment often ran short, because of inadequate fuel storage facilities. Any aircraft that landed with battle damage had to be given spot, one time repairs, and then flown to Japan for rework. If the damage was excessive, the aircraft was simply cannibalized for spare parts.

Ground support missions from K-13 were the norm until October 20 when the pilots were given an opportunity to fly a fighter escort mission to cover paratroop drops in the Sunchon area. The North Korean Air Force did not show up, so the Mustang pilots were able to cavort at an altitude out of antiaircraft fire range for awhile. The paratroop drop had turned out to be one of the more successful efforts of the war, involving 2,860 paratroopers and 111 C-119s and C-47s. It secured the Pyongyang area for the UN's drive to the north. But the following day it was back to the air-to-mud role once again.

On October 23 the 8th FBG started to move to Kimpo Air Base, K-14, with the ground support personnel and equipment being transferred by ship and rail from Japan. The following day an advance party of pilots and their Mustangs flew into K-14 to start combat operations. On the 28th the remainder of the Group, along with the 35th FBS from Suwon arrived, and two days later they were joined by the remainder of the 36th FBS from Japan.

Again, due to logistical problems, six F-51s had to be placed on the AOCP list. They would be out of service for some time, as the required spare parts had been lost while enroute to Suwon. There was more than a little disgruntlement among the pilots and ground crews. All sorts of required items were back ordered from FEAMCOM,

and the requests for these items were not being acted upon. FEAMCOM, obviously, was "Not aware there was a war going on."

One major concern was that the Mustangs gun cameras had not been modified when the F-51s had gone through FEAMCOM's repair depots. There were no connectors for the gun camera relays. What few cameras that did work took pictures that had to be processed and assessed at Itazuke, because FEAMCOM had neglected to send any photography equipment to the 8th FBG. Pilots would attempt to photograph enemy activity while on their low-level missions, often at extreme hazard to themselves, but they never could find out of these targets were either strategically or tactically worthwhile.

Intelligence and communications with the 5th Air Force was a continuing problem, regardless of where the 8th FBG was located. The pilots had a great fear repeating the incident where the 18th FBG had strafed friendly troops the previous summer because of a lack of up to date information on where the UN troops were. The battle lines were moving northward at a furious pace, and it was more than difficult to keep the pilots appraised the current lines. A "Crop Line" was established from Manchuria across North Korea, which was not to be crossed except under direct orders from the JOC. Another line was established from Sinanju to Hamnung, which was called the "VFR Line." This line was not to be crossed unless the pilots were in visual flight conditions and where they could positively identify the targets they were to strike. The remainder of North Korea was divided into sections where the pilots could make their attacks while under direct control of a FAC.

Due to the lack of standardized communications, all gathered intelligence was flown to Seoul each night by a courier aircraft. Intelligence personnel would then assimi-

An armorer of the 8th FBW loading a Mustang's ammo bays. (O'Donnell)

Forward Air Controllers on detached service from the 8th FBW and attached to a Republic of Korea infantry division observe a ground battle. The colored panels on the foreground mark the location of the front lines. (O'Donnell)

"Mac's Revenge" at Pyongyang. The photograph was taken shortly before the Mustang was damaged by another pilot and had to be destroyed by O'Donnell lest it fall into enemy hands when the airstrip was evacuated in December 1950. The C-54 in the background was used to air-evac wounded GI's, with the red tail markings identifying it as being winterized. (O'Donnell)

late the information and prepare pilot briefings for individual squadrons use. If a "Frag Order" was late in arriving from FEAF, there could be problems, particularly if the order might require a change in aircraft ordnance. This change could cause the entire next day's missions to be thrown off schedule, because of the time required for unloading and reloading the aircraft.

Debriefing of the pilots was conducted at the Group level, as this permitted the intelligence officer to spread "the word" to the concerned pilots as quickly as possible. Again, the unfortunate thing was that they never did get any photographs to work with, and the intelligence received from FEAF was always a couple days old when it arrived.

Needless to state, October had been a very busy month for the 8th FBG. The 36th FBS was fortunate in that they lost neither pilot nor aircraft. The 35th FBS, carrying the brunt of the load, due to their proximity to the enemy, lost three Mustangs during one day's missions, and one more before the month ended.

On October 16 Captain Charles Brower was flying his first combat mission over Korea and his flight had been in the process of working over the North Korean airfield at Sinuiju when Brower completed a strafing pass. He pulled up directly into a spray of 20mm fire that was arcing over the Yalu River from Manchuria. Brower's Mustang was hit several times and he turned south along the western coast of North Korea, but soon his oil pressure started to drop, and then his propeller ran away.

Figuring that attempting to ditch in the Yellow Sea was not a good idea, Brower elected to bail out. After landing in the water he inflated his life raft and started to

paddle to a small rocky island, where he spent the night. The next morning a communist boat headed for Brower's refuge in an attempt to capture him, but he held them off with his personal Colt .45 caliber pistol. A RESCAP of Marine F7Fs soon arrived and sank the boat with cannon fire, and then they remained overhead until a SA-16 from the 17th Air Rescue Squadron arrived early in the afternoon to pick him up. Brower apparently became the first Mustang pilot in history to capture and hold an enemy island!

Also on October 16 Captain Ralph Hall was shot down. Hall was strafing near Haeju when his Mustang was severely shot up by ground fire and he was forced to bail out. over "no man's land." The North Koreans continued shooting at him while he descended in his parachute, cutting several his parachute's shroud lines and holing its canopy. Due to these holes, Hall's rate of descent increased, and he hit the ground hard enough to break his back.

Fortunately an American patrol from the 5th Cavalry Division was scouting the area and they picked Hall up without undue delay. This was the third Mustang that was shot up while Hall was flying it, which is indicative of the amount of firepower facing the fighter-bomber pilots. Hall was returned to the United States for further medical treatment.

The third loss for the day saw the death of 1st Lt. Wayne Rabun, 35th FBS. Rabun had made a strafing pass on the outskirts of Sinuiju and then pulled up into the smoke and haze generated by the previous attacks of his flight. In the murk he apparently never saw the L-17 that was serving as a FAC for the mission, and the two aircraft collided and spun to the ground. One parachute was seen to open, but a search of the area could not locate it on the ground, and the occupants of both aircraft were considered as KIA.

On October 24 Captain Fletcher Westors took off from Seoul to ferry a Mustang to Suwon for some repair work. His Merlin engine quit cold on him soon after breaking ground, and Westors wrenched his back as he bailed out. After a short recuperation period he returned to flying status.

Air traffic conditions at Kimpo were hectic. The control tower did not have the proper radio crystals for talking to the Mustangs of the 8th FBG. The Mustangs had to be mixed in with three squadrons of 51st FIW F-80s and a squadron of Marine F7Fs, along with four different types of transport aircraft, all of which flew different styles of traffic patterns. There was one "near-miss" between a flight of four combat laden Mustangs that were taking off and a C-54 that tried to land head-on to them. They missed by less than one hundred feet, and by the next day AACS had furnished the tower with the proper radio crystals.

Somewhat atypical of military life, when nothing permanent is the norm, yet you don't know from day to day what the future may bring, it was decided that Seoul was going to be the permanent home of the 8th FBG. Personnel started making improvements on their billeting area in what had previously been the prewar dependent housing area for United Nations people. This housing was located three miles from the 8th FBG's flight line, and there were heavy demands for transportation of personnel to the airstrip. The only answer was to leave ten men from each squadron in the tent area on the flight line each night to prepare the aircraft for the next day's missions.

This was cold duty, for winter clothing had not yet arrived, but it was far better than having to force everyone to live in tents. The buildings themselves, due to battle damage, had to be heated by kerosene, which was fed from barrels from outside the buildings. These fed into sand-beds, which were then ignited. The kerosene burned with heavy fumes and a constant "poof-poof" that everyone mistrusted.

On November 1 three ships were spotted in Inchon Harbor that were loaded with supplies intended for the 8th FBG on their initial move to Suwon. Two of these ships were soon unloaded, yet the third one castoff for Pusan! Naturally it carried the most critically needed items of the three, including all of the desired photographic equipment. Eventually it was unloaded at Pusan and everything was trucked to Seoul, arriving just in time to be repacked for the next move.

On November 3 the 8th FBG started to fly armed reconnaissance missions along the Yalu River north of the previously mentioned Crop Line. These F-51s roamed at will, destroying thirteen vehicles that the North Koreans failed to camouflage. They also started to mount a daily CAP over the Sinuiju airfield, since some Yak-9s had been seen operating in the area.

Three days later the skies broke open with the first aerial combat between Mustangs and enemy fighters in several months. A flight of 35th FBS Mustangs led by 1st Lt. Robert Deward spotted a single MiG 15 overhead at 15,000 feet heading southeast toward Sanchon. The MiG was seen to turn around and commence a dive on the Mustangs, so Deward ordered his flight to also turn, so as to meet the interloper head on. Major Raymond Schillereff, flying in the Number Three position, was the

The famed "Itazuke Tower," the contact point for a sick Mustang immortalized in song. "Itazuke Tower, this is Air Force eight-oh-one/I'm turning on downwind, and I'm running on one lung," etc. (O'Donnell)

What's left of a North Korean based train after it was hit by a flight of 8th FBW Mustangs somewhere south of Suwon. (O'Donnell)

only F-51 pilot to be able to get into a firing position. Schillereff and the MiG exchanged bursts of fire as they passed by each other, but neither pilot was able to hit the other. Apparently the MiG pilot had seen enough, however, for he was last seen crossing the Yalu River heading for Manchuria. (Schillereff had shot down an Il-10 while flying a F-80 with the 36th FBS in June).

A few moments later "Cousin Baker," a flight of 36th FBS Mustangs led by Captain James Gasser, was passing over Sinuiju when another MiG met them head on. The MiG cut loose a long burst of cannon fire at the Mustang flown by Captain James Carnahan, who was in the flight's Number Four position. Gasser then swung the flight around to meet the MiG, who had also reversed course, and at 9, 500 feet the five aircraft entered into a swirling dogfight. Two of the Mustang pilots got off at least two bursts of fire at the MiG, but again neither side scored a hit on the other. To say that the Mustang pilots were disgruntled would be an understatement. The lack of hits was laid upon the K-14C gunsight, which was the Mustangs standard sight modified for air-to-ground attack instead of aerial combat.

A hour later "Cousin George" flight, led by Captain Carlisle, spotted four MiGs high over Sinuiju heading north. These MiGs were seen to descend to 12,000 feet, but they ignored the Mustangs and crossed the Yalu River to land at Antung.

The following day another conflict occurred between the MiG-15 and the F-51. "Cousin William" flight, led by Lt. Colonel William O'Donnell, met a MiG-15 head on. In a dogfight with lasted between six and eight minutes, O'Donnell scored a probable kill. This flight was composed of Captain Howard Tanner, Major James Buckley,

"MiG shooters!" 1st Lt. Robert Rollfs, Lt. Colonel William O'Donnell, Major Jim Buckley and Captain Howard Tanner at debriefing on November 7, 1950. (USAF)

the 36th FBS's operations officer, and 1st Lt. Robert Rohlfs.

The MiG had descended to the Mustangs optimum altitude and the aircraft had started to scissor, with both O'Donnell and his wingmen believing that they were getting some hits on it. Finally O'Donnell was able to maneuver to where he was able to attack the MiG head on, and he started firing, with his first rounds passing over the top of the MiG. Adjusting his fire by eyesight, because he felt that the K-14 sight was not working properly, O'Donnell started getting solid hits on the MiG's nose and wing roots as they closed. The MiG swept by, guns still firing and trailing smoke as it headed out to sea while loosing altitude. Unfortunately none of the Mustangs gun cameras were working, and no positive claim could be made.

That afternoon another flight of 35th FBS Mustangs, led by their commanding officer, Major Rayburn Lancaster, spotted MiGs taking off from Antung. Two MiGs flew down the north side of the Yalu River, and two more come down the south side to intercept Lancaster's flight. Again shots were fired, but no hits were claimed as they passed. Lancaster took his Mustangs after them in "hot pursuit," but the MiGs were just to fast and they recrossed the Yalu out of firing range.

The next day was almost a repeat performance. "Cousin Willie" flight from the 36th FBS was CAPing Sinuiju when they were jumped by MiGs that made one quick pass on them before disappearing into the smoke over the city. The flight leader, Captain William Osborne, called "Cousin George" flight which was orbiting Sinuiju at 15,000 feet and warned him that MiGs were headed his way. The four Mustangs of George flight spotted the MiGs and turned to meet them head on to no avail, and after the MiGs passed out of shooting range, they also turned their Mustangs around to chase them back across the Yalu, but once again no hits were scored.

Following this encounter "Cousin Roger" flight, led by Captain Joseph Rogers saw four MiGs in the sun and climbed to meet them. The MiGs broke into two elements and started a head on attack on the Mustangs. Rogers' hit the lead MiG with two solid bursts of .50 caliber fire, and his Number Four man, Major William Betha, got hits on the lead MiG of the second element. The MiGs did not choose to continue the fight and they swung northward while descending at a high airspeed to cross the Yalu to safety.

The 35th FBS also had an encounter with the MiG-15 on November 8. "Contour William" flight had been jumped by four MiGs, but the Mustang pilots had their

Major William Betha. "Every Man a Tiger." Betha damaged a MiG-15 on November 8, 1950. (O'Donnell)

issued to Mustang pilots in early November by Captain Doyle, 5th Air Force Intelligence Officer, who also provided briefings on their contents and use.

On November 10 a Lt. Foss from one of the 8th FBG squadrons took off from Seoul and immediately thereafter encountered engine difficulties. He flew west to the coast, where he jettisoned his ordnance, and then turned back east, but his engine quit while he was twenty miles out from K-14 and Foss was forced to bailout. Since he was well south of the battle line and in friendly territory, he did not get a chance to try out any of the E&E equipment, but he at least demonstrated that it was possible to bailout of a Mustang with the kit attached to a parachute harness, which had been a point of concern among the pilots.

On November 22 1st Lt. Harold Kinison, 36th FBS Intelligence Officer, was hit by flak while attacking an airfield at Kanggye, the North Korean provisional capitol. Kinison had listened closely to the E&E briefings, both because of his role in the squadron, and due to his personal interests. He even went so far as to carry a collapsible .30 caliber carbine with him in his Mustang's cockpit. When he was shot down the rest of his flight flew a RESCAP for him, but since they were seventy miles north of the MLR at the time, there appeared to be little chance to effect a rescue.

The next day Captain David Brown flew a T-6 to the spot where Kinison had last been seen, but there was no sign of him. Just to be on the safe side, though, Brown dropped a survival kit in the general area before returning to Seoul. This was followed by Lt. E. Tomes with a Mustang carrying a converted drop tank that was also loaded with survival equipment. Tomes did not have any better luck than Brown in spotting Kinison, and he could not get the tank to drop, so he had to fly back to Seoul with it, only to have it fall off of its own volition while he was on his final landing approach.

The following morning, after a night's worth of coercion, Lt. Colonel O'Donnell convinced the Air Rescue Squadron at K-29, Sinanju, to launch one helicopter for at least one try at finding Kinison. The helicopter pilot was none to pleased with this mission, and he kept complaining of either engine troubles of fuel shortages, even though extra fuel was being carried in "jerry" cans. It got to the point where the pilots were arguing back and forth on the radio as to whether the mission in itself was worthwhile, and it came to the further point that the Mustang pilots flew along side of the chopper to "clear their guns" to make their point clear. The chopper pilot still was not totally convinced, so O'Donnell's wingman, Robert Fogg,

adrenaline up, for they had just finished fending off a flight of four F-80s that had mistaken them for Yak-9s. 1st Lt. Harris Boyce got one "probable" when he sent a MiG reeling across the Yalu trailing smoke and apparently out of control. Another pilot was credited with a "damaged," either Lt.'s Bradley or Pagan, who were Boyce's wingmen during the encounter, but records do not clarify which pilot was credited.

During these encounters the MiGs did not press their speed advantage, and obviously their pilots were poor marksmen. But it was also obvious that the Mustangs were now out of their element and the 8th FBG was no longer assigned CAP duties along the Yalu River.

With the advent of winter weather it became necessary to develop some sort of winter escape and survival kit for pilots that might be forced down behind enemy lines. Exposure to the elements was almost an equal threat as enemy soldiers might be during the harsh Korean winter. These Escape and Evasion, E&E, kits were told the chopper pilot to pick a place to land and he would exchange himself for the helicopter's observer and they would then continue accordingly.

The observer, naturally, did not want any part of being stranded in North Korea, and particularly along side of a very obvious parked F-51, so he convinced his pilot to press on.

Kinison spotted the approaching helicopter and fired off a red flare that he had been carrying in his survival vest. O'Donnell spotted the flare first, and then directed the helicopter in to effect the rescue of the weary pilot. Immediately upon entering the chopper Kinison got on the radio and started calling out targets that he had spotted while on the ground. All sorts of tanks and trucks had been moving through the area by night and hid in houses during the daylight hours. O'Donnell and Fogg worked over the area until they were out of firepower, and then they proceeded to escort the quite relieved chopper pilot back to Sinanju.

The end result of the saga was that the value of the E&E lectures had paid off for the downed pilot. The helicopter pilot got the Distinguished Flying Cross, and Headquarters FEAF would not believe Kinison when he said that Chinese troops were in the area. This was in spite of the fact that two of them had urinated on him from a bridge while he hid in the pilings below.

On November 23 the 8th FBG moved from Seoul to K-23, Pyongyang. This was the Group's fourth move since August 19, so it was no longer considered to be a major feat, as everyone had plenty of experience in packing, unpacking and setting up a new camp. The advance party of the Group was led by Major Betha, and it included the men of the 6131st Support Wing. under the code name of "Hobo." There was no break in combat missions being flown during this move, even though the number of available Mustangs was so low that most had to be flown at least three sorties this day to keep up with the 8th FBG's commitments to the 5th Air Force. It was well known by all that the F-51s were by now becoming quite "war weary," so once again a strong tribute should be made to the ground crews that insured that the Mustangs remained operational through this move without having any adequate place to work on them.

The runway's at Pyongyang's K-23 airdrome had been so chewed up by heavy transport aircraft that were using the airstrip as a staging base to supply front line troops that they were deemed as unsuitable for safe fighter-bomber operations. Thus it became necessary for the Mustangs to takeoff and land on grass strips, designated as "runways." This was not an uncommon situation for Mustangs, as they had been doing it throughout their history, and it was an advantage they held over the jet fighters. Yet as in the past, they raised a lot of dust in the process, which is one of the stronger memories of any of the troops that served in Korea.

Living conditions at K-23 were considered to be better than those at Seoul, primarily because the officers were billeted in a "U" shaped building that had previously served as the officers quarters for the North Korean Air Force. The enlisted men, as usual, set up a tent city for themselves, and the scroungers started searching for material to improve upon the basic tent-life fare. It did not take long for them to find enough brick among all the rubble to floor all the tents and to construct walkways between them, which made things considerably more habitable in the frosty cold.

The Reds struck back on November 27 when a single liaison-type aircraft dropped two small bombs on the 8th FBG that night. The bombs struck the 35th FBS Mustang parking area and the blasts killed Staff Sergeant Alvin Clark the squadron's Technical Supply Sergeant. Clark was the only enlisted man to be killed in action while the 8th FBG was flying Mustangs in Korea. Eleven Mustangs suffered some sort of damage in this attack, but within two days nine of them had been repaired.

As November ended there was little doubt among the 8th FBG personnel that Kinison had been right when he said that the Chinese had entered the war. All the logistical support that FEAF could provide was now being delivered to the ground forces, and there was a constant stream of transport aircraft moving in and out of Pyongyang as the cargo aircraft brought in supplies and evacuated the wounded. The North Koreans and the Chinese were pressing south all along the MLR and it

Captain Hughes and a 8th FBW Mustang. Hughes would later become a Lt. General and an aide to President Nixon. (O'Donnell)

Photographed at K-14, this 8th FBW two-seat Mustang was used to evaluate the feasibility of Mustangs carrying 12" "Tiny Tim" naval rockets. Only one attempt was made, with Lt. Colonel Samways flying and with 1st Lt. Jack Clark sitting in the rearward-facing extra seat to observe the rockets blasts. The test was made on November 6, 1950 against bridges across the Yalu River, but the "Tiny Tim's" were not considered as accurate as the 5" HVAR's, so the experiment was abandoned. (Tanner via Davis)

was quickly discovered that K-23 was to far north now to be provided proper logistical support for combat operations. Even though the Mustangs were in heavy demand for ground support missions, they had to yield to higher priority transport aircraft, which reduced their effectiveness.

An advance party of 35th FBS personnel led the return trip back to Seoul and K-16 on November 30 with a heavy heart, there would be no "home by Christmas" as everyone had thought. On December 1 the 6131st Tactical Support Wing was deactivated and its personnel and equipment was absorbed by the 8th FBW. Although there was no break in operations, all classified documents had to destroyed at Pyongyang as the men prepared to surrender back to the Reds all of the time and improvements they had made during the previous week to their living areas.

When flying from Pyongyang the mission lengths averaged one to one and one-half hours, since the Reds were only thirty miles away. The pilots were distressed, however, that they could not provide more support to the UN ground forces, but there simply were not enough

Mustangs nor available ordnance. Each of the two squadrons should have had twenty-four Mustangs, but attrition had reduced this number to ten! Both the 35th and 36th FBS's flew as many combat sorties as they could get into the air on December 1 and 2, and then they prepared to abandon K-23 on December 3.

On the morning of December 3 three C-119s and a C-54 arrived to evacuate 8th FBG personnel and equipment. The first transport left at 0900 KST, and the last at 1315. The 36th FBS flew their last mission out of K-23 that afternoon, while the 35th FBS held on until the next morning, to fly one last strike before returning to Seoul. Everything had been evacuated except for a few chairs, some vehicles, and the F-51s that had been damaged during the attack of November 27.

The returning transports that had evacuated the 8th FBG had to land at K-14, to prevent tearing up the runways at K-16, which would become the new temporary home for the 8th FBG. This again meant that all of the supplies had to be transported by truck between the two airfields. And once again the Mustangs had to be flown off of grass runways, while army engineers laid PSP. "Although it was a little rough in spots, it served the purpose nicely." All of the Mustangs were now dispersed, as a result of the lesson learned at Pyongyang, and the men dug themselves foxholes just to be on the safe side.

On December 5 2nd Lt. Paul Carlsen, 35th FBS, had to make an emergency landing at K-23 because of engine problems. Since the airstrip was still in UN hands, a crew chief was flown up from Seoul to attempt to repair the Mustang, but the necessary parts were not available, and it had to be destroyed.

The next day another Mustang was lost at Pyongyang when its pilot flew through some power lines on takeoff. Its canopy was jammed by the impact with the wires, so its pilot could not bailout, thus it had to be crash landed. This particular Mustang had been the personal mount of Lt. Colonel O'Donnell, and had been named "Mac's Revenge" in honor of Major McNees. Lt. Colonel Samways and O'Donnell gave it a Viking send off with their Zippo's before evacuating K-23. It just would not have been proper to let an aircraft named in honor of a fallen pilot to be taken by the enemy.

December 9 was the last day for combat operations with the F-51 by the 8th FBG, for finally a sufficient number of F-80s had arrived in Japan to reequip the Group with Shooting Stars. Their last Mustang mission ended on a tragic note with the loss of 1st Lt. Robert Williams, 36th FBS. Williams was making a strafing run near the Pyongyang racetrack on an undetermined target and the Mustang was still carrying two 110 gallon napalm tanks when it hit the ground. There was no chance of survival. It had been Williams first combat mission.

All 8th FBG Mustang pilots were flown from Seoul to Iwakuni Air base the night of December 9, while the Group's Headquarters staff and all pertinent equipment were flown to Japan the next day. The Group's remaining Mustangs were transferred to the 18th and 35th Fighter Groups, who immediately recognized them as being in "deplorable shape." Those that were truly war weary were rejected and sent on to FEAMCOM for overhaul, while the rest were pressed into service, for both of these group's were also short of aircraft.

The 8th FBG reequipped with F-80Cs during mid December, and with the return to them of the 80th FBS from the 49th FBW on December 27 they officially were back into the war by the end of the year with a full complement of squadrons and aircraft. Once again it was a period of rapid transitions, for by this time twenty-two pilots from the 36th FBS were totally inexperienced in jet aircraft. Lt. Colonel Samways was promoted to "Bird" Colonel on December 28, Lt. Colonel O'Donnell became the 8th FBW Air Inspector. Major James Buckley became the commanding officer, 36th FBS; while Major Lancaster continued as commanding officer 35th FBS.

In the four and one half months that the two squadrons of the 8th FBW had flown the Mustang in combat they knew for sure that they had lost ten pilots to enemy action. They had fired 3,068,027 rounds of .50 caliber ammunition and fired 12,685 rockets, they lost track of all the napalm they had dropped.

CHAPTER SIX

The 35th Fighter Interceptor Wing

When the Korean Conflict started the 35th Fighter Interceptor Wing was involved with routine training and occupation duties at Yokota Air Base, J-38, on Japan's main home island of Honshu. The three fighter squadrons that were the basis of the 35th FIW were the 39th, 40th, and 41st Fighter Interceptor Squadrons, all of which were flying the Lockheed F-80C as daylight air superiority fighters. As the 40th FIS was charged with the defense of the Kanto Plains at this time, they were informed that they would probably not become involved in any action at all, because of their strategic location. The other two fighter squadrons were immediately placed on alert status, however.

A high percentage of the Wing personnel that composed the three squadrons were enjoying the weekend off, for the 35th Fighter Interceptor Group and the three tactical squadrons had just been released for a "stand down" a result of passing an Operational Readiness In-

Snugged in tight in "show formation" Lt. George Lukakis in F-51D 44-73728 formates with Lt. Robert Dunnavant during the fall of 1949, just before the 35th Fighter Interceptor Wing converted to F-80Cs. #728 was then placed in storage, only to be recalled back into the 39th Fighter Interceptor Squadron. The dual antennas on the fuselage spine are for the AN/ARA-8 Airborne Homing equipment, (Which worked like DF, only in reverse.) while the single antenna under the fuselage was for the SCR-522 VHF radio. Dunnavant was injured in a bailout on September 18, 1950 while Lukakis was killed on November 6 at Po'hang. (Dunnavant)

Loaded and ready to go this 39th FIS F-51D is on the flight line at Tsuiki Air Base in August 1950. The spinner is all-blue, which was later repainted as a "split-spinner," with one-half blue and the other white, and the 39th FIS then became known as the "Blinker Noses." (Penrose)

spection. As expected, there was a mad scramble to get all of the concerned personnel back to their respective bases to get the squadrons ready for any eventuality.

On July 2, 1950 Major Gerald Brown, commanding officer of the 39th FIS conducted a squadron briefing, informing his men that they would soon move from Yokota to another, undetermined at this time, air base and they would start flying combat missions over Korea. (Brown was the first P-38 pilot in the 55th Fighter Group during World War II to complete 120 combat missions. He also became an ace while flying with the 55th FG, and then went on to fly a tour in Mustangs with the 4th FG).

Two days later the 35th FIG, under the command of Lt. Colonel Jack Dale, was alerted for a move to Po'hang, Korea and a combat assignment, but this was quickly changed to Ashiya Air Base, on Japan's southern most island of Kyushu, because of the rapid communist advances and the questionable status of Po'hang. On July 7 the 40th FIS, commanded by Lt. Colonel James Kirkendall, was also ordered to Ashiya and they were informed that they should expect to start flying missions the following day. The 41st FIS, located at Misawa Air Base, J-27, was informed at this time that they would be the squadron held in reserve and that they now had the sole responsibility for daylight air defense duties over southern and middle Japan.

At 12:30 hours on July 7 sixteen F-80s of the 40th FIS headed for Ashiya, and the 39th FIS started their move to the southern base the following day. The 35th FIG launched their first combat sorties at 1120 hours on July 8 with pilots of the 40th FIS flying armed reconnaissance along the fluid battle line. The 39th FIS entered the war the next day by flying fifteen sorties over Osan where they shot-up a string of boxcars.

Amongst all the confusion, the Headquarters section of the 35th FIG and the Headquarters section of the 40th FIS departed Japan for Po'hang Air base, K-3, Korea on July 9 after all. Also included with this group were personnel of the 39th FIS who were charged with opening the airstrip, itself, and who would formally establish the 6131st Base Unit (BASUT) for all support functions required by he 35th FIG. (This role was usually covered by a Wing's support squadrons, of which there were normally seven, including mail, medical, airfield maintenance, etc.) Headquarters 35th FIW, then under Colonel Virgil Zoller, would remain in Japan until December 1, 1950.

On July 10 the 40th FIS was informed that they would be the first 5th Air Force squadron to transition back into the F-51 from the Shooting Star. This was because they had been the last 5th Air Force squadron to have converted from the F-51 when FEAF reequipped with F-80s the previous spring. The first F-51s actually started to arrive before the day was out, and for a period the squadron's pilots were flying combat missions in both types of fighters. The move was not totally unexpected, nor was it reported as particularly upsetting to the pilots. Many of them had already flown the F-51 over Korea as ferry pilots delivering the aircraft to the ROKAF or in combat air patrol (CAP) roles. But the rumors within the 35th FIG were that the pilots would go back into the F-51 willingly enough if they could get in on the action. The received Mustangs were not in too good of a shape since they were quickly being pulled from storage and only received a "once-over" inspection before being committed to action. The usual snafu that had to be both expected and accepted.

On July 11 the remainder of the 40th FIS was informed that they were going to move to Po'hang with the actual move taking place as soon as the squadron was up to strength with F-51s. They made this move on the afternoon of July 14, and started flying combat missions out of K-3 the following morning. The attached elements of the 35th FIG and the 40th FIS attempted to make Po'hang a usable airstrip, but it was a logistical nightmare, The 40th FIS quickly started to launch up to forty sorties per day, and everything necessary for these operations had to be flown in to K-3, assembled, and then loaded on the fighters. The armorers worked a straight thirty-six hours without relief during the first two days after the move. Except for some support provided by the 35th FIG's maintenance section, additional support was virtually nil, particularly in respect to items that should have been supplied by the 5th Air Force.

On August 3 the 39th FIS also turned over their F-80s to the 41st FIS and accepted their F-51s from the

39th FIS Mustangs undergoing maintenance at Tsuiki Air Base. The closest F-51 was later transferred to 2 Squadron, SAAF as their # 372 and it was written-off in an accident on January 15, 1952. (Penrose)

storage depot at Johnson Air base The contrast of opinions shared by the pilots of the 39th FIS versus those of the 8th Fighter Bomber Wing pilots is of some interest. Most of the 8th FBW pilots preferred to keep their F-80s, while the 39th FIS pilots were eager to get back into the F-5l. Yet the 8th FBW had already suffered the loss of several F-80 pilots in combat, while the 39th FIS had only two aircraft damaged. (Lt. Leroy Lette flew through a tree top, gouging out the wings leading edge back to the main wing-spar. Lt. Robert Dunnavant became "hoist with own petard" when he and a 5" rocket that he had fired arrived over the target at the same time. The belly of his F-80 was ripped open under the engine. Both pilots returned to Ashiya for safe landings).

Full scale combat operations in the F-5l by the 39th FIS started on August 5, although they did not "officially" become a F-51 squadron until August 7 when they moved to Po'hang. The delay was partially a result of having their ranks depleted by men being transferred into the "Bout 1" contingent and into the 40th FIS to make up for shortages in that squadron. However, they did receive eleven fresh Mustang pilots that had arrived on the aircraft carrier Boxer from the United States.

With the arrival of the 39th FIS at Po'hang, the 35th FIG was considered as combat operational. And also at this time the 35th FIG became subordinate to the 6131st Fighter Bomber Wing (Single Engine), which had rapidly expanded from the 6131st BASUT. The 35th FIW would remain in Japan on garrison duties for the duration with only the 41st FIS as an operational squadron.

The 6131st Fighter Bomber Wing and the 35th FIG lost their first Mustang on August 10. 1st Lt. Harold Hillery, the only black pilot in the 39th FIS at the time, had to

A flight of 39th FIS Mustangs over Korea while returning to Japan from a strike. The nearest Mustang is piloted by Captain Earnest Biggs. (Penrose)

Two 35th FIW pilots engaged in conversation in front of what is left of a World War II Japanese hangar at Tsuiki Air Base. Major Charles Bowers, left, hearing what 1st Lt. Clarence Harris has to say about his stint as a FAC. (Penrose)

bailout off the east coast of Korea after his F-51s engine quit. (Integration had not moved too fast within FEAF under President Truman's desegregation order. Each of the three F-80 squadrons of the 35th FIG had one black pilot assigned at the beginning of the conflict. They were all "under the gun," as was the baseball player Jackie Robinson in such a circumstance, but Hillery was noted for being a good pilot). He was picked up by a U.S. submarine, but was not returned to the squadron for some time, as the submarine was "on station" performing air-sea rescue duties. It was reported that he was not too great of a poker player, however, and that he had lost quite a bit of money to the sub's crew while he was on board.

Approximately at the same time that Hillery was forced bail out 1st Lt. Robert Dunnavant and his wingman, 1st Lt. James Mathis, took off for a strike against Andong. After strafing various targets they climbed out of the area and headed for Yongdok for some additional strafing runs. Mathis reported that his engine was overheating, but never said anything more. After dodging some hills Dunnavant realized that he was now alone, so he completed the mission and flew back to Po'hang to discover that Mathis was overdue. He then rearmed and refueled and flew back to Andong to see if he could discover where Mathis' might have disappeared to. There was no sign of a downed aircraft. Mathis's body was finally found in January 1951 and it was interned in the UN cemetery at Taegu. He was the first of the pilots that had arrived on the aircraft carrier Boxer to be lost.

Po'hang, came under enemy artillery fire for the first time on August 10, with shells falling in the hills surrounding the base, but lucky, not within the perimeter itself.

Pilots of both squadrons were pressed into flying ground support missions to protect their own base. Due to enemy pressure and to protect the Mustangs, staging during the day was conducted through K-2 at Taegu, but the aircraft were retained for the night of August 10-11 at Po'hang. The morning hours of August 11 saw even increased enemy activity and thus plans had to be developed to evacuate the aircraft before nightfall. There was a great fear that sappers would sneak through during the dark hours and sabotage the aircraft and associated equipment. Airmen of all units were pressed into perimeter defense, a roll for which they had never been trained.

The next day passed without incident, since the communists were aware, from their observations from the hills surrounding the base, that the Mustangs were not there during the night. The F-51s returned late on the night of August 12, and so did the rain, which turned the airstrip into a quagmire so deep that the fighters could not be moved. All airmen were once again pressed into airfield defense and they found themselves knee deep in water standing in their foxholes. For a time the weather was so bad that the North Koreans themselves could not mount an attack, and again the period passed without incident.

To say that things were a mess would be to understate the matter. The 6131st FBW was attempting to operate with their squadrons at a peacetime staffing level, for this was all the men that were available to them, and this was an impossibility. Each man was working a minimum of eighteen hours day, seven day a week. Since there were no non-rated officers (non pilots) in the flying squadrons, each assigned pilot was also given collateral duties. They had to fly their assigned missions, and then

Between the roads on the left side of this photograph the Mustang flown by 1st Lt. Robert Easer can just be seen against the green background after Easer has just napalmed the village of Roryang on August 31, 1950. Napalm was particularly effective against the thatched roofed huts in Korea. (Penrose)

catch up with the more mundane administrative paper-work each night, such as censoring mail. Headquarters FEAF was neither supportive nor sympathetic, for the paper mill had to be fed, regardless.

Even though the 6131st FBW was located only forty-five miles from the temporary 5th Air Force Headquarters at Taegu, communications were almost non existent. Weather reports were always inadequate, and pilots own weather observations, Pireps, were not disseminated. There were still no reliable navigational aids, and there was a lack of proper radio frequencies. Everything was in short supply, or non existent. There were no light bulbs for the fighters wing and tail lights. There were no flood-lights, or even flashlights for maintenance at night or for preflighting the aircraft. In fact, it was so dark that pilots had problems even in finding their assigned aircraft in the dark, having to rely upon shouted exchanges between themselves and their crew chiefs. There were no replace-ment instruments, either for navigation or engine moni-toring, throttle quadrants, external fuel tank fittings, or maps. Bomb hoists had to be modified so that F-80 equip-ment could be used on the F-51. Rocket racks had to be modified also, so that the rockets could be used inter-changeably between the two aircraft. Napalm had to be hand pumped from barrels into the drop tanks. Most of the spare parts came from cannibalized aircraft.

On August 13 the 6131st FBW was forced to evacu-ate Po'hang and return to Ashiya. The 35th FIG, itself, moved the following day to Tsuiki Air Base, J-36, on Kyushu, to alleviate the air traffic congestion at Ashiya. Tsuiki had been a Kamikaze base during the previous war, and had been heavily bombed as a result. When the 35th FIG arrived they found that only two hangars and buildings still had anything resembling roofs, and there were full of holes. A tent city was erected, and it was back to war as usual the next day.

The 39th and 40th Fighter Interceptor Squadron's were not involved air-to-air combat, for which most of the pilots appeared to be grateful. The consensus was that they were not proficient enough in the F-51 to take on an aerial opponent. (This attitude may seem somewhat strange, for the pilots had always trained for the inter-ceptor role and practiced air combat maneuvers. Most of them had not been away from the Mustang all that long to begin with and were now getting in plenty of flying time in the type (The 35th Fighter Interceptor Group and their associated squadrons refused to change their designa-tion from Fighter Interceptor to Fighter Bomber in spite of their new role). All of the missions presently being flown by the Group were those of close air support, usually

39th FIS squadron commander Gerald Brown, in the Jeep, and his operations officer, Major Charles Bowers, during a lighter moment at Po'hang, South Korea. (Penrose)

under the control of an airborne controller in a liaison aircraft, which was a function they had little if any training for. Few pilots had even ever fired a 5" rocket before, and less than 50% of the pilots had ever dropped a 500 pound bomb or a napalm tank prior to flying combat over Korea.

While attempting to learn how to become an effec-tive tactical fighter pilot they had to contend with heavy small arms fire. This ground fire was horrific, which caused the loss of six of the nine downed pilots from the 40th FIS in August. Four of these pilots are known to have been killed, W.R. Brisco, Jr., Meade M. Brown, Marlin T. Nolan and Thelbert B. Wormack. It may be assumed that the other two pilots were taken prisoner of war, but due to poor record keeping their identities are unknown, along with their ranks and eventual fate. The remaining three aircraft losses came as a result of a crash during a pre-dawn takeoff, a pilot snagging a wing on a mountain top while making a strafing pass, and another pilot flying into his own rocket blast. All three of these pilots again are unidentified in 40th FIS records but it was evident that the war was going to b a long ordeal.

To enhance survival, the pilots were forced to devise a gunnery pattern that would reduce their potential of being seen and hit by enemy gunners. The pattern was rectangular, with a final approach angle toward the tar-get between 30 and 45 degrees. The base leg was flown at three thousand feet to stay above as much of the small arms fire as possible and not to give away the final direc-tion of the attack until the last possible moment. The fighter would then be turned toward the target as tightly as pos-sible, and the strafing pass made to no lower than one thousand feet slant range from the target itself, or at 1,500 feet if rockets were to be fired. The latter would prevent ricochet damage when firing over rocky terrain. Bombing runs were flown with a similar pattern to the rocket pattern, with a dive angle of thirty degrees and a minimum pullout at 1,500 feet. For dropping napalm the pattern was changed to a fifteen degree dive and a recovery altitude of 1,000 feet. This permitted the tank to strike the ground some fifty to one hundred feet short of the target and splash the jellied gasoline against the target "quite nicely."

September 1950 opened with both of the 35th FIG squadrons still flying out of Japan for their missions over Korea. The Group remained attached to the 6131st Tactical Support Wing until September 5 when a new unit, the 6150th Tactical Support Wing was formed at Tsuiki to support 35th FIG functions and the 6131st TSW was relived to prepare to return to Korea. All combat missions were flown in support of the ground forces that were now attempting to hold the Pusan Perimeter until the Inchon Landing could take place. After this event, targets to strike soon became quite hard to find, because the communists scattered into the hills and continued to use judicious camouflage during daylight hours.

The 35th FIG was released against targets of opportunity after the Inchon beachhead was established. They then started flying far beyond Pyongyang into an area known as "Area 5" in order to find worthwhile targets. This area would be renamed as "MiG Alley" within another year.

Losses for September included Robert Dunnavant who was shot down after attacking a target spotted by a T-6 Mosquito twenty miles southwest of Taegu. Dunnavant dropped two bombs, which were both duds, and then

A flight of 39th FIS Mustangs takes to the air from Po'hang Air Base, K-3. The mobile control tower had been constructed from a Mustang canopy by members of the 18th FBG. (USAF via Davis)

started strafing runs against the objective, which was supposed to be an enemy troop concentration. He and his wingman did not like the looks of the target area as it was surrounded by hills on three sides, but the T-6 pilot assured them that the hills were in friendly hands. On Dunnavant's third pass he was hit in an oil line by enemy ground fire and oil soon covered the Mustang's windshield and his engine started running rough.

"He (Dunnavant) immediately climbed out on a southeast heading for altitude and to reach friendly terrain. He located road with a truck convoy, slowed to 150, trimmed and 'scratched' over the side." On the bailout his right knee struck the stabilizer and broke his leg, He then landed in a rice paddy, with his F-51 crashing nearby where it exploded on impact and its rockets started "cooking-off." He was picked up by a jeep from the convoy and taken to an aid station, and eventually returned to the United States for further medical treatment. Dunnavant had flown thirty-five F-80 missions and thirty-five additional missions in the F-51 to this time, and include the destruction of a North Korean liaison aircraft with a napalm tank among his exploits. (The claim was not credited by the USAF).

The 40th FIS lost two Mustang pilots while flying combat missions in September. 1st Lt. William Levi was killed on September 7, and 1st Lt. Donald E, Lee on September 27. The details of these two losses were not recorded by the 40th FIS historian. On September 28 1st Lt. Donald Pitchford, 39th FIS, was shot down by a Yak-9, which was the first enemy aircraft encountered by pilots of the 35th FIG since they started flying the F-51. Pitchford bailed out over friendly territory, but he was to low for his parachute to open in time to save his life.

On October 7 the 39th and 40th FIS's returned to Po'hang. The airfield and living conditions were now much improved over their previous stay, thanks to the men of the 6401st Field Maintenance Squadron who had gone in right after the airstrip had been declared secured and started to "put things right." They built a mess hall near the flight line, which featured welcome cold drinks and hot food for the pilots and ground crews.

Between the two squadrons 704 combat sorties were flown in October 1950. The pilots still found themselves fighting a determined enemy that was more than willing to shoot back while they were on the run northward. The 35th FIG had started the month with forty-nine F-51s assigned, and finished with eighty-one, but in the meantime twenty-five were lost as a result of enemy action and sixteen more through operational accidents. (These figures are from the 35th FIG history and appear to be

A line-up of 39th FIS Mustangs at K-14, Kimpo Air Base, Seoul in September 1950. 44-74809 is "Blanket Ass," which was later transferred to the 18th FBG. It survived the war. (Clark via Davis)

incorrect. They may have been intended to be a cumulative total. According to the Individual F-51 Aircraft Record Cards the 35th FIG lost only eighteen aircraft this month to all causes). The 40th FIS did loose two pilots, however, Captain Glenn Schlitz was declared as missing in action on October 6, and his death was soon confirmed. 1st Lt. Woodrow Burton was also declared as MIA, but his death was not made official until March 1954. The 39th FIS lost Captain Beriger Anderson on October 21. He had just joined the squadron on the first of the month, and his death came as the result of being hit by enemy ground fire near Sanchon. Otherwise, there were so many bailouts and forced landings taking place that the squadron historians did not bother to report them.

In November 1950 the two squadrons mounted 801 combat sorties. The Mustangs always flew with 5" rockets now, but they were not always effective. The early rockets just bounced off of the Russian built T-34 tanks, and the later ones, with shaped charges, still required an accurate hit. Major Gerald Brown commented that it was practically impossible to stop a T-34 with a rocket, you needed napalm." Correspondingly, the F-5ls started carrying a mixed load of one napalm tank and one long range fuel tank to help them reach the target areas and to attack effectively.

This mixed load created an interesting problem for the pilots, for approximately 50% of the fuel in the drop tank had to be burned off before the napalm tank could be dropped, to keep the Mustang in trim. Even after the external fuel was consumed the tank had to be retained, unless some sort of an emergency developed, as there were not enough belly tank fittings available to provide replacements. The induced drag from carrying the one

empty tank back from a sortie was just something that had to be endured. A pilot that returned without his drop tank had to explain why in writing to Lt. Colonel Dale.

The "Fighting Fortieth" finally had a good month in November, by not loosing a single pilot or aircraft. The 39th FIS lost 1st Lt. George "Luke" Lukakis, who was also the 35th FIG's Mess Officer, on November 6. He had just departed Po'hang far his second mission of the day when his engine started running rough. He reported turning base-leg in the traffic pattern for an emergency landing, but for some reason he was still carrying his two napalm tanks and four rockets. A crosswind was blowing and the laden Mustang started to veer-off, and then spun-in 500 yards short of the runway. There was no chance of survival.

On November 13 1st Lt. Allen C. Durgin, 39th FIS, was shot down over North Korea. He bailed out, but broke his leg in the process and was immediately captured by the North Koreans, before he even had a chance to free himself from his parachute harness. With extraordinary luck, and probably only due to the rapid northbound movement of the UN ground forces, his North Korean captors decided that Durgin would not make a very good prisoner in his physical condition and they gave him first aid and set him free. He was soon picked up by an advance UN patrol and was evacuated to a hospital at Osaka, Japan.

One of the assignments that often fell to the tactical fighter bomber pilots was that of pulling a stint as a forward air controller. Actually this duty went to only to a few, and usually was through the luck of the draw among their squadron mates. It was not a task that most en-

Three 35th FIW pilots head for the debriefing tent after a combat mission. Left to right: 1st Lt. George McKee, Captain Samuel Sanders and Captain Leroy Roberts. McKee and Sanders were activated Air National Guardsmen from Texas's 136th FBG, while Roberts had been a Tuskegee Airman. (USAF)

"Admiration Dwag," the mascot of the 39th FIS. It is claimed that he had at least ten combat missions under his collar. The pilot is Lt. J.V. Leroy. (Olmsted)

credit for pulling one of these tours, which also lowered their morale, for they were not getting in their flying missions, nor were they receiving any points for rotation home under the system then in use. In spite of the problems the duty was definitely worthwhile, for they were able to communicate with their airborne counterparts via the radio equipped jeeps they were assigned. Thus they were able to visually vector the fighters to targets not easily seen from the air. This also provided an element of safety for our own troops, for it reduced confusion on the radio frequencies, and, when a FAC was on the air, it reduced he chance of the aircraft striking the wrong troops to virtually zero.

One of the 39th FIS pilots was lost while pulling this FAC assignment, on November 16. 1st Lt. Aaron Abercrombie was TDY to the Republic of Korea's 6th Division when the company he was assigned to was overrun. The ROK troops were routed and they fled to the south in an area near Huschon. This was the last time he was ever seen, and he was declared as missing in action, and later declared as killed.

The 35th FIG moved again on November 17, this time into North Korea. They became operational at Yonpo, K-27, the following day, with the two squadrons having moved into the single hangar that FEAF bombers had not destroyed. The men were billeted in tents in an area that was quite sandy, and they found it difficult to peg down the tents and keep them in place because of the

joyed. Pulling front line duty with the ground forces was an educational experience, with more than its share of hazards, as those selected were ill prepared or trained for such a role. They had to live with the army contingent to which they were assigned for a period, normally two weeks. In the beginning they did not receive any type of

A 39th FIS 'Stang pulls into the arming pits at Chinhae Air Base, K-10. The areas around the gun ports are heavily blackened with soot from the many ground support missions it has flown. There was little time to keep the aircraft cleaned up. (via Davis)

The insignia of the 40th FIS, as posted at Johnson Air Base, J-16, Japan. Major T. "Tomcat" Bailey was a recalled ANG officer who has since retired from the Guard. The officer shown, Tom Blackstone, reportedly remains one of the Korean War MIA's, although his name does not appear on causality lists. (Chard)

members of his flight against all new targets observed in the area." Wakehouse was personally credited with killing forty communists, while his wingmen killed sixty more, along with destroying "numerous enemy bunkers." Wakehouse was awarded a DFC for leading this mission.

On November 30 the 39th FIS lost its Commanding Officer to enemy ground fire, (now) Lt. Colonel Gerald Brown was leading a four-ship flight of Mustangs and was working with a airborne FAC who wanted an estimated twenty communist vehicles that were stopped at a roadblock destroyed. The Mustang pilots accomplished this task, and then were directed to Tokchon to strike a motor pool that had been spotted. The flight was in a "wing down gunnery pattern" when Brown's Mustang took hits that entered through the bottom of the fuselage, blasted through the coolant system and then penetrated the cockpit where the bullets tore away the throttle quadrant, gunsight, and the goggles off of Brown's helmet.

Too low to bailout, and without the ability to advance the throttle and power-up the Merlin engine, Brown had to make an immediate forced landing in his Mustang that was by now on fire. Brown spotted the only open area that he could get to, and put the fighter down successfully, only to discover that the open area he had found was the bivouac area of an entire Chinese infantry division. He was immediately captured. Since Brown was a ranking officer he became the senior officer in every POW camp that he was held in. By the time he repatriated, on September 7, 1953, his weight had dropped to 120 pounds, which actually was a rise from the low point of approximately 100 pounds that he had weighed before the communists had started to feed the POW's adequately after Operation Little Switch in April 1953.

prevalent high winds. The tents came equipped with stoves that burned diesel fuel, and the men were issued muk-luk pac's for their feet, which were necessary with the approach of winter. In fact, the pac's were obtained by "aggressive methods." Generally, it was considered with high morale that this move was made, in spite of the cold, for the men were assured that the war would soon be over and they would be heading for home. Yet, with the enemy's potential for sporadic attacks, slit trenches were dug. It is stated that these came about as a method to prevent panic among the airmen, for they still did not have much knowledge of the objectives of the Korean War. But they were not the only ones.

On November 18 1st Lt. Ernest Wakehouse, 39th FIS, led a flight of four Mustangs against entrenched Red troops near Songdong-ni under low clouds. "Despite poor visibility and the intense enemy opposition encountered, Lt. Wakehouse repeatedly pressed attacks and directed

A 40th FIS Mustang undergoing maintenance in Japan. The 40th FIS used red as their squadron color. The oil header tank on the firewall in front of the windscreen was a particularly vulnerable place to be hit by enemy fire. (Foote)

When the 35th FIG had returned to Korea in October they had stayed with their then parent 6150th Tactical Support Wing. The 6150th TSW was deactivated on December 1, 1950 and at this time the 35th FIG and their Headquarters Squadron became autonomous from FEAF constraints. The 35th FIG returned to the control of their original parent unit, the 35th Fighter Interceptor Wing, located at Johnson Air Base, J-16, near Tokyo, Japan. Lt. Colonel Dale remained as the commanding officer of the 35th FIG, while Colonel Frederic Gray replaced Colonel Thomas Hall this same date as 35th FIW commander. (On August 14 Colonel Zoller had been transferred to the B-26 equipped 3rd Bomb Wing (Light) to replace their commanding officer who had been giving 77 Squadron RAAF a hard time). On December 7 the 35th FIW joined the 35th FIG at Pusan East. Coinciding with these actions, 77 Squadron, RAAF, was assigned to the 35th FIG for combat operations.

These moves all came, in part, as a result of the success of the UN forces, and it was felt, by Headquarters 5th Air Force, that they could once again control the air war from Japan. In less than a week the 5th Air Force would get their chance to find out whether they were correct in their thinking, or not.

The 39th and 40th FIS's continued to fly out of Yonpo until December 4 when they had to be withdrawn because of the Chinese onslaught. The two squadrons, along with 77 Squadron, RAAF, were evacuated to Pusan East Airdrome, K-9. It was announced, somewhat proudly, that they were able to evacuate all of their equipment without a material loss, either by air or by LST, depending upon its weight.

The F-51s landing gear was not particularly strong when it came to imposing side loads upon it. This 35th FIW Mustang came to grief "somewhere in Korea" while still carrying its underwing ordnance. (USAF via Ethell)

Three days later they were once again on operational status from the K-9 base (More commonly known as "Dogpatch." For the first time since they entered the war they now had clean new buildings for housing, for FEAF had started a massive construction effort in South Korea while the squadrons were stationed in the north. It had been decided that no matter which way the war might go FEAF would no longer leave South Korea on its own, and the USAF was going to be there to stay.

Major Kenneth S. Hodges, Assistant 35th FIG S-3, was killed on December 6 during a mission over North Korea, His death was bracketed by the losses of two 40th FIS pilots. 1st Lt. Olin W. Johnson's Mustang was seen to crash in North Korea on December 1, and Major Neil Johnson went down during his fifth mission of the month on December 12. Both of the Johnson's were originally posted as missing in action and later officially declared as killed in action. Enemy ground fire was responsible for all three of the deaths.

VMF-311, the first U.S. Marine squadron to fly the F9F Panther over Korea had been attached to the 35th Fighter Interceptor Wing for operational support when they arrived in the Theater. On December 14 they were further attached to the 35th FIG at K-9. Although they received their mission orders from the 1st Marine Air Wing, all of their mission briefings and debriefings were conducted jointly with the 35th FIG Mustang pilots. This way they could exchange target and weather information and discuss tactics quickly, which gave them up to date information on targets and antiaircraft emplacements. It was noted that there was a real spirit of cooperation among the pilots and ground crews of the Marines, the 35th FIG and the Australians that were flying out of K-9, which made the Korean air war a true UN effort in this example.

Still, there were problems involved with flying the F9Fs out of K-9. The air base runways had not been rebuilt in anticipation of jet operations, consequently they were far too short in length for safe operations. The Marine pilots had to use maximum power to get their Panthers rolling under combat loads. This blasted the dirt off the runway overruns and out from under the PSP planking. This eventually undermined the PSP and eventually caused the runway undulate as the planking contorted under the aircraft's weight as it moved along the surface in a cloud of dust. The dust then got into everything, which added to the 35th FIG's operational problems with the F-51. Eventually to alleviate the problems VMF-311 was transferred to another base and replaced by VMF-513 that was flying Corsairs.

This Marine F4U squadron always seemed to be creating some sort of excitement on the airstrip. During December one of their Corsair's had attempted an emergency landing while still carrying two 1,000 pound bombs. When the Corsair touched down hard on the runway its bombs tore free from its shackles and the bombs had gone skittering down the runway where one exploded. It damaged another F4U and three C-46s of the 437th Troop Carrier Wing.

The 39th FIS lost three Mustangs during a rash of accidents on December 18 and 19. Captain Ralph M. Olson was killed on the 18th when his F-51 crashed into the sea off the end of the runway, while Captain Robert Shipley was injured on the 19th when he was forced to belly land his Mustang in a rice paddy after an engine failure on takeoff. A third pilot escaped the crash of his Mustang unharmed. This last loss was believed to be the result of dust ingested into the carburetor of a heavily loaded Mustang that was taking off behind a F9F. When the engine failed soon after the aircraft became airborne the pilot had little choice but to bail out. His careening F-51 then crashed into a POW compound that adjoined K-9, and forty-two prisoners of war were killed in the explosions that resulted.

The first two of these crashes were believed to be the result of fuel contamination. And before the cause of the contamination could be found two more Mustangs from the 39th FIS were destroyed. Injured were Captain Warren Nicholes and Captain Harold Hillery. Both of these engine failures and the resultant crashes injured the pilots severely enough to force hospitalization in Japan, and in Hillery's case, a return to the United States for further treatment.

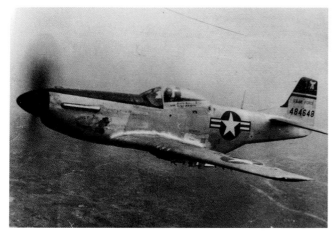

Lt. Paul "Pappy" Murry flying Lt. Dick Chard's "Surley Tis" over Japan. Murry was killed when he bailed out of a disabled Mustang in July 1952. (Chard)

All of these losses, and some additional ones of 77 Squadron, brought an order for all 35th FIW Mustangs to be grounded until their fuel systems could be flushed. Fuel segregators and filters were cleaned, and all aircraft fuel lines and tanks were purged of foreign particles. Additional fuel segregators were installed on the base fuel systems as an additional precaution.

The cause of all of these problems, it was ascertained, was due to work having been improperly accomplished on the fuel farm pipelines, and a poor arrangement of the refueling system in the first place, which allowed salt water to enter in to the system. All of these foreign salt particles were found to foul the Mustangs spark plugs, where the lead from the fuel, deposits of salt, and silica from the airborne dust would fuse on the electrodes under the heat and pressure of combustion to a point where the sparkplugs could no longer fire.

After a forced three day stand-down all of the F-51s were to be flown with their carburetors in the filtered air position, where the air was drawn through the "cheese holes" in the engine cowling instead of through the air scoop under the propeller spinner. This at least prevented ingestion of the silica dust into the engine.

In spite of the temporary grounding the 35th FIW, they managed to launch over one thousand combat sorties during December. As it was, these were barely enough, for the United Nations ground forces were reeling from both the winter cold and the relentless communist pressure. The best the Mustang pilots could hope for was that their efforts would at least help reduce the losses of the men on the ground while the UN made their "strategic withdrawal."

Most of the missions flown as 1951 began were those of armed reconnaissance, but these missions found few suitable targets. Both sides were holing up now to conserve their strength in the bitter cold. During the daylight flights along the battle lines nothing indicating any movement on the ground could be seen from the air to even indicate exactly were the battle lines actually were. Enemy vehicle movement behind the lines was also curtailed during the day, with one reason being that the cold temperatures caused the vehicles to leave their own exhaust gas vapor trails, which no camouflage effort on the communists part could hide.

Two 39th FIS pilots did get a chance to engage in a little air-to-air combat near Pyongyang on January 23, however. A flight of seven Mustangs was jumped by two Yak-3's and Captain Alexander Currie and his wingman, Captain Thomas Manjack, took after them in hot pursuit. Currie shot down one, while Manjack claimed a probable

The 40th FIS gunnery team gather in front of a F-51 at Johnson Air Base prior to the 1952 FEAF Gunnery Meet. The 40th placed second in the meet. "Beautiful Betty Boop" was transferred to the ROKAF, then returned to the USAF for salvage. (Chard)

on the other. These were the first kills claimed by the 35th FIG since they had converted from the F-80 so there was quite a bit of elation among the pilots over the feat. Yet, for an unknown reason, and in spite of gun camera film, the claims were not upheld by the USAF.

The 35th FIG flew its first major mission as an entire Group on January 29. Thirty-nine Mustangs from the 39th, 40th, and 77 Squadron were fully loaded with napalm, 5" HVAR's, and .50 caliber machine guns when they went after an enemy stronghold north of Suwon. Reports from FEAF Intelligence indicated that the effort was quite satisfactory, for the UN ground forces were able to move their front line in the area four miles to the north after the Mustangs headed for home.

There were few fighter escort missions assigned to the 35th FIG after the advent of the MiG-15 into the war the previous fall. But the 35th FIG did manage to catch seventeen of these during the winter of 1951, mostly shepherding RB-29s south of the Yalu River or up and down the coastlines of North Korea. The pilots were not known to jump for joy over these assignments, for they either had to carry their long-range fuel tanks on the longer missions or napalm tanks on the shorter ones, so they could hit targets of opportunity on their way home. The Mustangs were hard to maneuver with the underslung tanks, but of even greater concern was the fact that they often hung up when the pilot tried to drop them, either because of the cold or because of ice that accumulated on the shackles as they flew through clouds or rain/snow showers. And, of course, the tanks would have to be jettisoned if the Superforts were jumped by enemy fighters. In all, the idea of still using a F-51 as an escort fighter in

this period sparked of lunacy, but orders were orders, and if someone in FEAF was still living in the dark ages, so be it. The pilots felt that whom ever was giving such orders "ought to be shot." but they followed these orders anyhow, knowing that they were little more than sitting ducks along side of geese on these missions and that they would be of little value in any case.

The 35th FIG lost three Mustangs on combat missions during January 1951. Two of the pilots were killed, and the other pilot injured. Three additional Mustangs were damaged beyond economical repair through accidents. One of these had been written off in a belly landing in December 1950 but it had been repaired by personnel of the 35th Maintenance and Support Squadron, so actually the Group was only down five fighters for the reporting period.

On January 5, Captain William Hook, 40th FIS, was killed when his Mustang crashed shortly after takeoff from K-9. An oil line had ruptured, spraying the windshield with oil and destroying his forward flight visibility, but still Hook tried to save his fighter, and he stayed with it until the engine started to seize. At this point he tried to bailout, but by then he was too low for his parachute to have time to open. Hook had been one of the better know pilots within the 35th FIG and was noted for his leadership qualities, being considered "a real motivator." At the time of his death he was on his second combat tour with the 35th FIG, being lost on his 117th mission with the Group. Nobody knew for sure exactly how many missions he had flown previously while assigned to Dean Hess' 6146th BASUT/Republic of Korea Air Force.

On January 19 Captain William Matusz was killed when his F-51 went down behind the enemy lines while flying an armed reconnaissance mission. He was seen to be hit by enemy ground fire while a low level sweep, and his Mustang was completely consumed by fire in the ensuing crash. After Matusz's death Lt. Colonel Dale, no longer permitted his pilots to carry napalm tanks while flying armed reconnaissance missions, The weight of the tanks and their volatility made the F-51 just to vulnerable to enemy fire at the altitudes these type of missions were flown.

Weather conditions for flying combat missions in February were "tolerable," with little rain to dampen down the dust on the ground at K-9. Living conditions were considered to be also "tolerable," although overcrowding in the billets was the main gripe of the airmen. The food was improving, and morale was considered to be remaining at a constant level of reasonably satisfied people waiting for a definite rotation policy.

Only the pilots had a definite goal to reach, one hundred missions before they were relieved of combat duty. Whether they got to go home or not remained an intangible, depending on how long they had spent in the Theater. If they were "short timers' in Korea after their mission totals reached one hundred, they would probably be transferred to the 41st FIS in Japan for cross training into the F-80 and be assigned as a fighter-interceptor pilot for awhile. This was considered to be a "good duty," particularly in the eyes of the airmen who had to plan on spending their entire three year overseas tour in Korea.

On February 11 Captain Justice Haythorne, 40th FIS, died as a result of having to bailout of his Mustang that was hit by antiaircraft fire over North Korea. Haythorne managed to reach the shoreline and jumped in the vicinity of a South Korean, naval vessel, which immediately pulled him from the water, but even the short immersion in the frigid winter waters was to much for his system and he perished from exposure.

The following day Captain Clifford Summers, 39th FIS, received heavy battle damage to his Mustang while flying an interdiction mission. He managed to nurse his crippled ship back to Taegu, where he bailed out. During the minutes prior to his bailing out Summers had gathered all of the Mustangs' maps and maintenance papers together and stuffed them into one of the pockets in his flight suit, but he broke his leg when he landed and had to be evacuated to Japan to have it set and to recuperate. He mailed the papers back to the squadron!

Also on February 12 Captain Currie had led a CAS mission to Hoengsong where his flight bombed and strafed Red troops that were entrenched upon a ridge that was close to being obscured by low clouds. They killed an estimated forty communist troops and destroyed five mortar positions, and their efforts permitted the UN ground forces "to advance to carry out their mission." (Capture the ridge). Currie was awarded a second Oak Leaf Cluster to his previous DFC.

As in the previous months, an emphasis continued on flying the armed recce missions. For survivability, these were now being flown with a single F-51 at eight hundred feet, with the remainder of the flight at four thousand feet, which provided a top cover for the reconnaissance pilot. This permitted him to concentrate on his observations while the higher aircraft could look for enemy aircraft above them, or antiaircraft gun emplacements on the ground.

In a program similar to the "Circle 10" missions being flown by the Mustangs of the 45th Tactical Reconnaissance Squadron, the 5th Air Force started assigning specific areas for the 35th FIG pilots to reconnoiter. Each squadron received a certain geographical area which was then subdivided into four areas, for each of the four flights within a squadron to cover. The pilots soon began to discover more and more targets that had previously been unnoticed, strictly through their previous unfamiliarity with the topographical areas they had been looking at. Simple things, as a one room hutch that might appear the next day with a new room addition or a lean-to attached that would not have been noticed in the past now stood out to the observant pilot, and almost guaranteed him a worthwhile target, usually a stashed vehicle of some sort.

On February 21 another F4U crashed at K-9 when its pilot aborted his takeoff and retracted its landing gear in an attempt to get his "Hosenose" stopped. The Corsair was carrying two bombs and eight rockets at the time, and when it caught fire they started to cook-off. One 39th FIS Mustang was destroyed in the blasts, and two more suffered major damage, while four had minor damage. There were no personnel injuries, but it was reported that the relationship between the 35th FIG and the USMC was "starting to get a little strained."

Operation Killer started on February 23 and reportedly resulted in 10,000 enemy casualties. For their part in Operation Killer the 35th FIG was assigned the area between Hoengsong and Yondu-ri, due east of Seoul and midway across the Korean peninsula. Even though the air support phases of the UN attacks were hampered by bad weather, the 35th FIG squadrons roamed their assigned area strafing anything that moved. Operation Killer, in itself, did not have the desired effect in slowing down the Red movement, for the winter weather conditions re-

A 40th FIS Mustang enroute to the gunnery range at Miho, Japan. After the war toned down a bit and the 40th FIS was withdrawn from combat there was a bit more time to dress up their Mustangs. This F-51 belonged to the flight commander of "B Flight," as noted by the two fuselage stripes and the flying "B" on the rudder. It later became "Tomcat" Bailey's personal Mustang and then was transferred to the ROKAF. (Chard)

mained on their side. Thawing rivers, along with snow and ice caused the UN forces movements to almost a crawl along the east-west MLR. It was necessary for FEAF to air drop supplies and ammunition to the front line troops, just so they could hold the ground they had taken. Their premise had been great, the timing poor.

Antiaircraft fire increased during this period in both intensity and accuracy. The communists were now employing mobile antiaircraft batteries, which made their positions impossible to forecast for pilot briefings. As always, small arms fire continued to be a major hazard for the pilots, with the 35th FIG having seven Mustangs damaged during just one day's missions in February. It took a degree of fatalism for the pilots to have to face the fact that just one enemy soldier with one rifle and one round of ammunition could knock down one fighter-bomber. As the circumstance was, the Red soldier was not afraid to attempt to do so, for they knew that as long as the Mustang was not carrying its underslung belly tanks, which signified napalm to them, the communists would just stand there with their rifles and shoot at any attacking aircraft. It was great sport, and a strafing fighter could not get them all.

On the last day of February the 35th FIG set up a staging operation at Suwon, K-13. Lt. Colonel Thomas Robertson, commanding officer of the 39th FIS, took five F-51s to this recaptured airstrip in order to be able to provide a faster turnaround time for air support to the UN forces. Before the sun had set for the day they found that they had bitten off quite a task, for most of the involved pilots had flown four combat sorties a piece, and a couple had got in five. The 35th FIG set themselves a goal of staging eight F-51s at a time through K-13, but in actuality they were only able to manage four. The men were willing, but the weary Mustangs couldn't take the strain.

During the staging operation the pilots and aircraft were rotated between K-13 and K-9 every three days, which was designed to reduce the fatigue on the pilots, but 50% of the F-51s wound up either requiring an overhaul or repair of battle damage on a daily basis. Living conditions at Suwon were "primitive" but the pilots were reasonably satisfied with the assignment to the forward base. Their time in the cockpit was reduced by not having to fly the two hundred miles to and from K-9 to the target areas, and by being able to get in four missions per day they quickly built up their totals toward the magic one hundred mission goal. The airmen were not consulted as to whether they were satisfied, or not, with K-13's living conditions.

The 39th FIS had thirty-nine Mustangs on hand and flew 951 combat sorties in March, all without a loss. The 40th FIS continued with their string of bad luck, for in 989 combat sorties they lost four Mustangs and two pilots.

On March 3 Major Carl Aubrey and Captain Edward Williams were flying an armed recce mission when Williams was shot down by enemy ground fire. He was declared as missing in action. On March 12 Major Aubrey was also knocked down by ground fire. It was later determined that both of these men were killed in action.

The 40th FIS almost lost one additional pilot, on March 5, when Captain Allen Vanderyerk was shot down near Chunchon. A RESCAP was established over him and a helicopter managed to dodge its way through enemy gunfire and pick him up. To the chopper crew's amazement, Vanderyerk was sopping wet, as if he had been immersed in a pond or stream, but it was only perspiration. Vanderyerk estimated that in the fifty-seven minutes that he had been on the ground over 1,500 rounds had been fired at him while he was dodging from cover to cover while positioning himself so he could be rescued.

Emphasis was now placed upon armed recce all along all of the main roads in North Korea, along with the secondary roads that passed through the narrow ravines where the Reds might hide their vehicles or stockpile goods. This caught the communists off guard for a short period, for they had grown somewhat careless with their camouflaging of vehicles that were parked off of the main supply routes. The 35th FIG got in a couple of good days of truck busting before the Red's caught on and brought in more automatic weapons, and the pilots had to become wary once again.

Due to runway construction at Chinhae, the home of the 18th Fighter Bomber Wing, the 18th FBW's attached 2 Squadron, South African Air Force, moved to K-9 where they joined with the 35th FIG for fighter-bomber operations for a short period. On March 29 the 35th FIG also expanded their own operations by forming a Detachment 1. This unit consisted of only two officers and seven airmen, who then moved into some dilapidated buildings at Yonju, K-45, where they set up another Mustang staging base and a combat cargo depot.

Ten days later, on April 7, the 35th FIG ceased their combat staging operation at K-13 and moved this operation to K-16, Seoul Municipal Airport, which was actually a sub-base to Kimpo. This action coincided with the release of 77 Squadron, which was relieved of combat duties in the Mustang to return to Japan and conversion into the Meteor. Their withdrawal was envyingly noted, for not only was 77 Squadron going to get jet fighters but they were also getting out of the "smell-hole" of Korea. The UN airmen could never get over the fact that the Koreans used human waste for fertilizer.

Lt. Colonel Kirkendall was relieved as commander of the 40th FIS in April after flying 104 combat missions. He was replaced by Major Frank Malone, who had been transferred to the squadron from the 8th FBW's 36th FBS after flying fifty F-80 missions.

On April 3 Captain Thomas Manjack received major battle damage to his Mustang from Red gunfire while attacking Singye, 120 miles north of the MLR. Unable to make it home, Manjack had to settle for a crash landing, suffering a fractured forehead by striking the protruding K-14 gunsight in the process. Dazed, he was picked up by a H-19 after spending five hours evading communist search parties and flown to K-13 for first aid before being transferred to Japan for further treatment.

Four days later, on April 7 1st Lt. Siegel Dickman was also forced to make a crash landing, this time some twelve miles north of Singye. He also was rescued by a helicopter. Since he, Manjack and Vanderyerk were now considered as "evades," they were eligible for rotation out of the Theater.

On April 17 the 39th FIS suffered its first loss of a pilot through enemy action since December. Major Shelton Monroe was shot down by enemy ground fire while flying over Kumhwa. The crash site was RESCAPed by the rest of his flight and flights of F-80s and Marine F4Us, but heavy ground fire prevented a rescue attempt by a helicopter that had been dispatched for the effort. Monroe's body could be seen from the air in close proximity to his downed Mustang, but he showed no signs of life. Due to enemy gunfire, fuel considerations, and the fact that he already appeared to be dead, further attempts had to be abandoned. His body was never recovered.

44-63589 as belonging to Major Bailey with the squadron commander's three fuselage stripes. It is being bore-sighted prior to being placed on the alert pad for air defense duties at Johnson Air Base. It was scrapped in 1957. (Chard)

Luck ran out for another 39th FIS pilot on April 22 when Captain E.W. "Zack" Dean had to bailout over Sunchon. Dean's Mustang was heavily damaged by ground fire and he had only enough time to climb to 500 feet before a fire in his Mustang forced him to bailout prematurely. His wingman, Lt. Frank Bell, stated that it was unlikely that Dean survived the bailout, as his parachute had just started to stream out of its pack as he hit the ground. His death was confirmed after the war ended. Bell, himself, was barely able to escape the area, for while he was circling Dean's body his own Mustang was hit by 40mm fire in the right flap, rudder and engine. He was, however, able to return to K-14.

On April 22 Captain Duncan Palmer, 39th FIS, went down in enemy territory. He had just completed a strafing pass on his target and was seen climbing back up through a cloud layer when something went wrong with his Mustang. Colonel William McBride, the 35th FIG commanding officer since February, was leading the mission and he saw Palmer bailout, so he took his flight of Mustangs back down through the clouds to RESCAP the area. A helicopter was called for, but then was radioed to return home as McBride saw Palmer being taken prisoner and marched out of the area. Palmer was released by the Red's on September 5, 1953.

The MLR was now running from just north of Seoul to south of Chunchon. The communist "Spring Offensive" was thrown against this line on April 23, and it took all of the air power that the UN could muster to assist the ground forces hold their positions. The staging airstrips were surrounded by UN manned artillery for defensive purposes and the communists entered into cannon duels with these guns, but no enemy shells actually fell on the airstrips, themselves.

The 35th FIG and 2 Squadron SAAF flew over four hundred sorties during the four day period that marked the strongest activity of the Spring Offensive. Pilots that attained their 100 mission mark during this period were not released from further flying and they also continued to fly assigned missions. There was some expressed unhappiness over this development, but the pilots were quite aware of what would happen to those on the ground if they had to forego air support, so they stayed on and did the job at hand.

The communist "flak alley" increased in both quantity and accuracy of antiaircraft firepower during this period, also. It surpassed all numbers of guns and rounds of ammunition thrown up at the fighter-bomber. There was no longer any doubt that the Red's intended to continue the war without quarter. Destroyed communist villages were being rebuilt, being constructed to conceal their supply and POL dumps in the process. The communists once again began to show themselves during daylight hours. Construction crews were positioned along the main supply routes, and the roads that were "postholed" with bombs were under repair before the sounds of the fighter-bombers engines faded away. It became a most frustrating event for a pilot to bomb a road in the morning and then discover that it had been repaired and was open for traffic in the afternoon.

The 39th FIS was detached from the 35th FIG on May 7, 1951 and became attached to the 18th Fighter Bomber Wing. Although they were now totally and realistically relived of any form of fighter interceptor functions, they still refused to surrender their designation as a FIS, an apparent point of pride. They remained operational from K-9 and K-16 until May 10 when they relocated to K-10 to join with the 18th FBW for continuing service. Colonel Robertson, their commanding officer, went on record stating that he was not the least bit happy with the accommodations intended for his squadron. The area assigned to them for billeting had previously been the 18th FBW's napalm mixing dump and it stank from the residue. The area was also littered with fuel tanks and drums and was full of potholes. The tents that were issued to the squadron for quarters leaked, and there was nothing but mud for walkways between them. About the only highlight of the move was the reassignment of pilots to the 39th FIS from the 40th FIS, which for the first time brought them up to an actual TO&E strength.

Effective May 25, 1951 the 35th FIW was transferred from K-9 to Johnson Air Base, J-16, Japan. The move was made "Less Personnel and Equipment." All of the serviceable Mustangs were turned over to the 18th FBW, while the war weary examples were flown to Kisarazu Air Base, J-19, Japan for a major overhaul via Project Rebirth. A high percentage of both officers and airmen were also reassigned to units composing the 18th FBW to alleviate personnel shortages. A small cadre of ex 35th FIG people was all that were retained to rebuild the unit upon their return to Japan.

The "new" 35th FIG absorbed the "Personnel and Equipment" of the 6162nd Air Base Wing upon their arrival at J-16, and the expansion created the "new" 35th Fighter Interceptor Wing. Colonel Strother Hardwick assumed command of the new Wing until May 28, when he was replaced by Colonel William Schulgen. Lt. Colonel Homer Cox became the commanding officer of the 35th FIG.

The "new" 35th FIW was composed of the 40th and 41st FIS's with the 339th Fighter Interceptor Squadron serving as an attached squadron. The 40th FIS was assigned a temporary "on paper" assignment to Misawa Air Base, J-27, on Honshu, where the rebuilding of the squadron was to take place under the tutelage of the 41st FIS. At this time the 41st FIS was flying F-80s, but the 40th FIS was expected to receive F-51s once again. The 339th FIS, based at Johnson Air Base, was just completing a switch-over from F-82s to F-94s.

All of this action was highlighted by one of the stranger kills of the Korean Conflict when one of the 41st FIS pilots that was on TDY to the 40th FIS as an instructor was scrambled in his F-80 to shoot down a derelict C-119 whose crew had bailed out. This "kill" was the sole claim for the 41st FIS during the war.

June 1951 was spent in the rebuilding of the 40th FIS. New personnel were assigned and supplies were drawn. July opened with the assignment of three F-51s to the squadron, and by July 12 they were up to TO&E with both pilots and Mustangs. They made their first "Pass in Review" on July 24 when they formated with F-80s of the 41st FIS and F-86s of the 4th FIW's 336th FIS to salute the arrival of the U.S. aircraft carrier Sitka Bay. The carrier was bringing in the first of the activated Air National Guard Fighter Bomber Groups to Japan, the 116th.

The interim squadron commander of the 40th FIS, Major Jay Van Bloom, was promoted to Lt. Colonel and transferred to Korea. He was replaced by Major George Metcalf on September 1, 1951. Metcalf is previously noted for his flying with Bout One and the ROKAF.

Even though the 39th FIS was attached to the 18th FBW, the 35th FIW, through the 40th FIS, continued a direct connection to the 39th FIS by utilizing the 40th FIS as an operational training unit, OTU, for the squadron serving in Korea. To fulfill this role the 40th FIS flew in both air defense exercises and army cooperation missions over Japan for their pilots to become proficient in the F-51 before they were assigned to the 18th FBW as replacements.

The army cooperation missions gave the pilots realistic training and also helped to provide a scenario for the infantry units in training in Japan, themselves. The Mustangs were flown at low altitudes over Camp Fuji and varied in nature, with bombing, close air support and the laying of smoke screens over the heads of the men of the 40th Infantry Division and the 187th (Airborne) Regimental Combat Team.

These types of missions also had their hazards, for 1st Lt. Howard Kelley had an engine failure while flying in the air-to-air gunnery range near Miho Air Base, J-25. Kelley pointed the disabled Mustang out to sea and bailed out. He was rescued by a SA-16 of the 3rd Air Rescue Squadron within forty minutes. A second 40th FIS Mustang was lost on October 10, 1951 when its pilot had to bail out while on an aerial gunnery mission.

It was on this same day that the 40th FIS got in its last kill (of sorts) during the Korean Conflict. A radio controlled drone target escaped its operator while it was being flown for army antiaircraft gunners. A Lt. Lamb was scrambled to shoot it down, and he got it with one burst of .50 caliber fire.

All of these types of missions continued for the rest of 1951, being only interspersed by the occasional task of ferrying F-51s to Korea from FEAMCOM. Starting in 1952 the 40th FIS commenced flying "Classified Missions" with a RF-51D that had been assigned to them from the 45th TRS. Whatever these missions entailed remains a mystery yet today, for all that the USAF would admit was that the RF-51s contained modified radio equipment and those individuals connected with the 40th FIS at the time that have been contacted have forgotten the aircraft and missions.

Practice air defense exercises continued through April 1952 as the 40th FIS trained as an interceptor squadron in their role as a backup to the F-80s of the 41st FIS and the F-94s of the 339th FIS. In this capacity they stood strip-alert during the daylight hours at Johnson Air Base. As a part of this training they were also called upon to participate in the largest air defense exercise ever attempted over Japan, on April 23, 1952. Unfortunately the weather conditions were extremely bad at the time and it was felt by many of the pilots that the 40th FIS's portion of the exercise should have been canceled, but some of the more "gung ho" higher command officers ordered the squadron to fly, regardless.

Twenty Mustangs were launched to fly as intruder targets against the defenses at Itazuke Air Base in the midst of heavy thunderstorm activity and one Mustang, flown by 2nd Lt. Gerald "Jerry" Reynolds, became lost and crashed with fatal result near Beppo.

On May 25 the 40th FIS represented the 35th FIW in the FEAF Gunnery Meet in Japan. Mustangs flown by Lt.'s Richard Ernsberger, James Farley, Richard Chard and James Cook placed Third, which wasn't too bad for a bunch of rookie lieutenant pilots flying antiques against the experienced hot-shot jet jockies!

The 40th FIS had its second fatal accident since their reorganization on June 7, 1952. 1st Lt. Hildreth Payne, Jr., the squadron's Intelligence Officer, was involved in a mid-air collision with a Navy F4U over Oppana, Japan. Both of the pilots were killed. Payne's wife and family were only one day out of Japan at the time of the incident, and they had to be met by the Group's chaplain when their ship docked.

On July 15 1st Lt. Paul "Pappy" Murry took off on a practice scramble from Johnson Air Base. After making a few practice interceptions on another Mustang, Murry's engine started to run rough and he headed back towards Johnson. When his Merlin engine quit, Murry was forced to bail out, but he struck the aircraft's horizontal stabilizer and was decapitated.

A "Detachment 'E' (Provisional)" was formed within the 40th FIS during the early fall of 1952 that was equipped with F-86Es, and the era of the 35th FIW Mustangs began to draw to a close. This Detachment was soon transferred to Chitose Air Base, J-4, Japan to stand strip alert in the Sabres while also conducting training and proficiency missions.

The last major 35th FIW Mustang mission was flown on October 6, 1952 when the 40th FIS flew as a fighter escort for a U.S. Navy convoy that feigned an amphibious landing at Wonson, Korea, and then sailed through the Korea Strait to land its troops at Inchon.

After this, the Alert Flight of Mustangs at Johnson was moved to Yokota Air Base, J-38, in December when the Johnson Air Base runways were closed for construction, and when the runways were reopened, the Mustangs were left at Yokota for use in sundry roles by the tenant organization. The F-51s were replaced by a smattering of F-80s until additional F-86s could be obtained in early 1953.

Lt. Richard Chard, 40th FIS, while sitting cockpit alert at Johnson Air Base. This was tedious duty, for it required being strapped into a Mustang's cockpit for four hours at a time while waiting for a potential scramble. (Chard)

CHAPTER SEVEN

18th Fighter Bomber Wing

The 18th Fighter Bomber Wing was one of the 'hottest" fighter units in the USAF, having established an outstanding combat record during World War II. Post War this record and attitude continued, and they had been rewarded by being the first overseas recipient to receive the Lockheed P-80 Shooting Star. However, their experience with the P-80 was short lived at this time, as they were shipped back to the United States for refurbishment, and the Wing inactivated for a period, only to be reactivated with F-47Ns, and later F-51Ds in August 1948. In 1949 their Mustangs gave way to the now designated F-80Cs once again. At this time the 18th FBW was composed of the 12th, 44th and 67th Fighter Bomber Squadrons, all stationed at Clark Air Base, Philippines. One outstanding fact to the history of the 18th FBW is that they are the only combat wing within the Air Force to have never served in the United States!

The 18th FBW was directed by a 13th Air Force request on July 4, 1950 to supply a single fighter squadron for duty in Korea. The following day FEAF General Order 24 was received, which outlined the number of personnel and amount of equipment that the Wing was to furnish for this action. The effort was given the title of the "Dallas Project," and as soon as the contingent arrived in Japan they were renamed at the "Dallas Squadron." The original contingent was primarily composed of men from the 12th FBS, although volunteers were solicited from the Wing's other two squadrons to fill shortages in some specialties.

The original Dallas Squadron was composed of 36 officers and 302 Airmen, and it was commanded by Captain Harry H. Moreland. One of the items of interest in this action was that almost all of the volunteer pilots involved herein had completed, or nearly completed their peacetime tour in the Philippines and could have elected to remain at Clark, leaving the pilots of lessor experience to have taken their place. The Dallas Project departed Clark, via air transport, on July 10 and arrived at Johnson Air Base, Japan the following day.

The Dallas people picked up all of the needed and available equipment they could lay their hands on at Johnson and then moved to Ashiya Air Base, with the expectation of only being there a short time. Their original orders had indicated that their final destination would be Taegu Air Base, Korea. However, due to higher priority being given to other efforts, their movement to Taegu was not accomplished until July 27. Captain Moreland, in the interim, was faced with almost overwhelming problems. Except for having a "first class" operations officer, Captain Jerome Mau, Moreland was virtually on his own when it came to seeing to the billeting of his men and all of the more mundane chores involved with running a fighter squadron.

The unidentifiable burned out remains of a 12th Fighter Bomber Squadron Mustang in August 1950. (via Davis)

Most of all, Moreland's major task was to oversee the cross-training of F-80 pilots back into F-51s to satisfy USAF requirements. There was simply no way that this transition program could be accomplished, for there were but ten Mustangs available to them from Johnson Air Base. Finally the aircraft carrier Boxer arrived, and some of its 145 F-51s were then assigned to the Dallas Squadron. The pilots were required to receive a minimum of four transition sorties in the F-51 before entering combat: some got in only the single three hour flight between Johnson and Ashiya Air Bases, where they refueled and armed the Mustangs before setting out on their first combat mission.

Initially, and unknown to the men of the Dallas Squadron at the time, FEAF had cut General Orders #44, which intended to combine the Dallas Squadron with Dean Hess' Bout 1 and the 6002nd Air Base Squadron that had been created on July 6, 1950 at Sasebo, Japan. (The 6002nd Air Base Squadron was formed from men of Detachment 1, 36th Fighter Bomber Squadron, whose ranks were rapidly increased to include twenty officers and two hundred-fifty Airmen). These three combined units were to be identified as the 51st Fighter Bomber Squadron (Provisional). Major Hess, being of the higher rank, was named as the squadron's interim commanding officer.

This entire program then became a series of rapid moves and mobilizations. The 6002nd ABS was transferred from Japan to Pusan, Korea, arriving there on July 14, only to find their identification changed to that of the 6002nd Air Base Unit. Three days later they too were split, with a new Detachment 1 moving on to Taejon Air Base, Korea. On August 1 a further expansion brought the creation of the 6002nd Fighter Bomber Wing, while Detachment 1 was discontinued. (On November 24, 1950 the 6002nd FBW was inactivated and replaced in designation by the 18th Fighter Bomber Wing, while the original 18th FBW designation in the Philippines became the 6200th Air Base Wing. It would not be until 1957 when the 18th FBW designation was returned to Clark Air Base to replace the 6200th ABW).

Major Hess was neither overly impressed nor happy with his Bout 1 project being drafted into the 51st FBS(P), having just started to get them operational in support of the ROKAF. After some time, arguments, and effort, Hess was able to get his people released from the 51st FBS(P) contingent and returned to the support of Republic of Korea Air Force.

The 51st FBS (P) was considered as operational on July 10. The squadron was built around sixteen Mustangs, eight of which were obtained from the first allocation of

A Dallas Squadron Mustang at Taegu Air Base, K-2, Korea in July 1950. In the background are the squadron's operations, intelligence and maintenance control tents. South Korea's president Rhee visited the squadron and likened their volunteers to the World War II American Volunteer Group in China, so once Dallas became the 12th FBS again they painted the "shark mouth" on their Mustangs. (Biteman)

aircraft to the Dallas Squadron, and eight from Bout 1, although some of the latter had not actually been received by Bout 1 as yet. Acceptance checks started from scratch on these aircraft, as no aircraft maintenance forms could be found. The ground crews gave each F-51 a thorough inspection, and then started a new logbook on them showing a zero-time engine and airframe hours. In theory, each aircraft was at this time in perfect, brand new condition, and should be able to be flown for twenty-five hours with minimal attention. Yet due to the prevalent dust that was encountered in southern Korea, maintenance turned out to be a never ending chore. Carburetor and brake seals had to be flushed daily. Oil screens had to be cleaned every fifteen operating hours. When it rained, everything turned to mud, which created even more work as muddy water was thrown up by propwash or the aircraft's tires and it went directly into the aircraft's radiator scoop and clogged the radiator cores with a crust as it dried. None of the aircraft had a complete set of working navigational instruments, and in one instance it took a four-ship flight to get the mission back to Taegu, as one Mustang had a compass, but no artificial horizon, another had a radio, but no other aids, etc.!

At this point the history of the 51st FBS (P) runs simultaneous with that of the Dallas Squadron and the 12th FBS, and for clarities sake they will be referred to as the 12th FBS, for in reality they were all one and the same. When Major Hess returned to Bout 1 and the 6146th Base Unit on August 1 Captain Moreland once again became the squadron's commanding officer, and on August 5, 1950 the 51st FBS (P) was discontinued in favor of the 12th FBS.

The first 12th FBS combat mission was flown on July 15 when Lt. Frank Buzze flew along with a flight of Bout 1 Mustangs on a ground support strike. Between this date and the end of July the 12th FBS flew a total of 426 combat sorties. Due to the shortage of Mustangs, all of these missions were two-ship, with one flying as top cover for the other at 3,000 feet while the other pressed its attack at low level, followed by a reversal of positions when the first aircraft had expended its ordnance. After the first of August when more Mustangs became available, the 12th FBS was able to mount four-ship formations, with one two-ship element providing top cover for the other pair.

The combat mission situation required that the pilots alter their tactics from those that they had practiced in peacetime. Not only because the Mustangs flight characteristics were different from the previous F-80s, but because of the weather conditions and Korea's terrain features. Previously, and in peacetime, pilots had started their practice bombing runs at 6,000 feet, but because of the prevailing weather over Korea they now felt themselves lucky if they could start a bomb run from 1,000 feet. It was believed by both the pilots and the tacticians that the previous lack of realistic training caused the deaths of several of the Mustang pilots who perished early on in the war.

The weather problems and the terrain to be faced had been totally unforeseen and not covered by the training syllabus in the Philippine Island environment, and there were also peacetime flight restrictions on bombing altitudes in respect to maximum and minimum altitudes. The minimum altitude situation contributed to pilot deaths in a totally unexpected way, for many of the pilots flew into their own bomb bursts, as now their maximum starting altitude was well below the previous minimum altitudes and they never trained in how to avoid their own

A Dallas Squadron Mustang taxiing at Taegu, July 1950. 44-73592 was lost to Code M on April 5, 1951. (Biteman)

bomb blasts. The squadron's first death occurred when 2nd Lt. Billie Crabtree flew into the blast of his own 500 pound bombs while attacking near Kwangju on July 25.

In all, the 12th FBS lost ten of their scarce Mustangs in July. Pilot fatigue may well have been an additional factor in some of these losses, for several pilots were known to have flown up to eleven hours on the day that they were lost.

Due to the pressure brought on by the North Korean Army, many Mustang missions had to be flown at night. This was a role for which the F-51 was definitely not suited. The aircraft carried their normal ordnance loads on these missions, with the idea of attacking North Korean truck convoys. The communists would turn out the lights on their vehicles when they heard the fighter bombers overhead, which gave the pilots problems with target acquisition in the dark hilly terrain. Then, during the attack, the pilots had to guard themselves closely against loosing their night vision by closing one eye as they fired their rockets, for the flames of the rocket trails would render them virtually blind in the open eye for over an hour.

They also had to avoid the natural impulse to watch their bombs explode, so they were rarely sure whether they had hit their target, or not. Tracer fire from firing their .50 caliber machine guns likewise caused night blindness.

Also facing the pilots at the time of these night missions was the North Korean standard 20 mm antiaircraft guns. These guns normally remained silent when the Mustangs were overhead, for the gunners did not want to give away their positions by muzzle flashes. However, the North Korean gunners became adept at waiting until the Mustang pilot had made his attack and then they would fire at him as he was pulling away from the target and the guns were in his blind spot. One 12th FBS pilot returned to Ashiya to discover that his Mustang had been hit five times by 20 mm fire from an antiaircraft cannon that he never saw.

Navigation was a real problem, day or night. There were precious few maps available, and few of the Mustangs had any navigational radios installed. The radios would have proved to have little value anyhow, unless the pilot was headed for Japan, as the AACS troops had not yet been able to install any navigational aids in Korea. Lt. Duane Biteman had the Ashiya photo lab photograph the pilot's Sectional Charts for use in the cockpit, but the black and white prints were beyond difficult to read under the red night cockpit lighting.

As a follow-up to the Dallas project, on July 24, 1950 the 18th Fighter Bomber Group at Clark Air Base received orders for their transfer to Japan. The Group Headquarters and the 67th Fighter Bomber squadron were included in this move, but the 44th Fighter Bomber squadron would remain at Clark for the duration of the war. The 44th FBS and some attached units would serve as an Operational Training Unit for the 18th Fighter Bomber Wing at this time. The 18th FBG, under Lt. Colonel Ira "Ike" Wintermute, and the 67th FBS, under Major Louis Sebille, were airlifted from Clark Air Base to Johnson Air Base, Japan where they picked up their Mustangs and associated equipment before moving on to Taegu Air Base on July 28.

On August 4 Captain Moreland stepped down to the position of the squadron Operations Officer when Major Robert Dow arrived from Clark Air Base to assume command of the squadron. Dow had previously been one of the World War II 44th Fighter Squadron commanding officers and had become the commander of the 12th FBS in 1949. This action was not universally accepted, as Dow was a quiet and reserved individual, whereas Moreland was considered to be the better combat leader.

The Headquarters Section of the 18th FBG joined the 12th FBS at Taegu Air Base, K-2, on August 3, but due to the lack of adequate aircraft parking spaces, the 67th FBS had to remain at Ashiya Air Base, J-1, for the time being. Regardless, the 67th FBS immediately commenced combat missions, and lost their first pilot, Captain Robert Howell on a ground support strike near Waegwan on August 4. The following day, August 5, their squadron commander, Major Sebille, became the first of four USAF Medal of Honor recipients for their actions during the Korean Conflict. In fact, Sebille's Medal of Honor was the first awarded by the USAF since they had become an independent branch of the services in 1947. He was also the last of three Mustang pilots to have

earned this decoration, and was the first to receive it post-humously.

The 67th FBS's twenty-sixth combat mission was to have been a routine ground support strike against an enemy troop concentration near Hamchiang, some fifty miles northwest of Taegu. Arriving over the target area on his own fifth combat mission of this war, Sebille started down on a bomb run, and when he attempted to toggle-off the two 500 pound GP's he was carrying, he discovered that one had hung up on its shackle. The other two Mustangs in his flight, flown by Captain's Charles Morehouse and Maurice Martin, had followed him down and bombed successfully, with the Mosquito pilot they were working with reporting that the strike had destroyed four armored vehicles and had killed many enemy troops. Sebille, not wanting the encumbrance of the bomb under his wing when he landed, elected to attempt another run against the target in hopes that he could at least shake it off where it might be effective in some form. He dove down, and it is unclear whether he had been able to get rid of the bomb, or not. But, as he pulled up off the target he reported that he had taken several hits from antiaircraft fire. He then started a third attack, against the advice of his wingmen who had suggested that he head south toward a friendly ground patrol and bailout. Both the wingmen and the Mosquito pilot observed the Mustang, (Serial Number 44-74394, of which no photograph has ever surfaced.) dive into a half-track, "destroying target, aircraft, numerous troops, and himself."

Due to the indication that the Naktong River defense line could not be held, the 18th FBG Headquarters and the 12th FBS were evacuated back to Ashiya Air Base on August 6 and 7. They continued to provide uninterrupted support to the ground forces from Japan, however. The first missions of the day would leave Japan at dawn, and then stage succeeding strikes from Taegu through the day, and then they would time their last departure from K-2 to make a final strike and return to Japan just as darkness settled in. These were long and fatiguing days for the pilots, as they often did not even get a chance to get out of their cockpits at K-2 to stretch their legs while their Mustangs were being rearmed and refueled.

During the early morning hours of August 10 the 12th FBS carried out an experiment with two Mustangs, flown by Captain Jerry Mau and Lt. Biteman, to determine the feasibility of night attacks by F-51s. Armed with a napalm tank and a 500 pound GP bomb each, along with six HVAR's and machine guns, they flew to Songju on the Naktong River to attack North Korean convoys operating

The ever present dust at Taegu is kicked up into a storm at Taegu during a 18th Fighter Bomber Group takeoff. It got into everything, food and fuel, and made life miserable for all. (Biteman)

Loading a 500 lb. GP under a Mustang with improvised equipment. The bomb's arming vane is installed, and also the rockets electric arming wires. (Biteman)

in the dark. In all, the effort scared the pilots, for they both incurred bouts of vertigo and suffered flash-blindness from their ordnance explosions while not being able to ascertain whether they were successful in their attacks, or not. Future such exercises by Mustang pilots were definitely not recommended in such an unsuitable aircraft.

In all, August proved to be a busy and costly month for the 18th FBG. The 12th FBS had lost a total of ten Mustangs, with six of them going down to enemy ground fire and four of their pilots were declared as MIA. The 67th FBS, in addition to loosing their commanding officer and Captain Robert Howell also lost a Captain McVail to ground fire. Exactly what happened to McVail is unknown, as his name does not appear on USAF causality lists.

On the plus side, the first kills for the 18th FBG also occurred in August. On August 3 Captain's Edward Hoagland and Howard Price, 67th FBS, teamed up and each destroyed a Yak fighter during strafing runs. Seven days later Major Arnold "Moon" Mullins, Major Sebille's replacement as commanding officer of the 67th FBS, destroyed three more Yaks while strafing another North Korean airfield. The 18th FBG claimed four more enemy aircraft destroyed and one damaged, but Group records do not identify the pilots and FEAF disallowed the claims. Probably because the aircraft's gun cameras were not working and there were no other witnesses.

The 18th FBG returned to Korea on September 7, moving to an airstrip titled as K-9. On the east side of the port of Pusan, K-9 quickly became known as "Dogpatch," in a play on words from cartoonist Al Capp's "Li'l Abner," and it wasn't very long before someone contacted Capp and let him know about it. Capp, in turn, designed an insignia for the "Dogpatchers" that featured Li'l Abner and

Nancy O. taking a Mustang into action, and Capp was made an honorary member of the 18th FBG.

K-9 was a cultural shock to the men, for the transition from peacetime conditions at Clark Air Base, to the relative comforts of Ashiya, and then to the "camp out" experience at K-2, back to Ashiya, and then the "primitive" conditions at their newly occupied base was a bit hard to take. The runway was to be 6,000 feet long, but was of PSP construction. There were only a handful of weather-beaten buildings, and a shortage of tents, bedding, and potable water. The ground echelons of the squadrons had a stand-down for twenty-four hours while personal equipment and supplies were shipped to Pusan in a LST, but there was no break in flying missions, for during this period the Mustangs departed Ashiya to stage through K-2 and then to land on the uncompleted runway at K-9 to finish out their day.

At this time Dogpatch was but fifteen minutes flying time from the main line of resistance, and even though the weather was poor, the pilots were able to provide a continuous air support to the ground forces. There was no doubt that the movement of these Mustangs back into the Pusan Perimeter is what saved the perimeter itself from collapsing altogether while the UN attempted to bolster its ground forces. The U.S. Army, among others, said so. In one instance the 12th FBS was assigned the task of covering the withdrawal of a Republic of Korea infantry division north of Po'hang. Through the pilots judicious use of napalm and strafing runs, the ROK division was actually able to turn the situation around and managed to retake some of the ground previously lost to the North Koreans.

Two more enemy aircraft were damaged by 18th FBG pilots while making strafing attacks in September, but the loss rate of Mustangs remained in the enemy's favor. Both squadrons suffered their losses through communist antiaircraft fire, with the 67th FBS loosing four Mustangs and their pilots being declared MIA, while the 12th FBS lost two F-51s with one pilot MIA. Most of these losses occurred while the Group was flying missions over North Korea where there was heavy antiaircraft fire to contend with and whose gunners were not the least bit afraid of the Mustangs retaliating firepower. In all, during the first six weeks of combat from K-9 the losses mounted to two pilots confirmed as killed, four missing in action, and four wounded and removed from flying status.

During October the two squadrons continued to aid the UN forces to the best of their ability. During the Inchon Landing period, September 15-18, the 18th FBG had the task of supporting the U.S. 24th and 25th Infantry Divisions along with the 1st Cavalry Division along the Pusan Perimeter. This effort held the North Korean army in a position where they could not possibly interfere with MacArthur's invasion by withdrawing troops to support their own forces in the Seoul area.

When the Pusan Perimeter broke open on September 16, the day following the Inchon Invasion, air support provided by the 18th FBG and other FEAF air elements decimated the North Koreans fleeing to the north so severely that they no longer constituted a major threat. "After 75 days of combat the tide of Red terror went from a steam roller advance to a headlong and confused retreat along the entire front line perimeter."

Once again, though, the Mustang loss rate did not show any signs of abating. During October the 12th FBS lost four pilots to enemy action, while the 67th FBS lost one pilot and three Mustangs. Pilots were finding it necessary, during both their attacks and upon breakaway to have to take violent evasive action to avoid hostile fire. It hadn't taken very long for the communist gunners to discover that the pilots were still attempting to fly a "basic ground gunnery pattern" and were easy marks while in what amounted to a conventional air traffic pattern. To avoid this, a quick education program was instituted, and then reiterated under the threat of disciplinary action that the pilots had to fly their aircraft to the very up most of their ability, jinking and twisting while varying their target approaches in an effort to reduce their exposure to ground fire. All attacks were to be hit and run, to catch the enemy gunners off guard. If it appeared that the target would have to be hit a second time, the pilots were to fly off and stooge around somewhere for ten minutes or so before returning from a different direction, in hopes that the antiaircraft gunners would have reduced their vigilance.

The pilots also had to stop toggling off one bomb or napalm tank on each attack, for the asymmetrical aircraft balance afterwards made evasive action too difficult. Rocket attacks were revised from firing one rocket per attack to two. It was extremely difficult to hit a moving armored T-34 tank with just one rocket, anyhow, and it had to be hit square or the rocket's blast would be defused against the armor plate. The accepted practice was to aim for the tank's tracks to disable it, although a 5" HVAR with a shaped charge would penetrate a tanks turret if squarely hit.

As combat losses took their toll the effective strength of both squadrons was reduced. The 12th FBS at the end of October found themselves down to only twenty-one pilots, from an authorized strength of thirty-five. Taking into consideration those pilots not able to fly missions

Captain Jerry Mau, 12th FBS, at Taegu in July 1950. (Biteman)

because of illness or having been detailed to forward air controller duties, an abnormal load was placed upon the remaining pilots. Each available pilot was having to fly at least once a day, and at this time the missions were averaging five hours in duration, which was a morale breaking stress. To alleviate some of these problems, on October 10 ten replacement pilots were transferred to the 18th FBG from the 44th FBS at Clark, but it would take some time before they would become acclimated to combat and become effective fighter-bomber pilots.

On October 2 Captain Edward Hodges, 67th FBS, became the first pilot from the 18th FBG to be rescued from deep within North Korea. Hodges was seen to bail-out of his Mustang at only 700 feet while twenty-five miles south of Pyongyang. He struck the horizontal stabilizer of the Mustang while in the process, which injured his back and sent his body tumbling. His flight leader, 1st Lt. Daniel Leake, had just about given up hope for his wingman's survival, but then he spotted Hodges' parachute opening just before he struck the ground. Leake immediately started circling the area and called for a RESCAP. A U.S. Marine unit at Kimpo intercepted Leake's radio transmission and dispatched a helicopter. For an hour and a half 18th FBG Mustangs RESCAPed the area, and then they had to head for home because of fuel constraints. They were replaced by a flight of Marine F9Fs which came in strafing with their 20 mm cannons and managed to hold off the encroaching North Korean soldiers until the helicopter was able to locate Hodges and effect the rescue. Hodges was then flown to Kimpo to receive first aid, and then air evacuated to Japan for treatment of his spinal injuries.

On October 2 the 12th FBS lost 1st Lt. Donald Bolt to circumstances censored in official records. What is known is that he was flying F-51D 44-84982 when he went down after being hit by Red antiaircraft fire and he bellied-in in an open field east of Pyongyang. A RESCAP was set up and under the direction of Mellow Control the CAP continued through the day, but the site was beyond the range of any available rescue helicopter and by the time darkness arrived Bolt was seen to be totally surrounded by the enemy. It was reported back to the Group later that Bolt's body had been recovered the following week after UN troops had taken the area and that he had been shot in the back of his head and buried in a shallow grave. This appears to be incorrect, as Bolt's name remains in the Korean War MIA listings.

Three days another 12th FBS pilot, 1st Lt. Ramon Davis was lost under similar censorship. He was flying F-51D 45-11606 and he remains MIA yet today. Likewise, on October 9 1st Lt. Alexander Padilla became MIA in 44-74107, and he too remains MIA today. Under standard USAF policy, all three officers were promoted to the rank of captain while missing.

On October 15 "Somewhere Able" flight of the 67th FBS was flying a close air support mission, being led by Lt. Philip Conserva and composed of Lt.'s Patterson, Billie Cothern and Owen Brewer. The Mustangs were working with Mosquito "Export 14" and they were attacking an enemy occupied hill south of Namchom-jon. As they pulled up from their first strafing run Cothern noticed that Brewer's Mustang was spraying coolant, and he suggested that Brewer had better prepare to bailout. The flight headed east for the point of the UN spearhead at Conserva's suggestion and Brewer started to climb, but by the time he reached 3,000 feet his Merlin engine seized. Brewer then unbuckled, unplugged, and bailed out over the Mustang's right wing in Tech Order drill. He was picked up by a patrol from the 7th Regiment, 1st Cavalry Division who were so happy with the support they were receiving from the USAF that they would not let him go, being "retained" for a few days as a "guest air force observer."

The 18th FBG had started using Wonsan, K-25, as a staging base on October 14. This permitted them to get to their target areas much faster than from K-9, since it was that much closer to the present MLR. On Sunday October 18 the 67th FBS flew its first "Three-in-one" mission that was led by Major Mullins. The F-51s provided a fighter escort for the paradrops at Sukchon and Sunchon where the 187th Airborne Regimental Combat Team was being dropped to cut off retreating North Korean troops. They then provided the escort home for General MacArthur's C-54 from which he had been observing the operation. They left the C-54 over the MLR, and then

dove down to provide close air support for ROK forces near Wonsan, and finished up the day after rearming and refueling by providing a fighter escort for B-26s of the 3rd Bomb Wing.

During the course of the ground support portion of the day's efforts (now) Captain Daniel Leake had to bail-out after being hit by numerous rounds of small arms fire. His Mustang was being flown at maximum speed when it was hit, and the fabric control surfaces were seen by his wingman to have been shot away. Unfortunately, Leake was at too low of an altitude when he cleared his Mustang and his parachute just had time to blossom as he hit the ground with a high impact. He was picked up by an air-rescue team, but he died from his injuries. See the poem in his honor at the end of this book.

On October 20 1st Lt. Claude "Spud" Taylor, 12th FBS was lost near Sukchon while the 18th FBG was in the process of softening the area prior to a parachute drop that was scheduled for that afternoon. Taylor bailed out successfully only to be killed while descending in his parachute by Red rifle fire.

Major Louis Sebille, commanding officer 67th FBS and the first USAF Medal of Honor recipient. (USAF)

94

The supply lines for Mustang spare parts started falling behind during this period, due in part to the rapid movement of the UN forces, and also because of logistical shortcomings within the USAF. This situation started to create a bit of bitterness among the pilots who felt that the Air Force should have been able to have "gotten their act together" by this time. The supply of external fuel tanks was at a critical level, and they were the main object of ridicule. These tanks were either being shipped from the United States or were being manufactured under contract in Japan. In either case they were not being delivered to the squadrons in a timely fashion. The pilots were ordered to retain their empty tanks after the fuel had been used, or explain in writing, under the threat of disciplinary action, why they had dropped them.

There was also a critical shortage of M-16 fuses that were used to ignite napalm tanks upon impact. Since there were not enough fuses to go around, the fuse holes on the tanks were plugged with wooden inserts, which allowed the napalm to seep out. Prior to dropping the tanks the pilots were to fire their machine guns so the flash from the tracers would ignite the napalm residue, and then the flaming tank could be dropped to explode on impact. This, obviously, provided quite a thrill to the pilots that was surrounded by the question of what would happen if the tanks hung up on the shackles?

Another critical item was replacement barrels for the Browning M-3 machine guns installed in the F-51s. Some sixty percent of the barrels received as spares proved to be faulty, usually because of deterioration in storage after World War II. It was a common occurrence to have a barrel rupture during firing, with resultant damage to the aircraft's wing. In one instance on October 25 when 1st Lt. Billie Cothern led a flight of four Mustangs against a truck convoy near Mupyong-ni, on the Hoichon-Kangye highway, the Mustangs destroyed sixty communist vehicles. This was in spite of the fact that each F-51 had only one remaining machine gun left after the strafing runs, as all the other five gun barrels on each aircraft had ruptured. The only battle damage incurred to each Mustang was 'host with one's petard," as all four aircraft had wing damage as a result of the barrels rupturing. The pilots took all of this with the atypical GI "grain of salt," considering that the supply and personnel sections were all "flat on their asses the whole time."

To continue: even though it appeared that the USAF was not supporting the war, at least the army appreciated the pilots efforts. On one mission towards the end of October 1st Lt. William Foster, 67th FBS, went in to attack a communist regiment near Chong-san. One by one

his machine guns quit as their barrels burst, but Foster continued to press his attacks until all six of his machine guns had quit. The result of his attacks saw what was left of the regiment throw their hands into the air and surrender to the UN battalion that was waiting to advance after Foster had completed his strafing.

Through the encouraging efforts of the UN ground forces it appeared that the North Koreans would soon be driven across the Yalu River into Manchuria and that the war would soon be over. On November 8 a 6002nd Fighter Bomber Wing refueling and rearming party had moved to Pyongyang East, K-24, and set up combat operations just six miles east of the North Korean capital. For the next two weeks the 18th FBG would average thirty-six combat sorties a day from K-24, while flying a dozen more from K-9.

On November 20-21 the 18th FBG moved to Pyongyang-East and the pilots were elated. A mission out of K-9 had averaged five hours in flying time, and was equal to one from K-24, yet from K-9 he could get in but one per day, while he could fly three or four out of K-24. One hundred missions was the criteria to go home, and the quicker the better!

The actual move to K-24 was a full scale logistical exercise that started from scratch. A tent city had to be built on what had previously been either a corn field or a rice paddy. Happily the ground already was frozen, as the North Koreans used human feces for fertilizer. But no matter as the word was out, it would be "Home for Christmas," or so it was said by "those in the know."

Combat operations increased two-fold, due to the proximity to the targets and the infusion of 2 Squadron,

Major Arnold "Moon" Mullins, Sebille's replacement as commanding officer 67th FBS, and also the highest scoring Mustang pilot in the Korean War shows how it was done when he shot down a Yak-9 on February 5, 1951. His Mustang, serial number unknown, was named "Moon's Folly." (USAF)

South African Air Force into the 18th FBG. The new SAAF pilots were initially assigned to the 67th FBS for indoctrination flights, being assigned to the number two and four positions within the four-ship formations until they gained experience in the Mustangs. This is not what they had expected, since most believed that they should have received more transition time into the Mustang since their most recent aircraft had been the jet propelled Vampire. But a pilot is a pilot, and a few had experience in Mustangs or Spitfires in World War II and the war had to go on. For the history of 2 Squadron see the separate chapter.

The fighter bomber pilots soon found that their best hunting could be found in the mountains of northeastern North Korea. This appears to be somewhat strange, as the focal point of the war was to the northwest, and the northeastern mountainous areas were in the backwaters of the war. Yet the communists were not quite as vigilant in these areas. They did have to fly carefully while flying through the canyons and passes, while looking for tanks and other vehicles, because of the knife-edged mountains that rose on either side of the roads that left little room for error. But these same mountains made it difficult for the North Koreans to hide their rolling stock, too. In the south they had hidden their vehicles in houses and haystacks, but in the mountains the best that they could do was to construct camouflaged sheds to blend in with the rocks, or to park in dry creek beds or along secondary roads. From the air these vehicles were easy to spot, and to counter the problems of the mountains, one element would go in low to do the attacking, while the other element remained high to do the navigating and to provide radio warning of rocky terrain or box canyons ahead.

Due to attrition the problem of having an insufficient number of available Mustangs was starting to become critical. In October the group had averaged forty-six F-51s on hand, but by mid November the number was down to forty-two, and these figures did not reflect those aircraft down for maintenance or out of commission awaiting spare parts, AOCP. Except for the initial assignment of Mustangs that had come off the Boxer, replacement aircraft were hard to come by. Each F-51 now averaged 750 hours since they had been zero-timed, and several had already exceeded the one thousand hour mark. On the average, each Mustang was being flown over seventy hours each month. As in October, eight 18th FBG Mustangs were lost in November, either through combat action or accidents.

In the air, November had opened with the snarl of inline engines engaged in aerial combat. For the first time

in several months enemy air opposition was encountered, and the results were far in favor of the Mustangs.

On November 1 a flight of four 67th FBS Mustangs led by Captain Herbert Andridge, Jr. was on an armed reconnaissance mission when they heard a B-26 pilot calling for some fighter cover. The second element of the Mustang flight, led by Captain Alma Flake, with Captain Robert Thresher as his wingman, was the first to see the enemy aircraft. "I saw it come down at the six o'clock on the tail of a B-26. I told the others to watch for Yak's in the area," said Flake.

"In the mean time, the '26' had shot down the Yak. I guess it was the turret gunner who got him. The Yak pulled up into what looked like a high speed stall, and then crashed," Flake related. (In spite of the conformation, credit for the kill was not given to the 730th Bomb Squadron crew by the USAF). "The Mustang pilots then went down to look at the wreckage, and while they were reconnoitering they heard a T-6 Mosquito calling for help. They dropped their ordnance, rockets and bombs and flew to his aid."

"He kept diving and climbing," said Thresher. "We could out run and out dive him, but he gave us hell on the turns and climbing. I finally got a short burst into him, and he started to smoke. Just about then I caught him peeling off to dive again. I got on his tail and followed him all the way to the deck giving him short bursts all the way. He stopped smoking and 'fanned' his prop, and I overshot him."

"I came in then," said Flake. "I pulled in on top of him and gave him a couple short bursts. He burst into flame, did a snap roll and piled into the ground." Flake and Thresher each received credit for their kills.

Major Mullins points out on the map where he destroyed three Yaks. (USAF)

That afternoon, at 1345 hours KST, another Mosquito found himself trapped by enemy fighters ten miles south of Sinanju. He started calling for help, which only served to get the momentary attention of some 67th FBS pilots that were involved in a fracas of their own. This Mustang flight was led by 1st Lt. William Foster, with 1st Lt.'s George Olsen, Charles Morehouse and Henry Reynolds as wingmen: "Olsen and I went down to drop our napalm," Foster said, "and then went up to cover while Morehouse and Reynolds went down. While we were up I heard Olsen yell 'They're on us!' I knew what he meant. There were two on my tail."

"I was pulling out of my attack on the deck," continued Morehouse. "When I saw a bogie come in at eleven o'clock. I saw blotches of red spurting from his wings as he fired at me. He flew about five feet under me and I got a good look."

"Upstairs Foster and Olsen fought it out with six jets. Foster got one in a turn, gave it a burst and saw it start smoking. The jet turned and ran off in a northwesterly direction."

"Olsen hit another in the wing during a head on attack, and Reynolds joined the dogfight while Morehouse covered the Mosquito down below."

"While Foster regrouped the Flight, Olsen was jumped again, but he dove away and the MiG's headed for home." The 67th FBS was credited with three "damaged" during this encounter, and they were able to provide the first gun camera film that showed a MiG-15 in action.

Before the day closed a reconnaissance RF-80 spotted fifteen Yak's in revetments at Sinuiju Airdrome. A squadron of F-80s was then called in to bomb and strafe the field, but they only destroyed one and damaged six for their efforts. The following day the remaining Yak's were back in the air. Captain Flake, with his wingman 1st Lt. Harold Ausman, joined with two pilots from the 12th FBS, 1st Lt. James Glessner and 2nd Lt. Paul Buttry, to take them on.

"Ausman was the first to spot the four Yak's, and one broke off to attack Glessner. Flake followed him down."

"He was twisting and turning, but I managed to stay on his tail, pumping bullets into him. Pieces of him kept flying off and finally his wing tore off and he crashed. I was flying right behind him all the time," said Ausman. "When Flake shot him up, I was catching a lot of debris." "You can say that he (Ausman) is the best damned wingman in the whole Far East Air Forces," continued Flake. "He stuck to me like glue during the whole thing."

In the meantime, Glessner had picked up a Yak that had come in behind Ausman. "I finally caught him near

the ground. I climbed within 100 feet of his tail and let him have it. Debris was flying off of him. He peeled off and spun down a couple of times, then he took off for the border," said Glessner.

"He was doing all sorts of stunts," said Buttry. "All I could think of was it was a hell of a time for aerobatics."

"I went after him again," continued Glessner. "Before I could get at him, he did a wingover and bailed out. I saw his plane crash. Buttry was on my wing for protection all that time." Flake and Glessner were each credited with a kill during this encounter.

On November 6 the Yak's were back once again. Captain Howard Price was leading a flight of three 67th FBS Mustangs on a recce mission just west of Sinuiju when they spotted six Yak's coming at them from across the Yalu River.

"It was just 9:02 am when 'Olie' (1st Lt. George Olsen) called bogies at two o'clock. I made an identification pass

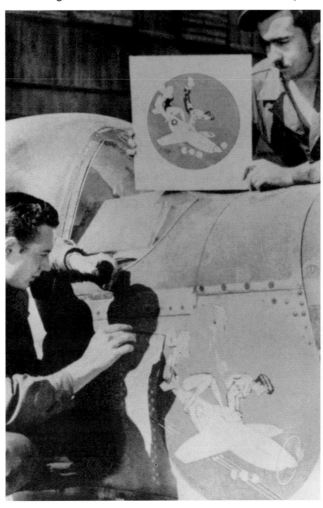

When the 18th FBG was at K-9, "Dogpatch," the noted cartoonist Al Capp designed an insignia for them. However it did not show up on many of their aircraft, as there just wasn't enough time to paint it on them. (USAF)

Yak's was given credit for one and one-half kills, while Reynolds, who had not made a claim, was given credit for one-half kill).

Of interest is the pilots observations on the enemies tactics, which were discussed during mission debriefings. One particularly noted was the MiG's tactic of "Yo-yoing," ie: making rapid vertical climbs and reversals when attacking or breaking away. The Yak pilots, in contrast, would usually attempt to turn inside of the F-51s, to try and take advantage of their greater maneuverability. When they found that this technique would not work, they would then start a series of three or four snap-rolls, and then dive away in a split-ess. The Mustang pilots felt that this sort of evasive action was detrimental to the enemy pilot, for it appeared to only disorientate him, and all the Mustang pilot had to do to shoot him down was to stay behind him and fire when he stopped playing games.

By the end of the first week of November six Yak's had been officially confirmed as shot down by FEAF F-51s. Considering that no enemy air opposition had been observed during October, it appeared that the dry spell was over, and almost all of the FEAF fighter pilots were looking forward to getting a piece of the aerial combat action.

On November 7 they got their chance, in spades. On this day there occurred five separate engagements between MiG-15s and F-51s. The 12th FBS had the greatest chance to score among the 18th FBG squadrons. A flight of four Mustangs was patrolling along the Yalu River when its flight leader, Major Kendall Carlson spotted four MiG's taking off from Antung, Manchuria. The MiG's didn't waste any time in forming up or to build up their airspeed,

Major Robert "Bob" Dow, commanding officer 12th FBS November 1950. (Biteman)

and called out to the others. "They're Yak's, go get them," stated Price.

"We turned," said Price, "and caught them in the middle of a turn. I went after one, but he snapped rolled and dived. I let him go and picked another. He did the same thing, but I followed him down. When I hit him, he started smoking and then pieces flew off him and he bailed out."

1st Lt. Harry Reynolds, in the meantime, had one of the Yak's in a kill position. "I climbed right on his tail and then my guns jammed. I was so mad, I shot my rockets at him. They missed and went under him."

"I saw him peel off and dive when the rockets went by," continued Price. "He dove right into my sights. I followed him down and when he broke to climb again, I let him have it. I caught him in the coolant and he started burning and crashed. Olie was on my wing throughout the whole thing. The other Yak's had disappeared, so we came home." (In this case, Price, who knocked down two

67th FBS Mustangs in the arming pits prior to another mission. The 5" HVAR's in the foreground were one of the most effective weapons of the war. 44-74037 was lost on New Years Day 1952. (USAF via Greenhalgh)

Lt. James Glessner's Mustang after he got his Yak kill on November 2, 1950. Glessner was declared as killed in action on December 31, 1953. His Mustang, 45-11736, was named "My Ass is Dragon" and it was lost on April 13, 1952 with another pilot. (Dave Crooks via Olmsted)

they simply crossed the Yalu and waded into the Mustangs. They struck head on in their first firing pass, but failed to hit any of the F-51s. They then pulled up to start a yo-yo, and when they came back down Carlson and his wingman, Lt. Lee Gomes, were waiting for them to bottom out. Carlson got several hits with a cluster of .50 caliber fire along the side of a MiG's fuselage at its wingroot, and then had to break off the attack to evade another MiG that was swinging in to attack him. It zipped past the Mustangs and crossed back over the Yalu with its two remaining wingmen without a further exchange of gun or cannon fire. The wreckage of the MiG that Carlson had hit was seen to be burning on the ground, but since none of the F-51 pilots had seen the actual MiG crash Carlson's claim was not upheld by the USAF. (A short blurb in "Naval Aviation News" in November 1952 does credit Carlson for this kill.)

(There is also some bitterness within the Mustang crowd regarding this incident, for it was felt that Carlson was deliberately "shafted" by FEAF, as he was not what is today considered to be a "politically correct" individual, concentrating his efforts on combat flying instead of USAF politics).

After this day's encounters all of the Mustang pilots returned home realizing that they were out of their element when it came to aerial combat, even though they had scored three damaged and one probable against none of their own being damaged. It had been to their advantage that the MiG pilots were poor shots, often commencing firing while still out of range, and then ceasing to fire to soon, which was unexplainable.

Three "good" things did come out of these encounters, though. The 18th FBG was released from flying

fighter escort missions for B-29s along the Yalu River where their value was dubious at best. They were also taken off combat air patrols along the Yalu, where they felt like they were only serving as decoys in the first place. And, for a two week period they were authorized a "Hot Pursuit" for "two or three minutes" across the Yalu River into Manchuria if they did have a chance to chase down an enemy aircraft. But due to political considerations, this order was rescinded before any of the Mustang pilots actually had an opportunity to take advantage of this pursuit while it was authorized.

On November 11 a four-ship strike of 67th FBS F-51s took off from K-24. The flight leader, 1st Lt. Billie Cothern took the formation to the target area where they started strafing at 1400 KST. At 1410 the Number Four Mustang, flown by Captain Solom, advised Cothern that his element leader, 1st Lt. Bernard Pearson, had been hit by small arms fire. Nevertheless, Pearson commenced another strafing run on the top of a North Korean held ridge. His Mustang was seen to hit the top of the ridge and simply disappear. He was KIA.

The 67th FBS lost another pilot through one of the other factors of war that faced fighter-bomber pilots. Captain Edward Mason was assigned duty as a forward air controller and the unit that he was attached to was overrun during a firefight. Mason although wounded, managed to escape and was evacuated to Japan for treatment.

The 67th FBS lost a second Mustang just before Thanksgiving Day when 1st Lt. Edwin Henley was hit by small arms fire while strafing near Anju. He bellied in his F-51 in a dry river bed, and the rest of his flight provided

The horizontal stabilizer of Captain Al Wagnor's Mustang after a raid on Pyongyang on August 14, 1951. Anti-aircraft fire could be hard on Mustangs. (USAF)

a RESCAP for him until a helicopter was able to effect his rescue.

The only reported 12th FBS loss for the month occurred on November 22 when 1st Lt. Frederick Hudson, III, was shot down by ground fire over Sinuiju. He had been the squadron's supply officer when he was killed. Two other Mustangs were written off during the month in landing incidents at K-24. Both of these were from the 67th FBS and the cause was laid upon the poor condition of the 4,500 foot runway, which varied between muddy and dusty, depending upon precipitation. Captain Frederick Blesse was trying to land after a combat sortie during one of the extremely dusty periods when cross winds reduced visibility to where he could not see a truck that was trying to pull another disabled Mustang off the runway. Blesse was uninjured, but both the truck and the two F-51s were destroyed. Apparently the first Mustang was that which 1st Lt. Patrick O'Connell had attempted to fly, only he had hit a rough spot on the PSP runway and jarred loose one of his napalm tanks. He lost control of the imbalanced aircraft and it cart wheeled, but he was uninjured.

Higher wisdom within FEAF decided that squadron commanders should now be of a higher rank than that of a major. Correspondingly, Major Mullins was demoted to 67th FBS executive officer, and he was replaced by Lt. Colonel William May. All other positions were also dropped down a slot, with Captain "Charlie" McGee being demoted to operations officer, and many flight leaders being demoted to element leaders. In one administrative order, FEAF had done more damage to the squadron's morale than the attacks by the MiG-15s had, or so it was felt by members of the squadron.

Proof positive with smoke and flames, a gun camera frame of Lt. Colonel R.H. Saltsman's probable kill against a heavily armored Il-10 on June 20, 1951. (USAF)

Mustang maintenance May 1951. Cpl. Weldon Wilson is in the cockpit while S/Sgt. Gordon McRee inspects the F-51's landing gear. It was a Code M loss on June 2, 1951. (USAF)

On November 24 the parent 6002nd Fighter Bomber Wing was redesignated as the 18th Fighter Bomber Wing. This too came as a result of FEAF's attempts toward numerical consolidation, for internal logistical purposes. In effect it had no bearing upon combat operations and Colonel Ira Wintermute remained as Wing Commander. (With this action, the original 18th FBW at Clark Air Base was replaced in designation by the 6200th Air Base Wing).

At this time it also became necessary to commence the evacuation of K-24 because of the potential of it's being overrun by the intervention of the communist Chinese forces. The 18th FBW, including the advance section of 2 Squadron, SAAF, withdrew to K-13 at Suwon, with the remainder of the Group and squadrons following and being in place at K-13 by December 3. The move had been carried off without a hitch, due to preplanning and the staging of C-119s, which took care of transporting ground personnel and equipment. During the move there had been no let up in combat operations. In fact, they increased from the November 30 Wing total of fifty-five sorties to seventy-five sorties on December 1.

Suwon, itself, was described as a "mess." The runway was 5,500 feet by 150 feet, ample enough for a loaded Mustang to operate safely. But it had been laid over a rice paddy with PSP and mud and dust constantly seeped up through the perforations while it became undermined. The runway had to be torn up and underlaid with rice bags and then relayed to create a reasonably smooth surface. The rattling and undulating of the PSP was particularly disconcerting to the pilots and those who had to work alongside of the runway. The runway was also lighted along one side, which, supposedly, made K-13 an all-weather airstrip. Fuel drums were lighted at night to show both ends of the runway and its orientation. The one major advantage to K-13 came with the installation of a Low Frequency non-directional Homer for navigation, which took a lot of sweat out of trying to find the airfield after dark or in low visibility.

The living areas were also a mess. They were also set up on a soggy rice paddy where the soil was either frozen or mud. The supplied tents were not insulated for winter and only had M-41 stoves for heating. These stoves thawed the ground underneath, and the only way to keep from living in a quagmire was to make a "midnight requisition" on the rice bag supply for runway repairs to floor the tents. There was no mess hall, so food had to be eaten from any handy shelf, jeep hood or oil drum. It took two weeks to set up a proper mess hall, and by then it was time for the 18th FBW to evacuate to the south once again as a result of the communist onslaught.

Flying and combat conditions became a confusing and chaotic situation, much like the previous summer during the Pusan Perimeter period. Due to the pressure brought on by the Red's, flight commanders often found themselves diverted from their briefed missions in order to recce areas where FEAF needed more information on the ground situation. This action took the Mustangs that had been intended to provide ground support for the UN troops away from their intended missions, which did not set well with the ground forces who thought that air support should be virtually instantaneous upon demand.

The pilots themselves were not happy with these continual revisions to their missions, either, for several reasons. There had always been difficulty in getting their observations through to the Control Centers, because of poor radio coverage and radio frequency congestion. They were expected to use grid type maps over North Korea for their reporting, but without suitable navigational aids for cross-checking their positions, it was difficult for them to positively ascertain where they were at in respect to the grid coordinates. In short, nobody knew exactly what was going on where except for the communists.

The 18th FBW withdrew to Chinhae, K-10, on December 22 and this would become their permanent home for the remainder of their Mustang era. They would, however, continue to use K-13 as a staging base for the duration. At this time Chinhae was described as "restorable" with a few quonset huts that at least got the men out of the wind and mud. Permanent facilities were being constructed as quickly as possible, with mess halls, clubs, and a Post Exchange being set up. Those men who had to remain at K-13 considered their counterparts at K-10 as being billeted "on the Riviera."

The Wing's Mustangs were still encountering MiGs as the year closed, but the pilots were not the least bit proud when it came to calling down their jet fighter escorts for help when they were bounced by the MiGs. In fact, many of the Mustang pilots were beginning to feel that they were being sent out as decoys to sucker in the MiGs so that the newly arrived USAF jet jockeys could get a crack at them. (This would be the 4th Fighter Interceptor Wing with F-86s and the 27th Fighter Escort Wing with F-84s). In reality, they were not to far off in their perceptions, for a high percentage of their December missions were RESCAP's for pilots and crews that were shot down in an area that would become known as MiG Alley. The F-51 was the only available USAF fighter that had the range to go up to northwestern North Korea and CAP an area for any length of time at low altitude to assist in effecting a rescue, which made them an easy target for MiG's zipping back and forth across the Yalu River.

The most notable day in December for the 67th FBS was on December 28 when Major Charles McGee led a flight of four Mustangs on a close support mission near the H'wachon Reservoir. The communist troops had closed to within fifty yards of the UN lines when McGee's flight swept in and napalmed their positions. Over 150 enemy troops surrendered after the Mustangs finished their attacks, and the bodies of those killed by the napalm and the strafing were to numerous to count.

Later that afternoon Captain Norman Soles and 1st Lt. Edwin Henley accomplished a similar feat, only with two Mustangs instead of four. Their attacks resulted in a mass surrender of many Reds. On the first reading, this

A flight of 18th FBG Mustangs prepare for takeoff from Hoengsong, K-46, in July 1951. The napalm tanks in the foreground already have their igniters installed while awaiting hanging on the 'Stangs for their next mission. Note the hulk of a F-51 laying on its side and another Mustang with a bent prop, hardly an inspiring sight for a departing pilot. (USAF via Greenhalgh)

The 12th FBS finally had their own maintenance hangar at Chinhae in 1951. There was always plenty of work to be done on the Mustang, the Red's saw to that! (Olmsted)

may not seem to be so notable, but there was a critical factor that makes the situation astounding. Due to the winter weather, snow and ice would pack on the Mustang's bomb racks, which caused the napalm tanks to freeze to the shackles. The only way to loosen them was to first make a strafing attack, where upon the vibration of the machine guns and the high "G's pulled on the passes' recovery would break the ice loose so that the tanks could be dropped on the succeeding attack. These tactics, obviously, made the F-51s quite vulnerable to communist antiaircraft fire, since their maneuverability was so reduced by the drag and weight of the tanks, themselves. No pilot relished the thought of having a tank of napalm explode under his wing if hit by enemy gunfire, particularly if it was stuck to its rack.

In spite of the deplorable December flying conditions, the 12th FBS only lost one Mustang in December, and this occurred during a landing incident where the pilot was uninjured. The 67th FBS lost Captain William Hydorn when communist small arms fire holed his Mustang's cooling system and forced him to make a belly landing near Sariwon. He received head injuries from striking the gunsight, but he was rescued and evacuated to Japan for treatment. In another incident 1st Lt. Morehouse had been cleared for takeoff by the control tower at K-13, and just as his F-51 broke ground he hit a C-47 that was taxiing across the runway. Morehouse jettisoned his external ordnance in a safe area and returned for a safe landing. (With a few choice words to the tower operator).

On December 16 Captain Joseph Lane was strafing a target on the outskirts of Pyongyang when his target blew up in his face. The Mustang was riddled with shrapnel and had gaping holes in both wings and its coolant lines were damaged. Lane managed to nurse his F-51

all the way back to K-13 for a successful emergency landing, which was a real rarity considering the Mustang's vulnerability to cooling system damage.

Everything considered the 18th FBW closed out 1950 rather well, for the loss rate of pilots was way down from the first months of the war and their accident rate was only .53% per 100,000 flying hours. (The average in the United states at this time was .11% for F-51 operations).

Eight new pilots were transferred into the 18th FBW in December, and all eight of these men were only experienced in jet aircraft. The Wing set up a training program for these men, only to discover that it was taking an inordinate length of time to get them cross-trained into the F-51. This was due, in part, to the lack of Mustangs available for training, for it meant that one or more F-51 had to be removed from combat operations to accomplish the task. Colonel Wintermute decided that it would be more advantageous to the war effort to have these pilots transferred to another unit where their talent could be more readily utilized, so he went to FEAF for permission to make trades for Mustang pilots. The jet pilots were transferred elsewhere, but replacements were not forthcoming. This faux pas was just another determent to morale, for seven F-51 pilots had just completed their 100 mission requirement and six more had between eighty and one hundred missions, and their was no relief in sight for them.

The 18th FBW did gain eight F-51s from the 8th Fighter Bomber Group when they were withdrawn to Ja-

A winter takeoff from K-46 with swirling snow and ice crystals. Korean winters were known for their brutally cold temperatures. (Barasky via Thompson)

pan in December, but these aircraft were considered to be too battered to be safe for more combat missions. The wear and tear from flying out of K-13 and K-24 had jarred just about everything loose on the aircraft. Yet, even with these additional aircraft the 18th FBW had only thirty-eight Mustangs available between their two USAF squadrons. It was hoped that both replacement aircraft and necessary tools would soon be forthcoming so that a major overhaul could be accomplished at K-10 on each aircraft, as the 18th FBW was attempting to establish their own maintenance depot there.

Flying in and out of K-10 itself was not without its own hazards. This was particularly true when mission planning called for a predawn takeoff. There were not nearly enough obstruction lights available to mark all of the obstructions surrounding the airstrip. On one end of the runway was Chinhae-man (Bay), and on the other a line of mountains which rose to a height of two thousand feet, which eventually circled the airstrip on three sides within a three mile radius. Inside this radius, water was on one side of the runway, and a steel hangar and other buildings were within fifty feet on the other side. The runway, itself, was constructed of sod and dirt fill and it was far too narrow. The margin for pilot error was zero.

The 18th FBW finally received an Executive Officer on December 18 when Lt. Colonel Eugene Wilson was transferred to K-10 from Clark Air Base. This action permitted Lt. Colonel Wintermute to start flying missions on a regular basis, which at least served to enhance his morale by pushing up his mission totals.

As of January 1, 1951 the Wing had flown 8,053 combat sorties and amassed over 20,000 flying hours, which was a feather in Wintermute's cap. Wintermute was promoted to full Colonel on January 19. Lt. Colonel Wilson was now delegated to establishing a workable rotation policy for the men of the Wing since they were not receiving any substantial support from FEAF on the topic. It was hoped that with Wintermute's rank and the Wing's combat record, maybe enough clout existed to get at least some of the men headed home from Korea.

Wilson decided that the men of the original Dallas Project should have first priority, and that they would be allowed to leave in four increments, so as to not reduce the Wing's effectiveness. Replacements would come from either the 44th FBS at Clark Air Base or from the 6200th Air Base Wing, also at Clark. By going directly through the parent 13th Air Force instead of the FEAF controlled 5th Air Force, to which they were only "attached," maybe they could "luck out."

There is a noted contradiction in this situation. In November 1950 several of the Dallas Project pilots had been permitted to return to Clark Air Base, regardless of the number of missions that they had flown. In May 1951 these same pilots were ordered back to Korea to complete a requisite tour of one hundred combat missions. At the same time there were several known F-51 pilots in Japan who were able to avoid being assigned to combat flying altogether. This created an extreme bitterness among the effected pilots, particularly when they saw several of their colleagues shot down and killed.

Once again, due to the press of the communist forces K-13 had to be given up as a staging base on January 4. Seoul had to be evacuated once again and conditions along the MLR were both critical and confused. The UN ground forces withdrew to the south side of the Han River, but it soon appeared that they would not be able to hold onto these positions. The 18th FBW and the 35th Fighter Interceptor Group were alerted for a possible withdrawal to Japan because of the onslaught and the possible failure of Operation Wolfhound, which was intended to counteract the communist drive to the south.

All non essential 18th FBW personnel were airlifted to Ozuki Air Base, Japan (Under British control.) on January 10, while the remainder of the 18th FBW was expected to be able to be withdrawn with only a twenty-four hour notice. Fortunately, the ground forces managed to stop the Red offensive and the remainder of the 18th FBWs evacuation was not necessary.

Most of the 18th FBW missions flown in January were armed reconnaissance, with the focal point being the

Although this appears to be a winter scene, it is not. A ground collision could be as bad as a mid-air. Lt. Brook's Mustang although covered with fire suppressing foam, is still burning while fire rescue troops attempt to extract him from the cockpit. They did rescue him, but the F-51 was consumed by fire. Note the broken wing just outboard of the napalm tank. (Kepthorn via Davis)

roads between Seoul and Sinanju. The remainder of the missions were close air support, which the pilots preferred since they were of a short duration, and if they were hit, they stood a better chance of making it back to friendly territory. They also flew some "post-holing" strikes against roads and enemy airfields.

These post-holing missions were dive bombing strikes where the Mustangs carried 500 pound GP's that were fitted with M-124 long-delay fuses. One to one hundred-forty four hours with anti-removal devices. Although it was evident that the enemy airstrips were in use, no enemy aircraft were to be seen on the airfields. It was believed that the communists were keeping them hidden in underground shelters, but the Mustang pilots were reluctant to go down for a closer look for the airfields were surrounded by antiaircraft guns. Nevertheless, the runways were postholed in an attempt to keep them non-operational.

The first Wing combat loss of the new year occurred on January 18 while attacking one of these airstrips. Captain Joseph Powers, 67th FBS, was hit by several rounds of antiaircraft fire as he pulled up from a dive bombing run. Realizing that he could not make it to safety, Powers settled for a controlled crash landing in North Korea. He was declared KIA in December.

"New" Mustangs finally started to be supplied to the Wing in late January. These were actually brand new aircraft that had been in storage at Kelly AFB, Texas since they had been delivered to the Air Force at the end of World War II. But it had taken six months to refurbish them from open air storage deterioration and get them shipped to Korea. The "war weary" F-51s were then sent to Kisarazu Air Base, Japan for major overhaul by FEAMCOM. It was hoped that the new Mustangs would not have all the problems that the older ones had suffered from, but the fouling of the LE-45 spark plugs continued, just as they had with the other Mustang units. The problem was traced to the high amounts of silicon in the prevalent dust in Korea. This dust, under the heat and compression in the Merlin engines when the plugs sparked built up deposits which soon closed the plugs' electrode gaps. The only way to resolve the problem was to keep a close watch on the carburetor air filters and change them as often as necessary. Kotex was found to be the most expedient filter.

"Operation Thunderbolt," a combined air-ground maneuver, started on January 25. This effort was supported by 18th FBW Mustangs which flew armed reconnaissance and interdiction missions. It began as a "reconnaissance in force," but gradually reduced itself to a limited objective counter-offensive. Thunderbolt did result in the UN ground forces being able to retake K-13 and Suwon proper on January 26, which permitted a new Detachment 1 from the 18th FBW to move from K-10 to K-13 in order to support elements of the Combat Cargo Command, who in turn went into action in supporting Operation Roundup, which began on February 5. Roundup was initiated with objectives similar to Thunderbolt, only its focus was on the central front in support of the U.S. X and ROK III Corps.

To attempt to deter the communists ability to camouflage anything and everything wherever they wanted to without the fear of detection, the 18th FBW now started an operation similar to the 45th Tactical Reconnaissance Squadron's "Circle Ten" program. Each squadron, and each flight within was given a specific area of communist controlled Korea to reconnoiter on a daily basis. This permitted the pilots to become intimately familiar with the typography in their assigned areas and helped them to spot any thing extraordinary in the way of changes. Mustang flights operated with the low element between one hundred and three hundred feet above the ground, while the second element flew between five hundred and a thousand feet, accomplishing the navigating and watching for antiaircraft emplacements. The Mustangs were flown under "cruise control" power settings, which reduced the wear and tear on the engines and also extended their loiter time during the recce.

It was during this period that the 18th FBW earned the sobriquet of "Truckbusters." For this was a role where they truly excelled. The 12th FBS destroyed over five hundred vehicles in February, alone. In fact, in one day they destroyed one hundred-eight. To do this it meant

Chinhae Air Base was in a constant state of activity for Mustang missions over Korea. 44-64004 in the second row was lost on October 6, 1951 with 1st Lt. Richard Olcott, 39th FIS. (USAF via Greenhalgh)

A flight line shot of 12th and 67th FBS Mustangs in 1952. 44-12943 was "Red Raider" & "Was That Too Fast?" It was written off in an accident in November 1953. (via Davis)

getting down in the trenches with their aircraft to find and nail their targets, which also resulted in a lot of casualties. During February the 12th FBS lost five Mustangs and had six others damaged. The 67th FBS lost two to enemy action, and had one more wrecked on takeoff. Details on these losses are sketchy for the squadron historians gave low priority in going into detail on them when writing their reports at the end of the month.

On February 2 the 18th FBW lost Lt. Colonel Milton Gloesner from their Headquarters Squadron. The exact cause has been censored from the official records, but a CAP set up over his downed Mustang the following day saw many footprints around the crashed aircraft in the snow and no sign of a body. He remains MIA yet today. On the same date Captain E.J. Deschamps, 67th FBS, went down in enemy territory and initially was declared MIA, but since has been declared as KIA. This established a "to date" figure for the 18th FBW of fourteen pilots MIA and six more known to have been killed. The 12th FBS did have it a little better in spite of loosing more aircraft. Their only reported casualty was Lt. Burton Cameron who was injured in a crash landing and had to be evacuated to Japan to recuperate.

On February 5 the twenty-seven year old Major Mullins became the highest scoring Mustang pilot during the Korean Conflict when he got his fourth kill. He now was tied with Colonel William Samways for the highest

total number of kills scored so far by FEAF pilots, and Samways obtained all of his kills while flying F-80s. Mullins was also the only FEAF pilot to obtain a kill during February. As it would turn out, Mullins and Samways records would stand for their respective types of aircraft.

Mullins was leading a flight of three Mustangs against ground targets near Sunan, northwest of Pyongyang, where they destroyed two locomotives and ten trucks. "I was pulling up from a strafing pass," Mullins related, "when I spotted a Yak directly above me. I let loose with a few bursts from my .50 caliber machine guns and scored direct hits in the cockpit and fuselage. The pilot must have been dead because he made a sloppy turn and just kept going. When he crashed it looked like two napalm bombs were exploding."

February 9 was a miserable day with rain, low clouds and extremely poor visibility. Four 18th FBW Mustangs were dispatched regardless, just to let the communists know that they hadn't been forgotten. The mission became disorientated over North Korea, but were finally able to obtain a DF steer towards home in increasing darkness. As the F-51s headed south their mission leader decided that the weather was just too bad for them to make it to K-10, so they headed for K-7, Kwanju for an emergency landing. The leader landed safely, but the Number Two pilot nosed his Mustang over in the mud at the end of the runway. Upon seeing this, the Number

Three pilot attempted a go-around, only to loose control and crash into a house, totally destroying the house and aircraft, but only incurring minor injuries to himself. The Number Four pilot tried to land next, but he slid into an embankment and also "washed out" his Mustang. The one good remaining Mustang was flown out the next day, while a repair crew replaced the propeller on the second F-51, and salvaged as much of the third as they could, and trucked the remains of the fourth back to K-10.

The 18th FBW had a change of command on February 20 when Lt. Colonel Homer Cox replaced Colonel Wintermute. Cox had previously been the Executive Office of the 6200nd Air Base Wing. Wintermute, in turn, rotated back to Clark Air Base to be assigned to Headquarters 13th Air Force. This rotation was a part of Operation Fort Worth, which Lt. Colonel Wilson had set up to allow the Dallas Project people to leave Korea. The first of the pilots that were permitted to leave under Project Ft. Worth were those who had completed their normal overseas tour prior to September 1, 1950 and had been forced to remain in the Far East because of the exigency of the war. The second batch left three days later, on February 23, and the third and fourth batches were scheduled for March 3 and 4. These transfers saw a total of 70% of the enlisted men from the Dallas Project leave, and it became "analogous to a blood transfusion" to the morale of everyone.

In contrast to Operation Fort Worth came a revision in FEAF's policy of assigning pilots to forward air controller duties. The original policy had called for a three week assignment as a FAC, but the revision extended the tour with the ground forces to sixty days. On paper the change appeared feasible as far as the utilization of the pilots was concerned, for the 18th FBW had only to supply five pilots for FAC duty instead of seven, which gave them two more pilots available for combat missions. Yet for the selected pilots it meant that their tour in Korea would be for at least for six months, instead of the anticipated three and one half. In addition, their proficiency in the F-51 would be lost, which tended to make the pilots apprehensive about returning to combat after such an extended layoff from flying. Since the average pilot selected for FAC assignment had somewhere around twenty-four missions already under his belt at the time of selection, it was felt that the policy should have been changed to select pilots who had at least sixty missions, and then give them credit for the remainder of their combat missions as a result of their FAC tour and then send them home instead of forcing them back into a cockpit.

More and more Mustangs were having mechanical problems as a result of the poor conditions at K-10, as they were plagued with blowing tires on the sharp-edged PSP. One received major damage, while another was consumed by fire as a result of blown tires. An attempt was made to obtain ten-ply tires for the Mustangs after these incidents, but few were available and they were only a stop gap remedy at best. Landing gear struts were starting to show fatigue cracks, which required a lengthy time in tear-down inspections and overhauls. Numerous fatigue cracks were also appearing in the Mustangs aluminum skins, particularly around the flap hinges.

"Little beast II" from the 12th FBS is being waved off by a South African flagman. These pilots served as a safety factor, as they could see down the runway far better than a pilot could over the nose of his Mustang. 44-84602 was a Code M loss on September 5, 1952. (USAF via Ethell)

Lt. Fred Thomas, a recalled ANG pilot from the 167th Fighter Squadron, West Virginia ANG, inspects the battle damage to his Mustang. His F-51 took a single round of a small caliber through its oil header tank, which caused all of his engine's oil to be lost, and he barely made it home. After returning to the States, Thomas rejoined the 167th FS and rose to the rank of colonel, and as the 167th was the last ANG Mustang squadron, he also was one of the last ANG F-51 pilots. (Thomas)

March 1951 was another physically active month, for it marked the seventh move for the Wing's operational squadrons, abet just a TDY to a base just a short distance away from Chinhae. On March 23 the squadrons were transported by truck and air to K-1, Pusan-West Airdrome, so that the runways at K-10 could be resurfaced.

In an incident unrelated to the runway's condition at K-10, one pilot was lost on March 18. 1st Lt. Francis Holcomb was taking off on a mission and when he reached the half way point down the runway his Mustang started emitting black and white smoke. Holcomb salvoed his napalm tanks on the runway and horsed the F-51 into the air, but it only climbed to ninety feet before it rolled inverted and dove into the bay a quarter mile offshore.

Combat missions were also remained full of perils. On March 1 Lt. Colonel Robert May, commanding officer 67th FBS, was hit by intense ground fire over North Korea. When his cockpit burst into flames May was forced to bailout. He was rescued by a helicopter dispatched from the U.S. heavy cruiser St. Paul. On March 8 Captain Lucian Schuler, 67th FBS, was also hit by ground fire while strafing enemy troops near Kaesong. Schuler headed for K-13 with his Mustang's engine getting hotter and hotter. He pulled the emergency release on the radiator shutter and pumped the engine primer furiously, to pump raw fuel into the engine, which detonated at a lower temperature and consequently helped the Merlin run a little cooler. These efforts were successful and Schuler made it back to K-13 for a belly landing. The next day 1st

Lt. Gerald Heagney, 67th FBS, wasn't so fortunate. Heagney crashed into a hillside in North Korea after being raked from prop to rudder by a burst of enemy groundfire. On March 20 Captain James Kuntz, also from the 67th FBS, had to bailout after being hit by groundfire over Kaesong. Kuntz headed south and managed to keep his Mustang in the air long enough to reach Suwon to effect a successful bailout.

Two 12th FBS pilots were also lost during March. 1st Lt.'s James Heath and Willis Brown. Both of their Mustangs went down in enemy territory to undetermined causes: Brown on the 15th and Heath on the 31st. Both pilots were carried as MIA for the duration and later declared as KIA.

In general, most of the missions being flown at this time were those of interdiction. The 12th FBS claimed 611 vehicles destroyed and seventy-eight more damaged. In an attempt to destroy more vehicles and posthole more roads the ordnance was changed from napalm to 500 pound General Purpose bombs once again. This change also tended to make the pilots feel more comfortable as they required a change in tactics that actually reduced their vulnerability to enemy fire. However, the dependability of the ordnance was a major irritant. The 18th FBW's records for March show that 34% of their machine guns malfunctioned, either because of faulty barrels or bad primers in the .50 caliber rounds. Of the 7,262 5" HVAR's attempted to be fired, 50% failed either because of electrical problems or that they exploded on their launching posts! Four hundred fifty-eight 500 pound GP's were dropped with a thirty to sixty percent failure to deto-

The personal Mustang of Colonel William Clark, commanding officer 18th FBW, March 7, 1952 - January 1, 1953. His F-51 bore fuselage bands of the 67th FBS (Red),12th FBS, (Yellow) and 2 Squadron SAAF (Red, white & blue: Which became orange during their F-86 era). On the left side of its fuselage it carried all three squadron insignias, while on the right it bore the 18th FBW insignia. (David Bickel via Thompson/Davis)

nate, either due to faulty M-16A1 nose or M-113 tail fuses. In all, twenty-nine F-51s suffered battle damage and fourteen more were lost with at least five of these as a direct result of enemy action.

April 1951 opened on much of the same note, as the Wing was frustrated by further ordnance failures during heavy exposure to combat. The 12th FBS had twenty-five Mustangs assigned went the month began and they finished with twenty-one. But to arrive at this total they had received six additional Mustangs as replacements, and had reported nine Mustangs lost to combat related incidents. They also had twenty-four Mustangs receive battle damage, ie: every surviving F-51 had been hit by enemy fire!

From the 18th FBW, itself, eight aircraft were reported lost as a result of enemy action and seventeen more lost to other causes. Of the latter, not all were write-off's, as several had been returned to FEAMCOM for maintenance while others were non-operational to AOCP.

There is no concrete explanation for all of these combat losses, for although the 12th FBS records show nine F-51s as combat losses, they only indicate five of these as actually being shot down. Known is that Captain S. G. Wilkerson was shot down behind enemy lines and that he spent two hours awaiting a rescue by helicopter. Captain George Grey was lost on April 4. Captain Chauncy Bennett, (Who was lost on his 100th mission.); Captain Graham Smith, and 1st. Lt. Harry Middleton are all listed as MIA on April 30.

The 67th FBS lost 1st Lt. Jack Wright on April 2 to an unidentified cause. Major Herbert Anderidge on April 10, also to an unidentified cause, and 1st Lt. William Haskett when he bailed out over enemy territory on April 14 and was believed to have been taken prisoner. His name, rank and serial number was discovered written on a wall in a communist bunker on April 29 by another POW, and Haskett remains a MIA.

April was also the month when the Air Rescue Service endeared themselves to the 67th FBS. for three out of four additional pilots that had been downed by enemy fire were plucked from communist hands through the efforts of ARS helicopter crews. On April 19 1st Lt. Robert Pasqualicchio had the radiator shot off his Mustang while on a strafing run. He made it back to just north of the Han River just before his Merlin seized and he had to effect a belly landing. He was picked up by a chopper dispatched from Seoul. On April 20 Captain James Corn was flying a CAS mission along the MLR when his controls were shot away by ground fire. Corn had little choice but to bailout at a high air speed and at a critically low altitude. He was

"Jeannie" of the 67th FBS in the process of having her tail wheel permanently locked down. She was lost on August 2, 1952. (USAF via Ethell)

severely injured when he hit the Mustang's tail in the bailout attempt, and then his parachute carried him down into "no man's land." But the helicopter crew beat out the communists that were trying to get to him first. They usually dispatched fighter-bomber pilots with a blast from a burp gun.

Three days later Captain Carl Allen was flying a CAP over the Imjin River where the Mustangs were trying to keep the Red's from using the water-way. Allen's F-51 was hit in an oil line and he headed south for Suwon, but he had to belly land north of Seoul when the Merlin engine seized. He also was picked up by an ARS chopper out of Seoul.

A goodly portion of all this activity and the corresponding losses stemmed from the efforts involved with Operation Rugged which had commenced on April 3. Rugged was designed not only to kill the enemy but to place friendly forces in a position to be able to take the infamous "Iron Triangle" area. During the operation the UN forces recrossed the 38th Parallel between Yongp'yong and Yongong and eventually established the "Kansas Line." Chorwan was retaken between April 11 and April 22 through the efforts of Operation Dauntless," and this ground fighting gave the UN domination of the "Triangle."

Following these moves, with all of the required air support, came communist retaliation through their own "Spring Offensive." This began on April 22 at 2300 KST and the Red offensive forced a general retreat, "bugging out" in GI parlance, of all UN forces along all the Kansas Line. By April 27 the UN again had been forced back to the outskirts of Seoul and formed what is often, and incorrectly termed as the Lincoln Line, (Correct is The Army Defense Line). This line managed to curtail the Red offensive, but it required a terrific amount of air support to do so.

In order to provide the most expeditious air support, 18th FBW staging operations were moved back to K-16 on May 8. Ninety percent of the Wing's operations were then conducted from this Seoul air base, including a record 155 combat sorties in one day. (This record was only eclipsed by the 18th FBW themselves after they received F-86s in 1953 and flew a phenomenal 190 sorties one day in June).

The ability to increase to this high sortie rate came as a result of the 18th FBW gaining the 39th Fighter Interceptor Squadron from the 35th Fighter Interceptor Wing on May 7. Along with the attachment of the 39th FIS came many experienced Mustang pilots from the 40th FIS and headquarters sections of the 35th FIW who still had a 100 mission requirement to meet, but not so many remaining missions that would justify retraining them into the F-80 that the 35th FIW was regaining.

Also, it was at this time that those original pilots from the Dallas Project were impressed back from Clark Air Base to complete a 100 combat mission tour. This action came as a directive from General Stratermeyer's office in Japan and needless to say it was both unsettling and a travesty.

The inconsistency of this combat mission requirements and the rotation policy was almost incomprehensible to the Mustang pilots. As mentioned, during the previous months there had been periods of extreme bitterness that centered around the fact that there was not an adequate pipeline of replacement F-51 pilots to replace those who had completed their 100 mission combat tour. These effected pilots found it hard to believe that there were not enough qualified Mustang pilots within the USAF to provide them relief, particularly since nearly all of the

Arming "Dottie" for another combat mission by the 67th FBS. Hanging a bomb on a Mustang's shackles required some muscle. 44-74874 started with the 35th FIW and post war went to the ROKAF. (USAF via Davis)

Air National Guard squadrons that had been flying Mustangs had been recalled to Federal Service since the conflict started. Yet few of these qualified ANG Mustang pilots had yet to appear in Korea and FEAF's rotation policy for pilots to return to the United States was still unclear at even this late date in the war.

Following this envisioned travesty was the situation effecting many individual Mustang pilots that had been relieved after their one hundredth mission was completed: they either had to go to either Japan or somewhere else in FEAF's domain to complete a three year tour of overseas duty. Whereas the one hundred mission jet pilot was permitted to return to the States, most receiving a "cushy" Air Training Command assignment. To clinch it all, replacement pilots that were arriving from Nellis Air Force Base, Nevada did not have the desired flying proficiency expected. They reportedly had little ability to fly formation or perform in the various phases of ground attack.

"Four replacement pilots from Nellis refused to fly combat, either before their first combat mission or prior to their fifth. It was (also) recommended that replacement pilots be more thoroughly screened so as to avoid incidents like this in the future."

The problem continued into the next month when the 39th FIS "Received pilots from the ZI who were neither proficient in combat training nor possessed of the necessary aggressiveness so necessary for a fighter pilot. After giving them further intensive training, it was found necessary to ground them."

The additional strike capability gained by the 18th FBW, however, meant that more pilots were exposed to the dangers of combat through more scheduled missions. During May a total of thirty-two Mustangs were lost, with twenty-five of them going down as a direct result of combat operations. This figure represented over one full squadron's actual complement of TO&E, (Table of Organization and Equipment.) or authorized number of aircraft. Twenty-six more F-51s were damaged, again equating to a squadron's full complement of aircraft.

The addition of the 39th FIS now gave the 18th FBW a total of four operational combat squadrons. The 39th FIS joined the 18th FBW at K-16 after moving up from K-9. This action also created a shuffle within the 18th FBW hierarchy as Colonel William McBride, nee commanding officer 35th Fighter Interceptor Group, now became the commanding officer of the 18th FBG. Lt. Colonel Cox was thusly transferred to FEAF Headquarters in Japan. The Wing's operations officer, Lt. Colonel Jack Cartwright, was also transferred to Japan, and he was replaced by Lt. Colonel Francis Bodine from the 35th FIG. The 39th FIS

"Lil' Warrior" and "Trudy" (aka "Connie") all bombed-up and ready to go. When the 67th FBS converted to F-86Fs both of these Mustangs were transferred to the ROKAF. (Loffler via Davis)

continued to be led by Lt. Colonel Tom Robertson. (Coinciding with this action, the 39th FIS personnel were ordered by FEAF supply to turn in their winter clothing. Robertson responded, "Go to hell; it's cold!")

The EUSAF offensive started on May 23 and this was the first time that the UN forces were able to mount an immediate counter-offensive against a previous communist attack. In the air and on the ground the objective was to cut the Red's main supply routes and to destroy both the enemy soldier and his equipment. The 18th FBW was again assigned the task of postholing roads and bombing tunnels. An indication of the intensity of this action was the fact that four 18th FBW F-51s were damaged on May 23, and one was lost, this being Lt. Richard Seguin, 39th FIS, whose Mustang was hit as he started a bomb run and he crashed in a "fiery ball." Four more Mustangs were damaged on May 24. The offensive continued through June 15 and the losses of pilots and aircraft is indicative of the combat situation.

During the first weeks of June the 67th FBS lost four pilots and six Mustangs, with five of the six aircraft being shot down by ground fire. The sixth was last seen south of Sinuiju in a dive with four MiG's on its tail. The 12th FBS lost two Mustangs to Red firepower, and a third to a combat related accident.

To encapsulate. June 1 Captain Harry Moore, 67th FBS as a result of the MiG attack. June 2: Captain Philip Kuhn, 12th FBS, had to belly-in after being hit by ground fire. He was rescued by a helicopter, hospitalized, and returned to flying duties. June 3: Lt. Eric O'Briant, 12th FBS, attempted to takeoff from K-16 with a fully loaded F-51. Engine trouble resulted in a crash landing from which O'Briant had to be hospitalized in Japan. June 5:

1st Lt. Ronald "Ross" Cree, 67th FBS, attempted a belly landing in North Korea after being hit by groundfire. "Just after he had it made antiaircraft fire blew him out of the sky." Colonel McBride, 18th FBW commanding officer, was leading a four-ship strike when he was hit in the temple by shrapnel. He was led back to K-10 by 1st Lt. Bud Biteman for a safe landing. (This episode marked Biteman's 100th mission, and with the loss of Lt. Cree, another of General Stratermeyer's "shaftees," 18th FBG commander Colonel Ralph Saltsman, (Who had replaced the injured Colonel McBride.) decreed that there would be no more combat missions flown by the mandated returnees from Clark Air Base). June 9: Captain Jack Hederstrom, 67th FBS to an unknown cause. June 11: Captain Jack Thompson, 39th FIS, was looking over a possible target when he was hit by antiaircraft fire. His F-51 exploded against a hillside, but his name does not appear on any causality lists. June 14: 1st Lt. Bernard Percy, 12th FBS, had to bailout after being hit by groundfire while RESCAPing a crash site. He was rescued by a SA-16 crew. June 16: 1st Lt. Francis Escott, 67th FBS, due to an unknown cause. June 19: Lt. Lee Harper, 39th FIS, was hit by groundfire and could have elected to bailout, but attempted to belly land his Mustang instead, and then it appeared that he changed his mind and bailed out too low for his parachute to open. 1st Lt. Vernon Burke, 67th FBS, was hit by groundfire five miles north of Yonan. This area was considered "safe," an "Old Ladies Home." He was rescued by a helicopter.

Captain Kenneth Stewart, 67th FBS, was also involved in one of the more spectacular rescues of a downed pilot during the Korean War when he was shot down in June. His Mustang was hit just after he pulled up off a target north of Sariwon, along the Sariwon-Pyongyang road.

"Stewart kept cool, and thought fast, and headed his sick Mustang west. Reaching the (Chaeryong) estuary east of Chinnampo he had to leave it, and bailed out successfully, landing in the water. He immediately inflated his May west and dinghy, crawled into the dinghy and began to paddle down the river. He soon came under some small arms fire from the banks, and realizing his dinghy was a good target, abandoned it. He then floated on his back, just keeping his nose above water to present as small a target as possible. This gave him a good chance to observe the remainder of his flight working up and down the river banks on strafing runs.

"A RESCAP flight, led by Lt. Joseph Babasa, kept the Mustangs on assigned runs, avoiding the pilot in the water and watched the arrival of a SA-16. Babasa observed heavy flak coming from the city of Kyomi-po, which was silenced by .50 caliber and rocket fire as Stewart drifted by.

The SA-16 took two hours to get to the area, having to fly up the coast line and avoid the hot spot Yonan Peninsula. Darkness arrived, and Stewart was hard to spot, but he had a flashlight with him which was used for signaling. The Dumbo pilot made a night water landing, difficult during peacetime conditions, and picked up Stewart in completely unfamiliar conditions."

The 18th FBW got back into the air-to-air war again on June 20. Intelligence had indicated that the Reds were going to invade the Semni-do Islands, three miles off the western coast and seventy miles south of the Yalu River, which were islands friendly to the UN. To thwart this threat, twenty-four 18th FBW Mustangs were ordered into the area on a CAP. While they were reconnoitering they spotted a mixed gaggle of twelve Il-10s and Yak 9s north of Pyongyang.

Captain James Harrison, 67th FBS, flying the Number Three position in his flight, spotted one Yak and zapped him with a full deflection shot that was witnessed by the other seven pilots in his section. This brought Harrison's total to eight kills in two wars, and prompted one of the better quotes from the Korean War. "Those Yaks are flown by a bunch of yuks and they ain't no sweat."

Two 12th FBS pilots also claimed kills, Captain's Bruce Clark and Landell Hames, while commanding officer of the 18th FBG, Colonel Saltsman, got a probable and Lt. James Reints claimed one damaged. Officially, only Harrison's kill was credited by the USAF, which was the last officially credited Mustang kill of the war.

On the negative side during this encounter a top cover was supposed to have been provided by 4th FIW F-86s, but two MiGs broke through their screen and one managed to shoot the wings off the Mustang flown by Captain John Coleman, 39th FIS. His F-51 went down in flames and he did not have a chance to bailout.

Two days later the MiGs were encountered again when a flight of four Mustangs were jumped by six MiGs while they were on a rail cutting mission. The F-51s turned into the MiGs and made a frontal attack on them. Lt. Babasa almost got one, as he was scoring effective hits all over its nose, but he ran out of ammunition before he could bring it down. He was credited with a damaged. Babasa would be lost on July 9 during a mission over North Korea, a loss that was keenly felt for he was already recognized for his leadership and talent.

On June 30 Captain Charles Sumner, "B" Flight commander, 39th FIS, received heavy antiaircraft fire damage to his F-51's right wing and wheel well. His Mustang caught on fire, but Sumner side-slipped it away from the flames and managed to blow the fire out. He headed south for K-16 and upon arriving there he set the aircraft up for a belly landing only to discover that he could not open his canopy. He set the Mustang down along side of the run-

A 67th FBS crew chief warms up his charge prior to a mission in January 1952. Note that the flying surfaces have been covered with canvas boots to keep them clear of snow and ice, which would destroy their lift. In the spring 44-84945 would undergo an in-the-field conversion to a two-seater, but it would be lost in April. (USAF)

way, and it caught on fire once again, with Sumner trapped in the cockpit. Lt. Colonel Thomas Robertson and the K-16 crash crew ran to the wreckage and physically yanked the canopy off the fuselage to free the trapped Sumner. He suffered a wrenched back and second degree burns. Robertson, Staff Sergeant Lester Dick and Technical Sergeant Coleman were all recommended for the Soldier's Medal for their rescue efforts.

During July the 39th FIS rounded out their first year of combat operations. During this period they had seen a complete turn over of personnel within the squadron. Although still technically a Fighter Interceptor Squadron, their role remained that of a Fighter Bomber Squadron, and they noted with wry amusement that they had moved some eight times during the course of the war, so far, and they had established a record for PCS or TDY relocations for a FIS.

The 39th FIS did appear to be jinxed during the first part of July. On July 4 Captain Raymond Carlson was hit by ground fire while in the area of Huichon. He headed south for friendly territory and started a slow descent over a reservoir near Pyonggang, anticipating a belly landing. Yet when Carlson released his canopy it appeared to strike him in the forehead and the Mustang went into a fifty degree dive, crashing into the side of the reservoir. His body was recovered by Canadian troops who stated that he had been hit five times by .50 caliber fire as he crossed over the communist-controlled side of the reservoir.

The next day Captain Walter Pittman departed K-16 to lead "Charlie Flight" on an armed reconnaissance and rail cutting mission. Just after dropping his bombs Pittman started an easy pull-out to recover from his dive when his

"Ol' NaDSoB," (Old Napalm Dropping Son of a Bitch) 45-11742, belonged to the 67th FBS. She was the last F-51D built by North American Aviation, and she was lost on October 18, 1951. (USAF)

Mustang caught fire and exploded. It was not determined whether he had been hit by enemy fire or whether his Mustang had suffered some sort of a malfunction. Pittman had started his combat tour with a chain of 100 links, and after each mission he would clip one off. He had less than five links to go when he was lost.

On July 7 1st Lt. Howard Arnold, Jr. was leading that day's "Baker Flight," (The second mission for the day.) on a strike against Haeju. After receiving heavy ground fire, Arnold decided that he would have to bailout over the sea. He landed almost within arms reach of a SA-16 that was on station performing picket duty, and was immediately recovered.

Two days later 1st Lt. Joseph Babasa, 67th FBS was lost to an undetermined cause over Pyongyang.

Although there were several more 18th FBW Mustangs lost through accidents during the remainder of July, no more fell through combat related incidents until July 30. On the 30th the 18th FBW launched their largest attack to date, hitting Pyongyang with sixty-four Mustangs. Each F-51 carried two 110 gallon drop tanks filled with napalm, and each of the four squadrons was assigned specific targets within the town. Attacks were concentrated, with flights of four aircraft flying in "line abreast" formation with additional flights coming along in trail.

1st Lt. Eric O'Briant, 12th FBS, who had just returned to combat operations, was lost on this strike. O'Briant's Mustang exploded for an unknown reason over the city.

One of the 39th FIS pilots, 2nd Lt. James Gleoggler, was declared "Luckiest pilot of the year." His Mustang took a 20mm hit through the side of its canopy, which then plowed a hot "furrow" across his back before it penetrated his parachute and exploded. Although "quite shook-up" he flew back to K-16 for a normal landing.

Lt. David Grey, 67th FBS, would become quite experienced in belly landing aircraft during his tour in Korea, sliding-in two Mustangs and a Texan. (USAF)

The rains of the monsoon season fell, and fell some more commencing in mid July. "Operation Punchbowl," which began on July 26 became largely a ground force operation because of the incessant rains and the low clouds facing the fighter-bomber pilots. The UN forces wanted air support, but there was just no way that the pilots could penetrate the weather to get through to the MLR. Eventually all of these rain storms caused K-16 to become totally flooded, so the 18th FBW staging personnel based there had to return to K-10 for operations. Missions were flown en total from Chinhae between August 9 and the 18th, but they were not considered to be as nearly effective as those from K-16, as the bombs had to be replaced by external fuel tanks for the longer ranged missions. K-10, in turn, had to be evacuated to K-16 because of Typhoon Marge" before the month was over. As always, the fluid situation was considered by the GI's to be "situation normal."

One of the more famous photographs of the Korean War was taken on the morning of August 14, 1951 over Pyongyang. Major Murrit Davis, (now) commanding officer of the 39th FIS, was captured at the moment of release as he was dropping napalm tanks on the North Korean capitol. In the photographs' background was the Mustang of Captain Al Wagner, busily dodging smokestacks. The photograph was taken by Captain John Horn from his own Mustang.

Soon after the photograph was taken Major Davis hit a cable, which sheared off his right wing tip, and Captain Wagner had a large portion of his right horizontal stabilizer shot away. Both pilots made it back to K-16 to exchange their battered Mustangs for good ones, and then they returned to Pyongyang.

The second time over the target Major Davis' Mustang was hit in the coolant system, but he insisted in circling over the target to see if he could see where the offending antiaircraft fire was coming from. After spotting the gun battery for future reference Davis headed for home, but his Merlin engine seized and the Mustang crashed before he could bailout.

Captain Horn, the squadron's operations officer, was in a Mustang fitted with a K-250 camera behind the pilot's armor plated headrest on this mission. After his flight made their napalm drops, Horn made a 180 degree turn back over the target to take strike photos and to see if he could see what had happened to his own wingman, Captain John Grossman. Grossman was only on his second mission, and he had been hit on his way across the target. His Mustang had been seen to roll inverted and crash into a canal that traversed through the city. Horn, apparently, wanted to see if Grossman had any chance of survival, but Horn was also shot down and killed.

The 5th Air Force started a "Rail Interdiction Program" on August 18. This was an entirely new plan that replaced Operation Strangle that had not been a particularly successful effort, and often the Rail Interdiction Program, RIP, is considered to be just a continuation of that effort by historians, but the aerial tactics were entirely different.

The 18th FBW participated in RIP by furnishing thirty-six F-51s to operate in conjunction with other 5th Air Force units. It was not a pleasant way to make a living, for there was always antiaircraft fire to be encountered. The 18th FBW records for the period mention that "many pilots are getting a 'fear of combat,' which was attributed to having to fly in F-51s, and (an) over consciousness of enemy flak concentrations. However, a bad day of losses does not seem to affect most pilots: a big factor is the 'pick-up' program of the 3rd Air Rescue Squadron, which increased survivability."

There is little doubt that it took a lot of courage to fly these missions, for many pilots threw-up both before and after flying as a matter of course, and were often so physi-

44-72914 of the 18th FBW but of an unidentified squadron at Kimpo in 1951. "Susan" was lost on April 5, 1952. (Stoltz via Dorr)

The personal Mustang of Major William Meyers, maintenance officer of the 67th FBS. This 'Stang was "built" by the men of the 67th from wrecks. The drop tanks are painted blue and were used to spray DDT over K-10 to keep down the fly population. (Milt Tarr via Menard/Thompson)

cally and emotionally drained that they had to be assisted from their cockpits when they returned from a mission.

On August 18 1st Lt. Richard Heilands, 39th FIS, took off from K-10 on a napalm strike mission. Shortly after his flight joined in formation it was recalled by the JOC because of adverse weather over the front lines. The flight was told by the Chinhae control tower to salvo their ordnance in the sea south of the base, and the flight leader stated that they did as instructed, but this was the last observation of Lt. Heilands. Search aircraft later spotted oil and napalm slicks on the water east of Koje-do Island, but there was no sign of the Mustang or its pilot.

The 67th FBS averaged twelve ground support missions per day, in addition to strikes upon Pyongyang and the RIP missions. Even though the first of the peace talks had already begun at Kaesong and there was some optimism, there was no let-up along the front lines in the ground war and the Red's continued to knock down Mustangs.

Captain David French, 18th FBW Headquarters, was flying a mission with the 67th FBS on August 25 when he was hit and attempted to bail out at only 200 feet directly over the front lines after being hit by ground fire. His parachute only partially opened before he struck the ground. A helicopter pilot tried to get to him, but it was driven off by heavy groundfire, and its pilot believed that French had already died. His body was later recovered by an army patrol.

Up to this point recent events had gone fairly well for the 12th FBS, but disaster struck for them also on August 25. Three Mustangs were lost this day, but fortunately just one pilot. 1st Lt. Raymond Stewart was killed while on a

ground support mission along the MLR. 2nd Lt. Ralph Clark had to bail out of his F-51 over enemy territory after being hit by ground fire. He was picked up by a 5th Air Force rescue team after only twenty minutes on the ground. The last Mustang lost this day was flown by Captain Lawrence Cookman. He too was hit by ground fire, but he was able to nurse his aircraft back to friendly territory before bailing out. He was hospitalized for burns caused by flames from a burning wing tank that he had to bailout through during his escape.

The last loss of the month was on August 31 when Lt. John Hoke, 39th FIS, was flying a CAS mission. His flight had made their napalm runs against Red positions, and then completed their rocket attacks and started to swing around to commence several strafing runs when Hoke's Mustang crashed into a hill. It was not known whether Hoke's loss was a result of enemy fire or whether he just got to low while ducking under some low hanging clouds in the twilight.

At this time interdiction missions were being flown with three of the 18th FBW's squadrons putting up eight to twelve Mustangs per strike. The fourth Wing squadron, which was a rotating assignment, was assigned to ground support strikes for the day. This provided some relief from the longer duration interdiction missions, and the potential of encountering the more prevalent antiaircraft batteries further behind the main battle lines. With the major emphasis on rail cutting, the Red's were forced to rely more and more on slower and less quantitative vehicular traffic to supply their front lines. By September The Truckbusters had done their job so well that the communists were forced to use horse drawn wagons, and occasionally, (Believe it or not.) camel caravans to move their supplies.

Supporting this interdiction role came the modification of the Mustang's K-14 gunsight. Originally, this sight had been developed by the British for air-to-air combat, and it contained its own gyroscope for deflection firing. The sight progressed through several changes which resulted in the K-14C that was set for air-to-ground harmony, and it was particularly accurate in the dive bombing role. To increase accuracy, and help the pilot have a better "sight picture," the pilots entered the bombing pattern at 6,000 feet with an airspeed of 350 mph. The bombs were released at 1,500 feet, which, with the addition of a 4-5 second delay fuse allowed the pilot plenty of time to avoid the bombs blasts.

As often apparent, one of the major deficiencies of the F-51 is its coolant system. The pilot sits above and in front of the coolant and oil radiators, and any damage to them or to their transmission lines or to the engine itself creates the potential of sending scalding oil, steam or glycol into the cockpit. The cockpit is also located over the aircraft's wings, which contain two fuel tanks, and the pilot's seat is just in front of the fuselage fuel tank. In spite of their being self-sealing, there is potential for an inferno. The fuselage fuel tank was only used during longer ranged missions in Korea because of its adverse effect upon the aircraft's center of gravity, particularly when bombs or napalm were carried. When the F-51 was thrown into the ground support and interdiction roles these vulnerabilities became quickly apparent. Yet the cockpit was also a "sweat box" and early on in the war the pilots liked to be both macho and cool by not wearing gloves and having their sleeves rolled up, etc. It didn't take too many Mustang pilot injuries before they realized just how vulnerable pilots were to severe burns with these aircraft shortcomings. The pilots then had but little choice but to sweat, for the USAF supply system was slow in getting summer flying suits to them. Most of the pilots started to wear the enlisted men's GI fatigues, which were both looser and cooler, or continued to wear their winter flying suits. Finally the USAF started to issue them nylon flying suits, which had further disastrous results as in a fire or at high temperatures the nylon would melt and fuse to their skin. Most of the pilots then reverted to wearing their winter flying suits all year around to protect themselves from fire or scalds.

Finally, after all the delays, a permanent and positive rotation policy was established by FEAF. There still remained several pilots within the 39th FIS that had finished their 100 missions in October 1950 that were still forced to remain in Korea in administrative positions, and they had become quite vocal in expressing their dissatisfaction with the USAF, which had an obvious effect upon the morale of the newer people. The enlisted men were also, and finally, included in the rotation policy, and those who had finished their overseas tours between October 1950 and April 1951 finally received their orders allowing them to go home in September. These transfers left several sections within the squadron short of manpower, but with the motivation of being able to go home at the end of their official tours, everyone doubled-up on the work that needed to be accomplished without a great amount of additional complaint.

Although no USAF Reserve units were flying F-51s when the Korean War started, there were plenty of previously experienced Mustang pilots still in reserve units that were flying other types of aircraft. Virtually all of the reservists and their units were activated, and then incorpo-

rated within the regular USAF during the immediate months after June 1950. Likewise, many Air National Guard Wings had been activated in the fall of 1950.

It had initially been USAF policy to activate individuals from the Reserve as needed, since the units they were drawn from, technically, belonged to the USAF to begin with, but the Air National Guard personnel were under State Control and by law they could not be activated without their entire unit being called to Federal Service in a national emergency. However, once these men were within the clutches of the USAF they also began receiving orders transferring them from unit to unit just like any other service man.

The activation of the Reserve and ANG units had been announced in their respective home town newspapers when they were called-up, for the early months of the Korean war was good news copy, but by the time the individual airman received orders to Korea the American attitude had become one of much indifference to the war and it attracted little attention in the press when the "home town boys" headed off to the actual war.

All of this apathy placed a real damper on the morale of the recalled men, but their reception in Korea was a real shot in the arm to those men of the 18th FBW who received these experienced people into their fold. The 67th FBS noted with glee that they received eight new qualified Mustang pilots in August from Reserve and ANG squadrons, including World War II ace Lt. James Ayers.

Aircraft losses for September continued along the average number with eight 18th FBW Mustangs falling to enemy fire and four more being lost through accidents. On September 1 2nd Lt. Robert Wood, 12th FBS, was declared MIA after being hit by groundfire. He was taken prisoner of war and returned on September 3, 1953. 1st

"Miss Dee" of the 67th FBS with the rarely appearing "Fighting Cock" squadron insignia. (Loeffler via Davis)

Lt. Leland Wolf, 67th FBS, fell to ground fire on September 13. Wolf was hit at an altitude where he was too low to bail out and he had to make a high-speed crash landing. An LTA-6 Mosquito pilot went down to see if Wolf had any chance of survival, and he also was shot down. A helicopter was called in to try and rescue the Mosquito pilot and his observer, and it also was shot down. All four involved airmen were listed as MIA and Wolf's death was confirmed after the fighting was concluded. (The never declared war has never been declared as over, either).

The MiG's also were back on September 13. The 39th FIS was on a rail cutting mission near Sambongdong, and the first three Mustangs in the flight of four were already on their bomb runs when the Number Four pilot, 2nd Lt. William Jackson, was jumped by three MiG's. His flight leader saw them first, just as he was pulling out from his own bomb run, and he radioed for the rest of the flight to "break." The Number Two pilot continued his run, hitting the target square on center, while the Number Three pilot salvoed his ordnance, and then all three pilots started violent evasive maneuvers to escape the MiG's. Apparently Jackson was either to engrossed in spotting the target or his radio had failed, for a MiG hit him with a blast of cannon fire just as he was starting his dive. The F-51 dove straight into the mud flats, and a reconnaissance of the site after the MiG's had left saw that the Mustang's cockpit had been obliterated by cannon fire.

The Flight Commander of the 67th FBS's "Easy Flight" on September 22, Lt. George Coyle was downed while on an armed reconnaissance mission. He bailed out right over a Red gun battery and the rest of his flight saw him

being taken prisoner. He was repatriated in September 1953. Captain James Moore, Flight Commander of "Dog Fight,' 67th FBS, had better luck. He made it back to friendly territory for a crash landing after being hit by ground fire. Moore did receive severe burns, however, and was off flying status for three months.

The leader of the 39th FIS's "Dog Flight" went down on his fifty-second mission. 1st Lt. Orval Tandy had a good chute when he bailed out and was last seen running into a wooded area. The rest of his flight RESCAPed the area but when a helicopter arrived, to trace of Tandy could be seen. He was taken prisoner and he was released with Lt. Wood.

The 18th FBW started staging operations out of K-46 on October 1, 1951. This airstrip was approximately five miles southeast of Hoengsong, or six miles from Wonjo, and is often identified by either name. Since the airstrip was only sixty miles from the MLR, and centrally located on the Korean Peninsula, the Wing's effectiveness was increased, particularly in respect to ground support operations. K-46's runway was newly laid with asphalt and gravel instead of PSP, thanks to Air Force engineers that had preceded the Wing and made the improvements after the area had been recaptured. A Low Frequency Radio Beacon had also been installed, which made the strip more suitable for all-weather operations. And to top things off, permanent living and messing quarters had been erected, which made everything a marked improvement over K-16.

Tactics were changed once again in October. Instead of flying "group gaggles," the Mustangs were now only flown in squadron strength, with larger Wing missions separated by a five minute interval between squadrons. This prevented the F-51s from jamming-up over the target prior to starting their bombing runs, and gave the first squadron in to the area an opportunity to fly flak suppression strikes prior to the other squadrons commencing their own attacks. Also, under these conditions, the first squadron into the area had an option of climbing up to provide a top cover for the succeeding squadrons, as more and more MiG activity was being observed.

Dive bombing tactics were once again revised, for no one ever seemed satisfied with their effectiveness. The initial altitude was lowered to 5,000 feet with an airspeed of 250 mph. This kept the Mustang's speed from building up too high in the actual dive and reduced the Merlin engine's torque factor, which hampered accuracy. The individual flights would attack from either an echelon left or right formation, and all pilots made their runs simultaneously. Upon bomb release the flight leader would

"Vendetta" of the 12th FBS. The yellow stripes across the top of the wing are to assist the pilot in lining up on a target for a rocket attack. (USAF)

A 67th FBS Mustang loaded with rockets and napalm trundles to the runway. The yellow napalm tanks were manufactured in Japan. (USAF via Davis)

make a quick 180 degree turn, which was followed by a ninety degree turn to bring him back towards the target, while the remainder of the flight only made a ninety degree breakaway. This permitted the flight leader to make a quick assessment of the mission's effectiveness and then to rejoin the remainder of his flight as rapidly as possible for defensive purposes without exposing anyone to ground fire any longer than necessary.

The 18th FBW historian noted that there were still some pilots suffering from a "fear complex" during October, although combat losses were down to just eight Mustangs, with only four to enemy groundfire.

Captain James McCable, 67th FBS, was shot down over enemy territory, but he had a chance to bail out at the last moment and only suffered a sprained knee and ankle in the process. He was rescued by a helicopter. 1st Lt. Lyle Moore, 67th FBS, got his Mustang back to friendly territory after it was shot-up, and he pulled off a successful belly landing in a rice paddy.

On October 17 1st Lt. Newman Golden, 39th FIS, was flying in the Number Four position in "Mongoose Easy" flight when he radioed that he had been hit and was bailing out. Due to heavy smoke in the area from previous napalm strikes, no one saw Golden's Mustang at the time, but one pilot later reported that he saw the burning hulk of a F-51 on the ground five miles south of the target area. A RESCAP was established over the site for three hours, but no trace of Golden could be seen. Golden had been a member of the Tuskegee Airmen and had previously been a POW in Germany during World War II. He remains MIA today as a result of this incident.

On October 28 1st Lt. George Jones, 39th FIS, was killed on a routine training flight while he was practicing rocket firing techniques against a small hill on an island just off shore from K-10. Without apparent warning his Mustang snap-rolled and dove into the water. Another Jones, 1st Lt. Oliver Jones, 12th FBS, was also lost on October 28 when he was declared MIA on his thirty-third mission over North Korea. His wingman, 1st Lt. Ralph Clark, reported that Jones stated that "his engine was failing, the aircraft rolled to the right, throwing flame and smoke from the exhaust ports." Jones bailed out when the nose of his Mustang was pointed straight down, but his parachute was not seen to open. Neither Clark nor another wingman, 1st Lt. Robert Morrison, who RESCAPed the area could see any trace of Jones on the ground. He remains MIA.

The commanding officer of the 67th FBS, Major Carl "Skoshi" Colson, was replaced by Major Julian Crow in November. Crow previously had been the operations officer of the 12th FBS. Colonel Saltsman was also relieved at this time, being replaced by Colonel Seymour Levenson. In part, these changes in command stemmed from, finally, the availability of experienced higher ranking officers from the United States.

There was also a large influx of new pilots at this time into the 18th FBW from Pilot Graduate Schools in the US. These new pilots were truly green, and four of them had never flown a Mustang. Very few had yet to practice the dropping of bombs or firing of rockets, and their limited instrument training had always been conducted in visual flight conditions. To resolve these shortcomings a training course had to be reestablished at K-10. Colonel Saltsman went on record by stating that the "UN cause would have been better served if these pilots had been better trained, and screened in the US, for the training program kept several aircraft out of their combat roles."

Vice President Alben Barkley visited Korea during this period, and he was provided a fighter escort on his travels by the "Flying Tigers" of the 12th FBS. (They had been so named by Syngman Rhee in July 1950 after he likened them to the early World War II American Volunteer Group. But the squadron preferred their own nickname of the "Foxy Few").

Combat missions were reduced during this period, for the peace talks continued at Kaesong and the UN did not desire to create any changes to the status quo at this time. With the reduction in the number of missions flown also came a reduction in aircraft losses. During November there were only five Mustangs downed, which was the lowest number since the 18th FBW had joined the war, and this number was spread over the four Wing squadrons instead of just two.

The 39th FIS lost 1st Lt. Ned Frankart on November 3 when he was flying as the Number Two man in a flight of four F-51s that were making a series of rocket attacks against a tunnel entrance. He got too low and flew into a hillside. The 12th FBS lost 1st Lt. Robert Lucas on November 17 to an unidentified cause. 2nd Lt. Donald Lynd, 39th FIS, was killed while attempting to land at K-10 after ferrying a Mustang south from K-46. He stalled-out on final approach and dove straight into the ground. The 67th FBS had one incident where Lt. Max Tomich had to bail-out while in the traffic pattern at K-46 as he was returning from a mission after darkness had set in. His Mustang's engine quit, and Tomich wisely went over the side instead of risking a night belly dead-stick landing.

The 67th FBS also had a series of incidents involving a pilot named McCamish, which makes one wonder just how lucky any one pilot can be expected to be. In fact, he was so lucky that "Lucky" became his nickname.

Lt. Carl McCamish flew his first combat mission with the 67th FBS on September 25, 1951 and in ninety-two days he had amassed ninety-two missions, and he had crash landed three Mustangs during the course of events. The first one was in October when he was flying as "Poker Stake Three," leading the second element in a flight of four F-51s. "Poker Stake Two," Captain James McCabe, and his own element leader had just finished strafing some enemy troops when McCabe's Mustang was hit and

started emitting black smoke, which increased in intensity until McCabe was forced to bail out. The remainder of the flight set up a RESCAP over the location, only a mile from the Red position they had been working over, and called in a rescue chopper. During the RESCAP the Mustangs came under antiaircraft fire and McCamish's was hit, knocking out his hydraulic system. He returned to K-46 and discovered that his left landing gear would not extend, while the right one locked into position. Without hydraulic pressure he could not retract the right wheel again. The ensuing groundloop gave him a wild ride, and although his Mustang was a write-off McCamish was uninjured.

His second belly landing came after a raid on a supply dump at Songbung-ni. This village had always been a major target for it was on the main highway and railroad between Sariwon and Manchuria. It was considered as one of the heaviest defended targets in North Korea. McCamish had led a flight of seven Mustangs up there, and they had made six separate attacks without a problem before starting a seventh run-in. McCamish's Mustang was hit, blowing off his entire left aileron. He then had to fight for control all the way back to K-46, and when he got there he found that his minimum controllable airspeed was 190 mph, which was too fast to permit lowering the landing gear and still maintain controllability with the resultant drag. He slid the Mustang in with all the tenderness that he could, using almost all of the available runway in the process. There were over fifty-eight bullet holes on one side of his F-51, and over 200 on the other, plus a 20mm hole up through the fighter's floorboard from a round that had passed through the cockpit without exploding.

McCamish's third incident occurred as he was in the process of taking off on a napalm strike with eleven other Mustangs. There is a point in every airplane's flight where, on the takeoff roll it is not quite yet flying, but is no longer bound to the ground, either. Just as McCamish reached this critical point his F-51 got caught in the propwash from the preceding Mustang and it started to slew on him. The F-51 was light on it's landing gear and it's tail wheel was off the ground, yet his airspeed had not reached the point where it's flying controls were effective and it started to skitter off to the side of the runway where the left wheel struck an obstacle and the left napalm tank ruptured, flinging flaming jelly over the canopy. Just as the burning wreck slid to a stop the starboard wing tank exploded, but fortunately the wing itself blanked out the flames long enough for McCamish to escape from the cockpit with only minor burns.

McCamish went on to fly nineteen more missions and on Christmas Day Colonel Seymour Levenson, (Who had replaced Colonel Saltsman as 18th FBG commander in November.) decided that McCamish had seen enough combat and credited him with the remaining number of required missions and ordered his return to the United States to finish out his remaining obligation to the USAF as an instructor pilot.

Eight more Mustangs were lost to enemy action in December. Most of these went down during rail cutting missions against the tracks radiating from Sunchon. Three F-51s were downed by groundfire east of Sunchon along the tracks to Unsan, and a fourth to the north.

Additional missions of note were against communists entrenched in front of the British Division along the western section of the I Corps areas. Support was also given to ROK troops operating south of Taejon in Operation Ratkiller which was a program to curtail guerrilla activity behind UN lines. "Ratkiller" actually was a four-phase

The burned out remains of a 67th FBS Mustang near K-46. (Dittmer via Isham)

effort which continued into 1952 that amounted to virtually sweeping South Korea from end to end from the air in search of enemy troops that had either been bypassed after the Inchon Landing or had infiltrated into the woods and hills. Largely this was a ROK effort that utilized both their air and ground forces, but it also included the USAF's F-51s, F-80s and F-84s. It never was totally successful in eradicating the guerrilla problem.

In mid December the 18th FBW was assigned targets between Kyomipo and Sariwon, south of Pyongyang, where the Red antiaircraft fire was noted to be particularly intense. Additional interdiction missions, identified as "Hammer" were flown in conjunction with the 45th Tactical Reconnaissance Squadron. The 45th TRS Mustangs at this time were only the RF-51D version, which did not have rocket launching racks, and their pilots were forced to mark their targets with .50 caliber API, armor piercing incendiary, rounds, which were difficult to spot when they struck their target; but they did permit their 18th FBW counterparts to locate and hit the intended objective.

In spite of the bad winter weather and the high loss rate during the early part of December, pilot morale "continued at a moderate level." This was due, mostly, to the high success rate of the helicopter rescue units who had proven themselves to be the most courageous individuals ever assembled into a unit.

To aid in the escape and evasion of downed pilots the 18th FBW ordered emergency substance kits and a seat-type survival kit to be carried on combat missions. These A-1 survival packs arrived only to be discovered that they were to large to be installed within the limited space of a F-51s cockpit. To get around this problem the pilot's dinghies were removed, for they would be of little value during the winter months. If a pilot went down in the frigid waters off Korea hypothermia would get him before he could get into the dinghy, anyhow. There wasn't room for a Mustang pilot to wear the new waterproof "poopy-suits" that the jet pilots were receiving, either.

For the heavier or larger pilot, forty foot diameter parachutes were furnished, which reduced their rate of descent. These large parachutes were all white, and they did not show up against the snow, which was good in helping in evading enemy troops but bad in aiding a rescue attempt. Thus the 18th FBW reverted back to the considerably smaller diameter twenty-eight foot parachutes which had alternating orange and white panels. Larger pilots then had to take their chances on sustaining injuries when they hit the ground at a faster rate of descent, but at least their impact point could be seen from the air!

In all, it was highly recommended that a pilot should bail out if his aircraft was damaged over enemy held territory. Experience had shown all to clearly that when communist gunners became aware that they had hit an aircraft they would cease fire and see what the pilot was going to do next. If it appeared that he was going to attempt a forced landing they would hold their fire until they saw that he was committed to the landing, and then cut loose on him again, usually blowing the defenseless aircraft out of the sky.

Of the eight F-51s lost by the 18th FBW during December the 12th FBS lost three. On December 3 2nd Lt. Donald Hoffman; December 13 1st Lt. John Swanson, and on December 23 1st Lt. Clarence McGowan. All three pilots were KIA. 1st Lt. Max Tomich, 67th FBS, had to bail out again on December 1 and he suffered minor injuries. Colonel Levenson then gave him credit for 100 missions and he was relieved of flying duties.

The 67th FBS lost 1st Lt. Lyle Moore. Moore was hit by ground fire on December 15 while on a bombing run and his Mustang dove straight into the ground. On the 18th the 67th FBS also lost Captain Joe Powers, but the circumstances are unknown.

One other 18th FBW pilot , Harold Forster, 12th FBS is listed as killed in December, but there is no mention of him in unit histories. It is suspected that he may have been killed sometime during the previous year and was carried as MIA until a determination of his status was ascertained.

The 39th FIS lost three Mustangs: On December 10 Captain Robert Ramsey was leading "Mongoose Zebra" Flight on a rail interdiction mission, and he never pulled out of his dive bombing run against the tracks. On December 14 1st Lt. Robert Smith was flying in the Number Two position in his flight when he radioed that he had been hit and was bailing out. At 5,000 feet Smith released his canopy, but the canopy bow struck him across his forehead and his Mustang went into an uncontrollable spin and crashed. On December 21 2nd Lt. Thurston Baxter was the Number Two man in his flight on a flak suppression mission that was to precede a rail strike. He started a strafing pass at 11,000 feet and simply never pulled out.

Nine Mustangs were lost in January 1952, and this month saw the second lowest number of combat missions flown since the 18th FBW had entered into the conflict. A bare 385 combat sorties were flown, with this low figure stemming from the extreme shortage of Mustangs available for operations and the adverse winter weather.

The high number of losses was due to the increasing proficiency of the communist antiaircraft gunners. Because of this, the 18th FBW issued "Direct Orders" to all pilots to make but one, and one only pass, on any target declared of "secondary importance." Obviously, if it was decreed a primary target, it was to be worked over, but there was little point of risking a pilot and his aircraft on a target of only secondary value or one of just opportunity.

The 12th FBS lost their first F-51 on January 6 when 1st Lt. Kenneth Shoemaker had to bailout, but he was rescued by a friendly patrol. Lt. Bill Elsom disappeared this same day over North Korea, and he was later declared as KIA. On January 31 Captain Frederick Irwin was also lost over North Korea, for an unknown reason, and he also was KIA.

The 67th FBS had the highest number of losses for January. On January 1 2nd Lt. John Strait was shot down by ground fire and was taken POW. He was released in September 1953. 2nd Lt. Morton Britten was hit by ground fire on January 8 while on an interdiction mission. His status remains unknown yet today. 2nd Lt. George Michalberger was also lost on an interdiction mission, on January 15, and his is listed as KIA. On January 27 2nd Lt. George Patton had to bailout behind enemy lines after being hit by ground fire. He was rescued with minor injuries.

It was not a good month for Lieutenants in the "Blinker Nose" squadron, either. The 39th FIS lost 1st Lt. Thomas Lafferty on January 31. He was flying as the Number Four man in "Put Put Yoke Flight" and was just starting a rocket attack when he was heard to exclaim "I'm hit!" Lafferty's Mustang was then seen to dive into the ground with no indication that he had bailed out. He was later declared as KIA.

Future four star general Lt. Daniel "Chappie" James. Even the apartheid-minded SAAF troops had nothing but the highest respect for him. (Spry)

Of some interest to the pilots of the 18th FBW was that of the two pilots who had managed successful bailouts in January, both landed in mine fields and their rescues had to be carried out with great finesse. The 18th FBW requested maps that would indicate the location of these fields, so that their pilots could be briefed accordingly in the future.

A serious training problem was now encountered by the 18th FBW which revolved around the replacements arriving from the United States. In the enlisted ranks either the airmen were fresh out of technical schools, or the senior non commissioned officers that were arriving lacked recent experience within their career fields. Similarly, within the officer grades, there were no non-rated officers being assigned to the Wing's staff sections to fill non-flying positions. This necessitated detailing rated combat pilots to these positions and shorting the Wing of operational pilots. A massive OJT instruction program had to be instituted for all ranks and grades to bring everyone up to speed, but fortunately there were now at least enough people available to both conduct and receive instruction and combat operations were not hampered by the programs.

The 18th FBW's Mustangs were becoming even more weary and this did effect combat operations. Most of the problems stemmed from the winter weather and leaks in the aircraft's coolant systems. Several engines had been allowed to overheat before an abnormal increase in temperature or a leak was noted, which then required an engine change before the Mustang could be flown again. Snow, ice, or tar deposits were found to be collecting in the F-51s tail wheel down-lock mechanisms, which caused several time consuming maintenance problems after the tail wheels either failed to extend or collapsed when the Mustangs landed. Starting in January all F-51 tail wheels were permanently locked down to resolve this problem, and eventually this procedure was instituted Air Force wide. The difference in aircraft performance was negligible, but it did destroy the clean lines of the fighter's profile.

Combat operations for February still remained at a lower level from those of the previous fall. This, again, was due to several factors, and did exclude the winter weather which was moderating. The main reason for the reduced number remained with the continuing shortage of F-51's assigned to the Wing. The 18th FBW's average number of F-51s on hand had dropped from sixty-six to fifty-seven, which was eighteen short of TO&E. (Not including those assigned to 2 Squadron). Also, the 18th FBW was not being tasked to fly as many ground sup-

port missions as previously, for the ground war had become stagnated, in part due to the peace talks taking place. In addition, there was now an excess of pilots, and each pilot assigned to the Wing now averaged but eight sorties each, which may be compared to the previous February where each pilot averaged twenty sorties.

The 12th FBS flew 350 effective sorties in February 1952 and for the first time since they left the Philippines they managed to go the entire month without loosing either a pilot or Mustang. The 67th FBS flew 458 sorties, but they lost three Mustangs in the process. On February 7 2nd Lt. Ralph Michael had engine trouble on takeoff from K-46 and landed too fast when he tried to get his Mustang back around and down, writing it off in a ditch across the end of the runway. On February 19 2nd Lt. Owen Nibley also had engine trouble on takeoff from K-46 and he had to settle for a crash landing in a river bed. Major Julian Crow, commanding officer 67th FBS, had his Mustang shot-up while on an interdiction mission that he was leading on February 22. He made it back to a friendly area for a belly landing in a rice paddy.

The 39th FIS was the hard luck squadron for February, for they had one pilot known to be killed at the time and two more become MIA. On February 5 1st Lt. James Clay was leading "Put Put Victor" Flight on a low-level recce mission which just happened to fly over a Red antiaircraft battery. Clay's Mustang was hit by gunfire in the radiator and immediately siphoned all of its coolant into the air. He headed south for Sol-to Island with the intention of bailing out. For some reason he delayed his abandonment of his Mustang until he was down to 500 feet and his parachute did not have time to open before he struck the water. His body was recovered by the Air Rescue Service.

On February 18 Captain Bruce Cram was leading "Put Put X-ray" on another armed recce mission and they spotted several trucks in a village. Cram went down for a closer look, and after completing his look-see he calmly announced that he had been hit and that he was going to bailout. He had a good chute, and after he landed he called his wingman on his survival radio stating that he was okay. A helicopter was called for and a RESCAP set up, but before the chopper arrived radio contact with Cram was lost and a recce of the area proved fruitless. Cram was taken POW and repatriated in September 1953.

On the same day 2nd Lt. Robert Hanner was flying as the Number Two man in "Put Put Willie" on a RESCAP for another pilot from another fighter group when his Mustang started loosing its coolant. His Merlin engine soon blew it's pop-off valve and Hanner was forced to bailout. Another chopper was called in, but before it could get to the area Hanner was seen to be captured. He was released on August 31, 1953.

The 12th FBS had another lucky month in March when they were again free from pilot losses. They did, however, loose three Mustangs with all three being writeoffs as a result of battle damage after their pilots brought them home to K-46. "Beyond economical repair" was the catch-all phrase.

The 67th FBS had two pilots declared MIA. 2nd Lt. Raymond Plevyak went down on March 1 and he was declared KIA after the Korean Conflict was concluded. 2nd Lt. Floyd O'Neal went down on March 4, but he was taken POW and he was returned on August 6, 1953. One additional 67th FBS pilot was lost on March 31 in a non combat related incident but his name and the circumstances are not known.

The 67th FBS encountered the wily MiG 15 during the second week in March. During a brief encounter over the lunch hour the Mustangs flown by 1st Lt. Shirley Tubbs and 2nd Lt. James Horsely were jumped by a pair of MiGs as they were chasing a truck down a lonely North Korean back road south of Pyongyang. The MiGs followed the Mustangs down the road as the pilots dove down as low as they dared in hopes of evading the MiGs cannon fire. One MiG fired over the top of Tubbs' canopy, with the rounds coming so close to him that he swore that he could feel their heat as they went by. No hits were scored by either side, and the MiGs, apparently low on fuel, made just the one pass on the F-51s and headed north to their sanctuary. Horsely, low on fuel himself, had to settle for an emergency landing at an abandoned airstrip while Tubbs' returned to K-46 to organize a refueling party to go and recover Horsely and his Mustang.

The 39th FIS lost one pilot on March 3 in an incident where a U.S. Silver Star would be awarded. 2nd Lt. Harry Rushing was flying in the Number Two slot in "Put Put Willie" Flight when his Mustang's engine started cutting out three miles north of the MLR. Rushing turned toward the friendly islands in the Han Estuary and climbed to 6,000 feet to search for a good place to make a forced landing. His Merlin engine then started to smoke and then caught on fire and Rushing was forced to bailout over the coastline. The drift of his parachute took him out to sea and he had to make a water landing near a sandbar. Rushing was observed to free himself from his parachute and its entangling shroud lines, but it was obvious that he was having trouble inflating his Mae West life jacket.

2nd Lt. Thomas Casserly went down on a low pass and was watching the whole situation unfold while his flight leader made radio contact with the Air Rescue Service, but he was advised that there would be at least a thirty minute delay before the ARS could get to the site. Under these circumstances things did not look good for Rushing, so Casserly elected to make a belly landing on the sandbar and try to swim to Rushing's assistance. After putting his Mustang down on the sandbar, no mean trick in itself, Casserly dove into the water to search for his wingman.

Unfortunately by this time Rushing had disappeared, and after fifteen minutes of fruitless searching Casserly had to swim back to his now partially submerged aircraft to await his own rescue. Rushing's body was never located. Casserly was awarded the Silver Star for his efforts. Later he was reported as killed, on October 1, 1952 in a 51st FIW F-86 crash at K-13 while trying to save his battle damaged Sabre.

The 18th FBW gained fifteen new pilots in April, which amounted to a fifteen percent overstaffing within the Wing. Each squadron now averaged forty-five Mustang pilots, but had only sixteen F-51s available for them to fly. This created yet again another morale problem as the pilots had too much time on their hands to dwell on the "what ifs?" of the war.

To assist in alleviating the aircraft shortage the 18th FBW established their own REMCO maintenance program at K-10. REMCO, Rear Echelon Maintenance Cooperative Organization, was a major FEAMCOM effort that was taking place at various air bases in Japan at the time. It amounted to the capability of either accomplishing a major overhaul or completely rebuilding an aircraft from the wheels up if necessary. The problem with the facilities in Japan was that they were to slow when it came to the F-51, since their priority went to the F-84s and F-86s. Thus the 18th FBW dedicated three hangars and their associated maintenance shops to their own REMCO and established a virtual Mustang production line to enhance and repair their own aircraft. The maintenance men had their hands full due with this effort because of the constant stream of weary or damaged F-51s brought south to them from K-46. The situation was a far cry from the World War II standard where an aircraft deemed as "war weary" was either scrapped or returned to the United States to serve in a training role and replaced by a brand new aircraft. At this time there were no replacement Mustangs available, and war weary or not, the F-51 had to be overhauled or rebuilt to fly again.

Not only had the Mustangs been subject to the high stress and combat fatigue from flying in a constant atmosphere of high G's during the various phases of ground attack, but they had been so subject to the damages incurred in flying from the rudimentary prepared air strips early on in the war. It had been hoped that by being able to operate off of runways laid with asphalt instead of PSP that the service life of the Mustangs would have been extended, due to the reduced vibrations and stress on the aircraft through the smoother runway surfaces. Yet it was found that the asphalt created its own problems.

As mentioned, thrown asphalt damaged the tail wheel retraction mechanisms. It also was spattered against the main landing gear struts after being thrown up by the tires, which caused abrasive wear to the struts themselves and destroyed the packing rings. Each Mustang that came off the 18th FBW's REMCO line was fitted with "boots" that covered the oleo struts in attempt to alleviate this problem.

Also coming from their REMCO was a modification to the Mustang's rocket racks that permitted them to carry 100 pound GP bombs. This required a modification to the A-2 Projector Control assembly that by-passed the rocket firing electrical circuits, but since the bombs were similar in weight to the 5" HVAR's, there were no discernible adverse effects to the Mustang's flight characteristics. The modification provided a very effective tool in attacking enemy ground positions.

It is not known to whom the credit should go for the rocket/bomb rack innovation, nor whose idea it was to establish the REMCO program for the 18th FBW, but to whomever the individuals were they deserve accolades for improving the serviceability of the F-51.

Combat losses continued true to form in April. On the 13th Lt. Allan Bettis, 12th FBS, was shot down while on a rail cutting mission and was killed. Four days later 1st Lt. William Starkley, 67th FBS, was wounded when he was shot down while on a RESCAP mission. He bailed out near Cho-do Island and was rescued by a helicopter. On April 23 1st Lt. Marvin Britting, 12th FBS, had to make a crash landing on a mud flat in North Korea after being hit by ground fire. He was rescued by a SA-16. Lt. Lawrence Wolfe, 12th FBS, was declared MIA while disappearing during a CAS mission on April 26, and was later declared as KIA. The following day two 67th FBS pilots were also declared MIA. 1st Lt. Starkley, who had recovered from his previous wounds in time to catch this mission, and 2nd Lt. Joel Rives. Both of them were killed while on an interdiction mission.

The 39th FIS had one pilot shot down during their last month of F-51 combat missions. On April 5 1st Lt. Grover Crocker was hit by both .50 caliber and 20 mm fire over the Chinnanpo Estuary. Coolant sprayed over

his canopy as he climbed and headed west to bailout over the Yellow Sea, but his engine froze before he could get to the coast and he had to bail out over the mud flats. Crocker landed three hundred yards out on the flats and only a hundred yards from where his Mustang plunked down. He then worked with the remainder of his flight on his survival radio, pin-pointing various antiaircraft batteries to them so they could be silenced. "Put Put Willie One and Two" both took hits from enemy fire while they were trying to knock out the guns and had to be replaced by a flight of F-84s, but the Thunderjets were able to stay around long enough to escort in a helicopter that rescued Crocker.

The "Cobra's" of the 39th FIS were released from combat operations on April 19. Two days later their Mustangs were dispersed to the other three 18th FBW squadrons. 39th FIS personnel were flown back to Chinhae to await further orders. The pilots then were assigned to various F-86 schools in Japan while airmen with less than four months remaining on their overseas tours were retained by the 18th FBW. Those with longer to serve were sent to either the 16th or 25th FIS's for OJT on Sabres. Although technically still assigned to the 35th Fighter Interceptor Wing, the 39th FIS was attached at this time to the 51st FIW at Suwon for further combat operations as a F-86E squadron.

During the twenty months that the 39th FIS had flown Mustangs in the Korean War they had flown a total of 13,535 combat sorties and amassed 27,337: 50 combat hours. The squadron and it's personnel earned every decoration awarded, plus the undying gratitude of the people of South Korea.

For combat operations the 18th FBW was now, finally, at the authorized TO&E strength for the standard three-squadron USAF Wing. Their primary assignment now was to support the UN ground forces in the "Punchbowl" area under the control of the 6147th Tactical Control Group's LTA-6 Mosquitos. Often they also would team-up with 1st Marine Air Wing F9Fs and the 8th Fighter Bomber Wing F-80s for rail cutting missions around Pyongyang, Sunchon and Chongju on the northwestern coast of North Korea.

Although most of these deep penetration missions were flown with a jet fighter escort, there were times when the jets had to be employed elsewhere or that the Mustang missions continued beyond the duration of the jets fuel. In these instances, F-86s would proceed to an assigned orbit point where they would circle as the Mustangs flew under them, and then head for home. Relieving flights would attempt to move in to cover the Mustangs at predetermined times in order to cover them during the missions return.

These missions were literal "white knuckle" sorties for the F-51 pilots, for they knew that they were operating directly on the Red's doorstep and that their "big brother" escort was many long blocks away. (This was during a period where there was a critical shortage of F-86 drop tanks within FEAF and Sabre missions had to be flown with just one external tank with corresponding limited range).

During one of these missions in April the 18th FBW Mustangs had just passed their initial point on the run-in to the target and the F-86s had long since departed, when they were jumped by a flight of MiG's. The MiGs swept in behind the last flight of Mustangs and using their greater speed they swept right up through the line of F-51 formations while firing upon each flight as they came upon them. Fortunately the MiG pilots were poor marksmen, for although a few Mustangs received minor damage, none were shot down.

To get around at least a part of this threat the 18th FBW started staggering their formations from side to side instead of flying in trail. Then when they were jumped by MiG's the individual flights were more flexible and were able to turn in toward the interlopers to provide mutual support for each other. Under these circumstances two of the attached 2 Squadron SAAF pilots were able to team up and managed to damage one of the MiG's and force the remainder of the MiG flight to break off their attack.

Indicative of the combat situation was the number of pilot and aircraft losses in May. Although there is a disparity between the 18th FBW's claim that nine Mustangs were lost and five pilots killed or missing, the individual squadron's do not indicate quite that heavy of a loss rate for the month.

On May 1 2nd Lt. David Gray had to belly-in a Mustang at K-14. On May 5 1st Lt. Robert Fluhr, 12th FBS, was killed when he was shot down on an interdiction mission. On May 13 1st Lt. Melvin Sousa, 67th FBS had to belly-in another Mustang at K-16. On May 14 2nd Lt. Leonard Olsen, 12th FBS, was up on his first training flight with the 18th FBW at Chinhae when his Mustang caught on fire. Olsen was killed when he crashed short of the runway as he tried to bring it back. At K-14 that afternoon 1st Lt. Harry Steffenson, 67th FBS, had a major accident as he was taxiing-in from a mission. His F-51 was a write-off, but he was uninjured. On May 22 1st Lt. Clayborn McCauley, 67th FBS, had to bail out at sea off of North Korea, but the reason for it was not indicated, and he was rescued, but by whom is not recorded.

The 18th FBW records indicated that they had pilots declared as MIA on May 15, 21 and 31, yet only Lt. Paul Kniss, 12th FBS, is mentioned, without detail. In a recent letter to the author, however, Kniss explained exactly what had transpired and it is worth going into in detail for it captures exactly what trying circumstances the pilots faced while fighting in far northwest North Korea.

The mission was what was termed as a "group gaggle," a rail interdiction strike to just north of Namsi, where all three squadrons were to bomb the same stretch of railroad track during the course of the day. The ordnance was 500 pound GP bombs with time-delay fuses varying between twelve and seventy-two hours to thwart communist repair crews in the hope that the track would be out of commission for at least a week.

The 12th FBS had dispatched about twenty Mustangs, but one had to abort, and it was escorted home by its wingman. The mission, itself, was led by 1st Lt. John Carlton and Lt. Kniss was training a new flight leader, 1st Lt. George Massey, so he was flying as "Love Two" with Massey as "Love One."

Approaching Sinanju they were jumped by a group of MiG-15s and the radar controller in South Korea told them to salvo their ordnance and abort the mission. Carlton did not hear the instructions and with his own wingman, Lt. Leonard Ranch, they continued north bound. Seeing this, Kniss instructed Lt. Massey to stay with them and they would attempt to cover Carlton's flight.

"Shortly thereafter, Massey said 'Love 2, break, there is a MiG on your ass.' I looked to my Number Two to see what was going on, and to see which direction he would break. Soon I realized that I was Number 2, and that it was me that was being hit.

"The MiG torched me almost immediately, and I turned to the water to bail out if necessary. 'Love 2, you

The remains of Lt. Brooks Mustang after his rescue. (Kempthorn via Davis)

124

are on fire,' yelled Massey. 'I know, I want to make the water,' I replied.

"One MiG 15 made a pass on me from my ten o'clock position. I turned into him and held my trigger switch down. I saw hits on him, and as he went by, he made what looked like a split S, so I don't know whether I got him or not. I had enough problems of my own.

"I was not going to make the water, so I stood up and looked down, and as I was doing so, the tail burned off, the nose pitched down and threw me out. I hit both the vertical and horizontal stabilizers with my head (in a helmet), and my ass. As I was floating down, one MiG almost hit me, and several went by and waved at me. None of the MiGs fired at me in the chute.

"After landing I slipped my chute into a rice paddy, so that I could be rescued by one of our choppers. After doing so, I ran to a large irrigation ditch and jumped in. I removed my classified information and buried it beneath the water and mud. I called my flight on my escape radio and told them to get a chopper up here 'Toute Suite.' By now I was drawing small arms fire, the purpose of which was to keep me in one spot, as none of the shots appeared to hit to close.

"Massey said, 'Are you okay?' 'Yes,' I replied. He sounded scared, as anyone in his position would be. 'The MiG's are shooting the hell out of us,' stated Massey. I said, 'Get the hell out of here!' I had never lost a wingman and I did not want to loose one now.

"I tried to run for the trees, but my leg gave way, and when I pushed myself up out of the rice paddy there was a group of civilians with guns, and one of them had a rifle shoved in front of my nose.

"They took my gun and all of my personal possessions, (watch, wedding ring, etc.) and the one in front of me, with my .45, fired a shot into the ground by me. In doing so, he held the gun by his leg, and in accidentally firing a shot, nearly took his foot off. I laughed – big mistake – he came over and hit me in the face with my gun.

"They took me to a Korean village, whereupon a Korean put a pistol in my face and pretended to pull the trigger. He would then remove the gun and all the people would laugh. He did this three or four times. I must have reacted properly, as he then gave me one of my own cigarettes and everyone smiled at me.

"The Chinese Army arrived in about five minutes and started me toward their AA (antiaircraft) positions. We met a group of Russians who in pantomime indicated that they wanted to hang me. The Chinese seemed like the best bet, so I leaned toward the Chinese and away from the Russian who was pulling my arm. This made him

angry, so he released me and hit me in the face three or four times.

"With this, the Chinese soldiers backed off and cocked their rifles and the Russians armed their machine guns, (tommy gun type, but air cooled) and here was our Hero in the middle of this with a stupid look on his face. This went on five seconds or fifty years, depending where you stood. Eventually, cooler heads prevailed and the Russians hopped back in their trucks and left us to continue our march.

"By a little tree, the Chinese stopped me and mounted their bayonets. They then put a blindfold on me and pushed me back against the tree. I remembered reading about the Rape of Nanking, the Japanese had used the Chinese for bayonet practice.

"Leaving me there for a minute or so, (To me it seemed like hours) they then led me to a large hut. Removing my blindfold, they took my flight suit and left me in my underwear. They eventually returned the suit. Someone had washed it. All day long I was the object of curiosity, as Russian and Chinese soldiers paraded by me all day.

"That night I traveled all night in the rain to Sinanju, where the fun started."

Kniss did not care to elaborate on his ordeals in the POW camp.

June 1952 was much more of the same for the men of the 18th FBW, although the 12th FBS did manage to get through the month unscathed. The 67th FBS declared two pilots as MIA. 1st Lt. George Patton on June 13 and 1st Lt. Archibald Conners on June 25. It was later found that both had been killed in action. 1st Lt. John McAlpine was known to have been killed outright, on June 24.

It also appeared that Lt. Gray was attempting to break McCamish's record for wiping out aircraft. On June 7 while flying a T-6 in marginal visibility he hit a cable which did quite a bit of damage to the Texan. On June 27 he then had to make another belly landing in a F-51 at K-46, because of battle damage. Little matter to the USAF, for he would retire as a Major General.

There were five stand down days in June because of the summer rains. K-46 was undulated by a six day deluge and flood control parties had to be established to attempt to protect the living quarters and operational areas of the base with sandbags and drainage ditches. When the Han River overflowed its banks everything became miserable for all.

In spite of many curtailed missions the 18th FBW flew 1179 sorties and 2345 combat hours during the month. Each Mustang averaged 23.6 sorties. The missions, themselves, varied, as usual, and included further attacks on "Ping Pong"(Pyongyang East airdrome, formally known as K-24). On June 14 the mission emphases shifted to ground support along the MLR once again. During one of these strikes Lt. Baxter, 12th FBS, earned a personal commendation from the new commanding officer of the 18th FBW, Colonel Shelton Brinson, for working his "Nan Flight" along the MLR in front of UN troops where they "caused great damage to the enemy."

The most powerful raids conducted by the 18th FBW were on June 23-26. These were attacks on the North Korean power plants at Suiho, Choshin and Fusen. The first were against the mammoth hydroelectric plant at Suiho, on the south fork of the Yalu River. This plant provided electricity for Pyongyang, Chinnampo, and much of Manchuria. Due to its location it was beyond the range of friendly fighter cover, so the 18th FBW had to make their way in and back out again on their own. But the MiG's did not show up, and the target was rendered useless without a loss.

The second attack was against Plant #2 at Choshin, and it was here that the Mustang flown by Lt. John McAlpine, 67th FBS, was shot down on June 24 by defending gunfire. The last attack was at Plant #4 at Fusen, and 1st Lt. Archibald Connors, 67th FBS, was lost on June 25. Both of these plants were put out of business for the duration. The exploits of the Mustang pilots were virtually ignored, however, for they were but a bit part of the largest concentrated effort put on by the jet propelled tactical units to date, and the jet jockeys managed to grab all the attention of both the press flacks and the official USAF historians.

As mentioned, during the early months of the war the 18th Fighter Bomber Group pilots had experimented with night missions in their F-51s to stop the North Korean onslaught. In July 1952 another attempt was made to fly these types of missions once again, even though it was recognized that the F-51 was hardly a feasible aircraft for this role. The purpose of these missions was to simply keep the Reds on their toes, and Headquarters FEAF decided that the Mustangs would be better than jets for this purpose. (Beginning in the early winter of 1952/53 they would change their mind and start using F-84s for these missions).

These strikes were of two different types, one working with LTA-6 Mosquitos along the MLR in total darkness to provide CAS for night infantry patrols. The other was in conjunction with a GCI site identified as "Hillbilly Control." These were MPG-2 radar attacks where the Mustangs were radar vectored to identified targets by the GCI controller where they bombed upon the controller's command. Normal loads for these flights of four Mustangs were eight 500 pound GP bombs. Since "Hillbilly" was physically located near the MLR, accuracy was considered to be quite good, often having as little as a two hundred foot error from a bomb release altitude of 1,000 feet.

Eventually this radar bombing program was expanded to include daylight operations with the Mustangs flying over solid cloud decks, which gave the enemy little respite regardless of weather conditions on the ground. Raymond Rice, James Kindelberger and Edgar Schmued, who had teamed up in 1940 to design the Mustang would have been astounded at the role that their progeny had assumed.

The 18th FBW flew their 45,000 effective combat sortie on July 9, just six days short of their second anniversary in Korea. This was the highest number of combat sorties flown up to this time by any unit in the war. The honor of flying this mission went to Captain Elliott Ayer, 67th FBS, but it was a dubious honor. Two weeks later, on July 25, Ayer would be killed on his own eighty-fourth mission. He was the Wing's only loss for the month.

In late summer 1952 the USAF's pilot training program finally caught up with the war's demand. All of a sudden there was an absolute glut of new pilots assigned to the 18th FBW. The 12th FBS picked up twenty-two new pilots, and they were not the least bit happy about it. The new pilots obviously did not have the experience of those pilots previously assigned from ANG or AFRES units and they required constant shepherding to get them trained in the Mustang. The 12th FBS had to stand down for five days just to get another new training program underway, "Which made the pilots stamp their feet with joy."

The pilots found it quite unrealistic, also, to return from a combat mission only to find themselves assigned to fly a training sortie with a rookie pilot to the gunnery range at Naktong. And of course, all of the new pilots were eager to start flying missions, which created competition for mission scheduling. There were not that many F-51s to go around. The high mission man for the month was 1st Lt. Bill Dursteller who flew seventeen, but most pilots only averaged a dozen sorties, averaging one every three days. This meant that all were going to have to spend more time in Korea than anticipated. In all, the training program, according to the pilots, "stinks."

The 67th FBS lost the only Mustang from the USAF portion of the 18th FBW in August when on August 2 Captain Charles Sargen had his canopy come off his

Mustang right after takeoff from K-46. Apparently it struck him on his forehead as it slid off of its rails, for Sargen bailed out twelve miles east of Hoensong, but he had no recollection of why he did so!

The Wing was forced to stand down for eight days again in September, either because of the continuing rainy season or their training commitments. The entire 18th FBW did fly 1,351 effective sorties in the operational periods, which averaged twenty-one missions per aircraft. There was an amount of elation involved in these figures, because for the first time since they entered the war there were no pilot losses.

One Mustang was written-off, however, as a result of battle damage on September 7 when "Mike Flight" from the 12th FBS found themselves jumped by MiG-15s near Pyongyang. The F-51s had to fight their way out of this encounter, but they did not score any hits upon the MiGs. The Mustang flown by Lt. William Dursteler took a 37mm hit in its left wing, which left a hole large enough to stand in. His wingman, 2nd Lt. Dick Kempthorn, escorted him back to K-14 for an emergency landing, while the rest of the flight diverted to K-16.

Rumors started flying around the squadrons in October that the 18th FBW was being slated to receive F-86s. Even though this appeared to be only a rumor at the time, it did create a rather unusual problem. There was a certainty among several of the pilots that there was more than a degree of truth to the rumor and from this time on they wanted no part of the Mustang at all. They started begging off combat missions, to keep from building up their individual mission totals in the event that they might have too many missions racked up and they would not be able to retrain into the Sabre. Other pilots, those who were eager to get out of Korea, or otherwise did not want any part of jet fighters, started snapping up all the missions that they could. This created havoc with both pilot proficiency and mission scheduling.

The 18th FBW was non-operational for eight days in October because of poor flying weather. Flying was restricted on thirteen more days during the morning hours because of prevalent ground fogs. Even with Mother Nature being on the Red's side the 12th FBS managed to fly 617 sorties, the 67th FBS 635 and 2 Squadron 326. This figure was only thirty-two short of the total number of sorties requested by the JOC.

Twenty-four Mustangs were led by Lt. Colonel Bradley, Deputy Group Commander, on October 6 against enemy troop concentrations at Piltae-ni. They dropped six tons of napalm and six more tons of 500 pound GP bombs with outstanding results. On October 12 Colonel

Sheldon Brinson, Commanding Officer 18th FBG, led twenty-four more Mustangs against Red troop concentrations and in the process they dropped or fired eleven tons of bombs or rockets. Again on October 27 Colonel Brinson took twenty-four Mustangs against Red supply dumps and storage shelters where they dropped seventeen tons of bombs.

Again there is a disparity in the number of reported aircraft losses during these raids. The 18th FBW historian stated that only one F-51 was lost during October, while the 18th FBG records indicate that actually four were lost, with one of these being shot down by a MiG-15. Neither historian reported who, what, where or when.

In actuality, 2 Squadron had Lt. T.V. Fryer shot down and taken prisoner of war on October 12. A Lt. P. Maxwell, 67th FBS, had to make a crash landing that wrote-off his F-51 on October 14. Captain Miguel "Mike" Encinas, 12th FBS, had to bail out of another Mustang, but the reason and date are unknown. There is a mention in the 18th FBW records of the death of Lt. Colonel Brenner as a result of an aircraft accident, but his name is not on the USAF causality listing.

Both combat losses in November involved pilots from the 12th FBS, but once again poor documentation leaves questions. On November 5 Lt. John Woliung was killed when he failed to pull out of a dive while on a close air support strike. The second pilot, whose identity is unknown, crashed during a low level bomb run and he was carried as MIA. A third 12th FBS pilot took a .30 caliber round through his buttocks, but flew, albeit uncomfortably, home for a safe landing.

Seventy-five percent of the missions flown by the 18th FBW in November were CAS while the remainder were JOC commitments in various roles. The 12th FBS also received orders to begin flying "Interceptor" missions during this period, but these were not true interception missions against unknown aircraft via radar vectors, but only consisted of flying CAP's along the front lines while keeping a lookout for unknown aircraft.

Multiple problems continued with the F-51s. As replacement Mustangs were ferried in from Japan there were constant complaints from their pilots of rough running engines. An inspection of the aircraft's magnetos showed that over twenty of them were badly corroded as a result of inadequate care. Problems with the landing gear retraction strut connecting rod assemblies showed that they were failing in compression. This was a result of their having exceeded their operational limits as the pilots cycled the landing gear up or down. Maladjustment of these parts was blamed on the lack of experienced maintenance men.

There were also problems with the napalm tanks, which were by now all of Japanese construction. The M-16 grenades which were used to ignite the tanks upon impact would not seat properly in the tank openings and caused napalm to seep out. If the pilots fired their machine guns before dropping the tanks the flash of gunfire would ignite the napalm residue, which shook up the pilots when they had a burning napalm tank hanging beneath their wing. What had been almost a matter of course technique during the early stages of the war was not well received any longer.

December mission totals included 395 interdiction, 824 close support, 162 RESCAP and twenty-six reconnaissance sorties. These totals were amassed during twenty-five days of flying, with the stand-down days resulting from either adverse weather conditions or during the period when General Eisenhower visited and the 18th FBW and stood "Ike's" inspection. This was also a period when the Wing had some of their lowest losses, for the 12th FBS had no accidents, no combat losses, and amazingly no aircraft reported as damaged by enemy fire.

The 67th FBS had only one damaged. On December 4 Captain Jack Hawley had a total engine failure on takeoff at K-46 and had to make a forced landing. 2 Squadron lost one Mustang also: On Christmas Day one of their Mustangs had an encounter with a USN Skyraider and its pilot was shot down for the Wing's only pilot loss.

The constant rumor of conversion to Sabres was finally verified in December when the 18th FBW received orders to move once again. Since neither K-10 nor K-46

was suitable for jet operations, the new base would be K-55 as Osan. Commencing on December 26 all personnel and equipment not essential for Mustang operations started their relocation to K-55. Logistically, this move was a major improvement in itself, for now all of the squadrons were to be colocated with both the 18th FBG and Wing headquarters at one location instead of being separated by over one hundred fifty miles. Advance parties from the 12th and 67th FBS's then started their move to Osan on January 6, 1953, with the main bodies of the two squadrons joining back up with them on January 11.

On January 8 the 12th FBS was withdrawn from combat operations and their pilots were instructed to ferry their Mustangs to J-19, Kisarazu Air base, Japan to be turned over to the 6401st Maintenance Squadron. A landing accident at J-13 marred this last 12th FBS Mustang operation when one flown by Lt. Rouke collided with another while landing at Itazuke, enroute to Kisarazu. Rouke was trapped in the wreckage of his aircraft, but 2nd Lt. Richard Kempthorn ran to the crash site and yanked Rouke free. Both pilots suffered burns, but both recovered in time to start jet transition training with the others of their squadron. Kempthorn was awarded the Soldiers Medal for his part in the rescue.

The 67th FBS lost one last Mustang to enemy action when its pilot had to bail out northwest of Sariwon after having his Merlin engine hit by small arms fire. The unidentified pilot was rescued by a helicopter and returned to K-46 with only minor injuries.

A "Maximum Effort" was flown by the 67th FBS on January 16 out of K-46, and upon the completion of the strike they flew their Mustangs to K-55. This action termi-

Do not tempt the gods of Mount Olympus. Lt. Paul Kniss has his photograph taken with 44-84638 on May 31, 1952. Two hours later he was a POW after being shot down by a MiG-15. (Kniss)

nated fighter-bomber operations from Hoengsong. The last 18th FBW Mustang missions were flown on January 23 and they consisted of two eight-ship CAS strikes.

At 1505 hours KST "Easy" and "Item" Flights, led by 1st Lt. George Hartwig, took off from K-55 to attack bunkers, automatic weapon and mortar positions. These attacks were reported to be with 100% coverage and 100% effectiveness. At 1520 hours Major Max King, commanding officer 67th FBS, led seven more Mustangs of "George" and "How" Flights on a similar strike against Red strong points. They destroyed four mortar positions, twenty personnel shelters, three command posts, and caused several secondary explosions. Major Jack Hawley, 67th FBS executive officer, was the last to return from these sorties, and thusly earned the distinction of flying the last official USAF combat sortie in a Mustang of the 18th FBW.

When the 18th FBW was relieved from combat operations there remained the problem of what to do with those pilots who could not economically be retrained in the F-86. A cut-off point of sixty missions was utilized, which did serve to create some hard feelings toward the USAF by a few disgruntled pilots. Most of these particular pilots were those who had been recalled from the reserves in 1951 and few had any jet experience, but they did want to gain some since they were there and felt that the opportunity existed for them to fly the F-86. From the 67th FBS eight pilots were forced against their desire to return to the United States, and twenty-one more were reassigned to other 5th Air Force units, including the 6146th Air Base group who continued to fly the Mustang in support of the ROKAF. The 12th FBS had thirty-nine Mustang pilots, of which six were rotated home, and thirty-three were entered into the Sabre training program. Of these, twenty-two were rotated back to the States prior to having completed their F-86 training, twelve against their will. It was not exactly a happy ending to what had been an era of great sacrifice. It was considered to be an atypical FEAF SNAFU.

Approaching Pyongyang on the morning of August 14, 1951 the Mustangs of Major Murrit Davis (In "Sexy Sally") and Captain Al Wagner were photographed by Captain John Horn. Both their F-51s were damaged by enemy fire, so they were exchanged for fresh ones and the 18th FBG returned to Pyongyang that afternoon. Both Davis and Horn were shot down and killed. (USAF via Ron Witt)

CHAPTER EIGHT

2 Squadron, South African Air Force

On August 4, 1950 the government of the Union of South Africa announced that they would place at the disposal of the United Nations one of their Air Force's fighter squadrons for use in the Korean War. Through a call for volunteers throughout all of the units and formations within the South African Air Force, SAAF, a contingent was formed that consisted of a liaison headquarters and a fighter-bomber squadron. It should be noted that every man involved was a true volunteer in the literal sense, as the South African Defense Act of 1912, as amended, provided that no citizen could fight outside of South Africa without his personal consent. Initially, all of the selected men were from the SAAF permanent force, although later on reservists were permitted to serve a tour in Korea, but again only upon their personal request.

By agreement, the aircraft to be flown in Korea, as well as all the necessary technical equipment would be purchased outright by the South African government from the United States. All of this material was to be made available to them upon their arrival in the Far East, which precluded a myriad of shipping problems for them. These items eventually were also to include some of the more necessary individual items, such as winter flying clothing, which never would have been available through their own supply channels, as they had no need for them in their own country. It has always been a point of pride with the SAAF that they paid the United States for every single item that they obtained.

The new volunteer squadron took the designation of 2 Squadron, a previously inactivated squadron that had a lineage dating back to the early days of World War II. The original 2 Squadron had fought and earned battle honors in East Africa, Albania, Sicily, Italy and other points in the Middle East. Their motto was "Su Suh Phors'que,"

The first USAF Mustang supplied to 2 Squadron, South African Air Force was ex 45-11370. It was lost on March 2, 1951 in an attempted ditching in Wonsan Harbor. Lt. D.A. Ruiter was killed. (USAF)

which translates from the Afrikains language as "Upwards and Onwards." In general, however, they became more commonly known as the "Flying Cheetahs," which derived from their individual squadron insignia, which was taken from two cheetah cub mascots that they took to Korea with them.

On August 27 Commandant S. "SV" van Breda Theron was "nominated" as commanding officer 2 Squadron. This nomination, or selection method, was carried through to all other members of the original squadron contingent. Theron, an ex-World War II fighter pilot, would lead a group composed of one hundred fifty-seven enlisted men and forty-seven pilots. (Of these, only eight had previous World War II combat experience). The new 2 Squadron assembled at Air Force Station Waterkloof, near Pretoria, on September 5. Twenty days later, with all of the initial training requirements behind them, they departed Pretoria by rail to Durban, where they boarded the H.V. Tjisadane to sail for Japan.

At this time the North Korean army was retreating back toward the 38th Parallel. Many of the South Africans were heard to express disappointment at this news, for they were sure that the war would be over before they could get into action. Almost all of October was spent in transient, for they stopped in Singapore, Hong Kong and other Commonwealth ports to visit Royal Air Force stations in goodwill gestures. Finally, on November 1 the "Tjisadane" docked at Kobe, Japan and everyone was broke, for they had all spent their allowances during their ports of call.

Three days later they departed Kobe with only the rumor that they were going to be assigned to the USAF's 35th Fighter Interceptor group. They arrived at Yokohama the following day and were finally allowed to disembark, being transported to Johnson Air Base to be greeted by Lt. General Sir Horace Robertson, Commander in Chief, British Commonwealth Occupation Forces, and Brigadier General Oliver Pricher, USAF. They were also greeted by an all-black USAF band, as someone had expected that the squadron would be composed of negroes, which did not set well with their apartheid views.

At Johnson Air Base a six week conversion training course commenced to teach the South Africans to fly the sixteen F-51s that had already been purchased by their government, while the ground crews set about learning the idiosyncrasies of the Mustangs. Again this lengthy program did not set too well with the squadron, as the combat veterans had all previously flown the Mustang with the Royal Air Force while the other pilots were experienced in the P-40, which they viewed as similar enough

to the F-51 to prepare them for combat. On November 8 the first of these Mustangs to bear the SAAF insignia of the Springbok took to the air over Japan on a training sortie. During the course of this training came more culture shocks, as in the field the South Africans were rationed (fed) by their government, so they did not expect to have to pay for their own meals in the USAF mess halls as was customary practice for USAF officers. Since they were still broke, their government had to make an emergency appropriation of funds so their men could eat. Inflation, in the form of pay scales was another shock, for their standards of pay was far lower than that of the USAF, and the American's dollar influence in Japan had brought on a rapid boost in the asking price of every available items in the stores. There was also the problem of integration, for the South Africans, who did not associate themselves with negroes, found themselves forced to dine, work and fly with USAF black airmen. One SAAF pilot's comment was, "Well, they must be far superior to ours."

On November 16 two C-47s carrying eight pilots and twenty-two maintenance personnel departed Johnson Air Base to join the 6002nd Tactical Support Wing at Taegu Air Base, K-2, Korea for further on-the-job training. Due to a change in plans, 2 Squadron now became attached to the 18th Fighter Bomber Group instead of the 35th FIW. At K-2 the men of 2 Squadron were assigned to the 12th Fighter Bomber Squadron to continue their OJT in a more realistic fashion. Three days later, after several orientation flights, Commander Theron, with Captain C.B. "Lippy" Lipawsky as wingman, flew the squadron's first combat mission of the Korean War. Their flight hit a communist supply line with bombs and rockets, and then they

In the arming pits at K-46. SAAF # 366 is prepared for a mission over North Korea. This Mustang was supplied to 2 Squadron on April 7, 1951. When 2 Squadron converted to F-86Fs, it was returned to the USAF, who in turn transferred it to the ROKAF. (USAF)

"Miss Marunduchi" was SAAF # 361, ex-USAF 44-74863.She is shown here awaiting takeoff clearance from K-10 with four rockets and two 500 lb. GP bombs. The fatigue of the wing walker speaks for itself. (USAF)

landed at Mirim-Ni Airdrome, K-24, (Pyongyang East) where the rest of the 18th FBG was staging at the time.

The UN forces had been preparing for an all-out offensive against the North Korean Army, which was scheduled for November 24. The attack started on schedule and 2 Squadron flew four major missions in support of this effort. With continual air support the UN ground forces were able to push northwards at a rate of five to eight miles per day against only scattered resistance until November 26 when the drive stalled, and then they suffered a massive reversal when the communist counter attacks turned out to be a massive offensive on the Red's part.

The remainder of 2 Squadron had been scheduled to join their contingent in Korea on November 29, but the communist counter attacks caused a revision to this plan. It had become obvious that the UN forces had over extended their supply lines and the Red's took advantage of this situation. They managed to drive a wedge into the Republic of Korea's II Corps line, and soon thereafter the entire front collapsed. To consolidate the MLR the UN forces attempted to pull back, but they encountered heavy fire from guerrillas and other forces that had infiltrated in behind them to set up roadblocks. It appeared that the men of 2 Squadron were going to get their wish for extensive combat, for the war was far from over.

With the close proximity of the North Korean Army to the UN outposts and with the belief that 200,000 Chinese troops were just over the boarder in Manchuria, a decision was made to retain the rest of 2 Squadron in Japan until it could be determined just how strong the communist winter offensive might be. At this time there were only the four SAAF Mustangs involved in the stag-

ing operations at Mirim-Ni and this appeared that this would be the maximum contribution that the squadron would be able to make out of the small airstrip. K-24, in itself, was within hearing distance of the gunfire at the MLR, and several armored cars and tanks were brought by the army to assist in airfield defense. They almost had a chance to test these antiaircraft defenses on November 29 when a MiG-15 zipped overhead, but he was gone before anyone could bring a gun to bear. Later that afternoon another unidentified aircraft intruded into their airspace again, but it also escaped unharmed. That night two North Korean guerrillas made an attempt at assassinating the base's commanding officer, but this was prevented by a number of GI's who captured them first.

Within a week enemy troops were attacking UN forces south of Pyongyang and it was clear that K-24 would have to be evacuated. On the morning of November 30 C-54s, C-47s and C-119s flew into K-24 through heavy Red ground fire to airlift out the 18th FBG's heavy equipment south to K-13, Suwon Air Base. While these efforts were taking place 2 Squadron launched three Mustangs to successfully break up a North Korean ambush near Kununi where they had set up two roadblocks that bottlenecked UN troops against the Taedong River. The contingent of 2 Squadron continued to give CAS of this nature to the UN forces as November closed, having flown 122 combat hours in sixty-seven sorties during their first two weeks of combat.

2 Squadron suffered its first casualty in a twist of irony and heroism on December 5. Captains J.F.D. "John" Davis and C.B. Lipawsky were ordered to destroy a UN supply train that was loaded with explosives some six miles north

of Sunan that had fallen into communist hands. The Mustangs were loaded with six 5" HVAR's each, and the pilots located the train without difficulty and commenced their attacks. Davis got a bit low on his last rocket run, and when the rocket blew up a boxcar a secondary explosion went off right in his face. The explosion's concussion blew off the Mustang's canopy and windshield, knocked out the controls to the elevators and blew both ailerons off the Mustang's wings! It also perforated the Mustang's cooling system, cheese holed the fuselage and knocked Davis unconscious.

What was left of the Mustang staggered through the sky and Davis recovered consciousness just as his Merlin engine quit. He had little choice but to attempt to belly his Mustang in at 180 mph. Meanwhile, Lipawsky set up an orbit over the area and called for a rescue helicopter. There were no USAF helicopters in the area, but a U.S. Army chopper flown by Captain Jim Lawrence and carrying Captain Lewis Millet, from the 25th Infantry Division as an observer, heard the distress calls.

Lawrence lowered the chopper down between jagged rocks and Millet climbed out, giving his seat to the well shaken Davis who had somehow survived the high-speed crash landing with only minor injuries. Davis was airlifted to safety. Millet was rescued, and would later the following year be awarded for his bravery on Bayonet Hill.

To bolster the squadron, five more pilots and their Mustangs flew to K-13 from Johnson during the first week of December. They were accompanied by a C-54 with twenty enlisted men, along with more supplies. Most of these "supplies" had been "requisitioned" from unserviceable Mustangs in Japan, because of shortcomings in FEAF's supply system. Resorting to cannibalism was any soldiers expedient method of obtaining parts. Also on board the C-54 was a large supply of winter clothing, which was gratefully received by the men who had never expected to experience such a thing as a Korean winter. December in South Africa was the middle of their summer season.

From Suwon Air Base the pilots occupied themselves by launching attacks against shipping in the Sinuiju Harbor. Other than these, missions for the most part were those of interdiction and ground support. But also during December some pilots drew the opportunity of flying a fighter escort mission for B-29s, which was a role that most had never experienced. The Mustangs were jumped by a flight of MiG-15s and the SAAF pilots quickly discovered that the jets were far superior to the Mustangs that they were flying, but they managed to evade the MiG's

Captain C.B. Lipawsky takes off on a combat strike on December 17, 1950. His Mustang is carrying two napalm tanks in addition to six rockets. Captain J.F.O. Davis was killed in this F-51 on March 3, 1951 at Yongdongwon-ni. (U.S. Army via Ethell)

fire and they returned home without receiving any damage to themselves or allowing the MiGs to attack the Superfortresses.

On December 17, the day after they had celebrated the South African version of Thanksgiving Day, the first section of the contingent remaining in Japan departed for Chinhae, K-10, where they were met by Colonel Curtis Low, who had just assumed command of the 18th Fighter Bomber Wing the first of the month. The remaining personnel would follow in small groups over the next five days. The movement seemed rather casual in contrast to the expectations of the men who had thought that they were going to be immediately committed to battle as a single unit. But it was a question of logistics and available space for them, as priority had to be given to those men and units that were having to be withdrawn from North Korea first. As it turned out, K-10 would be the squadron's permanent home in Korea during their relationship with the Mustang.

The men now busied themselves by setting up tents and establishing themselves at K-10 in general. They were heartened by a directive from Colonel Low that stated that they would be committed to combat as a unit, for they had feared that since they had arrived in Korea in a piecemeal fashion, they would then be dispersed throughout the 18th FBW, or become a political showpiece for the United Nations and not see much combat at all.

Meanwhile the original contingent at K-13 was not suffering from any illusions. They continued the grim business of aerial warfare, destroying a large compound of enemy troops that was located three miles south of Huach-on. Strafing troops on the ground was not a pleasant task.

Due to the fatigue already being incurred by the men at K-13 a rotation policy was established by the 18th FBW to bring up from K-10 fresh pilots and ground personnel. Although K-10 was neither home nor paradise it was a place of relative comfort in comparison to the wintry conditions at Suwon. A quick thaw had turned everything into a quagmire. The cold and damp had brought on a rash of head colds and flu symptoms and other body aches which hampered the effectiveness of everyone. With rumors that the Reds were going to invade the area, the men pressed themselves to keep the aircraft serviceable, for air support was going to be the only apparent way to stop the communist drive to the south.

Two days after Christmas it was learned that both North Korean and Chinese troops had crossed the 38th Parallel. Everything north of the bomb line was now "fair target," even targets that only looked like they might be worthwhile were fair game. With the beginning of the new year winter came with a vengeance. Low cloud ceilings, snow, rain and fog hampered both flight and ground operations. The maintenance personnel were issued additional winter clothing as they struggled to acclimate themselves to their new environment. Although the weather conditions were equal, or probably had an even more severe effect on the poorly clothed communists, they managed to break through the MLR in two locations and continued to push the UN forces south once again.

On January 3 Kimpo Air Base was lost to the communists for the second time. 5th Air Force units evacuated the two airfields at Seoul, K-14 and K-16 in the nick of time, and the staging operations at K-13 was also forced to commence the evacuation process soon thereafter. 2 Squadron and the elements of the 18th Fighter Bomber

A "Springbok" at K-9, Pusan, on April 2, 1951. The Springbok's were a part of the SAAF's National Insignia and identity, but 2 squadron preferred to be known as the "Flying Cheetahs," which came from their squadron insignia. (Reed)

Group rejoined the 18th Fighter Bomber Wing at K-10 without a loss of personnel or equipment, but casualties were incurred by members of the 3rd Bomb Group (Light) at Suwon when it was attacked by guerrillas prior to the onslaught of the regular communist army.

Fighter-bomber missions were then flown from K-10 without a break. Pilots attacked towns, bridges, individual buildings and anything else that appeared capable of providing support or comfort to the enemy. Reconnaissance flights over the snow covered ground spotted many camouflaged trucks, but no enemy troops were seen, which indicated that they were again moving only at night. All roads leading south were again crammed with refugees, and the pilots found themselves nauseated by the sight of so many civilians dead in the ditches where they had fallen after perishing from exposure or having been shot after they were no longer able to serve as a shield to the enemy.

The weather once again, (Although it may appear to be a preoccupation topic.) was the toughest of foes. Often it forced the Mustang pilots to have to abort their assigned missions because the clouds could not be penetrated in aircraft without adequate instrumentation or deicing equipment.

Pilots were not permitted to return to Chinhae with external ordnance, because of safety factors, so they had to jettison it somewhere if they could not locate their assigned targets. Intelligence reports had indicated that the communists were again utilizing K-16 for their own operations, so its hangars and runways became the target of choice for the pilots to pickle-off unexpended ordnance. The base, itself was in an geographical position where it was easy enough to find regardless of the weather conditions, because of its proximity to the Han River. In due course it was virtually obliterated.

On January 20, 1951 2 Squadron flew twenty combat sorties and during them they claimed forty buildings destroyed and twenty held enemy villages damaged. These attacks were being carried out only thirty miles from K-10, and it was confirmed that 511 enemy troops were killed and five villages destroyed, with six more being 50% destroyed. It was a sad fact of war that these villages had only recently been in friendly hands and the inhabitants had once had the sensation of freedom: they no longer existed, and their surviving civilian occupants were again forced out into the cold. (In a later war there would be the catch-phrase, "It had to be destroyed in order to save it).

18th FBW squadrons continued this general pace through the end of January with 2 Squadron averaging twenty-one sorties per day. In all, this rate was a strong tribute to the maintenance troops who managed to keep twenty-three of 2 Squadron's twenty-four assigned Mustangs in service, the highest percentage of operational aircraft among all of FEAF's squadrons.

February 1951 opened with an increase in the UN's efforts. The MLR had finally become stabilized, and the ground forces were starting a slow northward push to recapture lost territory. The communists, also, had just refused the first of the UN cease-fire proposals.

Up until this time 2 Squadron had not suffered any personal losses, but on February 2 the inevitable occurred. At 0725 KST Lt. W. Saint Elmer Wilson took off from Chinhae with three other Mustangs on an armed reconnaissance mission. The F-51s were flying in the Wonson-Hamhung-Chosen Reservoir area when Wilson's Mustang was hit by small arms fire. At first the damage did not appear to be too bad and Wilson turned east and started a climb towards the sea to evade further ground fire. But soon his Mustang started streaming its glycol coolant fluid and Wilson was forced to bailout. He was seen to have a good parachute, land in the sea and begin to tread water in high waves. A SA-16 arrived and landed, but the crew of the Albatross could not locate Wilson before he disappeared beneath the waves.

Less than a week later a second 2 Squadron pilot was lost. On February 7 Commandant Theron was leading a mission against some enemy vehicular traffic behind the MLR. One of the members of his flight, 2nd Lt. Doug Leah, started down on a strafing pass on a truck and was hit by Red ground fire. Leah's Mustang was seen to stream fire and then become a torch before it scraped a wingtip on a rocky outcrop and then cartwheel and disintegrate.

Unfortunately the weather continued to remain the communists greatest ally. Moving under the cover of low clouds the Reds were able to firmly entrench themselves in dugouts that bombs and rockets could not penetrate. With the first real break in the winter weather coming on February 15 another mission was launched, this time with the intention of burning the Reds out with napalm. The attacks were successful, turning the dugouts into char houses.

But these attacks were not with out a loss. Lt. G. Derek Doveton was killed when his Mustang was hit by ground fire while he was making a strafing attack on an enemy controlled hillside. His Mustang simply continued its course and flew into the ground and there was nothing left but for his wingman, Lt. Doug McKellar, to do but to return to K-10 and report the loss.

SAAF # 318, ex USAF 45-11419, which became named "Shy Talk." Photographed at K-18, Kangnung, South Korea on May 25, 1951. Lt. C.J. Baransky died in this Mustang on April 20, 1952. (Reed)

Flying had to be curtailed once again because of the weather on February 21. Winds as high as 56 mph struck K-10 and knocked down tents and damaged several buildings. All Wing personnel had to turn-to and secure maintenance stands and other equipment that was being flung around by the winds and endangering man and machine. Fortunately there were no casualties and no damage to the parked Mustangs.

On February 24 the first replacement pilots for 2 Squadron arrived from South Africa, including Commandant R.F. "Ray" Armstrong who would eventually assume command of the squadron. Many of the original pilots were rapidly approaching their magic seventy-five mission mark and were eagerly looking forward to returning home. (The SAAF required seventy-five missions, while the USAF required one hundred). It was reported that it wasn't the combat conditions that effected them the most; it was the rotten winter weather and the infernal smells of the human feces that the Koreans used for fertilizer that bothered them the most.

With the new pilots arriving, an operational training program had to be established. Captain W. J.J. "Badie" Badenhorst was placed in charge of the new pilots, but they didn't get much more than a briefing on the Mustang and a blind cockpit check because the promised training aids had not become available. USAF Captain Al Holet, 40th FIS, remarked that once he got into a conversation with a 2 Squadron Mustang pilot who had just returned from his third combat mission and he had just attained a total of nine hours of F-51 time under his belt.

On March 2 the ramifications of war once again became apparent when 2 Squadron lost two pilots. The first to fall was Lt. D.A. "Foxy" Ruiter who was forced to ditch his Mustang approximately 200 yards north of Yo-do Island off the coast of North Korea. Ruiter had been leading a flight of four Mustangs on an armed recce mission when his engine started running rough. He pulled up in an attempt to gain as much altitude as he could, in hopes of finding a place to make a forced landing. But before he could spot a good location his Merlin engine quit, and because he had not gained enough altitude for a bailout attempt, Ruiter was forced to attempt a ditching. The Mustang sank within three seconds of touching the water and there remained no trace of plane or pilot thereafter.

Later that afternoon Captain Badenhorst was leading another four-ship armed recce along the road from Sinanju to Chong-ju when his Mustang was hit by a barrage of heavy antiaircraft fire and was seen to crash in flames in the village of Sinanju. There was so much antiaircraft fire in the immediate area that the remaining three Mustangs could not chance to go down to a lower altitude to see if Badenhorst had escaped. He was carried as MIA for a period, and his death was eventually confirmed.

On March 4 another Mustang of 2 squadron was lost. Lt. F.A. Piet Swemmer had just become airborne at K-10 when his Mustang's engine coughed and then quit cold. Swemmer maintained the runways' heading and set his aircraft down in a rice paddy. The F-51 was a total write-off but Swemmer escaped without injury.

March was appearing to look like a bad month for flight leaders of 2 Squadron. Mid-day on March 10 Captain John Davis was leading a flight over Yangdogwon-ni to provide CAS for a UN contingent and as Davis was making his final turn to line up on a target his Mustang was seen to enter a spin, which continued until it crashed. Intense ground fire was credited for his downing.

The squadron was now flying up to twenty-eight sorties per day and quite a celebration was in order when Commandant Theron and Captain Lipawsky became the first two 2 Squadron pilots to complete their seventy-five mission requirements. Both of these pilots had been World War II veterans and had been a portion of the squadron's initial cadre, so it was of mixed emotions when these two pilots were relieved of their combat missions. On March 16 Theron relinquished his command to Commandant Armstrong.

Because the of incessant spring rains along the southern coast of Korea, which had an adverse effect on combat operations out of K-10, it was decided to relocate 2 Squadron and the 18th Fighter Bomber Group to other airfields while construction took place at K-10 to make it a more all-weather capable airfield. On March 23-24 2 Squadron moved to K-9, Pusan-East Airdrome, where they were temporally attached to the 35th Fighter Interceptor Group for combat operations. They did, however,

retain their administrative section at K-10 along with the staff sections of the 18th FBW.

Antiaircraft fire was increasing daily in both intensity and accuracy. Just how many guns the communists brought into Korea has never been determined, but their gunners were receiving daily practice against the Mustangs that were roaming overhead. On March 20 Commandant Armstrong was leading an armed recce patrol when one of his flight members, Lt. Steve Armstrong, (No known relation.) started having engine problems, presumably because of a small arms round having hit it. The Merlin engine soon caught on fire and Armstrong had to bailout over enemy territory. Fortunately the remainder of his flight was able to RESCAP him long enough for a helicopter to make its way in to rescue him.

Lt. F. "Pottie" Potgieter also had a narrow escape while flying a CAP in the Munsen-ni area. A .50 caliber slug penetrated his cockpit and blew away the radio control box near his right thigh and then struck him in the chest. He recovered the control of his Mustang that he had lost after being thumped so abrasively and returned to K-9 for a safe landing.

Toward the end of the first week of April the UN ground forces once again recrossed the 38th Parallel northbound. Resistance was vigorous and many Red vehicles were again in evidence during daylight hours, in spite of the constant threat of the fighter-bombers overhead. Intelligence at 5th Air Force Headquarters felt that the communists were preparing for an assault of their own, for otherwise they were sure that the communists would not be so brazen in their efforts.

SAAF # 385 had quite a history. Originally serving with the 357th Fighter Group during World War II it was coded as OS-R and belonged to Lt. Colonel Elder, who totaled twenty kills. Post War it was assigned to the 192nd Fighter Squadron, Nevada ANG. After 2 Squadron converted to Sabres both # 385 and #390, (in the background) were given to the ROKAF. (Ethell)

44-73068 was photographed at Moline, Illinois during World War II when it belonged to an Air Training Command unit. Post War she was stored at Kelly AFB, Texas, and then went to 2 Squadron as # 329. It crashed on takeoff at K-16, Seoul, on August 29, 1951. (Archive)

2 Squadron now gave up carrying napalm in favor of 500 pound general purpose, GP, bombs and they started flying "post holing" missions against roadways throughout all of North Korea. On April 14 two pilots, Lts J.H. Kruger and S.G. "Syd" De la Harpe had phenomenal success at Songwol-ni when they discovered a convoy of nineteen camouflaged vehicles, which they proceeded to destroy. They then proceeded to northeast of Sinmak where they shot up three more. Not bad for a morning's work. Kruger would receive a DFC for leading this strike. On the surface, shooting up a bunch of trucks does not appear to be that mean a feat, but it must be noted that these trucks did not move around undefended. In each convoy several trucks were always interspersed among the others that were equipped with antiaircraft guns of some nature. Additionally, gun emplacements lined either side of all of the major North Korean thorough-fares. On April 16 Captain J.R. "Horse" Sweeny also attacked similar targets in the Kunchon area in the face of heavy antiaircraft fire. He continued his attacks without regard for his personal safety, and although his Mustang was undamaged by enemy fire, Sweeny's act was considered brave enough to warrant a DFC.

Between April 23 and April 29 2 Squadron moved back to K-10 to rejoin the men of the 18th FBW. They were quite pleased with the transformation of their old base, for it was now a permanent installation with improvements in both living and flying conditions. Messing, billeting and sanitary improvements had all been accomplished, along with the resurfacing of the runway and the installation of navigational aids for instrument flying. Thanks to the AACS people, the pilots would now be able to fly a complete, and safe, instrument approach without having to rely on the sometimes erratic Direction Finding, DF, station, since an ADF radio beacon had been set up near the base.

The skies finally cleared with the advent of spring and on April 30 2 Squadron launched thirty combat sorties to celebrate, but in the process another Mustang was lost. Lt. Piet Celliers was attacking a railroad tunnel three miles east of Sinmak when he was hit in the leg by fragments of a 20 mm shell. These types of attacks were always hazardous for the pilots, as the tunnels were always located in rough terrain and consequently forced them to fly low to the ground along the tracks in order to skip-bomb their bombs into the tunnels entrances, and they had to make a hard pull-up to avoid the hillsides. The communist gunners obviously knew this predictable flight path and placed their antiaircraft guns accordingly. In Celliers' case he was lucky, as when his Mustang caught fire he had just cleared the ridge before having to bailout. Hampered by his leg injuries he had difficulty in getting out of his cockpit and diving for the wing's trailing edge in the prescribed procedure, and his parachute barely had time to open before he struck the ground. Fortunately, once again, with the ridge between him and the enemy, he was in a remote enough area that a helicopter was able to get to him before the Red's were able to find him.

The battle lines had now moved so far north that precious time and fuel was wasted in flying between K-10 and the targets that it was decided to once again start staging operations out of K-13. A detachment of twenty SAAF maintenance men were dispatched to Suwon Air Base to handle rearming and refueling of the 18th FBW Mustangs. The men stayed there for a week before the airstrip was declared unsuitable for sustained operations because of the damage that had been incurred while it was in communist hands, and so on May 7 the detachment relocated to K-16, Seoul, where thing really were not all that much better. K-16 was "beat-up" as a result of its also being heavily bombed, but Air Force engineers worked around the clock to get the runways reopened once again. K-16 would remain as the 18th FBW's staging base until October when a new base was opened at Wonju, K-46, usually known as Hoengsong.

On May 2 (now) Captain "Horse" Sweeny put on a noteworthy, if uncomfortable, performance with his F-51. Sweeny's Mustang had been hit in its left aileron and cockpit by small arms fire over North Korea, which gave him several lacerated wounds across his buttocks. In spite of loosing quite a bit of blood and the obvious discomfort involved he managed to keep the aircraft under control and effect a safe landing at K-16. He was off flying status for a month as a result of his wounds.

On May 9 the largest single air strike of the war to date was launched. Four USAF Wings that were composed of over three hundred fighters attacked the communist airfield at Sinuiju. 2 Squadron furnished sixteen Mustangs for their part in this effort, and the pilots were really spoiling for the communists, but their air force did not show up and the UN pilots had to be content with bombing and strafing the airfield.

May 11 marked the high point of heroism within the annals of 2 Squadron's history, and indeed within the history of the South African Air Force. At 1640 hours KST the last strike force of the day took off with four Mustangs on a interdiction mission. Lt. Vernon Kruger's Mustang was hit in the wing by ground fire, which quickly set the wing's internal fuel tank on fire and before long the wing itself started to buckle. Kruger bailed out and in the process incurred second degree burns on his hands and face while leaving the cockpit, and then he suffered a dislocated shoulder as he struck the Mustang's empennage before clearing the burning aircraft.

One of his wingmen, Lt. Pat Clulow, immediately climbed to a higher altitude for better radio reception and called for a RESCAP. Meanwhile Major Johann Blaauw and Lt. Martin Mentz went down low to CAP the downed pilot. Clulow's radio calls were unanswered and it was getting dark and something had to be done or else the downed Kruger was either expected to be captured or perish from his injuries.

Blaauw, rank having both privileges, and maybe obligations, ordered Mentz and Clulow to head for K-16 while they still had enough fuel to get there, and then he made a belly landing in his Mustang along side of Kruger. After an hour on the ground a rescue helicopter finally was able to pick its way through the darkness and find the pilots and airlift them to safety. Forty-five years later a reunion was held between Kruger, Celliers and the helicopter pilot who had rescued them both, Chuck Fields.

As Kruger had gone down on his seventy-fourth mission, he was credited for his seventy-fifth via his helicopter rescue and after hospitalization in Japan he returned to South Africa. Blaauw received the U.S. Silver Star and commented "Vergeet dit. Ons vlieeniers moet mos saamstaan." (Forget it. We pilots must stand together).

Not all of the Mustangs and pilots of 2 Squadron that were lost fell behind enemy lines. On May 15 one of the napalm loaded F-51s that was taking off for the last mission of the day went out of control at K-16 and crashed into a disabled B-26 off the end of the runway. Lt. M.H. "Micky" Rorke died in the ensuing fire. He was buried in the UN cemetery at Tangok, near Pusan.

June also got off to a poor start for the members of 2 Squadron. On the first day of the month a four-ship formation took off from K-16 for an interdiction mission and when the fighter-bombers attacked the village of Chorwon they came under heavy antiaircraft fire. Upon completing their bombing and strafing runs they reformed their formation and headed for Pyongyang, but they had difficulty in locating worthwhile targets in the early morning haze.

Just after they passed over the North Korean capitol's airstrip an excited voice came over the squadron's radio frequency stating that he had been hit by ground fire and that his aircraft was on fire and he was bailing out. Since the disembodied voice did not identify itself, the attacks were broken off and the formation rejoined to see who might be missing. It was found that Lt. Helton McDonald was missing and a search was started. Finally the burning wreckage of a Mustang was located seven miles south of Pyongyang. There was no sign of a pilot or a parachute. It was later learned that McDonald had been taken prisoner. Eventually McDonald was the first UN officer to be released during Operation Big Switch.

2nd Lt. Terry Liebenberg was assigned his first combat mission on June 9. It was to have been an interdiction mission and the Mustangs were loaded with six rockets and two 500 pound GP's. As his Mustang started its takeoff roll it started a swing to the port side, and it was evident that Liebenberg tried to control the torque, but the Mustang left the runway and ran across the ground, headed for the Wing's Mustang parking area. Liebenberg

South African Mustang being prepared for another mission as ground crews move napalm tanks on dollys from the pits to the aircraft. (USAF via Greenhalgh)

"Clank's Clink" under escort by a 3rd Air Rescue Squadron SA-16. There is no doubt that the 3rd ARS is the most unheralded unit from the Korean War era. (John Lord via Phillips)

poured on the power in an attempt to get the fighter airborne, but this just compounded the torque problem and the Mustang struck a ditch which tore off its landing gear and its external ordnance. The wreckage slid further across the ground and hit a parked Mustang and both aircraft burst into flames. Liebenberg perished in the fire and was buried in the UN cemetery at Tangok next to Rorke.

The middle of June brought excellent flying weather and missions were mounted daily. In fact the weather was so good that the previously virtually nonexistent North Korean Air Force even sent one of their PO-2s to attack K-14. It caused neither damage nor casualties, but it was the first aerial attack ever witnessed by 2 Squadron personnel and it did create quite a bit of excitement: along with the follow-up task of digging slit trenches for protection in case the attack might be repeated.

The morning of June 22 also brought on something else for a change, aerial opposition. While attacking targets in North Korea 18th FBW pilots encountered Red fighters for the first time in several months, and since the Red aircraft were not jet propelled, the Mustangs had a better than even chance to score. The Wing's Mustang pilots knocked down one Yak-9, two Il-2s, and scored probables or damages on three Il-10s. 2 Squadron, unfortunately, did not get a chance to claim any hits during the fracas. (Headquarters USAF only credited the Yak-9 to a 67th FBS pilot.)

June 22 also marked the loss of another 2 Squadron pilot. Lt. A.G. "Bob" Frisby's Mustang was hit by small arms fire while he was leading an interdiction mission to Namchanjom. Frisby's Mustang was seen to start to stream either glycol or fuel before Frisby jettisoned his canopy and bailed out, but his parachute did not open.

On June 23 the North Korean airfield at Sariwon was attacked by 2 Squadron. The mission was led by Captain John Swanepoel, and in spite of the target having been located in one of the more heavily defended areas in northwestern North Korea the Mustangs were able to break through the curtains of 20 and 40 mm automatic weapons fire and disable or destroy everything they could bring their guns to bear upon. Swanepoel received a DFC for leading the strike.

The following day was similar. Lt. G.H. "Gus" Marshall was leading a flight on an interdiction mission when he received a call from a FAC for assistance. A large concentration of enemy troops was discovered to be sequestered in a valley. The location, itself, was virtually inaccessible from the air, being ringed by mountains that had been planted with antiaircraft guns of all calibers. Yet without hesitation Marshall led his flight in for the attack, and they made repeated runs on the troops until both the defending guns and the troops were permanently disabled. Marshall also received a DFC.

July 1951 opened with one of the simple tragic incidents of war that can effect a pilot, that of being killed on a mundane ferry flight. At 1510 KST on July 1 Lt. J.P. Verster took off from K-10 to deliver a Mustang to K-16. At the time approximating his scheduled arrival time at Seoul the control tower heard an emergency radio transmission that gave Verster's radio call-sign and a "Mayday," the international distress signal. It was later reported by ground observers that they had seen a Mustang overhead trailing black smoke and the observers thought that they had seen the pilot attempting to bailout. The wreckage was found with the pilot's body half in and half out of its cockpit. Verster also was buried at Tangok, and he was posthumously awarded the U.S. Air Medal for having participated in the previous attacks led by Lt. Marshall.

Commandant Armstrong led two flights of four Mustangs each on July 8 as 2 Squadron's contribution to a thirty-two ship strike by the 18th FBW against the airfield at Kangdung, northeast of Pyongyang. 2 Squadron had been briefed to dive bomb the airfield after the remainder of the Wing had flown antiaircraft suppression sweeps across the area to silence the Red gunners. It was a textbook operation, as the Wing's Mustangs swept across the airfield in line-abreast formation strafing everything while 2 Squadron dove from on high from an echelon-right formation just as the last flight of strafers cleared the target. Fifteen of 2 Squadron's sixteen bombs post holed the runway and effectively put it out of commission.

As the 18th FBW Mustangs were reforming an exclamation was heard on the radio. "MiG's." A single MiG-15 was then seen trying to turn with a Mustang, but the MiG was firing without effect. Then more MiGs charged into the fray, meeting the Mustangs, which were now eastbound at seven thousand feet, head-on, while two more MiGs came in behind them from their eight o'clock position. Two additional MiGs approached from three o'clock, and two more were seen overhead, watching from their perch.

Armstrong called for an immediate one-eighty degree turn, and the SAAF Mustangs reversed course to meet the second MiG element head-on. The MiGs first pulled up into a vertical climb without firing, and then swung around for another attack, again being met head-on by the Mustangs. With fruitless results against the 18th FBW, the MiGs got into it with the 4th Fighter Interceptor Wing, and three MiGs were shot down by F-86s.

July 9 saw the loss of another 2 Squadron pilot during the course of another ferry flight between K-10 and K-16. A flight of four Mustangs had taken off on a rotational assignment to relieve another flight a Seoul, and while abeam of Mansan they encountered some bad weather. With mountains on one side of them and the weather on the other, the flight leader ordered a climb straight ahead in an attempt to get on top of the storm. Major L.B. Pierce, flying in the Number Two position lost sight of his flight leader and attempted to go "lost wingman." Apparently he soon suffered an attack of vertigo while attempting to transition to instrument flying from visual orientation to his flight leader, he lost control of his Mustang. Apparently although he attempted to bailout, he was too low to do so and his body was recovered from his Mustangs wreckage fifteen miles north of Chinhae.

With the summer's thunderstorm season now in progress, bad weather was again becoming as much of a problem as Red gunners. The number of combat sorties fluctuated on a daily basis because of the thunderstorms, which did give the maintenance crews a chance to catch up on their work. It also gave the communists a chance to install more antiaircraft guns just beyond the sight of the forward air controllers along the MLR. The pilots had to become extremely wary when operating along the MLR during this period, for as they were constantly ducking in and out and around the bases of thundershowers while fighting against the storms turbulence, they often discovered that an antiaircraft battery had been set up where none previously existed that was eagerly awaiting a chance to shoot at a Mustang that was silhouetted against the clouds.

2nd Lt. R.L. "Bob" Staats was flying his seventy-fourth combat mission and the Red gunners seemed to know it. At 1400 hours KST on July 22 Staats was dive bombing three miles east of Onjung-ni when ground fire riddled his Mustang. Knowing that it was reasonably warm and that the water temperature was survivable, Staats headed for Wonson Harbor to bailout. As he crossed the coastline his engine caught on fire and he had to leave his Mustang a little sooner than he wanted to, but he had a good parachute and a favorable on-shore wind that carried him into the harbor, and he was able to inflate his dingy after he landed in the water. He was soon picked up by an American destroyer and returned to the squadron four days later. Since the SAAF did not have a policy covering evaders as the USAF did, Staats had to fly again the following day to get in his seventy-fifth mission before returning home.

July 23, 1951 went into 2 Squadron's history as their blackest day. A flight of four Mustangs was led by Captain F.M. "Freddy" Bekker with wingmen Lt.'s Roy DuPlooy, D.A.R. "Tony" Green and M.I.B. "Mike" Halley. They departed K-16 at 1505 hours KST on what was to have been a simple weather reconnaissance mission, even though all of the Mustangs carried the standard six rockets and 500 pound GPs. The flight proceeded up the Han-gang River at 1,500 feet, but the cloud decks kept forced them to lower and lower altitudes as they attempted to keep in ground contact for navigation and any possible target acquisition. Captain Bekker finally gave up the mission as a lost cause and decided to take the flight home, but while they were in a turn he decided to see if they could find something worthwhile to expend their ordnance upon. There just didn't seem to be anything worthwhile to shoot at, so they proceeded back down the river to the point where it joined the Imjin River, and then they headed south in a line-astern formation.

At 1530 they came upon a bridge, which they proceeded to bomb in a non-standard manor because of the rain, turbulence and low clouds. Since by now they only ordnance they had left were their rockets, which had to be expended before they could land, they commenced looking for another target. Just as the flight was passing over the top of a low hill Bekker's Mustang was hit in it right wing's fuel tank by small arms fire. The wing immediately torched and Bekker jettisoned his canopy to bail-out, but the fire was sucked into the cockpit and the Mustang porpoised twice and plunged to the ground where it exploded.

2nd Lt. Green had been on Bekker's right wing when the incident happened and he was forced to break hard to the right to avoid Du Plooy who had also started evasive action. Green then went into the clouds with his directional gyro tumbled, and he came back down in a spin directly over the wreckage of Bekker's aircraft, where he managed to regain control at an altitude estimated to be at twenty feet. As he flashed by the crashed Mustang he looked to see if there could be any sign of life, but there was none, but he did see a parachute descending.

The pilot in the parachute was Lt. Halley, who appeared to be otherwise uninjured. Lt. Du Plooy started a RESCAP for Halley while Green climbed to establish radio contact with some sort of a rescue team. In doing this he was taking a chance in attempting to penetrate the clouds with his gyro out of commission, but as it turned out it probably saved his life. Even as he climbed he was being chased by 20 mm antiaircraft fire.

Contact with a rescue team was established and it was agreed that Green would meet them ten miles east of Kaesong where the weather was a bit better and they would have a better chance in finding each other. For forty-five minutes Du Plooy warded off the enemy soldiers that were attempting to capture Lt. Halley. Two other flights of fighters then offered their assistance after hearing the frantic radio conversations between Green and Du Plooy, but they could not make their way through the clouds.

Finally DuPlooy stated that he was running out of ammunition, and as Green was now in the process of shepherding a helicopter into the area, Du Plooy fired his last rounds and then helplessly watched the Red's take advantage of the situation and capture Halley. Then, just as Green and the helicopter arrived in the area they saw another parachute and the smoldering wreckage of another F-51. Repeated radio calls to Du Plooy went unanswered.

Both Green and the helicopter then came under intense ground fire, and Green was down to his last fifteen gallons of fuel. He escorted the chopper out of the area and headed for K-16 to land with virtually dry fuel tanks.

Lt. Halley became a POW and was repatriated on August 29, 1953. He died in South Africa on August 14, 1954 as a result of his confinement. Lt. Du Plooy was carried as MIA and it was later confirmed that he had died, although it was never known whether he died as a result of bailing out or as a POW. Du Plooy was the second, and last SAAF pilot to receive the U.S. Silver Star.

The next day was also another of poor flying conditions and 2 Squadron was able to only launch four interdiction and eight CAS strikes. It was on one of these CAS missions that another drama with the grim reaper occurred, and for a change, he lost. The Mustang flown by Captain Hardy Snyman was hit by ground fire and started streaming a trail of white glycol behind him, which was a good indicator that the life of this particular Mustang was over.

Snyman headed for the sea and decided to bailout rather than taking a chance on ditching, which was the last resort under the best of conditions. The belly air scoop on the F-51 would cause the Mustang to dive violently upon making contact with the surface of the water. (Maximum flotation time is given as two seconds in the F-51 Pilot's Handbook. Also see the Brackenreg incident in the chapter on 77 Squadron.)

As Snyman crawled out of the Mustang's cockpit in his bailout attempt he snagged his parachute on the canopy rail, which threw him off balance and then caused him to strike the Mustang's empennage. With a shoulder injury, Snyman found that he could not move his arm to free himself from his parachute that was now trying to drag him under the waves. Only through sheer determi-

Left to right: Commandant Ray F. Armstrong, Captain P.A. LeGrange, Captain J.W. Swanepoel and Major J.P.D. Blaauw. (SAAF)

nation was he able to free himself and inflate his survival dingy, and then it took all of his remaining energy to crawl into the dingy where he had to be content with just letting it drift.

A rescue helicopter appeared and its crew was able to assist Snyman aboard. He was flown to K-16, but he then had to be transported to Japan for hospitalization, and then back to South Africa for further treatment.

On July 26 Commandant Armstrong completed his tour of duty and relinquished command to Major J.P.D. Blaauw, who was then promoted to Commandant. Blaauw's first official duty was to handle the paperwork on the loss of 2nd Lt. J.F.G. Howe's Mustang that afternoon.

Howe had departed K-16 on a combat mission, but as he approached the MLR he saw that his coolant temperature go over the red line and then "peg-out." Since there was no way that he could continue the mission, Howe aborted the strike and turned back to K-16, but the Merlin engine blew its cooling system's pop-off valve, and there was no alternative but to bailout. Howe landed in friendly territory in a welcome change for the usual 2 Squadron's luck, and was soon back at K-16.

The first large batch of replacement pilots arrived from South Africa on August 11. Up until this time they had arrived in a piecemeal method. With the new batch of pilots also came sixty-seven enlisted men to replace some of the hard working ground crews. The replacements were flown in to K-10 on a USAF C-54, and immediately were welcomed with war stories. As usual, some of these stories were omens, and on the following day 2 squadron launched sixteen sorties and lost another Mustang.

2 Squadron Chaplin Captain Doempie Colete gives a thumb-up to a departing squadron Mustang. His presence at the end of the runway was traditional. (SAAF)

2nd Lt. A. "Mike" Muller was in the process of attacking a bridge in North Korea with 5" HVAR's when one of them hit the bridge, exploded, and sent its debris back up right into the path of Muller's Mustang. The F-51s control cables were cut by the fragments, but he was able to nurse it to Taegu for a belly landing.

The North Korean capitol of Pyongyang, itself, was singled out for special attention on August 14 by the four squadrons of the 18th FBW. Sixty-four Mustangs, including sixteen from 2 Squadron, were launched in the early morning for one attack, which was followed up by a second attack that afternoon with another sixty-four Mustangs.

Considerable antiaircraft fire was experienced on both of these raids, and four 2 Squadron Mustangs were damaged. One F-51 piloted by 2nd Lt. C.L. Ian de Jongh was hit in the coolant system during the afternoon mission and de Jongh headed west for the Korea Bay, but with so many Mustangs milling about, (Looking for three other lost 18th FBW Mustangs.) no one was able to discover which Mustang was his.

Feelings ran high afterwards that he might have made it to open water and either been able to evade or be taken prisoner. But this was not the case, as his Mustang had crashed northwest of Pyongyang and de Jongh had been killed. His loss was keenly felt for the interpersonal relationships within 2 Squadron were very close and one of his wingman, Willem van den Bos, had been the best man at the wedding of Ian's sister to Derek Doveton who had been killed on February 15. In addition to being a well known pilot, de Jongh had also represented South Africa in the 1949 Empire Games as a high-jumper.

Due to all sorts of bad weather conditions the 18th FBW had to cease their operations out of K-16 during the first week of August. They were finally able to return to K-16 on August 18 after the flood waters from the Han River had receded. The following day K-10 had to be evacuated because of the approach of Typhoon Marge, which struck on August 20 and left in its wake more bad flying weather. The skies were overcast with ceilings so low that virtually no flying could be accomplished until August 29 when they cleared enough to permit another large scale mission.

The target this time was Sunuiju. It appeared that the mission was off to a bad start when the Mustang of 2nd Lt. Tony Green, (The sole survivor of the July 23 mission.) blew its pop off valve. Green attempted to jettison his ordnance, but one of the 500 pound GP's hung up on its shackle, and by then Green was to low to bailout when the engine seized. Green selected a stretch of river bank along the Han and made a belly landing. He was knocked unconscious when his head struck the K-14 gunsight, but his luck continued and there was no fire or explosion and he escaped further injury. The mission, itself, came off with a resounding success.

Commandant Blaauw was involved in the next F-51 loss. While leading an interdiction mission near Hanchon Blaauw's Mustang was hit by ground fire which cut the rudder cables just below his seat. He headed back to K-16 where he attempted an emergency landing, but the Mustang started to swerve as soon as its main wheels touched the runway and without the rudder to give him directional control, Blaauw had to retract the landing gear to prevent a collision with a parked C-47. He was uninjured.

August closed with 2 Squadron having totaled 4,400 combat sorties in 10,100 combat hours so far in the war. Thus far thirty Mustangs had already been lost to one cause or another, and fourteen pilots were either already declared as KIA or MIA. The future did not look a bit better as far as casualties were concerned, for September opened with the loss of another pilot.

2nd Lt. M.O. "Mick" Grunder was leading a rail interdiction mission and after accomplishing three rail cuts the flight proceeded on a reconnaissance of a wooded area that Grunder thought that it might provide some worthwhile shooting. He ordered the remainder of his flight to stay at a higher altitude while he went down for a look-see. His wingmen reported that they could see Grunder firing his machine guns as he approached the woods, and then Grunder stated that he had come under enemy ground fire and thought that his Mustang had been hit.

Still Grunder proceeded to rocket and strafe the woods, and he reported that he had spotted six Red gun emplacements and the rest of the flight should come down and join him. As his wingman, Major. B.A.A. "Barry" Wiggett, pulled up into the sun to start his peel-off he saw a Mustang canopy and a wad of papers stream past his nose. A radio check of the flight was made and only Grunder failed to respond. The pilots then noticed that there were two fires on the ground. One was grass, and the other a burning Mustang. They RESCAPed the area for twenty minutes, but there was no sign of either a pilot or a parachute. It was later confirmed that Grunder had died in the crash.

On September 5 2 Squadron flew six missions, one of which was a RESCAP for a downed American pilot. The day's efforts cost the squadron two more Mustangs and another pilot. Lt. Willem van den Bos was working over a target in North Korea when his engine just quit

A SAAF Mustang starts to taxi for another mission from Chinhae during the early months of 2 Squadron's involvement in the Korean War. # 306 was one of the first F-51s supplied, and it was wrecked in a crash landing at K-10 on August 30, 1951. (SAAF)

cold. He made a successful belly landing and the remainder of his flight RESCAPed the area until relieved by another flight of SAAF Mustangs. One hour and forty minutes later a helicopter made its way in an pulled van den Bos out, flying him to an aircraft carrier in Wonson Harbor.

The second loss occurred when a T-6 Mosquito spotted a target east of Ipori near the infamous Punchbowl area and called in a flight of four SAAF Mustangs to take it out. Lt. N. Biden was seen dropping his napalm tanks on the target, but as the flight rejoined and made their customary radio check-in calls Biden did not answer. Two T-6s then joined with the remaining Mustangs to start a search but only a pyre of white and black smoke that continued long after the napalm fires had burned themselves out was still visible. "Flash" Biden had died in the crash.

September 9 saw the crash on one more SAAF Mustang and set a squadron record of sorts. Captain Dormie Barlow, one of the SAAF's World War II veterans, who had been shot down three times during that war and had to bailout twice, had to bailout once again. Just twenty minutes after taking off from K-16 his F-51s engine quit. Barlow injured his back when he hit the ground and he had to be sent to Japan for medical treatment, but he returned to the squadron to complete his tour.

Operation Strangle was well underway in September and 2 Squadron was participating to the best of their ability in this maximum effort. On September 20 they had launched twenty sorties, and again lost a pilot. The mission was led by Major Frank Montanari and they were reconnoitering the roads between Inch'on and Majon-ni

K-16, Seoul, was a mud hole during the spring of 1951 because of heavy rains and flooding. Lt. "Mickey" Rorke was killed in this Mustang when it crashed on takeoff from K-16 on May 15, 1951. (SAAF)

with one flight of four Mustangs. As they encountered more of the ever present instrument flight conditions they climbed to 8,000 feet until a break in the clouds was spotted and Montanari put the rest of his flight into an orbit while he descended to see if there was enough visibility under the clouds for effective work. On his descent he started encountering heavy antiaircraft fire, but he continued down to 300 feet, and then his Mustang was seen to start streaming some sort of fluid.

At this time Montanari was observed to climb back up to 3,000 feet, apparently heading for some cloud cover to hide in, but before he reached their safety his Mustang entered into a sweeping spiral and crashed into a dry river bed. The rest of his flight went down for a look-see to ascertain if there was any chance for the pilot to have survived, but they were driven off by more heavy antiaircraft fire. It was confirmed later that Montanari had died in the crash.

One of the most effective missions flown by 2 Squadron took place on September 17. A flight of four Mustangs led by Captain R.H. "Bob" Rogers attacked a bridge in North Korea, and after the bridge had been bombed they were just flying around looking for a target to expend their rockets upon before heading back to K-16. Just by luck they happened upon a Red train, which was the longest train that any of the pilots had ever seen. They immediately called for assistance, and a second flight of Mustangs, led by Lt. Jean DeWet, joined in on the fun. Between the two flights over one hundred-fifty boxcars were destroyed without communist opposition.

Lt. T. Severtson flew two combat missions on September 20. The first one was uneventful, but the second one brought a lifetime's worth of excitement. On the sec-

ond sortie Severtson's Mustang was severely damaged by antiaircraft fire over North Korea and for two hours he fought an aircraft that alternately threatened to either spin out of control, or just quit running altogether, apparently on its own whim. He took it all the way back to Chinhae for an off-runway belly landing that left the Mustang so torn up that it wasn't even worthwhile for spare parts.

But the incident was a good experience for the base crash crew, as later that day 2nd Lt. Ratief took off to give another Mustang a functional flight check. When Ratief attempted to retract the Mustang's landing gear the handle broke off in his hand, which left the landing gear down but unlocked. He returned to land and just as the tail wheel touched the runway the aircraft's left main gear collapsed. The Mustang skewed to a stop and the uninjured pilot was extracted from its cockpit by the crash crew that had followed him down the runway in their vehicles.

Exactly one year after 2 Squadron had departed South Africa the 18th FBW flew their largest number of combat sorties of the war. The Wing launched a total of one hundred twenty-two Mustangs, of which a forth were from 2 Squadron. This was the largest Mustang mission since World War II. Commandant Blaauw had just completed his 100th combat mission two days previously, having elected to continue his combat tour, and he did not intend to miss this effort. 2 Squadron was quite proud of the fact that Blaauw was selected to lead this mission, and all of the Mustangs except for one from the 67th FBS returned home safely.

That evening an anniversary party was held, which coincided with a change of command for 2 Squadron as Commandant Blaauw turned over the leadership of the

"My Boy" was 44-84761. Originally it had been assigned to the Air Force's first jet fighter group, the 412th, when they didn't yet have enough P-80As to become fully equipped. It eventually went to the ROKAF. Note the 2 squadron "Flying Cheetah" insignia on its fuselage. (SAAF)

squadron to Commandant B.A.A. "Barry" Wiggett. The party was festive, but there was a pause for reflection for the names of those who were lost were read. Of sixty-one F-51s supplied to the squadron so far, thirty-six had been lost to enemy action or otherwise written-off. Six 2 Squadron pilots had been confirmed as killed, while another sixteen were still considered as MIA. Four pilots had been wounded. The first year's ordnance has seen 5,097 napalm tanks and 3, 303 five hundred pound bombs had been dropped. 21,169 rockets and 3,051,468 .50 caliber machine gun rounds had been fired.

On September 27 Lt. Denis John Earp crashed at map coordinates CT0717, a non-descript portion of geography northeast of Keasong. A RESCAP was established, but Earp was taken captive by a Chinese soldier before a rescue could be effected. He was repatriated after the peace accord was signed and eventually became the Chief of the South African Air Force (1984-88).

As 2 Squadron began their second year in Korea they moved their operations to K-46, which was, roughly, straight east of Seoul on the 37th Parallel. The new base was not as yet improved from what it had been, a well bombed out World War II Japanese airstrip, but within a short span of time new buildings were erected, latrines dug and tents set up. Combat missions started from K-47 on October 1 and were typically effective: four rail cuts were made and a Red supply dump obliterated.

2nd Lt. A.W. "Mike" Muller was given an opportunity on October 2 to carry out one of the few successful escape and evasion, E&E, attempts by a Mustang pilot during the Korean War. An hour after takeoff and deep into North Korea a wingman noted that Muller's Mustang had started to stream glycol. At his flight commander's direction, Muller turned east and headed for open water, by the Mustang's temperature gauge soon pegged out and Muller decided that it would be a good idea for him to bailout before the Mustang caught on fire.

He went over the side, had a good parachute, and descended into a wooded area. The rest of his flight set up a RESCAP while Muller spread his parachute out on the ground so that it could easily be seen from the air. He waved his scarf to his mates so that they could see that he was okay, but his wingmen soon had to leave as they were running low on fuel. They were replaced by another flight of Mustangs, who were in turn replaced by a third flight. Ground fire was constantly being fired at the circling Mustangs, and the pilots could see Red soldiers starting to encircle the downed pilot.

Muller was ducking from tree to tree and bush in a life or death game of hide and seek that went on for four

The remains of several 2 Squadron Mustangs at Chinhae. # 326 was 44-74344, which was supposedly returned to the USAF. # 373 was 44-74021 that was written-off on March 6, 1952 by Lt. A.D. "Topper" van der Spuy. # 370 was 44-73073 that crashed on landing at K-10 on February 20, 1952. (USAF via Davis)

hours before a helicopter could make its way to the area. The chopper started taking hits from antiaircraft fire, but its pilot was able to spot the downed Muller and effect his rescue before it was to heavily damaged. Since Muller had gone down on his seventy-third mission he was given credit for another "mission" for his helicopter ride, a "pass" on his seventy-fifth mission and allowed to return to South Africa.

2 Squadron mounted its largest effort as a single squadron on October 4 when twelve Mustangs flew forty-eight effective sorties in support of the troops along the front lines. 45, 700 rounds of .50 caliber ammunition were fired and it was considered that all of the fired rockets and dropped bombs were effective against the entrenched enemy in the mountain ridges.

Another E&E attempt was made by a 2 Squadron pilot on October 11 as the squadron was flying another series of CAS missions, Lt. Chris Lombard and his flight had just pulled up off of one target and were heading for another when Lombard hand signaled to his flight leader that his radio had failed. His flight leader acknowledged and responded with the hand signal for Lombard to head for home, since North Korea was no place to be without an operable radio. The rest of the flight then swung in behind him, but soon a stream of smoke started to come from Lombard's Mustang.

Not too much later Lombard jettisoned his canopy and bailed out. The Mustang actually burst into flames before it hit the ground, so it appeared that Lombard had made a good decision. Two of his wingmen started to circled Lombard as he descended in his parachute, and as soon as he landed he waved that he was down okay, and then he pointed towards a hill, which was promptly strafed by the SAAF pilots.

The area where Chris Lombard had gone down was at the extreme range of the available helicopters. Still, a series of F-51s, F-80s and F4Us came into the area and set up a RESCAP until a chopper could make its way in. For a period Lombard's parachute was visible on the ground, and then it disappeared. Soon thereafter another pilot that was making a low pass over the area observed a man in a green uniform running with two men in white up a gully: one of which was thirty yards in front of the man in green, and the other an equal distance to the rear.

A few days later the word came in through intelligence sources that Lombard was in friendly hands and another rescue attempt was made, but it was fruitless. Lombard had been captured by the communists and was held as a POW for the duration.

Four SAAF Mustangs were flying a rail interdiction mission on October 29 when 2nd Lt. H. Theo Joyce reported having engine trouble. His wingman, "Bats" Maskell, started to escort him back home while the other two aircraft proceed with their assigned mission, but then Joyce decided that his Merlin had smoothed out enough, so the two pilots decided to seek out the assigned secondary target to see what they could accomplish with their .50 calibers, since they had already salvoed their bombs. The new target was Inch'on, and since it was on their way home, anyhow, there was little sense in passing up an opportunity in obtaining credit for a combat mission that they otherwise would not have received. (Joyce was on his first combat mission and obviously did not want an abort against his record and did desire credit for his first effort). Maskell made his first strafing pass and as he pulled up he noticed a vivid flash on a hillside near the town. He then descended and made a second pass, flying by the burning area where he had seen the explosion that was still burning with bright yellow flames and heavy black smoke. With no response to his radio calls, he flew back to K-46 to rejoin with the mission's original flight leader, and they then flew back to Inch'on to reconnoiter. The fire by now had consumed everything that could possibly be identified as an aircraft, so Joyce was initially declared as MIA and later confirmed as KIA.

The following day Lt. Joe Meirling was leading a flight on a CAS mission against a command post at Tosan. As he pulled up off his target his Mustang was hit by a burst of 40mm cannon rounds through it wing, fuselage and empennage. He immediately headed south towards the MLR, which was approximately fifteen miles away. Just as he crossed the MLR his Merlin engine quit, but he was by now to low to bailout and was traveling to fast to belly-in his Mustang, but he had little choice, so he selected as flat a spot as he could find and put the Mustang down in a cloud of dust. The Mustang was a total wreck but Meirling escaped the crash with only minor cuts.

Adverse weather conditions kept the fighter-bomber operations to a minimum until November 4 when sixteen sorties were launched on rail interdiction strikes. Five rail cuts were made, and after completing their bombing runs the last four Mustangs headed for a secondary target at Manam-ni where they encountered moderate 20mm antiaircraft fire.

The Mustang belonging to Lt. C.J. Pappas was last seen heading down into this gunfire as he attempted a rocket attack, but due to the heavy smoke from the gunfire and an unexplainable mass of silver flashes in the air he was never seen again. After the war ended Critton Pappas was declared as KIA.

After another day's stand-down because of the weather 2 Squadron went out in force on November 6. Thirty-two sorties were launched and they resulted in the destruction of five Red field positions and the deaths of an estimated one hundred twenty-eight enemy soldiers.

While making one of the strafing passes the Mustang of Captain J.C. "Cliff" Collins was hit and Collins headed south for friendly territory with his Mustang streaming glycol. The F-51 caught on fire before Collins could reach the MLR, but with fortuitous luck the prevailing winds permitted his parachute to drift him across the front lines and into the hands of the British Commonwealth Division. As it turned out the Britishers were so happy with the air support they were receiving from the SAAF that they didn't want to let Collins go home and they kept plying him with drinks. Through the efforts of a USAF helicopter crew he was "rescued" again and flown back to K-46.

During a subsequent mission a T-6 Mosquito was assigned a flight of SAAF Mustangs that were supposed to knock out a bridge that was heavily defended by antiaircraft fire. The mission leader, 2nd Lt. P.J. "Frank" Grober, made his first strafing pass to attempt to knock out some antiaircraft guns that the Mosquito pilot had marked with a smoke rocket, but in the process his own Mustang was hit, which knocked out his elevators. With a wingman as an escort Grober headed south, but the F-51 became more and more uncontrollable and soon the ailerons also froze. Grober waited until the Mustang got itself into a momentary stable attitude and then he bailed out, landing in 'no man's land" There was nothing for him to do but keep his head down in an attempt to keep from being hit by gunfire that was passing over his head from both directions until a helicopter could effect his rescue while his wingmen suppressed the communists guns.

The situation along the MLR stabilized for the moment in November so 2 Squadron returned to rail interdiction missions once again. These missions were not terribly popular with the pilots for their duration was longer and the hazards were greater. The ground support strikes along the MLR exposed them to small arms fire, but they had an immediate support to the ground pounders. The further they flew behind the lines the more antiaircraft fire they encountered, of larger calibers, and if downed their chances of being rescued diminished.

On November 24 2 Squadron was assigned to lead elements of the 18th FBW into North Korea on a rail interdiction strike south of Sunchon, and they lost another pilot. For the pilot involved, the entire mission had gotten off to a bad start, for as they taxied to the runway for takeoff Lt. George Krohn's Merlin engine started running rough. He taxied clear of the runway to let the other aircraft takeoff and did a quick troubleshoot of his problem, which apparently was a sticking radiator shutter that caused a temporary overheating of his engine. After the other Mustangs departed Krohn solicited permission from Flying Control to also takeoff and try to catch up with the rest of the mission.

By the time the 18th FBW arrived over the target the mission leader expected to find Krohn back in formation, but since Krohn hadn't shown up, he assumed that either Krohn had joined up with another element of Mustangs or turned around and gone back to K-46. The lead elements from 2 Squadron made their attacks, which were followed by the 18th FBW squadrons. By this time Krohn had checked in on the radio and declared that he was over the target and that he was starting his attack.

A USAF pilot reported that he saw a single SAAF Mustang climbing out on the prebriefed compass heading, but that it was lagging well behind the rest of its squadron. This was the last sighting of Krohn and he was declared as MIA when he did not return to base.

On November 28 Lt. Ken Whitehead crashed while he was landing at Chinhae. Whitehead had been in the process of delivering a F-51 from K-46 to K-10 for maintenance. He was unscathed but the Mustang was a write-off.

The next day another Mustang was lost, this time along with its pilot, and due to Red antiaircraft fire. Captain Amo Janse "Zulu" van Rensberg was leading a flight of four F-51s that attacked their primary target without encountering any hostile fire, and then he led them to a secondary target. The flight flew into a wall of antiaircraft fire and van Rensberg's F-51 took a hit in its vulnerable cooling system and lost a "concentration" of glycol.

Apparently van Rensberg also had suffered a mortal wound, for he made an attempt at transmitting on his radio that only came out as a groan and his wingman saw him slump down in his cockpit. The Mustang started to porpoise, fell off into a spin, caught fire and then exploded when it hit the ground.

December 1951 opened with considerable blasts of cold air coming down from Manchuria. All of the F-51 crew chiefs were having a great deal of problems with the tasks of winterizing the aircraft, which included having to double-clamp all of the coolant lines and inspect the insulation of all of the electrical wiring to make sure that they were adequately insulated against moisture. Another problem involved the physical size of the pilots, for by and large the SAAF pilots were larger men than the average USAF pilot. When these men of larger stature could not don the supplied winter clothing, or if they could not manage to get in or out of the cramped Mustang cockpits with it on; or much more, reach the proper cockpit levers or move the control stick to full travel: they had to be grounded for the duration of the winter flying season.

Two more Mustangs were lost on December 3. Two F-51s had gone out on a rail cutting strike that morning, and after accomplishing one and one-half rail cuts they proceeded to their secondary target. The second target was found to be obscured by clouds, so the pilots turned south for K-46 while flying on top of an overcast. Approaching Seoul they had to tighten their formation in order to penetrate the clouds without loosing sight of each other.

Lt. Ken Whitehead, as Number Two, closed in too fast on his leader and his propeller sliced into the tail section of Lt. P.I. Norman-Smith's Mustang, severing all of the empannage's control cables. Whitehead's prop tore off his Mustang, followed by his entire engine, and the Mustang tumbled into the Han River. Norman-Smith's Mustang was seen to roll over on its back and dive into the Han in an inverted attitude. The wreckage was embedded in the river's bottom and was unrecoverable. Whitehead's body was recovered and interned at Tangok.

A third loss of life for the month of December occurred to an enlisted men and it was the first of this nature for the squadron since they had entered the war. Air Corporal W.D. Patterson was standing in the rearm and refueling area at K-46 when refueling truck, its windshield frosted over in the cold, accidentally knocked him down. He died in the base hospital.

Some good news did arrive in December, though. Through the UN Peace Talk negotiations the communist delegates released the names of three SAAF pilots that were being held as POWs: Halley, Earp and McDonald.

The remainder of December was nothing but erratic flying conditions. Limited sorties were launched on any given day, only to be recalled because of icing or low clouds. What few targets that could be hit were, but they were few and far between, because the Reds were also holing up in the cold.

January 1952 was another story, for the skies cleared somewhat and all of FEAF's air units were besieged by call from the ground forces for air support. It was much easier to call for an air strike than to try and send out a ground patrol of cold infantry men to knock out an objective. With the peace talks in progress, no one wanted to leave their semi-comfortable bunkers to take a chance at being shot at. It was considered, (By the ground forces.) to be better to let something mechanical to take the chances, no matter if it did contain a pilot.

2 Squadron suffered their highest number of losses in January 1952 with eight Mustangs being destroyed. The first loss occurred on the first day of the New Year when Lt. J.H. "Pikkie" Rautenbach was making a strafing run on a supply dump and his Mustang was hit in its cooling system. He headed south with his F-51 streaming glycol, and just after he crossed the MLR the engine seized and he had to bailout at only seven hundred feet. His parachute swung twice and Rautenbach was on the ground suffering from shrapnel wounds and a back injury.

On January 3 sixteen combat sorties were dispatched, and fifteen of these were effective. The sixteenth was flown by Lt. G. Jimmie Newton whose Mustang was hit by ground fire before he reached the target area and he had to abort the mission. On the way back to K-46 the F-51 caught on fire and Newton took to the silk. He was picked up unscathed by one of the ever present and capable helicopter crews.

On January 6 fate struck once again. A flight of six SAAF Mustangs was attacking the North Korean rail system near Kumsong when Lt. L.W. "Jimmy" Parsonson made an unusually low strafing pass. As he pulled up off the target to the right he announced that he had been hit and that his Mustang was on fire. Parsonson climbed to 8,000 feet to bailout, but as he released the canopy the Mustang burst into flames that were sucked back into the cockpit and the Mustang stalled, falling off into a tight

spin that continued until it crashed. Apparently Parsonson had been incapacitated by the flames for he had made no attempt to bailout.

The squadron launched eighteen sorties on January 15 after enemy troops, billets and supply dumps. One F-51, flown by Lt. Reg Gasson, was seen climbing after making a strafing run, but it was trailing a stream of alternating black and white smoke. When a Mustang did this there was little doubt that it was soon either going to have its engine seize or catch on fire. Gasson soon released his canopy and bailed out, landing near the Imjin River.

For a few minutes Gasson was not visible, but then he appeared on the river's ice pack waving his scarf. The remainder of his flight set up a RESCAP until they were relieved by some USAF fighters. The second flight observed a considerable amount of ground fire in the area, and while they were watching this activity they also saw two men in dark clothing appear next to Gasson.

As the USAF fighters dove down for a better look one of the dark clothed men ran off, while Gasson was seen fighting with the other, and then he was seen to fall on the ice. A third man then ran out of the brush and grabbed Gasson under the arms and drug him off out of sight. A USAF helicopter arrived, but due to intense ground fire it could not land and the pilots overhead could only assume that Gasson had been taken prisoner. In April 1953 Gasson was the first pilot to be released during Project Little Switch. Due to his injuries received during his bailout, capture and internment, he was medically retired from the SAAF.

Bob Staats was reported as missing on January 17 after just returning to Korea for a second tour and while flying an orientation flight out of K-10 to refamiliarize him-

325 "Patsy Dawn" was the second SAAF Mustang to bear this number. It was rebuilt from the wreckages of #'s 364, 365 and 359. It was considered to be the fastest Mustang in Korea, being fifteen mph faster than any other 'Stang in the 18th FBW. (USAF via Davis)

self in the F-51. A report came in from some South Koreans that they had seen a Mustang plunge into the sea near Munsan, and three days later a diver was able to locate the wreck and recover Staats' body for internment at Tangok.

The last combat loss for the month occurred on January 31 as a flight of four SAAF Mustangs was working over the communist communications network. None of the pilots reported any battle damage from the heavy antiaircraft fire that they had encountered, but on the way back to K-46 Lt. Rex Earp-Jones radioed to his flight that his engine had quit. Since they were at 13,000 feet an attempt to glide to the MLR was attempted, but Earp-Jones decided that he was not going to be able to stretch his glide far enough and he bailed out.

Earp-Jones parachute decent drifted him towards a gully, and as his wingmen flew past his landing spot they observed a parachute hung up in a tree. As they came around for a second pass they were then able to see four men moving along a ditch, and as they flew overhead three of the men flattened themselves on the ground while the fourth waved his scarf at them until the other three rose and wrestled him to the ground. He was repatriated after the war.

Three additional Mustangs were lost in January but since they did not involve a loss of life or enemy action their reasons for their loss were not declared. It might be presumed that they were cannibalized for spare parts because of incurred airframe fatigue.

When King George died on February 5, 1952 the order came down from higher headquarters that since South Africa was a Commonwealth nation all members of 2 Squadron would have to wear mourning bands on their sleeves until the end of May. There were some feelings that it would have been more appropriate for these bands to be worn in honor of the lost pilots, but protocol has its privileges.

A rash of flying accidents seemed to hit 2 Squadron during February and March, causing a loss of aircraft when the enemy did not. On February 11 Captain R. Harbusch crashed while landing at K-46. On the 20th Lt. Jimmie Newton survived his second crash landing, this time at K-10. On February 24, 2nd Lt. David Taylor had the narrowest of narrow escapes while coming in to land at Chinhae. He flared-out over the end of the runway far to high and his Mustang stalled, bounced off the runway and commenced to cartwheel until it came to rest inverted in the bay. Two USAF Master Sergeants, S.M. Starks and R. Renaud, who had seen the crash dove into the water to free the trapped Taylor and saved his life.

Five days later, on February 29, a replacement pilot, 1st Lt. Jack Lellyet, crashed while on a milk run dive bombing mission against a bridge at Chong-du as a part of his "in-theater" operational training. Apparently he had failed to consume all of the fuel out of his fuselage fuel tank which rendered his Mustang unstable for dive bombing.

On March 20 the SAAF Mustangs had another brush with the MiG-15s. This was the first time that they had encountered any enemy fighters in almost a year. The 18th FBW had sent a concentration of Mustangs into MiG Alley to attack a rail system at "Butterfly Bend" that had started to operate there again, and the attacks were carried out successfully in spite of heavy and intense ground fire. As 2 Squadron's Able and Dog Flights pulled up off their target they were jumped by five MiG's and 2nd Lt. David Taylor's was chased down by a MiG swung that down behind him and hit his Mustang with a full blast of cannon fire. With his Mustang emitting heavy smoke Taylor headed south, but the MiG pilot was persistent and stayed on his tail until Taylor bailed out. He was declared as killed in action but it was not known whether he died of wounds or the result of bailing out.

The remainder of the SAAF flight also had their hands full. As the MiG's bore in on them, popping their speed brakes open as they jockeyed for position behind the slower F-51s that were twisting and turning in an effort to evade the MiG's heavy firepower. As one MiG slowed Lt. Hans Enslin whipped in behind him and fired back. The .50 caliber bullets were seen to strike the MiG's right wing and a large burst of black smoke erupted from its fuselage. The MiG pilot broke for the ground with Enslin in hot pursuit but the MiG crossed the Yalu River before he could bring his guns to bear again. Gun camera film assessment verified the hits upon the MiG and Enslin was awarded a "damaged."

In the meantime Lt. Vin F. Kuhn found himself separated from the rest of his flight by two more MiGs that had come in between them and had singled him out for their attention. Three times the MiG's bore in on him and three times Kuhn managed to evade their cannon fire by making hard turns that placed himself momentary behind the MiGs long enough for him to fire a few rounds before the MiG's speed advantage allowed them to get behind him once again. Kuhn felt that he may have scored a few hits himself, but he was happy enough to have been able to find a convenient cloud to duck into until the threat had passed and he could head for home.

The MiGs were again in evidence on April 6 when 2 Squadron was flying a rail interdiction mission. A flight of four Mustangs led by Lt. Al Rae was bounced by a flight of MiGs and Rae ordered his flight to salvo their ordnance and turn into the MiGs. One of the MiGs cut into the Mustangs turns and singled Rae out and Rae started a rapid series of ess turns himself until the MiG finally overshot him, where upon Rae fired a few shots at him in retaliation. No hits were scored by either side, but the MiGs had seen enough and broke north for Manchuria without pressing their advantage.

A bit of skullduggery took place two days later when Lt. J.O. "Holtzie" Holtzhausen and a USAF Mustang pilot were CAPing an area where a USAF pilot was reported down. The missing pilot's plane was spotted and the two Mustang's went down for a look-around. They spotted an individual on the ground, waving, so a helicopter was called for. The unknown individual waited for the chopper to get in close and then pulled out a concealed rifle and started shooting at it, holing a fuel tank. The Mustangs then began to come under antiaircraft fire and found them selves separated, so Holtzhausen escorted the chopper to a safer area and then flew back to rejoin the USAF Mustang pilot to escort him home. Two days later, on April 10, Holtzhausen was lost over North Korea when he became separated from his flight and radioed that he would rejoin with another flight of USAF Mustangs, but the rendezvous was not accomplished and he was never seen again.

Poor flying weather again set in and it wasn't until April 20 that effective combat missions could be flown. Lt. Gus Baransky was flying a Mustang named "Shy Talk" in his flight's Number Three position on a RESCAP mission staging from an orbit point off Chodo Island when they were instructed to proceed into North Korea to RESCAP two downed pilots near Sonchon. They had proceeded to their assigned area and contacted one of the downed pilots on their radios, but in order so as not to give away his position they set up an orbit four miles away from it and were just orbiting until a helicopter could arrive. At this point a F-84 pilot was seen to eject, and he landed five miles to the east of the first pilot's position. The Number Four man in the SAAF formation then climbed to a higher altitude to call for another helicopter when his radio transmission was overridden by a flat statement, "My God, there goes another" as the witnessing pilot saw Baransky dive straight into the ground.

On the following day 2 Squadron flew only RESCAP missions, but these did result in the rescues of three downed UN pilots, including the one that Baransky had attempted to RESCAP. For their assistance in these efforts 2 Squadron received the congratulations of Lt. General Frank Everest, Commanding Officer, 5th Air Force.

2 Squadron dispatched eight Mustangs on May 25 as their contribution to a mission that composed twelve other 18th FBW Mustangs. The twenty fighter-bombers were making rail-cutting strikes some twenty miles south of the Yalu River near Taegwondong when they were jumped by eight MiG-15s. Their flight leader, Captain Jan van der Merwe, immediately called for help from the F-86s that had been assigned their top cover, but by the time they got to the Mustangs location the sky was full of individual dogfights as the F-51s and the MiGs spared with each other. All of the F-51s pilots were getting off bursts of gunfire at the interlopers, but apparently neither side were able to score any hits and when the MiG pilots spotted the Sabres they broke for Manchuria with the whole show being over within five minutes.

During the morning of June 23 the 5th Air Force dispatched their surprise attacks against the hydroelectric plants in North Korea. Commandant Hendrik Burger, the present commanding officer of 2 Squadron, led six SAAF Mustangs and the 18th FBW's 67th FBS against one facility, which they completely destroyed. A secondary target, another power plant, was attacked by the remainder of 2 Squadron, with the two elements being led by Captain Ben Grove and Lt. Attie Bosch. This target was also wiped out.

The following day 2 Squadron went after the hydroelectric plants at Fusen and Chosin. Poor weather prevented an accurate assessment of the damage accomplished but it was believed to have been severe. The pilots and ground crews were obviously quite proud of their contributions to this effort, but the one thing that really made them feel better than anything else was the fact that they were able to close the month without sustaining the loss of a pilot.

Things would change for the worse in the not to distant future, though, for on July 9 Lt. Theodore Scott was leading a strike to provide CAS along the MLR and as the Mustangs arrived over the front lines they discovered that Scott's radio had failed and they could not contact their forward air controller. One of the wingmen, Lt. B.W. "Tubby" Singleton, went down to pick out a target, which he marked by firing a rocket, while the other three pilots positioned themselves to commence their attacks. No antiaircraft fire was observed, but as the three Mustangs dove down through three thousand feet pieces of Scott's Mustang were seen to fly off, and then the Mustang burst into flames before crashing a mile from the target. Since none of the other pilots had seen the canopy come off the aircraft or any sign of a parachute, Scott was declared as KIA.

A trailer load of 5" HVAR's waiting to be loaded on SAAF Mustangs at K-46 in the midst of the winter of 1952. (SAAF via Clyde Carstens)

A major portion of the missions flown in August were devoted to CAS of the UN ground troops along the MLR. On August 22 a flight led by Captain John Bolito was in the process of knocking out some artillery pieces that were bothering the ground pounders when another SAAF Mustang was lost.

The F-51s had swung into a line-astern formation and started their attacks, knocking out two gun emplacements and damaging two more, when Major Piet Kotzenberg, who was flying the Number Four position, lined up for his turn, but some where between the final turn to the target and the target he simply disappeared. No trace of the pilot or his Mustang was ever found.

On September 22 Commandant Burger departed for South Africa and Major Ralph Gerneke assumed command of 2 Squadron. The squadron continued flying CAS missions under Gerneke through the fall months and were grateful for decent flying weather along the front lines. 2 squadron became noted during this period for some of their outstanding close air support work, as on October 6 they had flown maximum effort missions in the defense of White Horse Mountain where they had protected the 9th ROK Infantry Division from several communist attacks. For these missions they received letters of appreciation from Lt. General Glenn Barcus, Commanding Officer, 5th Air Force, and from Major General Kim Chang O, commander of the 9th ROK Division.

Lt. T.R. "Chick" Fryer was shot down on October 12 after being jumped by MiG-15s while on a armed recce mission between Samdong and Kowon. He was one of the few lucky pilots that were shot down near the north side of the MLR and lived to tell about it, for most that had to bailout near the MLR that came down into enemy hands were simply dispatched by a burst of burp-gun fire, and usually before they even touched the ground. Fryer was truly fortunate, for his parachute had hung-up in a tree that left him dangling as he fumbled with burned hands to free himself while also contending with blurred vision and a burned face. He was captured almost immediately by some North Koreans, yet they even took the time to remove some shrapnel from the back of his head before incarcerating him. Fryer was repatriated on August 18, 1953.

On November 9 a flight of SAAF Mustangs led by 2nd Lt. John Moir was attacking some artillery positions near Kumwha as a part of Operation Showdown and after they finished this chore they commenced strafing the enemy trenches in front of the ROK 3rd Infantry Division near Kumsong. A T-6 Mosquito that was acting as their FAC came under some antiaircraft fire and was hit, so the Mustangs broke off their attacks and escorted the Mosquito back across the MLR. As the Mustang flight returned to K-46 2nd Lt. Brian Forsyth, who had just completed his third mission, received the honor of completing the 18th FBW's 50,000 combat sortie. Another record also was established later in the month when 2nd Lt. Anstan Mather flew the 10,000 combat sortie for 2 Squadron, which broke their previous mission record from World War II.

In December 1952 2 Squadron continued to fly CAS missions, and lost one more Mustang and its pilot in an ironical tragedy. On Christmas Day Captain John Nortje and Lt. John Moir were on patrol over Hwachon Reservoir when they spotted several unidentifiable aircraft passing underneath them. Nortje told Moir that he was going to go down for a closer look to see what type of aircraft that they might be and told Moir to climb to a higher altitude to be able to give a little better top cover in case they might be hostile.

Moir did not acknowledge these instructions, for apparently his radio had failed. Nortje dove down and the unidentified aircraft saw him coming and broke their own formation, which created a melee. The unsuspecting Moir was shot down in the ensuing action, with his Mustang crashing six miles south of the reservoir. Nortje, now justifiably assumed that the other aircraft were unfriendly and started radioing for help on his radio's emergency frequency. His calls were heard by the very aircraft that he was fighting with, U.S. Marine Corps AD Skyraiders, and the battle was terminated. The unfortunate Moir's body was later recovered.

The month of December 1952 began the closing of an era for 2 Squadron and their Mustangs as the squadron was informed that they would transition to F-86F Sabres in January 1953, becoming the first of the 18th FBW squadrons to receive jet fighters.

The last combat sorties by 2 Squadron Mustangs were flown on December 27 with two flights of four aircraft each to the Punchbowl area. Baker Flight, with Porkey Rich, Andre du Plessis, Shorty Dowden and Brian Forsyth all completed their seventy-fifth and final combat sorties of the war. The pilots of Able Flight all stuck around to fly Sabres. Following this, the squadrons' remaining F-51s were returned to the USAF in Japan for refurbishment and then most were passed on to the ROKAF.

During the two years that 2 Squadron had been in combat with the F-51 they had flown 2, 890 missions with 10, 337 individual combat sorties. Seventy-four Mustangs were lost with thirty-four SAAF pilots killed. Seven of 2 Squadron's Mustang pilots became POW's and were repatriated at the end of the hostilities, with two of these men dying soon thereafter as a result of their experiences. Two pilots were wounded in action. Mathematically these figures equated to one out of every six SAAF pilots serving in Korea becoming a casualty. One enlisted man also had died as a result of an accident.

The South African's didn't care much for winter weather, yet snow was something new to them and something that could be enjoyed (To a degree). (Air Force Museum)

There was little doubt that 2 Squadron had earned everyone of the two Silver Stars, twenty-six Distinguished Flying Crosses, one Soldier's Medal, eighteen Bronze Stars, and eighty-nine Air Medals (With fifty-one additional clusters.) which they received from the 5th Air Force: and an extensive list of medals which they received from their own government and the Republic of Korea.

CHAPTER NINE

The 45th Tactical Reconnaissance Squadron

Due to the demands of modern war for vital and current information, the role of aerial reconnaissance had come into its own during World War II. Several series of Air Force tactical aircraft had been modified for this role as a result of these needs, most notably the Lockheed F-5 (P-38) Lightning and North American Aviation's F-6 (P-51, which was redesignated as the RF-51 in 1948).

At the beginning of the Korean War the required aircraft for the gathering this photographic information was sadly lacking within FEAF. There was one strategic squadron, the 31st Strategic Reconnaissance Squadron, which flew RB-29s, while only the 8th Tactical Reconnaissance Squadron with the new RF-80s were available for tactical purposes. Both of these aircraft had their limitations for use in Korea, the RB-29 by the altitude they had to work from, and the RF-80 with its severely limited range, due to fuel considerations a low altitudes. To get around these difficulties, FEAF initially requested RF-51Ds, but then changed their minds in favor of obtaining more RF-80s when a sufficient number of the larger Misawa fuel tanks became available for use by the 8th TRS. FEAF also requested that the 162nd Tactical Reconnaissance Squadron, equipped with RB-26s, should be transferred from their home station at Langley AFB, Virginia to FEAF for their use in providing low to medium altitude tactical photography.

However, none of these aircraft were sufficient, as the war was proving to be too fluid and the enemy too wily. Initially, squadrons operating in or over Korea had to provide their own reconnaissance while flying their combat missions, or rely up the observations of airborne Forward Air Control aircraft for up to date information. This information came back to squadron intelligence officers in a piecemeal fashion, for pilots sightings while dodging enemy ground fire were not the most reliable sources, particularly since they were not trained for this sort of observation, and their gun camera films, when the cameras worked in the first place, lacked the necessary quality.

To gather this information in the most expeditious manor, only first-hand low-level "recce" by trained pilots would do. With the exception of the few in number RF-80s available to FEAF, there was only one other aircraft in the USAF inventory at the time that was capable of this type of reconnaissance, and that was the RF-51D: Yet almost all of the RF-51Ds that had once been in FEAF's inventory had been scrapped prior to the beginning of the Korean War.

"The smoothest running, watchlike, hummingest, most vibration free Mustang I ever flew." The personal Mustang of Lt. Perry Hunnicutt,45th Tactical Reconnaissance Squadron. This particular F-51 had the best reputation in the squadron and Hunnicutt had to "stand in line" to have it assigned to him. Considerable credit went to Sgt. H. Marshall, its crew chief. It survived the war and was assigned to the 105th TRS, Tennessee Air National Guard. (Hunnicutt)

In the United States, the allocation of the RF-51Ds had been indiscriminate. There had been three post World War II tactical reconnaissance groups equipped with these Mustangs, but when they reequipped with RF-80s the Mustangs either went to the Air National Guard, to storage or to scrap. For the most part, those to the ANG were scattered across the country to various units without actual regard to the unit's tactical commitment. Consequently, when the ANG Mustangs were mobilized it took quite awhile to get the RF-'s segregated from the F-'s and then transported to Korea to be assigned to the 45th Tactical reconnaissance Squadron. (As a result of budget cut-backs in 1948/49, the majority of the USAF photo reconnaissance squadrons were inactivated and their pilots discharged. Almost all of the admittedly and limitedly proficient aerial reconnaissance pilots were now in either the USAF Reserve or in the Air National Guard, and it would be over a year before these men were activated into Federal Service and assigned to Korea).

The RF- version of the Mustang was essentially a conventional F-51D with permanently installed camera mounts in its aft fuselage for vertical and oblique photography. Initially they were delivered without rocket launching posts under their wings, although many had the rocket firing capabilities installed after their arrival in Korea. The RF-51D continued to carry the standard six .50 caliber wing machine guns and bomb/fuel tank racks. North American Aviation had built 136 RF-51Ds and 163 F-51Ks during World War II. The K version was identical to the D except for an Aeroproducts propeller with automatic pitch control, which was standard for the Dallas, Texas built F-51K. The F/RF-51K was not as popular with the pilots as the D version because its propeller slammed between pitch settings in a disconcerting herky-jerky fashion. It was supposed to have been phased out of the USAF inventory by 1951, but they remained in service in Korea until 1953. There were also many other F-51s thrown into the photo reconnaissance role by simply bolting a Fairchild F-17 camera on to the back of the pilot's armored headrest.

Probably the greatest advantage to FEAF in having the Mustang made available to them in the reconnaissance capacity was the aircraft's range. The RF-51D had the range and combat duration to permit it to loiter all over North Korea on any given photo sortie for as long as required. The second advantage was that it did carry machine guns, which enabled its pilot to destroy many targets without having to call in additional air support, and they gave him a chance to fight his way out of a bad situation. A major advantage over the RF-80 and other

44-84522 at K-14 on November 21, 1951 while undergoing maintenance. The camera access panel on the aft fuselage is not usually noticeable when it is in place. This Mustang had previously belonged to Alabama's 160th TRS, and it was returned to them after the war. (Reed)

recce types that were unarmed. (Of interest is that of the two Medal of Honor's awarded to Mustang pilots during World War II, the one to Major William Shomo was for shooting down seven Japanese aircraft on a mission while flying a F-6).

The 45th Tactical Reconnaissance Squadron was reactivated at Itazuke Air Base, Japan on September 3, 1950, although the date did not become official until September 26 when the squadron was attached to the 543rd Tactical Support Group. (The 543rd TSG eventually expanded and was redesignated as the 67th Tactical Reconnaissance Wing on February 25, 1951).

It was not until December 3 before the 45th TRS received their first ten RF-51Ds. Only thirteen pilots composed the initial meager squadron, and they immediately started proficiency training only to discover that the cameras in their Mustangs had deteriorated during storage and transpacific shipment. All of the cameras had to be completely rebuilt before they could be utilized operationally. By December 8, however, the 45th TRS was considered as combat ready, only to have to go on standby status while an air base in Korea could be found for them to be assigned. It was during this period when their first Mustang was lost, when Captain C.S. West was forced to bailout after his engine quit on takeoff from Komaki Air Base, J-21, Japan on December 23. The bailout was successful.

On December 27 the 45th TRS sent an advance party to Taegu Air Base, South Korea and the following day the rest of the squadron followed. On December 29 Captains East and Simpson flew the squadron's first combat mission, an armed reconnaissance strike behind the MLR.

The 45th TRS ended the month with a bare 12:30 hours of combat time out of a total of 438 Mustang flying hours.

On January 5, 1951 the 45th TRS received permission to attack targets while on recce missions. Previously they had been limited to only firing their machine guns to protect themselves. This quickly proved to be a popular move, for the Mustang pilots gained some satisfaction in being able to strike back at antiaircraft gunners. On January 15 they were ordered to commence single-ship recce missions, in order to spread out their limited number of aircraft over a wider area. The pilots greeted this particular order with mixed emotions, for they would no longer have any sort of top fighter escort cover while they were flying at tree-top heights. In addition, if they were shot down, the incident would probably occur unseen by anyone else and they had there doubts that they would have time to make a distress radio transmission in hopes of someone hearing them and being able to establish a RESCAP for them on the ground. They viewed their chances at becoming a POW as virtually nil.

Combat and reconnaissance sorties got off to a rough start for the 45th TRS as there were four aborted missions in January because of radio failures alone, a critical item for a recce pilot. Sixteen more sorties had to be aborted because of engine problems, while eight other missions had to be cut short because of additional engine difficulties. These engine problems were found to result from fuel contamination, as someone from the 8th Fighter Bomber Group had filled the 45th TRS's fuel trucks with jet fuel that was intended for RF-80s.

On January 26 the Mustang flown by Captain Warren Hanks was hit by small arms fire, becoming the first 45th TRS aircraft to receive battle damage. Hanks' got the Mustang back to Taegu for a safe landing, much to the relief of the squadron's operations section, as this

"Tempe Queen" of the 45th TRS. Its serial number and the significance of its name are unknown. (USAF)

particular RF-51 was the only one in the squadron with an operating oblique Fairchild K-22 camera.

In February a new type of reconnaissance mission was started, titled as "Circle Ten," these missions called for a RF-51 to be sent to explore a specific ten mile radius of a given area on a daily basis. A major advantage of these missions was that the same pilot was always assigned to the same area where he became more and more familiar with the topography and thus could note any changes brought about by the enemies use of camouflage. Circle Ten was quite effective as the RF-51 pilot could observe the area for hours, and if a target was spotted he could either attack it himself or call for a larger air strike. But there was a major hazard, also, for the communists soon learned to expect the Mustang, so the pilot had to vary the time of day that he arrived and his route of flight inbound, lest he encounter antiaircraft fire upon his arrival. Yet once he was established in his area, the enemy gunners pretty well left him alone, because they also quickly discovered that they could incur his wrath in the form of an air strike if they fired upon him. In all Circle Ten kept the Reds at bay during daylight hours, but it was a odd way of running a war.

On February 1 the 45th TRS lost its first Mustang since they started combat operations. 2nd Lt. James Rice was flying an armed recce mission over North Korea when his Mustang was hit several times by 20mm antiaircraft fire. Rice managed to nurse it back to friendly territory before bailing out. He struck the stabilizer during the bailout attempt, breaking his ankle, but he was picked up by friendly forces without further difficulties.

Also during February the Mustang of Captain William Freeton took 20mm fire through the rear of its canopy. Freeton suffered shrapnel wounds and became the first squadron pilot to receive the Purple Heart. One other Mustang had to make an emergency landing at Changju after its pilot strafed a communist truck, which then blew up in front of him, throwing debris up into its radiator. Two other Mustangs had to make emergency landings as a result of enemy ground fire, while one more had a mechanical problem. In addition, two more were damaged as a result of the necessity of flying low level recce missions. One struck a cable the communists had strung across a valley, while the other had a mid-air collision with a goose.

On February 13 Lt.'s James Dolan and Clyde East flew the longest duration mission since the 45th TRS entered the war. In five and a half hours over enemy territory they photographed the entire rail line between Hoeryong and Tanchon. This was considered to be quite the feat, as the fatiguing mission had to be flown at telephone pole height while dodging small arms fire.

1st Lt. Marshall Summerlin was flying a visual recce mission in the Chorwon area on March 3 when he became the first 45th TRS pilot to be lost in action. Summerlin had reported a rough running engine while well into the mission, but he did not believe that it was enough of a problem to force him to abort. After completing his reconnaissance, Summerlin stated that the engine problems were continuing and that he might have to bailout. Nothing further was heard from him, and he was declared as KIA six months later.

Captain David Rust fared considerably better on March 17 when his Mustang was hit by communist gun fire. Rust was forced to bailout over the Imjin River southeast of Kaesong. After landing in the river, Rust swam to the shore and sought refuge in an abandoned foxhole. With a flight of Mustangs overhead providing a RESCAP, Rust kept his head down and waited for a successful rescue by an ARS helicopter a hour later.

Two days later a second 45th TRS Mustang pilot was killed in action. Lt. James Dolan was leading a flight of two Mustangs on a visual reconnaissance mission near Chorwon when they spotted an enemy troop concentration. Dolan led the pair of Mustangs down to attack the enemy, and his Mustang was seen by his wingman to stall-out and then snap roll into the ground without a chance for him to bailout.

Captain William Preston was the next 45th TRS pilot to be lost, as he disappeared while on a visual recce mission near Kaesong on March 26. A communications check was made between his flight members when it was real-

ized that one of their Mustangs was missing, but nothing was further heard from Preston and he was declared as MIA. Preston was taken prisoner and was repatriated on September 1, 1953.

April 1951 was another bad month for 45th TRS pilots, three being lost while on combat missions. On April 10 Captain John McCullum was hit by ground fire east of the Zwachon Reservoir. It was first reported by the JOC that McCullum had bailed out behind enemy lines and was probably taken prisoner. Pilots of the squadron started a search for him anyway, and as it turned out, McCullum had radioed conflicting position reports prior to his being hit, so the search was abandoned. His Mustang was later found crashed in friendly territory with his body still in its cockpit.

On April 14 1st Lt. Roma Foglesong was hit by ground fire. His Mustang caught on fire and dove straight into the ground. His wingman, 1st Lt. Ellison Carroll, saw the crash and stated that there was no chance of survival. Nevertheless, Foglesong was carried as MIA until December, when he was officially declared as KIA.

In an attempt to get around at least a part of the heavy enemy ground fire problem, two-ship 45th TRS Mustang missions were started on April 15. One recce Mustang would continue its work at low altitude, while the other one flew a bit higher in hopes of spotting antiaircraft batteries in time to avoid them. For two days the concept appeared to be valid.

On April 17 Captain Charles Brown and 1st Lt. Jackie Douglas took off from Taegu on an armed recce mission. Brown spotted a target that appeared to him as being worthwhile, so he dove on it to mark its position with his .50 caliber tracer fire so Douglas could make an accurate bomb run. Brown's Mustang was hit by ground fire just at the point where he should have started to pull up from his dive, and it continued its dive into the ground.

In addition to the three Mustangs lost during April thirteen more received battle damage. Two of these were on April 22 while their pilots were RESCAPing a downed pilot from another squadron. (Dean, 39th FIS.) By the middle of the month the 45th TRS remained equipped with just ten aircraft, as attrition equaled the number of replacement F-51s received since December. With the serviceable Mustangs being flown at least twice a day, an emergency message was sent to FEAF for more Mustangs, and those that were received in response were all the fighter versions. This meant that the ground crews had their hands full in keeping the remaining RF versions operational while the fighter versions were utilized as the higher top cover and photography was accomplished by

Future Father Boardman C. Reed, who became an Episcopalian minister, prepares to fly a functional flight check of a 45th TRS Mustang, a collateral duty. Reed, an ex World War II B-17 squadron commander later became a 5th Air Force Historical Officer before retiring from the USAF. (Reed)

the lower RF-51. As the regular F-51 was able to carry more ordnance than its counterpart on armed recce missions, they were considered to be an adequate trade-off.

In all, the spring of 1951 was a period of major problems in keeping the Mustangs operational during the intensive Communist Spring Offensive and the demands for up to date reconnaissance. Even though replacement Mustangs were now being shipped to Japan and Korea in large lots, fresh from Pacific Aeromotive Corporation's overhaul facility at Burbank, California or from Temco's facility at Dallas, Texas, spare parts did not always manage to find their way to where they were needed. All of the F-51 units were plagued with this problem, but the 45th TRS the most, because of the desired camera equipment. Crew Chiefs begged, borrowed and stole to keep their Mustangs operational, often being forced to pull parts off of one aircraft returning from a mission for installation on another being prepared for the next one. These efforts brought long hours for the crew chiefs and a duplication of work but they kept the aircraft loss and abort rate down, as the crew chiefs refused to let an aircraft leave with questionable equipment.

Due to this sort of professionalism the 45th TRS garnered a strong reputation among the fighter pilots from the other squadrons that they worked with on a daily basis. The fighter bomber pilots knew that if the 45th TRS called them in for a strike, there was definitely a worthwhile target and they would not find themselves exposed to hostile fire unjustly. Also, due to the 45th TRS pilots familiarity with their given recce areas, the strike orders were explicit, so the attacking pilots did not have to consume time nor fuel while orientating themselves to their targets.

All of this expertise did not come cheaply. The 45th TRS had eleven Mustangs damaged by Red ground fire in May, but none were lost. To reduce their exposure to the loss of an aircraft or pilot, orders were revised once again, with the pilots restricted to no lower than 1, 500 feet above the ground. The recce pilots felt that this restriction was just too tight, for it reduced their effectiveness. Previously they often flew low enough to look in doors and windows of the Korean "hooches" they passed. Fortunately at this time the war had become fairly static and it was no longer necessary for the pilots to take abnormal risks.

One rather interesting experiment was carried out during this lull to help the recce pilots pin-point targets for the fighter bombers. The Mustangs six .50 caliber machine guns were all loaded with tracer ammunition, instead of the usual one in four rounds. This turned out to

be helpful in identifying the targets for the attacking aircraft, but entirely unsatisfactory and hazardous for the recce pilot. It was discovered that reflex would cause the recce pilot to look at the fire emitting from his wings instead of the target, and then he would be momentarily blinded by the glare of the tracers. They then reduced the tracer ammunition to four guns, and then to two, where the tracers looked like fingers pointing at the target. But even this was hazardous, for the smoke from the tracers was found to help the Red gunners orientate their weapons on the Mustangs.

The 45th TRS flew 338 recce missions in June, of which 275 were considered to be effective. Fifty-two of the non-effective missions were the result of bad weather over the targeted areas. The efforts to get in these missions again took their toll of Mustangs.

On June 4 Captain Lloyd Simpson's F-51 incurred battle damage over enemy territory and Simpson headed south for Kimpo Air Base, but he had to bailout before he got there. Fortunately the winds were in his favor and his parachute drifted him to a safe landing south of the MLR. Two days later Lt. Willis Thatcher wasn't so lucky as he was killed by communist gunfire while on a low-level sortie. On June 28 Captain Johnny Crowell's F-51 was also hit by enemy fire over North Korea. As in Simpson's case, he got as far as the UN lines before he was forced to abandon his Mustang.

On July 1 the 67th Tactical Reconnaissance Wing lost its commanding officer. Colonel Karl "Pop" Polifka was killed after making a low pass on an enemy target while flying an armed recce mission. His F-51 took flak hits in its engine and coolant systems. Polifka almost made it back to the MLR before he was forced to bailout, but during the attempt his parachute fouled on the aircraft, itself, and he was carried with it to his death. Polifka had been considered to be the "Father of modern aerial reconnaissance" as a result of his World War II experiences. He was replaced by Colonel Bert Smiley until July 4 when Colonel Vincent Howard took over the Wing.

The next day 1st Lt. Eugene Ruiz was also killed as a result of enemy fire. Lt. Jackie Douglas was shot down on June 17, and exactly what occurred is an unknown. His name does not appear on USAF casualty, POW or MIA listings.

The 45th TRS moved their operations to Kimpo Air Base, K-14, on August 14, 1951. Because of the squadron's move there was a slight break in the action, so only 606 individual sorties were attempted. Due to their proximity to the front lines and the corresponding reduction in the amount of required flying time, the 45th TRS was able to increase their number of missions, but the figure remained well below the desired 800 sorties. During the period August 18-24 the typhoon season let up enough to allow them to perform at almost a maximum effort level, for during this period they averaged eighteen sorties per day. For the month of August they totaled 1,350 combat hours, and were accident free!

One Mustang was lost, however, as a result of enemy gunfire, on August 7. Lt. Donald Dishon was forced to make a forced landing in friendly territory while on his way home from a reconnaissance mission. He was uninjured.

During September the 45th TRS was committed by the 5th Air Force to a figure ranging between 25 and 30 reconnaissance sorties per day. These were all of short duration, ranging along the MLR, where in some cases the pilots were asked to double as FAC's. The F-51 wasn't particularly well suited for this FAC mission, due to its own inherent vulnerability, but it was felt by 5th Air Force planners that they had a better chance of survivability than the unarmed T-6s. In spite of the number of hours flown and the hazards over the MLR, no Mustangs were lost to enemy action, but six suffered major battle damage. One Mustang, flown by Lt. Raymond Schmitt, was hit by 40mm antiaircraft fire which put forty-two holes in it. Schmitt was cut about the face and his back by Plexiglas shards. Another Mustang, flown by Lt. Robert Grubaugh, came under .50 caliber fire and caused him many anxious moments. His right wing fuel tank and wing spar were holed, but the Mustang held together without catching fire and he made it back to K-14 for a safe landing. His Mustang required an entire new wing.

The 45th TRS reached the 5,000th combat sortie mark in October, just ten months after entering the conflict. Due to the proximity between Kimpo and the MLR, the recce missions were still of short duration, averaging two hours each. This was fine with the pilots as it gave them a chance to build up their missions totals without spending a lot of time in their cockpits or over enemy held ground. Atypical of military life though, just as they were starting to feel good about their situation, the "word" came down from Headquarters 5th Air Force for them to start expanding their reconnaissance areas further to the north, to look for any signs of the Reds reinforcing their own front lines.

On October 5 Captain Learnard was hit by small arms fire and had to bailout. He landed in friendly territory and was immediately picked up and returned to the squadron. On October 11 Lt. Donald Dishon was flying out of K-14 on a proficiency flight when he hit a cable that was

1st Lt. David Howard, 45th TRS. Howard was shot down, but escaped the enemys' clutches via the efforts of the 3rd ARS in February 1952. (Yost)

strung across a valley. These cables were a constant hazard to recce pilots for their position was rarely noted on their maps. They also were often strung across valleys by communist soldiers behind their lines, or by guerrillas at night while operating behind friendly lines. At the altitudes the recce pilots liked to fly these cables were rarely visible, due to their relative proximity to the horizon, in time for the pilots to see and avoid them.

The first fatal pilot casualty in several months occurred on the last day of October when Grant Madison was leading a fighter strike. His Mustang was seen to dive into the ground, for no apparent reason: and again there was no chance of survival.

The 45th TRS flew under the tactical radio callsign of "Topkick," and a new offensive program under this same name commenced with them in November. This program sent a 45th TRS reconnaissance flight to a specific area, as previously under Circle Ten, but they then would work directly under the control of a JOC. Also under "Topkick," the JOC would assign fighter-bombers in advance to the same area as the 45th TRS Mustang was assigned, to loiter at a fuel conserving altitude until one of the recce pilots discovered a target that he deemed as worthwhile, whereupon the recce pilot would serve as a FAC. This new program was found to work considerably better than the previous method where the recce pilot had to radio the JOC for a strike and then wait to see if any aircraft were going to become available. In twenty Topkick missions thirteen supply dumps, eight vehicles, nine tanks and six artillery positions were destroyed as quickly as they were spotted.

Seventeen "new" RF-51Ds were received in November, these having been taken out of storage at Kelly AFB, Texas and overhauled by Temco and then shipped to Korea. These were all brand-new six-year old Mustangs that had been placed in storage at Kelly after initial delivery to the Air Force at the end of World War II and the only flying time that they had on their airframes was from the North American Aviation factory to San Antonio. Seven of the weary 45th TRS F-51s were thusly transferred to the 18th FBW, while ten others were returned to Kisarazu Air Base, Japan to be placed in Theater storage awaiting further need. These transfers of aircraft fairly well, and finally, established the 45th TRS as a true reconnaissance squadron and correspondingly reduced their fighter-bomber commitments.

Almost all of the missions flown in December were of the Topkick variety, operating in conjunction with fighter bomber strikes. A few incidents were the only ones reflecting communist opposition. On December 1, 2nd Lt. Ross Carson was hit in the right wing by Red .50 caliber fire. Ten days later, while flying another Mustang, he was again hit in the right wing. From this time on he became noted for casting protective glances at this wing before and after missions. Also occurring on December 1 Captain Carl Burak came under antiaircraft fire and had to fight his damaged Mustang all the way back to friendly territory to belly land it on a beach. Burak was uninjured, but his Mustang was a total write-off and he reportedly had several angry words to say to it for its resisting his attempts to save it.

Now operating under the radio callsign of "Hammer," the 45th TRS started 1952 by getting back to aerial photography. The winter weather did make their job all the more difficult, as the cameras in their RF-51s often would freeze-up or the camera lenses would frost over if their heaters would fail; or mud, snow or slush would be thrown from the landing gear or prop wash over the camera ports

causing obscured photography. One hundred-eleven photo-reconnaissance sorties were unsuccessful due to these conditions or the cold weather effecting the aircraft. Two Mustangs suffered major damage because their tail wheels would not extend for landing, due to snow or ice being accumulated in the tail wheel wells as they took off and then freezing solid during the course of the mission.

The first combat loss of a 45th TRS Mustang for 1952 occurred on January 14 when Lt. Ralph Reighter had to belly one in after being hit by communist fire. He managed to nurse it to a position behind the UN lines before putting it down and he was uninjured.

Regardless of the weather there was no let up in attacking the communists. On January 17 Lt.'s Perry Hunnicutt and Carson flew a Topkick mission for a flight of six F4Us against a concentration of thirty Red tanks, which effectively put them out of commission. One Corsair was lost. The month ended with the loss of 1st Lt. Bill Bing. Bing had to bailout over North Korea on January 31 and he was carried as MIA. He was released as a POW on August 30, 1953.

During February 1952 the ground war was at a virtual standstill, but for the 45th TRS it was a period of high activity, and of high losses. 1,442 combat hours were flown during 670 reconnaissance sorties. Four pilots were declared as missing in action while Lt. David Howard managed to get back to friendly territory before he had to bailout of his shot up Mustang.

Lt. Donald Dishon's luck ran out of February 2 after his two previous incidents. He disappeared over North Korea without any indication as to why, but this was not an uncommon circumstance considering that many of the squadrons missions continued to be solo flights at altitudes below both radar and radio coverage. Dishon be-

"Miss Freckleface" was the personal Mustang of Lt. John Yost. 44-84520 came to Korea from the 153rd TRS, and returned to the 105th TRS. (Yost)

came a POW and was released on September 5, 1953 during Operation Big Switch.

Lt. Charles Price was the next to disappear, on February 17, and again the was no indication as to why. He was released as a POW on August 31, 1953 during Operation Little Switch.

On February 21 Captain William Mauldin was shot down, Mauldin was able to make radio contact with a RESCAP flight via his URC-4 survival radio, but he was captured before a helicopter could make its way to him. It is not known whether he was killed while being taken prisoner or whether he died as a POW, but his death was confirmed after the cease fire took effect. Captain Robert Burns, the squadrons operations officer, was shot down on February 28 and also was carried as MIA. He was repatriated with Lt. Dishon.

The compliment of assigned Mustangs for March stood at twenty-two RF-51Ds and two F-51Ds. One of the F-51Ds was written-off on March 7 when being flown by Lt. Thornsel. It was hit by enemy ground fire and Thornsel had to make a forced landing in "no man's land," but he managed to escape both injury and the enemy. This particular Mustang just happened to be one of the oldest ones in the 5th Air Force inventory, having been built in 1944 and having evaded the post war scrappers' torch. One additional Mustang received major combat damage and two more had minor damage as a result of hostile action. The mission count was increased to 738 sorties, thus, percentage wise, the 45th TRS was far ahead of the previous month in the relationship between sorties and combat losses.

Sometime in April 1952 1st Lt. Curtis Ash spotted and destroyed an Il-10 which was parked in the open on the North Korean airstrip at Wonsan, (the ex K-25). This was the first, and only, kill to be claimed by a 45th TRS Mustang pilot, although it was not officially credited by the USAF.

An improvement in the weather and combat conditions in the late spring gave the 45th TRS crew chiefs an opportunity to finally start painting the squadron's Mustangs in a blue and white polka dot paint scheme. This was something that Lt. Dishon had originated when he purchased a bolt of silk in Japan for use in making scarves for squadron pilots. (This scheme was carried through on all of the squadron's aircraft ever since).

The 10,000th combat sortie for the 45th TRS was flown on May 5 by the squadron's commanding officer, Lt. Colonel Hudson. Even though mission lengths were still averaging only two hours each, the number of take-offs and landings amassed on the Mustangs was beginning to take its toll. For the pilots there was the fatigue factor of being flung around in the cockpit while pulling lots of "g's" while dodging hostile gunfire. All of these factors contributed to one Mustang being lost as a result of battle damage and four more being damaged or written-off through belly landings. One incident was charged to maintenance error, one to pilot error, one to a combination of maintenance and pilot error after its Merlin engine quit on takeoff, and one to material failure.

Due to the increasing fatigue of the Mustangs FEAF decided that it was time to consider replacing them with another type of reconnaissance aircraft. They wanted RF-88s, but since the USAF had not ordered this aircraft into production to begin with, they had to settle for more RF-80s. The exchange of Mustangs for Shooting Stars by the 45th TRS would then compliment the 67th Tactical Reconnaissance Wing's other RF-80 squadron, the 15th TRS for the time being.

During June 1952 the transition to jets began with the receipt of five RF-80As and five F-80Cs. Some of the new RF-80As were delivered with an olive drab paint scheme on their top surfaces, with natural aluminum undersides, in an attempt to camouflage them. An advantage the Mustangs never had in Korea.

In spite of the anticipation of receiving jet aircraft, the war had to be continued with Mustangs for the time being. In one instance Lt. John Yost led in a squadron of sixteen F-80s to attack four Red artillery positions. Yost marked the target with tracer fire, which was difficult for the F-80 pilots to see from their higher altitudes, so he had to go down even lower to re-mark them again. In the process he spotted and then reported the ever prevalent antiaircraft gun emplacements, which were then dispatched, along with the artillery positions. Yost then made

45-11613 "Linda & Bobby Jr." at K-14 on September 3, 1951. It had previously belonged to the 35th FIW, and it was lost on November 2, 1951 as a result of enemy action. (Reed)

three low-level recce passes to ascertain the damage, and for his efforts he received the DFC.

In an attempt to improve the versatility of the RF-51 while they were still being utilized by the 45th TRS, camera pods were attached to the underside of the Mustangs wings. These turned out not to be feasible, as they created undesirable aerodynamic stability problems by disrupting the wing's lift.

Even though jet aircraft had been using K-14 for over a year, it was decided to extend the runways length at Kimpo for greater safety. Consequently all of the 45th TRS Mustang operations were moved to K-16, Seoul Air Base, in August 1952 while the construction took place. The temporary relocation did not curtail any tactical operations, but it did create certain hardships on squadron personnel, particularly the enlisted men who had to live and work in still more primitive conditions than they had in their tent area over at K-14.

Three squadron aircraft were lost during August. One was an F-80 that was involved in a mid-air collision, but its pilot made a successful ejection. One Mustang was

"The Thing" was named after a popular song of the era. The crew chief usually named the right side of an aircraft, the pilot the left, which was "Oh Kay II." It survived the war and was assigned to the 154th TRS, Mississippi ANG. (Reed)

lost when its pilot bailed out over friendly territory after he encountered vertigo while flying on instruments. The third loss was as a result of enemy action when on August 15 Lt. Fred Partridge was killed after being hit by enemy ground fire.

"Ok Kaye Baby." The 45th TRS polka dot colors came as a result of Lt. Don Dishon's R&R trip to Japan where he purchased a bolt of blue and white polka dot silk to make scarves for the pilots. (Major General S. Newman via Menard)

It had started raining in August with the beginning of the traditional typhoon season, and heavy rains continued into September. Only 562 effective sorties were flown during September because of the incessant storms and low cloud ceilings. One Mustang was hit by small arms fire and gave its pilot many bad moments while he was directing fire for a U.S. Navy battleship that was firing 3.5" while phosphorus rockets. With his Merlin engine shaking in its mounts, the pilot headed for K-16 with great concern, for occasionally a Mustang was known to have its entire engine tear loose from the fuselage. If this would occur there was little likelihood of a pilot being able to escape the then tumbling fuselage. But the Mustang held together long enough for him to make a safe emergency landing. It took the ground crew two days to replace the damaged engine and its mounts.

The 45th TRS was at half their authorized strength of RF-80s by October and they decided to test the feasibility of working the Shooting Stars and the Mustangs as a team. The evaluation proved to be a satisfactory one, as long as the jets could remain at a higher altitude, to reduce their fuel consumption. The photographic results of the teamwork efforts were deemed as 'excellent." The purpose of these efforts were to supply the U.S. Eighth Army with current front line photography. The Eighth Army was single minded in its demands, as they wanted 3,

44-84517 "Betty Jane" with some unusual nose art for a 45th TRS Mustang. The airman is believed to be Sgt. Marshall. (Colbert via Menard)

600 photographic negatives a day, ranging from the MLR to a depth of fifteen miles behind the battle lines at a minimum, to as far as the Yalu River at a maximum! Logistically and realistically there was just no possible way that the 5th Air Force could meet these demands, but they still attempted to cover the areas from the MLR to as deep within North Korea as they could. One problem, it was found, was that the RF-80 was just a bit too fast for its cameras to operate effectively, which resulted in blurred images. When they operated in conjunction with the RF-51s some of these deficits were alleviated.

One of the oldest 45th TRS Mustangs was this RF-51K which was photographed in Korea a year after it was supposedly scrapped. It was the second "Tulie, Scotty & ?" to serve in Korea. (Picciani Aircraft Slides)

45-11679, previously of the 45th TRS, all cleaned up and ready for its next assignment to where? Photographed at Itazuke Air Base in September 1953. (Brian Stainer via Menard)

Captain Ted Giermek taxiing-in after completing his 100th combat mission in 44-84852 in May 1952. "Marynia" appears war weary but she was cleaned-up and returned to the ANG. (Yost)

During these missions in October two Mustangs were shot down by enemy ground fire while four received battle damage. Lt. Mathis Martin bailed out over friendly territory, while Lt. Davis settled for a belly landing, also in friendly territory. Both were uninjured.

One thing was known for sure by all of the 45th TRS pilots and that was that although the ground war was static, Red activity behind the lines was not. The communists, since they were not actively attacking the MLR, busied themselves installing more and more antiaircraft batteries. Again it was claimed that there were more antiaircraft guns in North Korea than there had been in all of Europe during World War II. Which may, or may not have been a numerical fact, but the point was that all of these existing guns were concentrated in an area one-

half the size of the state of Minnesota, and all of the Red gun crews were excellent marksmen. One result of this knowledge came the placement of a 9,000 foot minimum altitude restriction for pilots while conducting visual reconnaissance. This was a marked increase from the previous 4,000 foot minimum that had been mandated the previous February. Some pilots complained about the higher restriction, believing that it hampered their recce, but it did help increase their longevity.

Because of the continuing poor weather into November, there were only nine days where good weather permitted reconnaissance operations. The 45th TRS had officially become a jet squadron in October, but they still had fourteen RF-51s and one F-51 for use in their recce missions. One RF-51D, "Connie," amassed 88:30 hours

Curtis Ash, John Knight and David Howard in the cold and snow at Kimpo. Ash may have been the last USAF pilot to score a kill while flying a Mustang. (Yost)

Karl Polifka, seated center at desk, in Italy during World War II. He was considered to be the father of modern tactical reconnaissance. He died bailing out of a 45th TRS F-51 on July 1, 1951. (Karl Polifka, Jr.)

The war is over for two. Lt's John Knight and Walt Elflein with the symbolic lucky 100 mission horseshoe. (Hunnicutt)

Lt. Walt Flint sporting an insignia on his A-2 jacket that was not approved by the USAF. It reads: "Search and Destroy, Korea 1951, 45th Tactical Recon Squadron ." (Hunnicutt)

flying time, which wasn't bad for nine days work in an "official" jet squadron. In spite of the adverse weather and the fact that there were now, and finally, an adequate number of pilots, 399 combat sorties were flown in the

Lt. Perry Hunnicutt and Captain Ted Giermek at K-14. Note the "Sylvester" insignia of the 45th TRS. (Hunnicutt)

Mustang out of a total of 483 launched by the 45th TRS.

Two more Mustang pilots became MIA in December 1952. Lt. Warren Lull was shot down by Red ground fire on December 27 and became a POW. He was released on September 6, 1953. Lt. Frank Salazar went down on December 31, and he was declared as KIA on January 1, 1954. The reason for his loss was never determined.

For all practicality the era of the photo-reconnaissance Mustang in Korea ended in January 1953, coinciding with the withdrawal of the Mustang from the 18th Fighter Bomber Wing.

During the Korean War the 45th TRS Mustang pilots had photographed 83% of their assigned objectives with 48% effectiveness, by the U.S. Eighth Army's unrealistic demands. The 45th TRS alone averaged more aerial photography than any single 9th Air Force Photo Group had during World War II, and the 67th TRW had more than doubled the 9th Air Force's photographic missions. In fact, they had quadrupled the amount of photography. The 45th TRS had averaged sixty-two assigned photographic targets per month of Mustang operations, which was only 10% of their assigned missions. All other of their missions being armed reconnaissance, which equated to picking out a target of opportunity, destroy it if you can, and report back with what you have seen or accomplished.

This was a rough business, considering that the 45th TRS averaged 666 combat sorties each month and paid the price of loosing thirty-seven Mustangs. Fourteen squadron Mustang pilots were killed in action, six became prisoners of war.

"California or Bust"/"Sweet Lorraine," 44-84840 (Which would have made an acceptable poker hand). She was lost to enemy action on August 7, 1951. (Reed)

A "piggy-back" conversion of a F-51D that was utilized for orientation and training flights by the 45th TRS. She was transferred to the ROKAF after the war. (Esposito)

"Big Bertha" came to an untimely end on October 5, 1951 when Captain Learnard had to bailout after being hit by enemy ground fire. Fortunately his parachute drifted him into friendly territory. (Reed)

A nice line-up of 45th TRS Mustangs at Taegu on July 18, 1951. 45-11735 was one of those F-51s later transferred to the Philippine Air Force. (Reed)

Epilogue

Statistics can be boring, but some figures can be illuminating. The F-51 Mustang, as a fighter bomber in the Korean War ranked as number four within the USAF committed units for the total number of combat sorties flown, 62, 607. Fully one third less than the F-80 Shooting Star that totaled 98, 515. By comparison, they had a considerably higher loss rate, 341 to enemy action, while only 143 F-80s were lost to enemy action. Total losses, due to all causes, show that 474 Mustangs were lost, in relation to the F-80 that totaled 373. However, the pilot casualties in relationship to the total number of sorties flown are virtually identical.

Mustang pilots dropped 12, 909 tons of bombs, which placed them number three in this catagory behind the F-80 and F-84 Thunderjet. However, they fired more .50 caliber ammunition and dropped more napalm than the F-80, F-84 and F-86F Sabre combined. They fired 183, 034 rockets, two-thirds more than the other three types combined.

In fighting enemy aircraft they shot down sixteen, and destroyed eight more on the ground. According to USAF Historical Study Number 81, which gives the "Credits for the Destruction of Enemy Aircraft, Korean War," (June 1963) they were credited with twelve of the mentioned sixteen in the air and seven on the ground. The USAF Statistical Digest, Fiscal 1953, credits the Mustang with higher figures, thirty-seven enemy aircraft destroyed, and that Mustang pilots also were credited with eleven probably destroyed and twenty-seven damaged. Official unit records only indicate claims for five probables and eight damaged. Choose the statistics of your choice.

It might be fitting to state that the 18th FBW, which flew the Mustang in combat longer than any other unit in the history of the Air Force, (Including the post World War II period.) produced more future General Officers for the USAF than any other unit that was involved in the Korean War, but this claim cannot be proven. The ideal closing is probably more in keeping with the following tribute to one of the pilots that did not survive.

In Memoriam

I walked among the crosses on the hill,
I looked for names of those I know.
Many crosses, white and still
Until, at last, I came to you.
Your name was there in letters small,
Day of birth and day you died;
"In memory of," it said ... that's all,
Not who cared, or not who cried.
Many things it does not tell-
That cross that's over your head,
Nothing there of why you fell;
"In memory of," is all it said.
People will recall each year
On a certain day in May;
They'll kneel and maybe shed a tear
And put some flowers where you lay.
But we will remember every day
You who gave his all.
Not just once a year in May
We will your name recall.
For we who knew and called you friend,
For we who saw you fall,
We will remember to the end
The day you gave your all,
If only people could but see
Into our Hearts they'd know
While your name will always be
With us where 'ere we go.
Burned upon our hearts they'd find,
If they could take a peek
The mark that you left behind.

"In memory of," Captain Danny Leake

M/Sgt. Maynard A. Boynton, 18th FBG
His Crew Chief

From "Truckbusters," 18th FBW Yearbook, 1951

Appendix 1:
Confirmed Mustang Pilot Losses
in the Korean Conflict

The date given is the actual date of loss, if known, or the later date if declared as killed in action.

2 Squadron, SAAF

Badenhorst, W.J.J. Captain	March 2, 1951
Baransky, G.J. Lt.	April 20, 1952
Bekker, F.M. Lt.	July 23, 1951
Biden, N. Lt.	September 5, 1951
Botha, M.C. Lt.	August 28, 1951
Davis, J.F.O. Captain	March 10, 1951
Doveton, G.D. Lt.	February 15, 1951
duPlooy, R.N. Lt.	July 23, 1951
deJongh, C.L. Lt.	August 14, 1951
Frisby, A.G. Lt.	June 22, 1951
Grunder, M.O. Lt.	September 1, 1951
Harburn, R.A. Captain	February 11, 1952
Holtzhauzen, J.O. Lt.	April 10, 1952
Janse van Rensburg, A. Captain	November 29, 1951
Joyce, H.T.R. Lt.	October 29, 1951
Kotzenberg, R.P.G. Captain	August 22, 1952
Krohn, G.H. Lt.	November 24, 1951
Leah, D.R. Lt.	February 7, 1951
Lellyet, J.N. Lt.	February 29, 1952
Leibenberg, T. Lt.	June 10, 1951
Montanari, F.A. Lt.	September 12, 1951
Moir, J. Lt.	December 25, 1952
Norman-Smith, P.I. Lt.	December 3, 1951
Pearce, L.B. Major	July 9, 1951
Parsonson, L.W. Lt.	January 6, 1952
Pappas, C.J. Lt.	November 4, 1951
Rorke, M.H. Lt.	May 15, 1951
Ruiter, D.A. Lt.	March 2, 1951
Scott, T.C. Lt.	August 9, 1952
Staats, R.L. Lt.	January 17, 1952
Taylor, D.L. Lt.	March 20, 1952
Verster, J.P. Lt.	July 1, 1951
Wilson, W.E. Lt.	February 2, 1951
Whitehead, K.R. Lt.	December 3, 1951

35th Fighter Bomber Squadron

Gilliam, Patterson 1st Lt.	August 22, 1950
Mullet, Arlin A. 1st Lt.	August 27, 1950
Munkres, John N. 1st Lt.	August 15, 1950
Rabun, Wayne J. 1st Lt.	October 16, 1950

36th Fighter Bomber Squadron

Anderlie, James 1st Lt.	September 2, 1950

Onze, Edward J. Captain	September 18, 1950
Webster, H. D., Jr. Captain	September 14, 1950
Williams, Robert 1st Lt.	December 9, 1950

18th Fighter Bomber Group (& Wing) Pilot Losses

18th Fighter Bomber Group

Bolt, Donald D. Captain	October 2, 1950/March 31, 1954, remains MIA (Flying w/12th FBS)
Edens, Malcom B. Captain	November 26, 1950 as a FAC, remains MIA but believed to have died as a POW
French, David J. Captain	August 25, 1951
Glessner, Milton Jr., Lt. Colonel	February 2, 1951/December 31, 1953, remains MIA
Jones, George D. 1st. Lt.	October 28, 1951 (Flying w/39th FIS)
Lynd, Donald 1st Lt.	November 20, 1951 (Flying w/39th FIS)

12th Fighter Bomber Squadron

Bennett, Chauncy A. Captain	April 30, 1951
Bettis, Allan S. 1st Lt.	April 13, 1952
Brown, Willis R. 1st Lt.	March 15, 1951
David, Mike S. 2nd Lt.	October 8, 1950
Davis, Raymond, R. Captain	October 5, 1951 remains MIA
Elsom, William Captain	January 6, 1952
Fluhr, Robert S. Lt.	May 6, 1952
Forster, Harold S.	December 17, 1951
Gray, George E. Captain	April 5, 1951
Heath, James D. 1st Lt.	March 8, 1951
Hoffman, Donald E. 1st Lt.	December 8, 1951
Hudson, Fred G. Capt.	November 27, 1950
Irwin, Frederick Captain	January 31, 1952
Jones, Oliver E. 1st Lt.	October 22, 1951, remains MIA
Lucas, Robert J. 1st Lt.	November 17, 1951
McGowan, Clarence 1st Lt.	December 23, 1951
Middleton, Harry B. 1st Lt.	April 30, 1951
Olson, Leonard S. Lt.	May 14, 1952
Padilla, Alex B. 1st Lt.	October 9, 1950, remains MIA
Smith, Graham Captain	April 30, 1951

Stewart, Raymond S. 1st Lt.	August 25, 1951 As POW
Swanson, John A. 1st Lt.	December 13, 1951
Taylor, Claude R. 1st Lt.	October 20, 1950
Tyler, Harry M.	December 25, 1951
Wolfe, Lawrence E. 1st Lt.	April 26, 1952
Woliung, John J. Captain	November 5, 1952

51st Fighter Bomber Squadron (Provisional)

Haines, George E.	December 21, 1950
Higgins, John J.	July 6, 1950
Smith, Howard E.	December 30, 1950

67th Fighter Bomber Squadron

Andridge, Herbert W., Jr. Captain	April 10, 1951
Ausman, Harold J. 1st Lt.	December 4, 1950
Ayer, Elliott D. Captain	July 31, 1951
Babasa, Joseph M. 1st Lt.	July 9, 1951/July 30, 1951
Bitzer, Morton A. 1st Lt.	January 8, 1952
Connors, Archibald 1st Lt.	June 25, 1952
Cree, Ronald R. Captain	June 5, 1951
Deschamps, Elzeard Captain	February 2, 1951
Eichelberger, George 1st Lt.	January 15, 1952
Escott, Francis 1st Lt.	June 16, 1951
Flentke, Donald D. Captain	September 28, 1950/December 28, 1950
Greene, William J. Major	August 14, 1951
Harkness, Grant D. 1st Lt.	December 5, 1951
Haskett, William T., Jr. Captain	April 14, 1951, remains MIA
Heagney, Gerald J. 1st Lt.	March 9, 1951
Holcomb, Francis A. 1st Lt.	March 18, 1951
Howell, Robert N. Captain	August 4, 1950
Leake, Daniel B. Captain	October 18, 1950
Lighter, Jack A. 1st Lt.	September 7, 1950/December 7, 1950
McAlpine, John M. 1st Lt.	June 24, 1952
Mederstrom, Jack A. Captain	June 1, 1951
Michelberger, George 1st Lt.	February 8, 1952 Remains MIA
Moore, Harry C. Captain	June 1, 1951
Moore, Lyle E. 1st Lt.	December 15, 1951
Murray, Joseph J. 1st Lt.	July 18, 1951
Patton, George V. 1st Lt.	June 13, 1951/June 13, 1952
Pearson. Benard 1st Lt.	November 11, 1950
Plevyak, Raymond 1st Lt.	March 1, 1952
Powers, Joseph E. Captain	January 18, 1951
Rives, Joel O. 1st Lt.	April 27, 1952/April 27, 1953
Sankey, William C. 1st Lt.	April 27, 1952
Sebille, Louis J. Major	August 5, 1950
Solom, ? Captain	November 11, 1950
Steckel, Richard E. Major	May 15, 1952
Wolf, Leland H. 1st Lt.	September 13, 1951
Wright, Jack M. 1st Lt.	April 2, 1951

35th Fighter Interceptor Wing

Hodges, Kenneth S. Major	December 6, 1950

39th Fighter Interceptor Squadron

Abercrombie A.R.	November 16, 1950 As FAC
Anderson, Berger A. Captain	October 21, 1950
Baxter, Thurston R. Lt.	December 21, 1951
Carlson, Raymond J. Captain	July 4, 1951
Clay, James E. 1st Lt.	February 5, 1952
Coleman, John J. Captain	June 20, 1951
Davis, Murrit H. Major	August 14, 1951
Dean, Zack W. Captain	April 20, 1951
Frankart, Ned C. 1st Lt.	November 3, 1951
Golden, Newman C. 1st Lt.	October 17, 1951, remains MIA
Grossman, John F. Captain	August 14, 1951
Harper, Lee A. Lt.	June 19, 1951
Heilands, Richard 1st Lt.	August 18, 1951
Hoke, John D.	August 31, 1951
Horn, John L. Captain	August 14, 1951
Jackson, William E. Lt.	September 13, 1951
Lafferty, Thomas C. 1st Lt.	January 31, 1952
Longshire, Lamar B.	October 19, 1950
Lukakis, George M. 1st Lt.	November 6, 1950
Lynd, Donald Lt.	November 20, 1951
Mathis, James I. 1st Lt.	August 10, 1950
Monroe, Sheldon, W. Major	April 17, 1951
Olcutt, Richard L.	October 6, 1951
Olson, Ralph M. Captain	December 19, 1950
Pitchford, Donald E. 1st Lt.	September 28, 1950
Pittman, Walter E. Captain	July 5, 1951
Ramsey, Robert D. Captain	December 10, 1951
Rushing, Harry E. Lt.	March 3, 1952
Smith, Robert L. 1st Lt.	December 14, 1951
Thompson, Jack F. Captain	June 11, 1951

40th Fighter Interceptor Squadron

Aubrey, Carl L. Major	March 12, 1951
Briscoe, W. R., Jr.	December 6, 1950
Brown, Meade M.	December 25, 1950
Burton, Woodrow 1st lt.	October 31, 1950 remains MIA
Haythorne, Justice Captain	February 11, 1951
Hook, William, E. Captain	January 5, 1951
Johnson, Neil Major	December 12, 1950
Johnson, Olin W. 1st Lt.	December 1, 1950
Lee, William J. 1st lt.	September 7, 1950
Matusz, William T. Captain	January 19, 1951
Murray, Paul 1st Lt.	July 15, 1952 in Japan
Nolan, Marlin T.	December 6, 1950
Payne, Hildreth 1st Lt.	July 6, 1952 in Japan
Reynolds, Gerald lt.	April ?, 1952 in Japan
Schlitz, Glenn D. Captain	October 6, 1950
Williams, Edward J. Captain	March 3, 1951
Wormack, Thelbert B.	March 31, 1954, remains MIA

45th Tactical Reconnaissance Squadron

Brown, Charles D. Captain	December 17, 1951
Dolan, James M. Lt.	March 19, 1951
Douglas, Jackie R. Lt.	July 17, 1951 remains MIA
Foglesong, Roma 1st Lt.	April 14, 1951

Madseon, D. Grant Lt.	October 30, 1951
McCollom, Francis N. Captain	April 10, 1951
Mauldin, William K. Captain	February 21, 1952
Polifka, Karl L. Colonel	July 1, 1951
Ruiz, Eugene L. Lt.	July 2, 1951
Salazar, Frank R. Lt.	December 31, 1952
Thatcher, Willis W. Lt.	June 6, 1951

77 Squadron, RAAF

Ellis, D.C. Sgt.	December 22, 1950
Harrop, W.P. Sgt.	September 3, 1950
Mathews, K.G. Flight Lt.	February 14, 1951
Robson, R. Sgt.	April 14, 1951
Royle, K.E. Sgt.	February 26, 1951
Spence, L.T. Wing Commander	September 9, 1950
Stephens, G.I. Sgt.	January 6, 1951
Strange, H.T. Sgt.	March 19, 1951
Strout, G. Squadron Leader	July 7, 1950
Squires, S.S. Warrant Officer	February 14, 1951

6002nd Fighter Wing

Thomas, Norbourn A.	December 3, 1950

6146th Air Base Unit (ROKAF)

Crowell, Dean L. Captain	October 1, 1950

The following pilots are listed in official records as flying the F-51 when they were killed during the Korean conflict, but they cannot be confirmed as actually doing so. It should be noted that several of the listed squadrons never flew the Mustang at all, while other listed units were never committed to the conflict.

Bach, Lawrence 335th FIS	December 22, 1950
Bass, Henry R. 154th FBG	December 15, 1950
Bush, William D. 335th FIS	December 26, 1951
Carey, Desmond 334th FIS	December 31, 1953
Dees, Robert F. 430th ?	December 31, 1953
Eason, Theon C. 25th FBS	October 19, 1950
Grisham, David H. 20th Weather Squadron	December 31, 1953
Jackman, W. E. 30th FIS	December 13, 1951
Johnson, William 750th ?	May 9, 1952
Johnson, Cameron ?	March 15, 1954
Leman, Jacob C. 162nd FBS	December 5, 1951
Losoyda, John 16th FIS	January 1, 1952
Nicaise, Leo J. 80th FBS	January 8, 1952
Pentecost, John, Jr. 428th FBS	January 13, 1953
Peuter, James V. ?	March 2, 1953
Ramsey, Robert J. 130th Bomb Sq.	December 31, 1953
Sluder, Amos L. 80th FBS	December 3, 1950
Wilkens, Bertram 80th FBS	December 29, 1950

Appendix 2:
Australian Mustangs
in the Korean Conflict

The 77 Squadron Mustangs were either those of Commonwealth Aircraft Corporation construction in Australia, being license-built from North American Aviation and were equivalent to the F-51D-20 or -25, or of US construction, as supplied under the WWII Lend-Lease programs.

After a period of time after replacement by the Meteor several of the Australian F-51s were obtained by the US Aeronautics Corporation, USAC, refurbished and sold to either foreign governments or on the US civilian market where they received "N" numbers and disappeared!

serial #	type	taken on strength by 77 Sq. or first flown	loss/disposal date	pilot, etc.
A68-121	CA-18	3-30-51	11-27-56	scrapped
A68-123	"	4-2-51	5-27-57	Crashed Mallal
A68-125	"	4-4-51	4-17-51	Crashed Japan: Robson
A68-130	XXIII	4-4-51	11-27-56	scrapped
A68-701	CA-21	12-10-50		
A68-702	"			used as target
A68-704	"	11-16-50	2-26-51	Crashed Kimpo Penisula: Royal
A68-705	"	9-9-50		Coburn bailed out
A68-706	"	2-15-51	2-23-53	to USAC
A68-707	"	4-1-52		used as target
A68-708	"	11-19-50	2-15-51	Crashed: Howe
A68-709	"	11-19-50	2-23-53	to USAC
A68-715	"	11-19-50	3-20-51	Crashed: Sly
A68-716	"	3-10-51	2-23-52	to USAC
A68-720	"	11-19-50	11-8-53	scrapped
A68-723	"	11-19-50	11-26-52	to ROKAF
A68-725	"	1-11-51	2-23-53	to USAC
A68-726	"	11-19-50	12-22-50	Crashed: Ellis
A68-729	"	11-19-50	11-8-53	scrapped
A68-732	"	3-13-51	2-23-53	to USAC
A68-733	"	3-12-51	4-1-52	used as target
A68-734	"	3-15-51	2-23-53	to USAC
A68-735	"	11-19-50		
A68-736	"	11-19-50	2-23-53	to USAC
A68-737	"	11-19-50	3-13-51	Crashed: Meggs
A68-738	"	3-19-51		
A68-739	"	11-19-50	2-23-53	to USAC
A68-741	"	3-27-51	2-23-53	to USAC
A68-750	"	4-1-52		used as target
A68-753	"	9-3-50		Crashed: Harrop
A68-754	"	11-19-50	1-11-51	Ditched Pusan: Brackenreg
A68-755	"	11-19-50	1-23-51	writeoff result of F4U crash
A68-756	"	11-19-50	2-23-53	to USAC
A68-757	"	7-7-50		Crashed: Strout
A68-759	"	12-26-50		
A68-760	"	11-19-50	8-11-53	scrapped
A68-761	"	12-3-50		

A68-763	"	11-19-50	2-23-52	to USAC
A68-765	"	11-19-50	1-6-51	Crashed: Stephens
A68-766	"	11-19-50		
A68-769	"	11-19-50	1-4-52	used as target
A68-772	"	1-19-51		Crashed: Harvey
A68-774	"	7-3-50		Crashed Iwakuni
A68-775	"	8-9-50		Crashed Korea
A68-776	"	11-19-50		
A68-779	"	1-4-52		used as target
A68-780	"	2-7-51	2-23-53	to USAC
A68-782	"	11-19-50	3-19-51	Crashed: Strange
A68-783	"	4-5-51		
A68-791	"	11-19-50	1-4-51	Crashed: Bessell
A68-792	"	1-1-51	2-23-53	to USAC
A68-793	"	1-4-51		used as target
A68-794	"	1-31-51		
A68-796	"	11-19-50	2-14-51	Crashed: Squires
A68-799	"	11-19-50	11-8-53	scrapped
A68-801	"	11-19-50	2-23-53	to USAC
A68-803	"	11-19-50	4-13-51	Crashed Iwakuni
A68-804	"	11-19-50	2-23-53	to USAC
A68-806	"	2-7-51	11-26-52	to ROKAF
A68-807	"	4-1-52		used as target
A68-808	"	2-7-51	11-8-53	scrapped
A68-809	"	9-9-50		Crashed: Spence
A68-810	"	2-20-51	2-23-53	to USAC
A68-812	"	12-12-50	2-14-51	Crashed: Mathews
A68-813	"	11-19-50	2-23-53	to USAC

Appendix 3:
USAF Mustangs
in the Korean Conflict

The loss codes for a particular aircraft are carried as a suffix to the aircraft's serial number if the aircraft is known to be written-off during the actual period of the Korean Conflict. The number of flying hours shown on the aircraft are either the those airframe hours on it when it was lost or when it was transferred to a foreign air force. For those Mustangs supplied to the ROKAF, the transfer date is shown. For those assigned to 2 Squadron, SAAF, the transfer date is not given, but the loss date is shown, (If it was, indeed lost). The location given is where the possessing unit was stationed at the time the aircraft was lost, and is not necessarily the actual location of the loss, itself. The name shown in parenthesis is that of the pilot flying the aircraft when it was lost, but this is only given if it could be confirmed through a primary source. Due to multiple losses on any given day by particular units and poor USAF record keeping, an extended aircraft serial number match-up with pilots losses has proven to be impossible. The aircraft's previous unit is given, if possibly pertinent, for us "serial number freaks" benefit.

A = Flying Accident
E = Salvaged, fair wear & tear: Stress or strain
G = Deterioration
J = Cannibalized
L = Transfered to a foreign government
M = Enemy Action on a combat mission
N = Flying accident on a combat mission
P = Cause unknown on a combat mission
R = Deterioration
Q = Enemy action not on a combat mission
TT = Total airframe hours

44-11913	45th TRS. "Tullie, Scotty & ?"
44-12065E	35th FIW. Salvaged 5-8-51. 1599 TT.
44-12237P	45th TRS. 12-31-52 (Salazar).
44-12534M	45th TRS 12-27-52 (Lull). "Belle Julie."
44-12851M	45th TRS. 2-21-52 (Mauldin).
44-12943A	12th FBS. 11-53. 1540 TT. "Was That Too Fast/Red Raider."
44-13035L	6408th M&S, Kisarazu 2-16-53. Destination listed as secret.
44-13220M	45th TRS. 6-28-51 Taegu. (Crowell). 374 TT.
44-13253M	18th FBG. Crash landed friendly territory ? date.
44-13256M	18th FBG. 10-22-51Chinhae.
44-13465M	18th FBG, 39th FIS. 10-28-51 Chinhae.
44-12594M	18th FBG, 39th FIS. 11-3-51 Chinhae (Frankart).
44-13851A	2 sq. as # 374. 1-17-52 (Staats).
44-13856M	18th FBG. 6-18-51. 474 TT.
44-14233	45th TRS. Returned to US, 105th TRS.
44-14268M	18th FBG, 39th FIS. 2-6-52 Chinhae "NoHeroHere."
44-14289M	45th TRS. 2-7-52 Kimpo (Price).
44-14297M	2 Sq. as # 356. 11-28-51 Chinhae (White head).
44-14445M	18th FBG. 8-25-51 Chinhae.
44-14449M	2 Sq. as # 350. 1-1-52 (Rautenbach).
44-14476M	18th FBG, 67th FBS. 2-22-52 Chinhae.
44-14484N	18th FBG 11-7-51 Chinhae.
44-14547P	45th TRS. 6-14-52 Kimpo. "Symons Lemon." ex-9th Air Force WWII.
44-14703M	45th TRS. 3-2-52 Kimpo (Thornsell).

44-14930M	2 Sq. as # 332. 6-1-51. 517 TT. (McDonald). ex-"P83Y, 'Miss Denver."
44-15047L	ROKAF. Assigned 5-3-51, 239 TT. ex-109th FS.
44-15053	18th FBG, 67th FBS.
44-15091M	2 sq. as # 323. 8-12-51 572 TT. (Muller). Previously w/18th FBG.
44-15236M	18th FBG 4-30-51 Chinhae. 596 TT.
44-15727M	18th FBG, 39th FIS. 3-3-52 Chinhae. ex-15th AF WWII.
44-63400L	2 Sq. as # 309. 5-11-51 (Kruger). 493 TT.
44-63515L	2 sq. as # 346. 11-29-51. (Rensburg).
44-63581L	ROKAF as # 21. 3-26-53 from 40th FIS.
44-63589L	ROKAF. 4-11-53 from 40th FIS. Salvaged 7-57.
44-63650L	ROKAF. 11-15-50 from 6146th ABG, 601 TT. ex-110th FS "Virginia Mayo"
44-63800L	ROKAF. 11-15-50 431 TT. ex-110th FS.
44-63822L	2 Sq. as # 374. Crashed on landing 8-16-51.
44-63824L	ROKAF. 5-51, 345 TT.
44-63846A	ROKAF. 5-51 088 TT. W/O 2-7-52. ex-9th AF WWII.
44-63853L	2 Sq. as # 363. 11-4-51 (Pappas).
44-63870M	18th FBG. 3-31-52.
44-63886M	18th FBG. 9-13-51.
44-64004M	18th FBG. 10-6-51 (Olcutt).
44-64079	40th FIS. Salvaged 10-17-50. "Jo Ellen V."
44-64101L	2 Sq. as # 351. 9-12-51 (Montanari).
44-64134M	51st FBS(P). 8-12-50 314 TT.
44-72043M	18th FBG. 12-13-51.
44-72055M	18th FBG. 3-1-52.

44-72085M	51st FBS (P). 8-12-50 Taegu. 1313 TT.
44-72087L	ROKAF. 4-51. 489 TT.
44-72091P	18th FBG. 3-15-51. 701 TT.
44-72134L	2 sq. as # 331. 7-23-52 (Halley). 547 TT.
44-72162N	40th FIS. 12-7-50,627 TT. Loss charged to 18th FBG.
44-72249M	18th FBG. 2-5-52.
44-72271L	2 sq. as # 349. 8-14-51 (deJongh).
44-72278E	18th FBG. 3-10-53. "Shoot You'r Faded."
44-72373L	ROKAF. 10-13-52. ex-335th FG, 357th FS, OS-H, WWII.
44-72427M	18th FBG, 39th FIS. 12-21-51.
44-72428L	ROKAF. 3-1-52. ex-18th FBG.
44-72531M	18th FBG, 39th FIS. 12-21-51.
44-72533M	18th FBG. 6-13-52.
44-72559M	51st FBS (P). 8-24-50 Taegu.
44-72620M	35th FIG. 7-30-50, Yongil. 934 TT. ex-462nd FS "Shawnee Princess."
44-72656N	2 Sq. as # 360. 10-14-52 (Maxwell). ex-35th FBS "Rosalle."
44-72691M	35th FIG. 8-24-50. 426 TT.
44-72726P	18th FBG. 3-9-51. 838 TT.
44-72733L	ROKAF. 9-18-52. ex-163rd FS.
44-72734M	18th FBG. 8-14-51.
44-72743M	35th FIG. 12-6-50 Pusan. 503 TT. ex-172nd FS.
44-72750L	ROKAF. 6-19-53. Salvaged 7-57. ex-18th FBW, ex-194th FS.
44-72792M	18th FBG. 10-8-50. 578 TT.
44-72800L	ROKAF. 2-5-53. ex-18th FBG, ex-35th FIG.
44-72806M	2 Sq. as # 391. 7-9-52 (Scott). ex-176th FS.
44-72847P	? unit. Lost 4-51. 1121 TT.
44-72895L	ROKAF. 1-6-53. Salvaged 7-57. ex-18th FBG, ex-176th FS.
44-72914M	18th FBG. 4-5-52. ex-170th FS.
44-72915M	8th FBG. 9-17-50 Tsuiki. 370 TT. ex-176th FS.
44-72916L	ROKAF. 5-15-53. ex-152nd & 175th FS's.
44-72917L	ROKAF. Returned to USAF & given to Philippine Air Force. ex-170th FS.
44-72930L	ROKAF. 1-30-53. Returned to USAF & given to Philippine Air Force.
44-72960M	18th FBG, 67th FBS. 12-5-50 K-24. 700 TT. ex-109th FS.
44-72969M	8th FBG. 9-19-50 Tsuiki. 174 TT. ex-176th FS.
44-72983L	2 Sq. as # 336. 7-26-51. (Howe). 516 TT.
44-73000L	ROKAF. 4-27-53. Still in inventory 1957. ex-18th FBG.
44-73006M	35th FIG. 10-8-50. ex-165th FS.
44-73022L	ROKAF. 4-6-53. Salvaged 7-57. ex-35th FIG.
44-73038M	18th FBG. 1-6-51.
44-73049L	2 Sq. as # 337. 6-22-51 (Frisby). 526 TT.
44-73050	18th FBG. 5-7-51 K-16. 1013 TT.
44-73055A	ROKAF. 9-11-53. Assigned 10-6-52. ex-18th FBG, 35th FIG, 8th FBG.
44-73058N	18th FBG. 12-16-50. 661 TT. ex-110th FS.
44-73064L	ROKAF. 5-16-53. Salvaged 7-57. ex-18th FBG, 67th FBS.
44-73065L	ROKAF. Returned USAF 12-52. ex-357th FS, OS-R. Lt. Col. Elder's w/20 Kills. "Bonnie."
44-73068L	2 Sq. as # 329. 8-29-51 (Green). 477 TT.
44-73073L	2 Sq. as # 370. 2-20-52 (Newton). ex-18th FBG, 12th FBS "Liz Plus 3."
44-73084L	2 Sq. as # 324. 12-3-51 (Whitehead). ex-8th FBG, ex-176th FS.
44-73092A	ROKAF. 9-9-53. "A" 10-16-54. ex-2 Sq. as # 378, assigned 4-30-52 & returned to USAF 12-28-52.
44-73096M	ROKAF. Lost 6-13-53. ex-110th FS.
44-73100M	8th FBG. 11-22-50. (Kinson) 570 TT. ex-4th FG WWII WD-B w/3 kills. ex-110th FS.
44-73104A	ROKAF. Write-off 11-13-53. ex-18th FBG, ex-124thFS.
44-73116M	18th FBG. 5-25-51. 1040 TT.
44-73122P	8th FBG, 36th FBS. 12-9-50 (Williams). 590 TT. ex-124th FS.
44-73139P	35th FIG, 39th FIS. 10-25-50. 632 TT. ex-192nd FS.
44-73154L	ROKAF. 10-25-53. ex-18th FBG, 12th FBS. ex-4th FG WWII, ex-165th FS.
44-73155A	ROKAF. "A" 5-17-53. ex-358th FS WWII "Ole III," ex-4th FG, 336th FS, ex-165th FS.
44-73157M	35th FIG. 3-30-51. 696 TT. ex-165th FS.
44-73166L	ROKAF. 11-9-53. ex-18th FBG, ex-163rd FS.
44-73180M	18th FBG, 39th FIS. 11-9-51.
44-73181M	18th FBG. 9-30-50. 478 TT. ex-35th FIG, ex-109th FS.
44-73183L	ROKAF. 3-14-53. Salvaged 7-57. ex-109th FS.
44-73185M	18th FBG, 67th FBS. 9-4-50. 462 TT. ex-176th FS.
44-73191M	2 sq. as # 310. 10-2-51 (Muller). 463 TT.
44-73194L	ROKAF. 8-9-52. Salvaged 7-57. ex-175th FS.
44-73205L	ROKAF. 8-50. 533 TT. ex-110th FS.
44-73208L	ROKAF. 4-6-63. Returned USAF, To Philippine Air Force.
44-73213M	35th FIG, 39th FIS. 9-4-50 Tsuiki. ex-124th FS.
44-73226	18th FBG.
44-73227A	2 Sq. as # 388. Crashed & repared. "Anne." To ROKAF 6-7-64. "A" 1-22-55. ex-111th FS.
44-73242A	18th FBG. 9-7-51 Chinhae.
44-73253L	ROKAF. 6-17-52. ex-123rd FS.
44-73255P	35th FIG. 10-15-50. 453 TT. ex-176th FS.
44-73258N	35th FIG, 40th FIS. 3-13-51. "Old Rattler." 1071 TT.
44-73263L	ROKAF. 11-7-52. ex-152nd FS.
44-73270L	ROKAF. 3-15-54. Salvaged 7-57. ex-18th FBG, 67th FBS, ex-123rd FS.
44-73273M	51st FBS(P) (sic). 1-10-51 Kimpo. 422 TT. ex-35th FBS.
44-73280N	35th FIG, 39th FIS. 10-29-50 (Pitchford, shot down by Yak). 652 TT. ex-163rd FS.
44-73282L	ROKAF. 3-14-53. Salvaged 7-57. ex-176th FS.
44-73284M	18th FBG, 67th FBS. 8-15-50, Ashiya. 499 TT. ex-165th FS.

44-73286L	ROKAF. 4-13-53. "A" 12-17-53. 862 TT. ex-175th FS.
44-73289M	18th FBG. 12-8-51. ex-110th FS.
44-73291A	ROKAF. 6-9-53. "A" 1-22-55. 459 TT. ex-18th FBG.
44-73313P	8th FBG, 36th FBS. 8-8-50 Itazuke (Richman). 276 T. ex-172nd FS.
44-73327P	18th FBG. 11-9-50 K-9. 772 TT.
44-73329L	ROKAF. 8-9-50. 509 TT.
44-73333L	ROKAF. 8-9-50. Lost 4-4-53. ex-176th FS.
44-73335L	ROKAF. 4-27-53. Returned USAF, to Philippine Air Force. ex-35th FIG, 40th FIS.
44-73338M	2 Sq. as # 317. 3-2-51 (Badenhorst). 437 TT.
44-73356L	ROKAF. 3-27-53. Salvaged 7-57.
44-73360L	ROKAF. 5-13-53. Salvaged 7-57. ex-35th FIG, 40th FIS, ex-156th FS.
44-73363N	18th FBG. 9-19-50 K-9. 778 TT.
44-73372L	ROKAF. Salvaged 1-54. 2116 TT. ex-18th FBG.
44-73396M	35th FIG. 11-8-50 Yongil. 1000 TT.
44-73399M	35th FIG. 7-30-50 Yongil. 814 TT.
44-73409L	2 Sq. as # 389. To ROKAF 6-9-53. Returned USAF, to Philippine Air Force.
44-73453N	45th TRS. 3-19-51 (Nolan). 609 TT.
44-73459A	ROKAF. 2-15-54. "A" 4-22-54. ex-18th FBG, 12th FBS "Kay Baby" & "Gika II."
44-73468P	35th FIG. 10-15-50. 400 TT.
44-73471N	35th FIG. 11-13-50. 659 TT. ex-109th FS.
44-73475M	45th TRS. 12-10-51. Cause layed to 39th FIS.
44-73494A	ROKAF. 7-1-52. "A" 7-16-52. ex-109th FS.
44-73504M	35th FIG. 10-8-50 Tsuiki. 1311 TT.
44-73514L	ROKAF. 5-14-53. Returned USAF, to Philippine Air Force. ex-35th FIG, 40th FIS, ex-172nd FS.
44-73526A	ROKAF. 8-26-52. "A" 7-28-52. ex-170th FS.
44-73531N	18th FBG. 2-7-51. 923 TT.
44-73532A	ROKAF. 8-8-52. "A" 3-17-53. ex-165th FS.
44-73533N	18th FBG. 10-20-52 Chinhae.
44-73544L	ROKAF. 5-31-52. Returned USAF, to Philippine Air Force. ex-155th FS. (Note: This s/n is erroneously shown for # 9544 with the RCAF).
44-73546M	51st FBS(P). 8-2-50 Taegu. 761 TT.
44-73547M	8th FBG. 8-12-50 Itazuke. 481 TT.
44-73549M	35th FIG. 8-17-50 Yongil. 281 TT.
44-73555L	ROKAF. 4-27-53. Returned USAF, to Philippine Air Force. ex-157th FS.
44-73556M	35th FIG, 39th FIS. 8-17-50 Yongil. 281 TT.
44-73560M	35th FIG, 39th FIS. 8-17-50. Tsuiki. 344 TT.
44-73564L	ROKAF. 1-6-53. ex-18th FBG, 12th FBS "Ruth's Ruthless Russ." ex-176th FS.
44-73570N	35th FIG. 11-8-50. 344 TT. ex-167th FS.
44-73571A	ROKAF. Crashed 2-21-52. ex-152nd FS.
44-73580L	ROKAF. 8-50. 1034 TT.
44-73581L	ROKAF. 4-6-53. ex-167th FS.
44-73582L	2 Sq. as # 386. Returned to USAF 12-28-52, to ROKAF 1-2-53. ex-175th FS.
44-73593M	18th FBG. 4-5-51. 607 TT.
44-73608M	51st FBS (P). 7-31-50. 973 TT.
44-73638M	18th FBG. 1-6-52. Supposedly scrapped 11-25-49.
44-73648M	18th FBG. 4-10-52.
44-73650M	18th FBG, 67th FBS 12-13-50 (Blesse). K-24. 684 TT.
44-73654N	18th FBG. 2-51. 755 TT. ex-172nd FS.
44-73679A	ROKAF. 3-28-53. "A" 7-18-53
44-73684M	18th FBG, 67th FBS. 2-15-51. 847 TT. ex-167th FS.
44-73688M	2 Sq. as # 339. Crashed 7-24-51 (Synman).
44-73713A	ROKAF. Lost 1-25-53. ex-163rd FS.
44-73728M	35th FIG, 39th FIS. 8-7-50 Yongil. 859 TT.
44-73737A	18th FBG. 8-30-50 Ashiya. ex-165th FS.
44-73740?	18th FBG. 5-13-51. 905 TT.
44-73754L	ROKAF. 8-9-50. 912 TT.
44-73805M	51st FBS (P). 8-12-50. 487 TT. ("M" 35th FIG Itazuke?)
44-73808L	ROKAF. 8-7-50. 639 TT.
44-73812M	35th FIG. 8-17-50 Yongil. 567 TT.
44-73816M	51st FBS (P). 8-12-50 Taegu. 371 TT.
44-73818L	ROKAF. 8-9-50. 999 TT.
44-73829M	51st FBS (P). 8-12-50. 837 TT. Repossessed ROKAF.
44-73842?	45th TRS. 7-2-51. (Ruiz).
44-73846L	ROKAF. 8-9-50. 799 TT.
44-73847A	18th FBG. 6-9-51. 453 TT.
44-73850L	ROKAF. 5-51. 313 TT.
44-73860A	45th TRS. 8-2-52. ex-18th FBG. "Betty."
44-73861P	35th FIG, 39th FBS. 11-9-51.
44-73863M	18th FBG. 9-5-51.
44-73865M	18th FBG. 4-23-51 (Allen). 472 TT.
44-73867M	? unit. 5-5-51. 473 TT.
44-73868?	18th FBG. Crash landing 7-5-51.
44-73870L	ROKAF. 7-23-53. ex-35th FIG. -Pilot defected to China. On display Peking.
44-73873M	18th FBG. 8-31-51 (Hoke).
44-73875M	18th FBG. 4-27-52. "Marilinn." ex-35th FIG & 45th TRS.
44-73879M	51st FBS (P). 8-2-50. 967 TT. Repossessed ROKAF.
44-73888M	18th FBG. 4-27-52. ex-8th FBG & 35th FIG, 39th FIS.
44-73892M	2 Sq. as # 330. 5-15-51 (Rorke).
44-73897L	ROKAF. 6-17-53. 651 TT. Returned USAF & scrapped 3-54. ex-18th FBG.
44-73898A	18th FBG, 39th FIS. 3-21-52.
44-73901L	ROKAF. 1-27-52. ex-18th FBG, ex-156th FS.
44-73903M	2 Sq. as # 362. 2-29-52 (Lellyet).
44-73911M	? unit. Lost 4-51. 590 TT.
44-73912L	ROKAF. 1-27-53. ex-45th TRS, ex-18th FBG, 67th FBS.
44-73935N	35th FIG. 9-24-50 Tsuiki. 673 TT.
44-73936L	ROKAF. 3-27-53. ex-111th FS.
44-73960N	2 Sq. as # 383. 12-25-52 (Moir). Shot down by USMC AD.
44-73962L	ROKAF. 1-11-53. ex-45th TRS, ex-18th FBG, 67th FBS "Angel Face."/"The Ridge Runner."
44-73981M	18th FBG. 7-9-51.
44-73983M	18th FBG. 4-2-51. 558 TT.

44-73984M	35th FIG. 3-12-51 K-9. 526 TT. ex-191st FS.	44-74322L	ROKAF. 5-13-54. ex-45th TRS "Shorted II."
44-73985A	ROKAF. Lost 10-14-52.	44-74343?	18th FBG. Crashed 12-3-51.
44-73991N	18th FBG. 7-8-51.	44-74344L	2 Sq. as # 326. w/753 TT. Returned USAF.
44-73992M	18th FBG. 8-14-51.		To ROKAF 1-18-53. ex-8th FBG, ex-18th
44-73994M	18th FBG. 3-8-51 (Schroder). 561 TT.		FBG.
44-73995M	18th FBG. 5-7-51. 419 TT.	44-74363M	18th FBG. 9-7-52.
44-73998L	ROKAF. 5-51. 447 TT.	44-74364A	ROKAF. Assigned 6-30-52, loss date ?. ex-
44-73999M	18th FBG. 1-31-52.		176th FS.
44-74014A	18th FBG. 9-17-51.	44-74366M	35th FIG, 40th FIS. 2-22-51 K-9 (Haythorne).
44-74016N	35th FIG. 2-20-51. 1024 TT.		932 TT.
44-74017L	ROKAF. 1-3-51. 383 TT.	44-74367N	35th FIG. 11-19-51. (Matusz). 749 TT.
44-74019L	ROKAF. 1-3-51. 403 TT.	44-74378M	18th FBG. 4-20-51 (Corn).
44-74021L	2 Sq. as # 373. 3-6-52 (Spry).	44-74379N	35th FIG. 1-20-51 K-9. 957 TT.
44-74029M	18th FBG. 4-30-51. 484 TT.	44-74383L	ROKAF. 2-10-52. Returned USAF, to Philip-
44-74030L	ROKAF. 4-6-53. ex-35th FIW, 40th FIS "Helen		pine Air Force. ex-170th FS.
	San."	44-74384M	18th FBG, 12th FBS. 3-4-52.
44-74032M	18th FBG. 3-30-51. 487 TT.	44-74385N	18th FBG. 8-30-51.
44-74034L	ROKAF. 1-8-51. 410 TT.	44-74392A	18th FBG. 7-3-51.
44-74035M	18th FBG. 8-14-51.	44-74394M	18th FBG, 67th FBS. 8-5-50 (Sebille, MOH).
44-74037M	18th FBG. 1-1-52.		ex-170th FS.
44-74046L	ROKAF. 9-10-53. ex-2 Sq. as # 379. "Jean."	44-74398M	8th FBG. 8-22-50 (Gilliam). 422 TT.
	ex-18th FBG "Spite."	44-74399P	35th FIG, 39th FIS. 8-17-50 Yongil. 664 TT.
44-74052M	18th FBG, 12th FBS. 1-12-53 Itazuke (Rock).	44-74401M	18th FBG, 67th FBS. 4-14-51 (Haskett). 585
	(Collision w/-74840). ex-45th TRS.		TT.
44-74072M	35th FIG. 10-2-50. 959 TT.	44-74408A	18th FBG. 7-18-51 (Murray).
44-74107P	18th FBG. 10-9-50. ex-35th FIG.	44-74412?	18th FBG, 12th FBS. 2-19-52. "Buchie."
44-74133N	18th FBG. 6-30-51. (O'Bryant) 785 TT.	44-74416N	18th FBG. 5-29-51. 577 TT.
44-74137N	? unit. Crashed on takeoff 7-9-51.	44-74428N	35th FIG, 39th FIS. 9-30-50. 1198 TT.
44-74138	8th FBG, 36th FBS. "My Baby II."	44-74432M	2 sq. as # 312. 7-22-51 (Staats). 604 TT.
44-74154M	18th FBG, 67th FBS. 4-19-51	44-74438N	35th FIG. 10-15-50 Yongil. ex-156th FS.
	(Pasqualicchio). 616 TT.		(Supposed s/n for RCAF 9589).
44-74158L	ROKAF. 5-4-53. ex-18th FBG.	44-74440A	8th FBG, 35th FBS. Salvaged 11-2-50. 1072
44-74165M	2 Sq. as # 380. 8-22-52 (Kotzenberg). ex-		TT. ex-197th FS.
	18th FBG.	44-74442N	18th FBG. 8-2-51.
44-74168P	2 Sq. as # 311. 12-5-50 (Davis). 757 TT. ex-	44-74460M	18th FBG, 12 FBS. 4-5-51 (Wilkerson). 654
	18th FBG, ex-126th FS.		TT.
44-74171L	ROKAF. 11-2-51. ex-18th FBG.	44-74461M	2 sq. as # 338. 7-23-51 (duPlooy). 432 TT.
44-74174M	2 Sq. as # 327. 11-13-51 (Collins). 377 TT.	44-74462A	18th FBG. 10-27-51.
44-74176M	18th FBG. 8-7-51.	44-74476P	8th FBG. 8-24-50 Tsuiki (Mullet). 627 TT. ex-
44-74177M	18th FBG. 6-2-51. 769 TT.		113th FS.
44-74189L	ROKAF. ex-2 Sq. # 394.	44-74479M	35th FIG. 3-17-51 K-9. 401 TT.
44-74192M	18th FBG. 9-9-51.	44-74484M	18th FBG. 4-26-51. 845 TT. ex-8th FBG, 36th
44-74205L	ROKAF. 1-14-52. Considered a write-off 12-		FBS "Deacon Butler II."
	18-50 w/35th FIG, 39th FIS (Shipley), but	44-74488N	18th FBG. 7-7-51 (Arnold).
	rebuilt 1-51.	44-74489M	2 Sq. as # 313. 4-30-51 (Gillers). 550 TT. ex-
44-74213L	ROKAF. 5-28-54. ex-35th FIG, 40th FIS.		156th FS.
44-74223?	18th FBG, 39th FIS. 8-16-52. "Dreamboat,"	44-74495A	18th FBG. 7-11-51.
	"Tulie Scottie & ?"	44-74503M	2 Sq. as # 333. 6-9-51 (Leinbenberg).
44-74228	35th FIG, 40th FIS. "Skippy."	44-74507M	18th FBG, 12th FBS. 4-26-52 Chinhae.
44-74235?	? unit. Salvaged 8-50. 642 TT.	44-74509N	18th FBG. 4-30-51. 530 TT.
44-74243?	18th FBG, 12th FBS. Salvaged 10-17-50.	44-74510P	18th FBG. 7-1-51.
44-74267N	35th FIG. 2-20-51. 1226 TT.	44-74511M	2 sq. as # 335. 7-23-51 (Bekker). 377 TT.
44-74276L	ROKAF. 8-9-50. ex-51st FBS (P).	44-74512M	35th FIG. 3-11-51. 456 TT.
44-74280N	35th FIG, 40th FIS. 10-14-50 Yongil. 925 TT.	44-74513M	18th FBG. 8-25-51.
44-74281P	35th FIG. 7-12-50 Yokota. 881 TT.	44-74515M	18th FBG. 1-8-52. "Bookle."
44-74297M	? unit. 4-51. 994 TT.	44-74516N	18th FBG, 39th FIS. 11-22-51.
44-74304J	35th FIG. 7-31-50 Yongil.	44-74518M	18th FBG, 67th FBS. 3-1-52. ex-176th FS.
44-74307	18th FBG. Major damage 11-8-51. Supposed	44-74520L	ROKAF. 4-30-51. Returned USAF, to Philip-
	write-off. Salvaged 2-27-50?		pine Air Force.

44-74521M	18th FBG, 67th FBS. 9-27-50. 927 TT. ex-169th FS.
44-74525P	45th TRS. 7-17-51 (Douglas).
44-74534M	18th FBG. 8-14-51.
44-74539M	18th FBG. 5-27-51. 375 TT.
44-74540	18th FBG. Returned to Kisarazu. ex-175th FS.
44-74550M	35th FIG, 39th FIS. 10-9-50 Ashiya. 943 TT. ex-170th FS.
44-74553N	18th FBG. 11-11-50. 1053 TT. ex-188th FS.
44-74565M	2 Sq. as # 352. 9-9-51 (Barlow).
44-74577M	2 Sq. as # 392. 10-12-52 (Fryer). ex-123rd FS.
44-74579A	FEAMCOM. "A" 8-5-50. 752 TT. ex-169th FS.
44-74587L	ROKAF. 6-10-52. ex-176th FS.
44-74588M	8th FBG. 8-16-50 Tsuiki. 633 TT. ex-186th FS.
44-74592N	18th FBG. 10-8-51.
44-74595M	18th FBG. 6-11-51. 420 TT.
44-74597M	18th FBG. 8-14-51.
44-74604M	18th FBG. 6-11-51. 281 TT.
44-74605A	35th FIG, 40th FIS. 7-15-52 (Murry).
44-74607?	18th FBG. 9-5-51
44-74608P	45th TRS.3-26-51 (Preston). 279 TT.
44-74609A	ROKAF. 3-3-51. "A" date ? 325 TT. ex-134th FS.
44-74611?	18th FBG. 7-1-51
44-74612M	18th FBG. 4-23-52. ex-45th TRS.
44-74614M	18th FBG. 6-1-51. 380 TT.
44-74615M	45th TRS.4-17-51 (Brown). 265 TT.
44-74617M	2 Sq. as # 371. 1-15-52 (Montgomery). ex-18th FBG, 12th FBS.
44-74618M	18th FBG. 6-9-51 prior to acceptance by 2 Sq. No SAAF #. 009 TT.
44-74619?	2 Sq. as #376. 1-14-51 (Vmzyl). ex-35th FIG, 39th FIS.
44-74621M	35th FIG. 10-15-50 Yongil. 808 TT. ex-170th FS.
44-74622?	18th FBG. 5-17-51. 159 TT.
44-74623	45th TRS.
44-74625A	ROKAF. 2-13-53. "A" 2-24-54. ex-18th FBG, 67th FBS "Rotation Blues."
44-74626L	ROKAF. 4-28-52. 928 TT.
44-74627L	ROKAF. 4-20-53. Returned USAF, to Philippine Air Force. ex-35th FIG.
44-74630L	ROKAF. 5-4-53. ex-45th TRS "Laura," "Gene." ex-18th FBG.
44-74631?	? unit. Crashed 5-51. 188 TT.
44-74632M	2 Sq. as # 342. 9-1-51 (Grunder). 009 TT!
44-74633L	ROKAF. 10-15-53. Returned USAF, to Philippine Air Force. ex-18th FBG.
44-74638M	45th TRS. 7-1-51 (Polifka).
44-74643M	18th FBG. 4-5-52
44-74646M	45th TRS. 6-6-51 (Thatcher). 281 TT.
44-74651L	ROKAF. 7-28-53. ex-18th FBG commanding officers Mustang.
44-74653A	18th FBG. 10-18-52 Hoesong.
44-74654N	51st FBS (P). 8-9-50 Taegu. 696 TT. ex-165th FS.
44-74655M	18th FBG. 7-25-52 Chinhae.
44-74658A	18th FBG. 10-18-52
44-74671M	ROKAF 7-15-52. "M" 6-3-53. ex-190th FS.
44-74677A	ROKAF. 3-9-53. "A" 7-17-54. ex-163rd FS.
44-74691N	18th FBG, 67th FBS. 10-9-50 K-9. 1041 TT. ex-163rd FS.
44-74692L	ROKAF as # 18. 10-8-50. Dean Hess's personal Mustang. "By Faith I Fly," "Last Chance." ex-18th FBG, ex-182nd FS.
44-74693M	18th FBG, 10-25-50 K-9. 802 TT.
44-74708L	ROKAF. ? date. Returned USAF, to Philippine Air Force. ex-35th FIG.
44-74712M	8th FBG. 10-30-50 Tsuiki. 1191 TT. ex-156th FS.
44-74716N	35th FIG. 12-19-50 K-9 (Olsen). 1188 TT. ex-124th FS.
44-74718M	2 Sq. as # 328. 7-1-51 (Verster). 086 TT.
44-74723N	8th FBG. 5-51. "Bad Check (Alway's Comes Back)." 980 TT. ex-186th FS.
44-74724L	ROKAF. 4-13-53. Returned USAF, to Philippine Air Force. ex-35th FIG.
44-74727?	18th FBG. 4-12-52. "The Old Crow," Lt. Col. J.F. Crow's Mustang.
44-74737	35th FIG, 40th FIS.
44-74738L	ROKAF. 5-24-53. ex-35th FIG.
44-74745M	2 Sq. as # 357. 9-20-51 Chinhae (Severtson).
44-74748L	2 Sq. as # 343. Returned USAF, to Philippine Air Force. "Hazel."
4474750M	2 Sq. as # 344. 9-8-51 (Van den bos).
44-74752M	18th FBG. 6-16-51 (Escott). 1194 TT.
44-74753M	18th FBG, 67th FBS. 2-2-51 Chinhae (Deschamps). 1127 TT. ex-174th FS.
44-74757M	2 Sq. as # 340. 10-29-51 (Joyce). 170 TT.
44-74758M	18th FBG, 67th FBS. 12-13-50 Yongil. ex-35th FIG, ex-171st FS.
44-74759M	2 Sq. as # 341. 2-3-51 (Norman-Smith). 252 TT.
44-74765N	? unit. 4-51 1056 TT.
44-74769M	35th FIG, 39th FIS. 11-30-50 Tsuiki. 492 TT. ex-160th FS.
44-74771M	35th FIG, 39th FIS. 12-5-50 K-9. 452 TT. ex-170th FS.
44-74780N	18th FBG. 9-24-51
44-74784A	18th FBG. 8-8-51
44-74786L	ROKAF. 4-8-54. ex-2 Sq. as # 387, ex-191st FS.
44-74787M	ROKAF. Lost 3-6-53. ex-192nd FS.
44-74788?	2 Sq. as # 314. 6-2-51 (Sherwood). 554 TT. ex-178th FS.
44-74792	8th FBG, 36th FBS.
44-74794M	18th FBG. 9-5-51
44-74801L	ROKAF. 10-21-53. ex-18th FBG, ex-123rd FS.
44-74803R	35th FIG. 12-5-50 Yongpo. 361 TT. ex-186th FS. (An obvious loss code error).
44-74809	18th FBG, 39th FIS. "Blanket Ass."
44-74814M	2 Sq. as # 315. 3-20-51 (Armstrong). 258 TT. ex-178th FS.

44-74840A	18th FBG, 12th FBS. 1-12-53 Itazuke (Ferguson). Collision w/-74052. ex-45th TRS.
44-74846M	18th FBG, 12th FBS. 10-2-51.
44-74862A	13th Air Base Group. 10-22-52. Intended for 2 Sq. but not delivered.
44-74863M	2 Sq. as # 361. 10-22-52 (Pearson). "Miss Marunouchi."
44-74867L	ROKAF. 5-2-53. ex-35th FIG.
44-74871?	18th FBG. 8-20-50 Ashiya. ex-169th FS.
44-74875M	18th FBG, 67th FBS. 12-4-52. ex-190th FS.
44-74877M	18th FBG. 3-11-52.
44-74879L	ROKAF. 3-17-54. ex-18th FBG, 67th FBS "Dottie." ex-35th FIG.
44-74881M	? unit. Lost 4-53. 483 TT.
44-74883N	35th FIG. 1-2-51 K-9. 604 TT. ex-188th FS
44-74890R	8th FBG, 35th FBS. 12-5-50 Kimpo. 644 TT. ex-192nd FS.
44-74901L	ROKAF. 9-21-54. ex-35th FIG.
44-74903L	ROKAF. 8-17-50. 331 TT. ex-188th FS.
44-74905P	18th FBG. 4-30-51
44-74925N	18th FBG. 2-27-51 K-10. 731 TT. ex-8th FBG, 36th FBS "Nightmare Alley." ex-188th FS.
44-74928A	ROKAF as # 142. "A" 5-5-54. ex-18th FBG, ex-163rd FS.
44-74933L	ROKAF. 1-19-53. ex-18th FBG, ex-35th FIG.
44-74941R	8th FBG, 35th FBS. 12-5-50 Kimpo. 766 TT. "Red Eraser," "Buckeye Blitz VI." ex-170th FS.
44-74943?	18th FBG. 4-11-51 K-13. 225 TT.
44-74953L	ROKAF. 6-3-52. ex-172nd FS.
44-74955A	ROKAF. 5-15-53. "A" 8-14-53. ex-35th FIG.
44-74971P	35th FIG, 39th FIS. 10-17-51.
44-74984M	2 Sq. as # 316. 7-9-51 (Pearce). 596 TT. ex-35th FIG, ex-182nd FS.
44-74989L	2 Sq. No # assigned, no dates.
44-74992L	2 Sq. as # 359. 10-29-51 (Shawe).
44-74993M	8th FBG, 35th FBS. 10-18-50 Suwon. 814 TT. ex-113th FS.
44-75000L	ROKAF. 10-29-53. ex-18th FBG, 67th FBS.
44-75001M	35th FIG, 39th FIS. 9-18-50 Tsuiki. 481 TT. ex-186th FS
44-75002M	8th FBG, 35th FBS. 1-10-50 Kimpo. 788 TT. ex-51st FBS (P), ex-113th FS
44-75010A	ROKAF. 10-22-53. "A" 5-12-54. ex-18th FBG, ex-123rd FS.
44-75016N	8th FBG. 9-17-50. 624 TT. ex-113th FS.
44-75021P	18th FBG. 8-17-51
44-75025A	ROKAF. 9-27-52. "A" 9-18-53. ex-45th TRS.
44-84517	45th TRS. "Blackie." Returned to 105th TRS 6-19-53.
44-84519	45th TRS. "Irish Lady."
44-84520	45th TRS. "Miss Freckleface." Returned to 153rd TRS 6-19-53.
44-84522	45th TRS. Returned to 160th TRS 9-8-53.
44-84523?	45th TRS. 12-1-51 (Burack).
44-84530	45th TRS. Damaged 12-50. Supposedly scrapped 8-49?
44-84537?	45th TRS. 7-19-52.
44-84544P	35th FIG, 39th FIS. 4-3-51. 931 TT. ex-169th FS.
44-84553M	2 Sq. as # 354. 10-3-51 (Meiring).
44-84560A	ROKAF. ? assignment date. "A" 2-20-53. ex-18th FBG, 12th FBS. 936 TT.
44-84564M	18th FBG. 2-18-52. ex-35th FIG.
44-84566M	45th TRS. 1-31-52 Kimpo (Bing).
44-84577E	Scrapped Kisarazu. EX-35th FIG, intended for ROKAF.
44-84589A	ROKAF. 3-30-53. "A" 7-29-53. ex-35th FIG, 40th FIS.
44-84597R	35th FIG. 12-14-50 Yonpo. 801 TT. ex-167th FS. (Loss code error).
44-84599L	ROKAF. 9-30-52.
44-84600A	35th FIG. 6-17-52 Johnson.
44-84602M	18th FBG, 12th FBS. 9-5-52 Chinhae. "Little Beast II."
44-84619N	ROKAF. "N" 10-3-52.
44-84621L	ROKAF. 3-28-53. Returned USAF, to Philippine Air Force. ex-35th FIG, 40th FIS.
44-84622L	ROKAF. 4-20-53. Returned USAF, to Philippine Air Force. ex-35th FIG.
44-84623M	18th FBG. 12-14-51 Chinhae. ex-35th FIG.
44-84625M	18th FBG. 12-15-51
44-84627A	ROKAF. 3-27-53. "A" 8-13-54. 2050 TT. ex-18th FBG, ex-197th FS.
44-84628M	18th FBG. 12-23-51.
44-84629L	ROKAF. 2-2-53. Crashed 11-56. ex-18th FBG.
44-84638M	18th FBG. 5-31-52 (Kniss) Chinhae "Little Dynamite."
44-84643L	ROKAF. ? date. ex-18th FBG, 67th FBS "Barbara Jean IV," "Dennis A II."
44-84647L	ROKAF. 9-21-53. ex-18th FBG, 67th FBS "Mouse Meat." ex-45th TRS.
44-84648	35th FIG, 40th FIS "Surely Tiz." (Dick Chard's personal Mustang).
44-84649L	2 Sq. as # 365. 11-13-51 (Grobler). Rebuilt, see -84887.
44-84650L	ROKAF. 2-19-54. ex-18th FBG.
44-84652L	ROKAF. 6-7-54. ex-18th FBG.
44-84653L	ROKAF. ex-18th FBG, 67th FBS.
44-84654	18th FBG, 67th FBS "Evelyn." TF-51D. Returned to 445th FBW, AFRES,
44-84656L	ROKAF. 4-6-54. TF-51D. ex-2589th FBW, AFRES.
44-84666L	ROKAF. 4-9-54. TF-51D. ex-2242nd FBW, AFRES.
44-84667L	ROKAF as # 137. 5-29-54. TF-51D. ex-3625th FBW, AFRES.
44-84669L	ROKAF. 4-9-64. TF-51D. ex-3625th PTW.
44-84670L	ROKAF. 4-6-64. TF-51D. ex-2242nd FBW, AFRES.
44-84672L	ROKAF. 7-24-53. ex-18th FBG.
44-84674A	ROKAF. 6-17-53. "A" 5-4-54. ex-18th FBG.
44-84676L	ROKAF. 4-9-54
44-84679A	ROKAF. 12-27-52. "A" 3-4-54. ex-18th FBG, 12th FBS. ex-111th FS. 1353 TT.

44-84744L	ROKAF. 6-12-54. ex-18th FBG.
44-84746?	35th FIG. Written-off 10-10-51 Johnson.
44-84749M	45th TRS. 4-14-51 Taegu (Foglesong). ex-111th FS.
44-84750M	2 sq. as # 358. 1-31-52 (Earp-Jones).
44-84752L	ROKAF. 4-2-54. ex-18th FBG, 67th FBS.
44-84754A	ROKAF. 8-21-52. "A" 9-23-54. 936 TT. ex-131st FBW.
44-84757L	ROKAF. 4-13-53. ex-35th FIG, 40th FIS "Beautyful Betty Boop."
44-84761L	2 Sq. as # 369, "My Boy." Returned to USAF, to ROKAF 3-17-54.
44-84763M	18th FBG, 67th FBS. 11-19-50 K-9. 808 TT. ex-172nd FS.
44-84766M	18th FBG. 10-27-51 Chinhae.
44-84771L	2 sq. as # 355. 9-27-51 (Earp).
44-84775	455th TRS "Connie." Returned to 105th TRS.
44-84778M	45th TRS. 10-14-52 Kimpo (Martin) "My Mimi."
44-84780M	45th TRS. 2-28-52 Kimpo (Burns).
44-84781M	45th TRS. 1-14-52 Kimpo (Righter).
44-84782?	45th TRS. Salvaged, no code or date.
44-84787M	45th TRS. 10-13-52 Kimpo (Davis).
44-84788M	45th TRS. 2-5-52 Kimpo (Dishon).
44-84791L	ROKAF. 3-23-54. ex-18th FBG.
44-84792P	18th FBG. 4-10-51 (Anderlige). 1052 TT. ex-113th FS.
44-84833	45th TRS. Damaged by ground fire 2-51. (A/C origionally intended for Australia).
44-84835	45th TRS. "Oh Kay II," "The Thing." Returned to 154th TRS.
44-84837	45th TRS. Returned to 154th TRS.
44-84838M	45th TRS. 6-10-51 "Betty" (Simpson).
44-84840M	45th TRS. 8-7-51 "California or Bust," "Sweet Lorrane" (Dishon).
44-84841M	45th TRS. 3-17-51 (Rust). 211 TT.
44-84844P	45th TRS. 2-1-51 (Rice).. 102 TT.
44-84845A	45th TRS. 12-23-50 Komaki (West).
44-84846P	45th TRS. 4-10-51 (McCollum). 199 TT.
44-84847	45th TRS. Returned to 154th TRS.
44-84848A	45th TRS. 8-15-52 (Partridge).
44-84849M	45th TRS. 10-30-51 (Madison).
44-84850	45th TRS. Returned 153rd TRS.
44-84851	45th TRS "Mike & Cindy." Returned to 153rd TRS.
44-84852	45th TRS "Sooner Snooper." Received from and returned to 153rd TRS.
44-84853	45th TRS "Oh Kaye Baby." Returned to 105th TRS.
44-84854	45th TRS. Returned to 153rd TRS.
44-84860	18th FBG, 12th FBS.
44-84862N	2 Sq. as # 348. 5-5-52 (Moir). "Lilian," "Sandra."
44-84863L	2 Sq. as # 353. 1-6-52 (Parsonson).
44-84865L	ROKAF. ex-18th FBG.
44-84867M	2 Sq. as # 345. 11-24-51 (Krohn). ex-18th FBG.
44-84868N	18th FBG, 39th FIS. 12-20-51.
44-84869M	2 Sq. No # assigned. Write-off 1-25-52.
44-84870P	18th FBG. 10-8-51. 702 TT. ex-172nd FS.
44-84872M	18th FBG. 6-6-52 Chinhae.
44-84874M	2 Sq. as # 368. 1-3-52 (Newson).
44-84875N	18th FBG. 10-22-51 Chinhae. ex-35th FIG, ex-186th FS.
44-84878M	35th FIG, 39th FIS. 9-10-50 Ashiya. 431 TT. ex-170th.
44-84880M	ROKAF. Lost 3-9-52.
44-84882L	2 Sq. as # 366. Returned to USAF, to ROKAF.
44-84884N	18th FBG, 39th FIS. 3-3-52 Chinhae.
44-84885A	ROKAF. "A" 4-4-54. 1021 TT. ex-8, FBG, ex-18th FBG, 67th FBS, ex-165th FS.
44-84886A	18th FBG. 8-12-51 Chinhae. ex-51st FBS (P).
44-84887L	ROKAF as # 138. ex-2 Sq. as # 364.
44-84890L	ROKAF. "A" 10-11-54. 369 TT. ex-2 sq. as # 393.
44-84891M	ROKAF. Lost 11-2-52.
44-84893R	8th FBG, 35th FBS. 12-5-50. 425 TT.
44-84894M	18th FBG. 11-5-52 K-46.
44-84895L	ROKAF. ex-18th FBG.
44-84898A	ROKAF. "A" 6-22-53. ex-18th FBG, 67th FBS "Connie," "Trudy."
44-84899M	18th FBG, 39th FIS. 4-20-51 K-9 (Dean). 370 TT.
44-84901L	ROKAF. ex-45th TRS "Jane II." ex-176th FS.
44-84902L	ROKAF. ex-2 Sq. as # 367. ex-18th FBG.
44-84903L	ROKAF. ex-2 Sq. as # 334 "Buggs.". ex-109th FS.
44-84904L	ROKAF. ex-18th FBG. ex-179th FS
44-84906M	18th FBG. 7-30-51 "Slo Mo Shun." ex-179th FS.
44-84908P	18th FBG. 7-30-51 Chinhae.
44-84909M	45th TRS. 10-5-51 Kimpo (Learnard) "Big Bertha."
44-84910M	18th FBG. 5-6-52. ex-35th FIG.
44-84912A	ROKAF. Salvaged 8-26-54. 1337 TT. ex-35th FIG, ex-109th FS.
44-84913M	18th FBG. 5-19-51. 348 TT. ex-35th FIG.
44-84914L	ROKAF. ex-45th TRS, ex-179th FS.
44-84916L	ROKAF. ex-18th FBG, 67th FBS.
44-84917M	35th FIG. 4-22-51 K-9 (Palmer). 296 TT.
44-84918A	ROKAF. Salvaged 3-25-54. 433 TT. ex-18th FBG, ex-179th FS.
44-84919M	18th FBG. 6-14-51 Chinhae. 328 TT.
44-84923A	ROKAF. "A" 2-24-51. 326 TT.
44-84925N	18th FBG, 67th FBS. 8-2-52 "Jeannie."
44-84926L	ROKAF. ex-18th FBG, 67th FBS "The Mad Gook," ex-35th FIG.
44-84929L	ROKAF. ex-2 Sq. as # 395.
44-84930A	ROKAF. "A" 1-2-52. 260 TT.
44-84932?	35th FIG. 3-25-51. 228 TT.
44-84939N	18th FBG. 8-5-51 "Mary & Lew." 854 TT.
44-84942A	ROKAF. Assigned 5-51. "A" 10-27-52. 261 TT.
44-84943M	18th FBG. 11-17-51
44-84945M	18th FBG. 4-1-52 as two-seat TF-51D.
44-84947A	ROKAF. "A" 7-23-53. ex-45th TRS.
44-84950M	ROKAF. Assigned 6-51. "M" 8-4-52. 269 TT.

44-84951M	18th FBG. 2-18-52. ex-35th FIG.
44-84956M	18th FBG, 12th FBS. 11-25-52 K-46. "Vendetta."
44-84959L	ROKAF. Scrapped 3-54. 1176 TT. ex-18th FBG, 12th FBS.
44-84962L	ROKAF. 9-30-52. Returned to USAF, to Indonesia Air Force. Returned to US as N9851P.
44-84963A	ROKAF. 4-30-51. "A" 7-23-52. 574 TT.
44-84964N	ROKAF. Lost 10-18-52. ex-195th FS.
44-84968L	ROKAF as # 97. ex-195th FS.
44-84969M	8th FBG, 36th FBS. 8-18-50 Taegu (Wuster). 413 TT,
44-84974M	8th FBG, 36th FBS. 12-5-50 K-24. "Mac's Revenge," "Old Anchor Ass." (O'Donnell's personal Mustang and burned by him).
44-84975L	ROKAF. ex-18th FBG, ex-179th FS.
44-84982M	18th FBG. 10-4-50. 442 TT. ex-192nd FS.
45-11350G	18th FBG, 67th FBS. 3-18-51 Chinhae (Holcomb). ex-113th FS.
45-11351L	ROKAF. ex-35th FIG, ex-178th FS.
45-11352M	35th FIG, 39th FIS. 8-19-50 Ashiya. 385 TT. ex-197th FS.
45-11356M	18th FBG, 67th FBS. 8-5-50 Ashiya. 453 TT. ex-113th Fs.
45-11358E	18th FBG, 12th FBS. 3-5-53 Kisarazu. ex-152nd FS.
45-11360N	2 sq. as # 303. 10-7-51 (Lombard). 357 TT. ex-35th FIG, ex-178th FS.
45-11362M	18th FBG, 12th FBS. 3-1-51. Chinhae "Mox Nix." ex-113th FS.
45-11363M	18th FBG. 4-13-51. 1065 TT. ex-51st FBS (P), ex-197th FS.
45-11365N	18th FBG. 7-5-51 K-46. ex-191st FS.
45-11369L	ROKAF. returned to USAF, to Philippine Air Force. ex-163rd FS.
45-11370M	2 Sq. as # 301. 3-2-51 (Ruiter). 442 TT. ex-178th FS.
45-11379M	18th FBG, 39th FIS. 5-18-51 Chinhae. 996 TT. ex-197th FS.
45-11382L	ROKAF. ex-8th FBG, ex-35th FIG, ex-18th FBG, 67th FBS "Lil Warrior," ex-116th FS.
45-11390M	2 Sq. as # 302. 9-5-51 (Biden). 423 TT. ex-35th FIG.
45-11393L	ROKAF. ex-35th FIG, ex-157th FS.
45-11398N	8th FBG, 35th FBS. 10-18-50 K-13 (Brower). 600 TT. ex-197th FS.
45-11399M	2 Sq. as # 304. 2-15-51 (Doveton). 412 TT. ex-35th FIG, ex-178th FS.
45-11404N	8th FBG, 35th FBS. 10-25-50 K-13. 541 TT. ex-197th FS.
45-11407N	18th FBG. 7-5-51. ex-35th FIG, ex-197th FIS.
45-11408M	35th FIG, 39th FIS. 11-30-50 Yonpo (Brown). 638 TT. ex-51st FBS (P), ex-109th FS.
45-11409L	Kisarazu. To Philippine Air Force.
45-11410L	ROKAF. ex-51st FBS (P), ex-18th FBG, ex-45th TRS, ex-167th FS.
45-11411L	2 Sq. as # 381. To ROKAF. ex-18th FBG "Connie," ex-167th FS.
45-11412L	ROKAF. ex-18th FGG, 12th FBS, ex-109th FS.
45-11415M	18th FBG. 4-27-52 Chinhae. ex-109th FS.
45-11417N	2 Sq. as # 375. 2-11-52 (Harburn). ex-8th FBG, ex-169th FS.
45-11419M	2 Sq. as # 318 4-20-52 (Baransky) "Shy Talk." 144 TT.
45-11420M	18th FBG. 4-25-51 Ashiya. 492 TT. ex-190th FS.
45-11421N	18th FBG, 67th FBS. 10-22-50 Ashiya. 492 TT. ex-160th FS.
45-11427M	18th FBG. 2-2-51. 763 TT. ex-191st FS.
45-11428L	ROKAF. 12-10-51. ex-35th FIG, ex-18th FBG, exz 190th FS.
45-11429M	2 Sq. as # 305. 3-4-51 (Swemmer). 483 TT. ex-35th FIG, ex-178th FS.
45-11430N	35th FIG. 12-19-50 K-9. 571 TT. ex-8th FBG, 35th FBS.
45-11432A	18th FBG, 12th FBS. 5-1-52. ex-35th FIG, ex-190th FS.
45-11434L	ROKAF. ex-179th FS.
45-11435L	ROKAF. ex-179th FS.
45-11438A	18th FBG. 9-4-50 Ashiya "Ann". 608 TT. ex-186th FS.
45-11440M	18th FBG. 1-2-52. ex-8th FBG, 36th FBS, ex-126th FS.
45-11451A	ROKAF. "A" 10-13-52. ex-191st FS.
45-11454N	8th FBG. 8-15-50 Tsuiki. 459 TT. ex-116th FS.
45-11456A	2 Sq. as # 325. Crashed on delivery to SAAF at Johnson AB. 043 TT. Parts used to rebuild #'s 364, 365 & 359). (Joubert). Reduced to further spares at end of war.
45-11470L	2 Sq. as # 382. returned to USAF.
45-11475M	2 Sq. as # 319. 2-2-51 (Wilson). 061 TT. ex-18th FBG.
45-11476N	? unit. Lost 1-51. 541 TT. ex-178th FS.
45-11477M	2 Sq. as # 322. 5-11-51 @ Syngye to aid downed pilot. (Blaauw).
45-11480M	ROKAF. Lost 11-2-52. ex-134th FS.
45-11484M	35th FIG, 39th FIS. 5-11-51 (Harper).
45-11486N	51st FBS (P). 9-7-50 Tsuiki. 368 TT. ex-160th FS.
45-11488M	51st FBS (P). 8-7-50 Yongil. ex-163rd FS.
45-11514M	18th FBG. 11-13-50 K-9. 769 TT. ex-197th FS.
45-11520P	8th FBG. 10-12-50. 385 TT. ex-116th FS.
45-11524M	18th FBG. 1-26-52. ex-156th FS.
45-11528M	8th FBG. 9-4-50 Tsuiki. 368 TT. ex-169th FS.
45-11529M	18th FBG, 67th FBS. 6-9-51. 913 TT. ex-113th FS.
45-11534M	8th FBG, 35th FBS. 11-13-50 Kimpo. 632 TT. ex-116th FS.
45-11536N	18th FBG, 67th FBS. 2-28-51 Chinhae. 964 TT. ex-8th FBG, ex-176th FS.
45-11537N	18th FBG, 67th FBS. 11-19-50 K-9. 043 TT. ex-197th FS.
45-11538M	18th FBG, 67th FBS. 10-21-52 K-46. ex-113th FS.

45-11539M	18th FBG. 1-14-53 Osan. ex-35th FIG, ex-113th FS.
45-11541M	2 Sq. as # 321. 3-10-51 (Davis). 439 TT. ex-18th FBG.
45-11551L	2 Sq. as # 377. To ROKAF. ex-8th FBG, ex-35th FIG, ex-188th FS.
45-11555M	35th FIG. 2-12-51 K-9 (Summers). 622 TT.ex-116th FS.
45-11560P	18th FBG. 11-27-50 K-24. 623 TT. ex-116th FS.
45-11563M	2 Sq. as # 306. 8-30-51 (Blaauw). 548 TT.
45-11567A	18th FBG, 67th FBS. 8-21-50 Ashiya. 376 TT. ex-172nd FS.
45-11570N	8th FBG, 36th FBS. 12-11-50. 624 TT. ex-186th FS.
45-11573L	ROKAF. Returned to USAF, to Philippine Air Force.
45-11576N	51st FBS (P). 8-9-50 Taegu. 325 TT. ex-170th FS.
45-11578N	45th TRS. 3-3-51 Taegu (Summerlin). 262 TT.
45-11579M	18th FBG, 67th FBS. 9-12-50 K-9. 553 TT. ex-169th FS.
45-11593M	18th FBG, 39th FIS. 6-20-51 (Coleman). 994 TT. ex-8th FBG, ex-110th FS.
45-11594?	18th FBG. 5-6-51 K-9. 790 TT. ex-126th FS.
45-11602N	18th FBG, 67th FBS. 2-8-52 Chinhae (Crashed on takeoff K-46). ex-163rd FS.
45-11605M	18th FBG, 67th FBS. 9-1-51 Chinhae. ex-197th FS.
45-11606M	18th FBG. 10-8-50. 795 TT. ex-163rd FS.
45-11607L	2 Sq. as # 384. 443 TT. Returned to USAF. Salvaged 3-54. ex-157th FS.
45-11609M	18th FBG. 12-6-50 Suwon. 803 TT. ex-110th FS.
45-11613A	45th TRS. 11-2-51 "Linda & Bobby Jr." ex-35th FIG.
45-11614R	8th FBG, 35th FBS. 12-5-50. 236 TT. ex-126th FS.
45-11615L	ROKAF
45-11619M	ROKAF. 6-26-52 from 18th FBG for salvage.
45-11624M	18th FBG. 8-20-50 Ashiya. 355 TT> ex-188th FS.
45-11627M	18th FBG. 6-24-52
45-11629?	18th FBG, 67th FBS. 7-14-51 Tachikawa. ex-169th FS.
45-11631L	Kisarazu. To Philippine Air Force.
45-11632M	2 sq. as # 307. 2-7-51 (Leah). 822 TT. ex-110th FS.
45-11637Q	35th FIG. 8-17-50 Yongil. SABOTAGE. 556 TT. ex-124th FS
45-11642A	35th FIG. 12-9-50 Johnson. 408 TT.
45-11646L	2 Sq. as # 390. To ROKAF. ex-18th FBG, 12th FBS.
45-11647N	18th FBG, 67th FBS. 11-8-51 Suwon. 849 TT.. ex-188th FS.
45-11648M	2 Sq. as # 308. 2-24-52 (Taylor). 547 TT. ex-18th FBG, ex-191st FS.
45-11649M	18th FBG. 9-24-50 Tsuiki. 547 TT.
45-11651M	18th FBG, 67th FBS. 10-10-50 K-9 (Leake). 684 TT. ex-188th FS.
45-11679	45th TRS.
45-11704M	2 Sq. as # 320. 3-20-52 (Taylor). 319 TT.
45-11705M	18th FBG. 6-5-51 (McBride). ex-8th FBG.
45-11707N	2 Sq. as # 372. 1-15-52 (Casson). ex-35th FIG, 39th FIS, ex-110th FS.
45-11712M	35th FIG. 10-22-50 Yongil. 535 TT. ex-116th FS.
45-11732M	18th FBG, 67th FBS. 9-22-51 Chinhae (Coyle). ex-8th FBG, ex-116th FS.
45-11735L	45th TRS. To Philippine Air Force.
45-11736M	18th FBG, 12th FBS. 4-13-52 "My Ass is Dragon."
45-11738L	2 Sq. as 3 396. returned to USAF. ex-45th TRS.
45-11740	45th TRS.
45-11742M	18th FBG, 67th FBS. 10-18-51 "Ol' NaDSob" (Old napalm dropping son of a bitch). To ROKAF for salvage. Last F-51D built!

Appendix 4:
Enemy Aircraft Destroyed by Mustang Pilots during the Korean War

* = Claim upheld by the USAF
D = Damaged
P = Probable kill

June 29, 1950
Il-10*   Burns, Richard J. 35th FBS
Il-10 (2)*   Fox, Orrin R.   8th FBS
La-7*   Sandlin, Harry T. 8th FBS

August 3, 1950
Yak*   Hoagland, Edward D. 67th FBS (Ground kill)
Yak*   Price, Howard I.   67th FBS (Ground kill)

August 10, 1950
Yak (3)*   Mullins, Arnold   67th FBS (Ground kills)

September 28, 1950
Prop*   Hall, Ralph G.   35th FBS (Ground kill)

November 1, 1950
Yak-3*   Thresher, Robert 67th FBS
Yak-3*   Flake, Alma R.   67th FBS
MiG-15 (D)   Foster, William G. 67th FBS
MiG-15 (D)   Olsen, George   67th FBS
MiG-15 (D)   Reynolds, Harry L. 67th FBS

November 2, 1950
Yak-9*   Flake, Alma R. 67th FBS
Yak-9*   Glessner, James L. 12th FBS

November 6, 1950
Yak-9*   Price, Howard I. 67th FBS (1 1/2 credits)
Yak-9*   Reynolds, Harry L. 67th FBS (1/2 credit)

November 7, 1950
MiG-15 (P)   O'Donnell, William 36th FBS
MiG-15   Carlson, Kendall 12th FBS
                    (This may well have been the first MiG-15 destroyed in aerial combat, but credit has been withheld for whatever reasons?)

November 8, 1950
MiG-15 (D)   Rogers, Joseph W. 36th FBS
MiG-15 (D)   Betha, William 36th FBS
MiG-15 (P)   Boyce, Harris S. 35th FBS

January 23, 1951
Yak-3   Currie, Alexander 39th FBS
Yak-3 (D)   Manjack, Thomas 39th FBS

February 5, 1951
Yak-9*   Mullins, Arnold 67th FBS

June 20, 1951
Yak-9*   Harrison, James B. 67th FBS
Il-10 (P)   Saltsman, R.H. 18th FBG
Yak-9   Clark, Bruce 12th FBS
Yak-9   Hames, Landell 12th FBS
Yak-9 (D)   Reins, James 12th FBS

June 22, 1951
MiG-15 (D)   Babsa, Joseph M. 67th FBS

March 20, 1952
MiG-15 (D)   Eslin, J.S. 2 Sq. SAAF

April ?, 1952
Il-10   Ash, Curtis 45th TRS (Ground kill)

Appendix 5:
Key to Korean Place-Name Endings and F-51 Air Bases in Korea

Key to Korean place-name endings

-bong = Mountain
-Chaing = river
-chon = river
-dan = point
-do = island
-dong = village, town
-gang = river
-gap = point
-get = point
-hang = harbor
-Ho = river
-kaykio = strait
-kundo = archipelago
-li = villiage, town
-man = bay
-ni = village, town
-ri = village, town
-saki = point
-san = mountain
-Shan - mountain
-shima = island
-shoto = archipelago
-tan = point
-Tao = island
-to - island
-tong = village, town
-tu = point

Major F-51 airbases in Korea

K-2, Taegu, South Korea
K-3, P'Ohang, South Korea
K-4, Sachon, South Korea
K-5, Taejon, South Korea
K-9, Pusan-East, South Korea
K-10. Chinhae, South Korea
K-13, Suwon, South Korea
K-14, Kimpo, Seoul, South Korea
K-16, Seoul, South Korea
K-23, Pyongyang, North Korea
K-24, Pyongyang-East, North Korea
K-25, Wonsan, North Korea
K-40, Chejo Island, South Korea
K-46, Hoengsong, South Korea
K-55, Osan, South Korea